Just Visiting:

A grumpy old fan's journey into English football's Promised Land

By S.B. Mann

With match reports

By Mark Gardiner

Through Contemporary Eyes Publishing

Foreword

It gives me great pleasure to write a few words in the front of Mike's "Just Visiting" which, you will soon find out is a real *Labour of Love* from a passionate Palace Fan. As the great man, Steve Coppell, once said, "The only loyalty in football is between the supporter and his club" and it would be hard to find a more loyal supporter than the author of this book. The story follows his journey up and down the country from pre-season in Dagenham to long trips north to Newcastle and Sunderland on successive Saturdays. Furthermore, the match reports here, from Mark Gardiner, are far more valuable and insightful than any that you will have read on the back pages of the Sunday papers.

The stadia of the Premier League may be a touch more glamorous than those to which we have become accustomed in our most recent sojourn in The Championship (or the Second Division in old money). Maybe many fans thought that 2013-4 would just be another of those brief visits for Palace before we dropped back down a division, as we have always done in the past. However, this season was a real roller-coaster ride that, fortunately for us, ended with a fantastic finish and Palace's 3rd highest league position in our 109 year history. Our club's name is now becoming better known to millions of football fans around the world and sometimes it's hard to believe how far the club has come since the dark days of 2010 when we were just hours from going into liquidation. This has, I suppose, made our recent successes even sweeter for the many long-suffering Palace fans who have followed the team on cold, wet, windy Tuesday nights to places like Barnsley, Preston and Huddersfield.

We'll have to wait and see if "Just Visiting" is an apt title for this book, or not. Maybe, just maybe, Crystal Palace F.C. can shake of the "yo-yo team" tag and establish itself as a regular member of the Premier League. It's been great to visit but it would be even better to stay.

Stephen Browett
Co-Owner CPFC.

In the process of writing a book there are always people who encourage and assist, without their input far less would be achieved. I would like to thank anybody who feels that they might fall into these categories, in particular James, whose feedback was invaluable.

However, as this book is about my journey, following Crystal Palace Football Club, it would be remiss of me not to also thank those people, who made this journey possible and so much fun. Firstly CPFC2010, without whom there would be no team to follow and thus no journey. Secondly, my travelling companions who kept me sane, when the journey seemed rather fruitless and unrewarding. Thirdly, Mum and Dad who encouraged me to follow whatever course in life I chose, as long as this included The Palace.
Finally, there would have been no journey for me personally, with my Grandfather, Alfred who watched his first Palace match in 1907 and brought up Dad, to continue his passion, which he has now passed onto a third and fourth generation of Glaziers and Eagles.

It is inevitable, as I grow older; that some people who have been part of the extended Palace experience, will pass away. In 2013/14 This has included Peggy Smith and Joyce "the Voice" True, both of whom were a regular part of my travelling experiences over many years. This book is dedicated to them and the many others supporters, players, and officials, watching from the terraces in the sky.

S.B.Mann

Introduction

"Is this your first trip to Anfield, first trip to Anfield?"

Palace fans, Anfield Saturday 5th October 2014

"Is this your last trip to Anfield, last trip to Anfield?"

The Kop two minutes later

This second chant, coming as it did from the previously silent Liverpool supporters, was something I guess we would get used too. What many of them would have failed to understand, was that we were taking the micky out of them, Manchester United, Chelsea and the English Premier League as a whole. OK, so we lost again, five out of six wasn't looking so good, but for many supporters, of average English football teams, it doesn't and didn't, really matter. We were there, supporting our team in the only way we could. We were loud, we were proud and we were Palace. If you 'support' one of the big boys, you probably don't get it and maybe you never will. If you want to read all about the wonders of the Premier League, (Am I even allowed to type that, without paying some royalty to somebody, somewhere?) then you are probably best getting your 200-page souvenir programme, brought off the internet obviously, wrapping yourself in your half-and-half scarf and watching Skysport. Alternatively, read on and I will give you the benefit of the doubt, that you want to learn what you are missing. For the rest of the 16 million supporters who watch football up and down the country in the largely vain hope of success, this is your story as well as mine. So, I support Crystal Palace and briefly, we are in the Premier League, wooppy do! (I most stop using their name or I'll go bankrupt.) However, I identify more with fans of Barnsley, Orient, Rochdale and yes, even Brighton, than I could ever do with the fans, whose expectation; not even hope; expectation, is the Champions League. (That actually has very few "champions" in it.)

Firstly a confession: I started this book with a little chanting exchange from Anfield because that was the point at which I decided to write it. I therefore admit that everything chronologically before this, was written from memory, not as the rest will try to be, without hindsight. However, I will still endeavour to recall how I felt at the time. So much of what is written about football, relies on what people know now, not what they knew then. I will use Ian Wright as an example, for reasons that will become clear in a few chapters time. Which Palace fan, genuinely thought that selling him for £2.5 million, (When that was a colossal amount of money) was bad business? Not me. Five seasons, a few England

1

appearances, a truck load of goals and Marco Gabbiadini later, it is easy to change your view.

 A second confession: things never really quite go to plan. When it came to compiling all my notes for this book, I realised that I hadn't written, quite as much as I thought I had. Bits were missing and bits were rubbish, but there was enough that I thought was OK, to inspire me to fill the gaps anyway. It was at this point that I called on Mark Gardiner. I had read his match reports on the bulletin boards and they seemed to be well regarded. The fact that, I didn't always agree with his assessment of players or performances, convinced me that his reports would not only add the nuts and bolts, they would at the same time offer an interesting, alternative viewpoint. Fortunately, for both you and me, he agreed that I could use his reports and my original idea for the book, needed further revision. Consequently the book, like the season, didn't quite end up how I thought it would, at the onset. Much like being a football fan, I hope that is part of its charm.

As with running a football club, writing a book is often a compromise between the desired and the practical, with a fair slice of the financial, thrown in for good measure. You can gamble your long-term finances, by hiring the best and most expensive players or in the case of a book, Proofreader, Editor and Designer. Alternatively, you can try to accomplish something worthwhile, within a reasonable budget. There is also the whole issue of timing. The transfer window or in my case publishing window, may close before you have everything perfect. You can then only sit back in your proverbial dugout, hands clasped, praying that you have done enough, to not embarrass yourself. The joys of new digital printing technology, means that there are no transfer windows as such, in publishing anymore. As a result, it is possible to tweak and tinker with your team selection and constantly improve what you are offering. If you are unfortunate enough to have a copy of this book, with version 1 in the opening information, I apologise in advance, for all the inevitable proof reading errors. However, like those people who attend the first match of any season, to watch a team full of players, that they thought were going to be good, but turned out to be a bit rubbish, you can at least say that you were there at the very beginning. If you have version three hundred and seventy-eight, you are less likely to be screaming, "Why has he capitalised that word?" There is a vague possibility that you may have a version 2, which is perfect, with no errors whatsoever. This will not mean that I have suddenly learnt the rudimentaries of English grammar; it is more likely that my publishing company has been brought out by an American Billionaire. They will have spent ten grand on editing and proof reading even though book sales will not justify this outlay. This would have been a ridiculous thing to do, but as the book is about the English Premier League, (Dear Liz, hope you are impressed that I used all upper case) it would not be entirely inconsistent.

Before I move onto the book proper, I feel that I must also make one further observation about the editing. Whilst my own pieces have been subjected to numerous reads, writes, deletes or rewrites, yet probably still contain numerous errors, Mark's reports, have not had the benefit of any such attention. They were used exactly as originally written and posted on the bulletin boards (BBS). Any small errors that may have appeared as a result, are not through any lack of attention on his behalf, but a desire for authenticity on mine. For reasons of editorial flow, I have also moved Mark's detail player analysis, to an appendix. However, they are in themselves a great read and an invaluable resource, for those who like a more detailed insight into individual performances.

Part 1: Holloway

In the Beginning

Our journey into the Promised Land, wasn't supposed to start with a tube journey to East London. After our exploits at Wembley, it was supposed to be far more Premier Leaguey. Now before any West Ham fans reading, get all defensive, although I might have made the same comment about a trip to the Boleyn Ground, I am not on this occasion, being detrimental about the soon to be residents of the Olympic legacy, which will be good business for *The Evening Standard* advertising department, even if it isn't for the nation. Although Hammerites, (New paint for my gates please.) might have us believe that there is only one footballing reason to travel to East London, there are in fact others. If I can start off, in the way I expect to continue, they also contain considerably more room, in the away section concourse. One of those reasons is Dagenham and Redbridge, which was the reason for this preseason tube journey. I don't normally do preseason, but this was the potential for a new ground and there was not a lot else happening. Away matches are normally planned with a little bit more consideration than this, but hey-ho, it was a sunny day and I have a Travelcard. It had also occurred to me that, in the sanitised world in which we now plied our trade, this might be the last time for a while, to visit a proper football ground. Terraces, quirky stands and supporters who don't expect multi-million pound signings, from every distant continent, were all appealing. I might even get to stand on a concrete step, lean on a crash barrier and jump up and down a bit, without concerns that I am obstructing someone's view.

The first thing to be said about Dagenham, is that it is a lot further East than you think. The tube journey is long and my Travelcard didn't after all, extend that far. If as a Londoner, all be it, one who has lived on the borders of Wales, for most of the past two decades, I didn't really appreciate this, then travellers from further afield may well get a shock. Therefore, my first recommendation to any would be away traveller is to plan your journey properly. This is especially true if you want a pre-match pint. On some journeys, missing out on a local hostile hostelry, might be seen as a wise choice, but today it was a shame. Dagenham have a nice old school clubhouse attached to the ground, which seemed to allow access for anybody wishing to enter, regardless of allegiance. On this occasion, I passed up a drink, in favour of a lunchtime kebab from the local chippy. I accompanied this with a chat in the sun with Joe, who is another long-suffering Eagle, who my family has known for many years. The best thing about a new season, is often catching up with fellow fans and just chatting football. The exact details of the conversations are almost immaterial, exemplified by the fact that I can't remember this one, only that it took place.

The match, like the conversation, was enjoyable and interesting at the time, but soon passed from memory. What I do remember, is that we used two completely different teams. There was a mixture of old, new and never to be seen again. In fact, this last category could actually be renamed, "No idea who they were in the first place." As with no names on the shirts and no announcements, the paying public was left in the dark, about some of the players identities. Fortunately, thanks to the wonders of mobile internet, player profiles were downloaded and passed around. One of these trialists did stand out, not because he was any good, but just because he was huge. Even the official team sheet, which I didn't even know existed until a few moments ago, just listed him as 'Trialist (no name)'. The conversation on the Palace BBS surrounding Mr Noname was almost frantic. Had a supporter from the away section, run onto the pitch and approached the bearded giant, it would not have been as an act of foolish drunken bravado, but just a response to the following plea from the user known as Seaguleater.
"Still don't know his name lol, would someone who is there, grab the fecker and ask him his bloody name,"

I personally would not have recommended this whole grabbing approach, but a more respectful.

"Excuse me Mr Noname, would it be possible that you could furnish me with your real name. We would all like to sing it for you, 'there's only one Mr Noname' seems a little disrespectful."

Although quite how we would have incorporated a response of, "Atdhe Nuhiu," spoken with and Albanio-Austrian accent into a song, I am not sure.

The one major disappointment of the day, was that the sizeable away following was placed behind the goal, in a seated section of the ground, not as I had hoped, on the side of the pitch were there was still an area of terracing. Oh well, let's just hope for a good away draw in the cup. I hope that this is somewhere, that is still removed from the effects of the misguided and politically influenced Taylor Report. [i][ii]

The return journey back to the familiar roads of South London, was not surprisingly, as long as the outward trip. I had however seen a game of football and chalked off another ground, although I have since discovered that the Ninety-Two Club, would not see it this way.

Before the season proper started, there was the theoretically more glamorous home friendly against Lazio. I must admit at this point, that I had actually forgotten that I even went to this match. It was only when trying to tot up my final spending for the season, that I came across the receipt. This prompted me to ask

Dad, if he had any idea, who I brought this ticket for? Then I remembered, it was for me. That tells me two things. Firstly, the match was not that memorable, so I will allow Mark to do the honours in that regard. Secondly, it indicates that writing the bits that I neglected at the time, could be a long and torturous process, if I cannot even remember going to the games.

Once the mind was jogged by Palacefantv[iii], on YouTube, there were a couple of points that I did remember. The Italian's seemed to have a very relaxed attitude to the whole affair, with headphones were much in abundance on the touchline, even during the match. They also seemed to have a total disregard, for our new electronic pitch side advertising boards. Treating them, more like a park bench than a symbol of our new found status, as a team with a ground in which, multinational companies want to advertise. Our Chairman once mentioned that in previous years, they would have cost a six-figure sum to install. That is one expensive park bench! Unlike some others around South London, it definitely wasn't occupied by out of work ex-footballers, down on their luck. [iv] With the current wages players earn, I can hardly see this happening again in the near future either. Their headphones alone, would have kept a soup kitchen in a good quality broth, for a few weeks.

The biggest shame about the day, was that there was very little atmosphere. Despite the high number of Italians, living in easy travelling distance of South London, there was only a handful present. The cynical amongst you, may be thinking that this is because Lazio were playing us and not Liverpool or Chelsea. True fans, particular the expatriates, will of course know that, opponents are largely immaterial and a chance to see your team, even in a friendly must not be passed over lightly. The truth of the matter was far more worrying and I hope it will not become an unpleasant feature of the season. One set of police, "Intelligence officers," suggested that the Lazio fans, were planning some vague and undefined act of violence. Rather than putting an action plan in place, which would intercept the obviously known criminal minority. The Met Police chose instead to "advise" that no Italians should be allowed at the game. [v] Now if I can just remind you, this was a preseason friendly, not the Champions League final. What the hell are they going to do when United come to town? Oh sorry forgot, they are already here, living amongst us. So instead of a fun, lively and friendly atmosphere, yes Mr Chief Constable, football supporters can be the later, it was largely a damp squib, but without the dampness, it was actually a nice sunny day.

Marks Match report

Friendlies are so bloody difficult to get into. You're not entirely sure how seriously both sides are taking it, so whatever we divine from the result usually means absolutely nothing. There are usually 40-odd players appearing during 90 minutes, so by the time you figure out that KG is playing right back, he's switched position twice. And the mind does wander: isn't the pitch looking great / worryingly warm, that reminds me, I must cut the grass, hope England have taken a wicket by now... Inevitably there are more players on both sides than the squad on the team sheet allows. I recall my first such sighting of Ian Wright, although I confused him with Andy Higginbotham.

This was on paper a decent warm up for Spurs, as Lazio are about the Italian equivalent, even if comparisons are worthless as the 19th substitute appears. And, to be honest, if the first hour is repeated next Sunday then I doubt Palace would only be one goal down. It was not that Palace were poor – in fact it is difficult to pick any individual who was outstanding or mediocre – just that when Lazio could be bothered the ball zipped around with some wonderful one-touch flowing moves that opened us up five or six times. Overall Delaney, Gabbidon and Speroni had very good games – Julian in particular with four or five good saves – but each made one terrible individual error that cost us one goal and could have seen another two conceded. Ward & Moxey looked good going forward, but were exposed at the back, with Ward in particular being given the run-around by Lulic, although it took a slow-motion goal line clearance from Dean to stop a second Lazio goal. Palace never quite forced a first half save out of Marchetti, despite some neat touches in midfield and some hard work from Wilbraham, but a comparison of Aaron with goal scorer Klose, one goal behind "Der Bomber" Gerd Muller's Germany record and second highest scorer in Word Cup finals, highlighted an area where Palace cannot afford a blunt edge. Nine seasons ago Palace had AJ knocking in goals all over the country but still went down.

Strangely it was a much-changed Palace team, with seven half-time changes, who eventually could have claimed a draw. There is definite raw material in Gayle, who dragged one shot wide, then showed immense skill in a first time shot from a deep free kick that drew an excellent save out of Marchetti, and he linked well with Phillips. The latter missed Palace's best chance, sent clear on goal only to see his shot hit the keeper's trailing leg. On an admittedly very restricted showing I'm not sure Gayle will be able to play the lone striker role, which might mean some employment for Wilbraham, but with the right partner & some courage from IH in playing two up front, I reckon Dwight may

4

shock the odd opposition. Just don't expect the second coming of Ian Wright: he had the benefit of 3 seasons playing in the (old) Second Division alongside Mark Bright before hitting the big time, and even then the step up in class was nowhere near the gulf that exists to the Premiership today. Palace were not far short of a draw in the end, even if Lazio spurned some good chances and probably eased off in anticipation of sampling a night out in Croydon.

The following were also good to some degree: O'Keefe: Probably our best player as a second half sub. Usually someone comes through you don't expect, and it looks like Stuart is continuing on from Wembley. Jedinak: Did you expect any less? Dobbie & Williams: (the short blond one) – Some good touches that helped make the best openings in the first half.
Garvan: Quietly efficient with an eye for a through pass, sadly not always executed to perfection or read / controlled by his team mates.
Grandin & Bolasie: Both took some time to settle after coming on at half-time but showed some good touches as they got into the game.

Disappointments? Well, no-one had a shocker, although Thomas didn't look match fit and soon departed with some kind of strain. I hope he won't suffer the same fate as Marco Gabbiadini, as Zaha's boots are big ones to fill. The late subs, including Williams (Jerome) and Boateng had little opportunity to impress.

So, the verdict is that the Jedi is key, our back four & keeper will have to remain focussed & strong. We are going to miss Wilf. While without Murray, goal scoring will be a major concern. Now, who would have thought that?

Spurs Home ~~Saturday 17th August 3pm~~ Sunday 18th August 1pm

First home game of the campaign and a taste of what is to face us this season, not just in a Spurs team, assembled with multi-millions, including £26 million for Soldado alone.

For a family, whose loyalties are split almost equally, between church and football, a kick off at 1pm, on a Sunday, is not particularly convenient. Combined with the rush and the expected extra demand on the Sainsbury's car park, I was glad to get a parking space, even if it did involve bumping Mum's car onto a grass verge, and destroying considerable amounts of a bush.

 Ian "Ollie" Holloway in his programme notes for today's game, asked us all to, "Stick together, no matter what is happening." As I walked up from the car park, past the new fans area, towards the Holmesdale Road, I definitely felt that sense of camaraderie. Some of the people you pass, we have known over many years, others, I had never seen before. Ollie also asked that we, "Keep a sense of reality about what we are trying to achieve." This second idea is sensible, and it is understandable that he should want to express it. However, today is perhaps not the day to do it, and certainly not for this glorious hour before kick off, on the first day of the season, when most people are probably reading his programme notes. For this short period, supporting my team is about dreams, hopes, and overcoming all realism. One of our owners Stephen Browett, in his own programme notes, wrote a sentiment that reveals his status; a genuine fan. For at least a few hours, I will hold this in my brain and above Ollie's possibly, wiser words.

"Nothing is impossible if we believe."

Maybe like in 1991, I could beat the bookies. Once again, I could walk into William Hills in May, to collect my returns on Palace winning the league. (Ok, it was an each way bet, but it was no less satisfying.) The change in those 23 years, is perhaps best expressed by the bookies themselves. My winning bet in 1991, from £5 each way was £66. This year, the same bet would net nearer to £10,000. I haven't placed that bet, yet, Maybe, buoyed by a wave of Steve Browett optimism, or some would suggest stupidity, if there is a Bookmakers in the Holmesdale, as there always used to be, I just might have a punt.

 I was denied this opportunity, as in ground betting has not returned, despite our new sponsors, and the bookies never got my 10 quid. More worryingly, I could have just squandered the chance to make, an easy ten grand; the next nine months will tell.

 The first chance for the crowd to show the collectivism that Ollie called for, was in the display, that the Holmesdale Fanatics, had set up for the players' entrance. The days of 30,000 balloons, at Wembley in 1990, are it seems long gone. The possibility of a state of the art, £200 football boot, or more likely a blade, or whatever is currently in vogue, being unable to remain static, when faced with a small piece of rubber, is too much for the health and safety brigade. The nice thing for me about balloons, was that once you had spent considerable amounts of time, blowing them up and storing them under your seat, or around your seat, or on your seat, or even on other peoples seat, you could simply launch them, towards the pitch. Then watch as they created a mass of floating colour. There was always the possibility, of added humour as well. Ground staff, police officers, players and sometimes officials, would all try to pop them, with differing degrees of success. It is perhaps indicative of the more orchestrated environment, in which we now operate, that a display that carries a message, is what the Fanatics had planned. However, the difference that Palace displays have, is that the fans instigate them.

Today's display, has been paid for by the fans, and designed by the fans. Free from interference by the club authorities, it will hopefully, show an originality, that big corporate banners, with sponsor's logos, never could. The only problem with these displays, is that sometimes, when you are actually part of the display, it is difficult to gauge its full meaning and affect. Glancing up from behind my square of red plastic, as the teams entered the pitch, I could see the swirls of red and blue on the electronic scoreboard, but I could not fully make out the central picture or the written message. Ollie later admitted that like me, he didn't really understand it, but at least Sky TV had paused long enough from their normal, `cut to adverts` routine to show the world the efforts that had been made. When I got home and witnessed the full effect on TV and YouTube as well as the photographs on Twitter, it was certainly impressive. [vi] Now I have also had the opportunity to Google (That's four bits of product placement, in two sentences. I think I am now officially Premier League) the movie 'Saw', I think that I also understand its theme and significance. Perhaps the very fact that it was a bit obscure and some may even suggest extreme, shows the independence from interference in its design. The 'Saw' movies are, I believe, a little tongue in cheek, the message also needs to viewed, that way. Along with the central picture of the lead character from the movies, the message read. 'The Palace are here. Let the games begin'. I believe these are lines from the film, (without the Palace bit, obviously,) which are used, just prior to torture and humiliation of his victims. Now I am sure, no one who took part in the display intends to torture visiting players or supporters. However, a little bit of fear, intimidation and even humiliation would be welcome. The concept that no opposing player, with their Lamborghini's, stupid haircuts and excessive body art should want to come to Selhurst, is a message that I whole-heartedly support. However, the removal of body parts is maybe just a little extreme.

On the pitch, I was pleased, that the boss had stayed faithful to, much of the team that gained promotion, just as he had done at Blackpool. If that little bit of momentum, can get us through the first few weeks, then we can look to incorporate the new players, six of whom were featured in today's programme. This is not necessarily a view, that was shared on the BBS this morning. The match day thread, [1] was already running to an impressive eleven pages, even

---

[1] A thread is a series of related messages on an internet message board.

before kick off. This is perhaps, also an indication of the added interest in top flight football. There was a fear on the BBS, that without Zaha and Murray, the team was actually weaker than last year, and considerably slower. I know that it is often said that, there is no room for sentiment in football, but I disagree. If players think that promotion, will leave them without a team, then what is the incentive, to give that little bit extra? These players deserve this moment, and I am proud that as a club, we have done this; whatever the outcome. After all, it will hardly be today's result, that dictates our fate, come Fulham in May.

Whilst there are a variety of changes around the ground, which I will return to at a later date, one of the most noticeable for me, was the expansion of the Crystals, cheerleaders. Please don't think at this point, that Nina et al have spent the summer, undergoing eye watering surgery and trying to outsize Samantha Fox, there were, just definitely, more of them, in terms of numbers. The Premier League does have some benefits it seems, and it could be argued, provides something for everyone. They also had new uniforms, based on our impressive evil sash away kit. These were slightly more modest than their previous wardrobe, which pleased some if not others. I am not revealing my camp on this point.

Mark will give you all the details of the match itself, in his match report. However, even though we lost, it was encouraging, that we were by no means outclassed. Was there a £100 Million, difference in the two teams? I don't think so, and despite the doom mongers, our defence held out well. As this is the first game of the season, and I am almost positive, that there will be other opportunities, to talk about refereeing, I will not go into a long rant. However, I find it very difficult to criticise Dean Moxey, for giving away a penalty today. It is almost impossible, to control what your hands are doing, when you are trying desperately to block a cross. This is far removed from what I used to understand, was meant by deliberate handball. (The clues in the words.) Let us just hope, that given the same scenario, against one of the top teams, we would get the same decision; but I have my doubts. Oh no! I've implied refs might favour the big teams, I expect my three-week touchline ban, to arrive by fax any moment now.

Marks Match report

Well, perhaps this season won't be such a long drudge as many of us feared. I don't think anyone would deny that Spurs were the better team, but Palace somehow hung in there to be in with a chance, however slim, of dragging back a point. Survival means we have to win the key games at home against lower & mid-table teams, and the display today gave us some indications that this will not be a forlorn hope. What will need to be addressed are the simple avoidable errors that cost us a goal and helped prevent our game gaining any rhythm until Holloway made a triple substitution.

8

Palace lined up with a 4-3-2-1 Christmas tree formation, with most of the team that started at Wembley. Jedinak, KG & Garvan formed the midfield trio, with Gayle & Dobbie slightly further forward in nominal support of Wilbraham. Unfortunately, both the formation and the personnel employed therein soon exhibited weaknesses, the primary one being a complete lack of width in attack. Ward & Moxey tried hard to cover 80 yards but that often exposed the rearguard when the ball was lost; in addition, they rarely had an outlet down the line. Attacks developed far too ponderously, with opportunities to cross or shoot being passed up in favour of laying the ball off and back; strangely, when the crosses were put in they were far too early with no-one in the box to take advantage. Wilbraham was too static and totally isolated up front, while Dobbie and Gayle looked far too lightweight and distant to provide support; Gayle in particular appeared overawed & nervous, playing at this level in an unfamiliar role, and lost the ball far too easily, including in the build up to the penalty. At the back there appeared a gap down our left between Garvan & Dobbie that Tottenham exploited several times, often outflanking Moxey. To add to this was the number of times simple passing moves were ruined by a poor pass or a misunderstanding between colleagues that saw balls left in favour of someone else.

As a result it should come as no surprise that Palace's sole "effort" on goal was a soft header by Wilbraham straight at Lloris. Spurs took their time to find the range on the Palace goal, although it took a smart save from Speroni to turn over Sigurdsson's effort from distance, while as the first half acme to a close Speroni had to act smartly to deny Soldado and there was a far post header that was missed. In some ways the match reminded me of our first game back in '89 against a functional Manchester United, when Wright grabbed a late equaliser. Tottenham made the same errors as our guys but not quite as frequently; their defence looked gawky at times, and despite a Palace team that had yet to change up from first gear, they did not look like a side that should be pressing at the upper echelons of the Premiership. Their favourite move was the long diagonal ball from Dawson to left back Rose, suspiciously like the long balls launched from Delaney & Gabbidon towards Wilbraham (although occasionally they found the midget Gayle).

9

The second half started much the same as the first, with Palace unable to build any momentum, mostly due to slack passing play, but finally Spurs made us pay. Gayle lost the ball far too easily in our half, Lennon worked some space on our left, and as Moxey slid in to block the cross the ball struck his outstretched arm; it was a clear, definite penalty, that Soldado finished coolly. Palace continued in their miss-firing way for some 10 minutes or so, during which Gayle showed that when acting instinctively he has the raw talent when he escaped and fired a shot not far over. Then Holloway introduced a triple substitution with Williams, Phillips and Chamakh on for Dobbie, Garvan and Wilbraham. Whether this was a predetermined strategy, similar to his plan that finished off Brighton at the Amex in holding on for an hour then going for the win, or an act of desperation, only Olly knows. The formation seemed to be far more fluid, with Chamakh appearing down the right & Williams buzzing on the left and through the middle, while Phillips went through the middle, but this also left Palace more exposed than previously.

As the game stretched Spurs really should have made the game safe. Twice Palace were brushed aside as first Sigurdsson then sub Defoe managed to slide clear chances wide of Julian's right hand post. Palace looked more dangerous as Williams in particular was able to use the ball to more effect, and two half chances arrived for veteran Phillips, one being blocked by good anticipation by Lloris and the other sent well wide. At the death a corner to the far post saw efforts from Delaney & KG blocked, while Spurs were happy to run down the clock. Despite the number of individual errors made by Palace players, perhaps due to nerves, and being unable to grasp a foothold in the match for over an hour, the result in the end gives us hope for the future – we have the spirit and foundations that we can build upon.

MARK'S MARKS

Speroni 7
Ward – 6
Moxey – 6
Delaney – 7
Gabbidon – 6

10

Dikgacoi — 6
Jedinak — 8
Garvan — 6
Dobbie — 5
Gayle — 4
Wilbraham — 5
Williams — 7
Phillips — 6
Chamakh — 6
Individual player reports for each match can be found
index on page 274

Eagles and Lions

Despite all the negatives of the F.A.'s (or is it the Premier League's) Elite Performance Programme, vii one of the developments that I have liked, is the U21 Development League. With some of the games being played at Selhurst Park, it is a nice opportunity, to see some of the younger players, and given our recent influx of new first team players, it is also an opportunity to evaluate some of these. It would be even better, in my opinion, if like in the old days, season ticket holders could attend for free. The clubs in the Premier League, are obviously still short of a bob or two, so in Palace's case, £8 is the on the gate price. Dad gets in for £1, whether he books or not, so a last minute decision is normally the policy. Last season, when we were entertaining the likes of Man City, with a team that including Kolo Taure and was Managed by the bald eagle himself, [2] we were getting approaching four figure gates, but ironically, since the first team have gone up, the U21's seem to have gone down. Thus our first game, is against Millwall. So, not surprisingly, the gate wasn't so high, although the club, presumably under "advice" from the police 'intelligence' officers, still made the precaution of having separate sections for home and away supporters. I was not consulted to provide my own intelligence, but it would have reported that, this section would in fact be empty and that the decision, was fundamentally silly.

I was able to get away from work a little sharp-ish, which enabled me to phone Dad, from the bus and ask if he wanted to come, which he did. I Therefore called in at home, picking up Dad and the car. The regular feature of these games, which hasn't improved, now we are in the Premier League, is the difficulty in finding a team sheet. If you are early, the office photocopier is still purring away somewhere, in a Porto cabin, and if you are late, they have all gone. Given the transient nature of these teams, and the addition of new unknown transfers, team sheets are a requirement. I was eventually able to find two. One for use during the game, and one to add to the programme collection, which hasn't been folded up, crushed into my pocket, or circulated amongst fellow fans, about twenty times each game. The first puzzle of the evening, was how we were allowed four, over aged players. This is apparently because goalkeepers don't count, which is a bit strange. given that if you are a young goalkeeper, you can hardly just ditch the gloves, and play up front for match practice. The second puzzle, which wasn't posed for another ninety minutes, was how, with these four players, plus our newly acquired Spanish U20 international in the side, we could lose, to what was basically, a full Millwall youth team? The answer, from a spectator's point of view, was that they wanted to win, a bit more than us. When you are playing Millwall, at any level, that's a bit annoying. I guess there must be, a bigger picture.

Jose Campaña, did look as you would expect, very comfortable on the ball. Chamakh looked a little laboured and Marange, our new desert defender, was OK, but a little bit too slow to produce the goods, for my liking. (Bad cookery jokes

---

[2] Attilio Lombardo

already and its only August.) The other two of our signings, didn't really live up to my expectations. One of the things, I do particularly like, about these youth matches, is sitting near enough to some of the other trainees, and finding out about different aspects of players, and the club. Ok, so admit it, I eaves drop the youngsters. No juicy gossip tonight, but it's good that the other players are encouraged to come and watch. From what I can gather, they could be called in at short notice, or left out in a similar way. Perhaps, like I did, on many occasions as a youngster these juniors, travel with boots in hand; just in case This perhaps explains the late printing of team sheets.

My final comment on the evening, was that it was great to see, some of the Holmesdale Fanatics there, as is often the case, cheering on the junior players. They can get a bit of stick, from some sections of the fan base, but they are certainly dedicated.

Stoke away Saturday 24th August 3pm: Statement of Principles

The first away game of the season, is always a bit special. As a newly promoted team, in the lofty world of the Barclays Premier League, this first game was going to have, added importance. Principles and precedents needed to be set. The first principle that has become obvious, is that ticketing, for away matches in the Premier League, is going to be a nightmare. The club has introduced an away season ticket, which is a brilliant idea and a loyalty point's scheme. I am not sure, which games I am going to this year, so have decided to rely on, my substantial accumulated loyalty points from last year, to see me through. Mum on the other hand, has brought her away season ticket, as she will probably do the whole lot, as normal, and this avoids her having to go backwards and forwards to the box office. This splitting of our tickets, also has another advantage, in that it gives two opportunities, to get a ticket which Mum at seventy-nine and less than 5 foot, might actually be able to use. The original thinking was, as away season tickets would be allocated first, they would get the best seats in the house. The problem for the box office being: what are the best seats in the house? It very much depends on your prospective, age and personal preference all have an influence, but more on that later, I'm sure. Added to this, is the thorny issue of the home clubs, restricting how the away club, sells tickets. It surely can't take the work of a genius, to come up with a booking system, that is fit for purpose. When you join the little the Premier League club, you have to have, according to our owners, about one million pounds worth of TV cabling, a recording studio, and probably hundreds of other little riders and controls. An integrated ticket system for away supporters, is not one of them. My decision, with regard to splitting my tickets, worked well. Mums ticket, apparently first off the production line, is half way up the back, and my ticket, brought by personal contact with the box office, is in the front row, A quick switch around and everybody's happy. Others, such as DorkingEagle, took a slightly different approach. His family, which include 5-year-old P., who are also away season ticket holders, were given largely useless tickets, near the back. So, they moved to the vacant disabled area, until a better, more appropriate seat could be found. On this occasion, fair play to Stoke City stewards, it was accomplished, but what if it wasn't possible, or if the stewards just didn't care, as much as they cared about me, taking my camera into the match. This was allowed, as long as I didn't take any photos, during the game. I initially thought, this was some kind of particular control, as my camera is big. However, it meets Wembley stadium, and the IOC regulations, on cameras. I had assumed incorrectly, that the Britannia Stadium, would be somewhat less restrictive. I soon found out, that I was not being picked on, because my equipment was larger than others. Liz, another away season ticket holder, was also told to stop taking pictures, almost as soon as the game began. The same vigilance on ground regulations, didn't appear to be implemented concerning standing, which was allowed and not questioned. Knowing that, Mum, was safely seated down the front and could see fine, made this not an issue for me today, and generally speaking, I prefer to stand, so everyone was happy. Let's hope, this accommodation of polarised preferences, continues for the rest of the season.

Just to touch on a practical observations, the coach parking at Stoke is great and just outside the away entrance. This made the job of Caroline, our coaches chief pusher, that little bit easier. Even though the push was short, I was still called upon to help, give Mandy a little shove, over an annoyingly steep ridge, into the ground. (Bear with me on this one; I can't explain the details of every member of the coach One Posse, in the first match. It would take far too long, and leave me scrabbling around with things to write, by Boxing Day)

Before passing you over to Mark for all the nuts and bolts, it was great that the Palace fans, joined in a minute's applause in the 14th minute of the game, for a 14-year-old Stoke fan, who had died. Sometimes, I think that the formally organised, minutes of this, or minutes of that, before games, have got a bit OTT. The ad hoc, fan organised tributes, are often better and more fitting. It also helps to ensure, that we all retain a sense of prospective. It was also nice that, a Stoke fan, took the trouble to thank us, via the BBS. This was appreciated, but also indicates that, perhaps not all fans that visit them, during a season, would have joined in so enthusiastically.

Marks Match Report

Saturday's match at Stoke reinforced two major lessons. First, the performance from every player is proof that we can survive in the Premier League, and are not doomed to be outclassed by every team we meet. Second that we can only do this if we can cut down on the number of simple errors we make, particularly at the back. Despite conceding a goal lead, this was a particularly difficult match to assign player ratings to, as every single player was superb, particularly in the first half, yet by the same token every player also made errors that contributed in a small way to our losing the match.

Holloway's initial selection raised some eyebrows. Instead of a defensive team sent out to hold Stoke, he selected what looked like an attacking side with full debuts for Chamakh, Campaña and Puncheon. The line-up was 4-3-3 with an exceptionally mobile & fluid front three of Chamakh, Gayle and Puncheon, with the width coming almost exclusively from the full backs pushing on. Senile old goats like me will recall Sir Alf Ramsey's wingless wonders, particularly the team from the 1970 Mexico World Cup which featured overlapping full backs like Cooper & Newton. This is not to say Palace are nailed on for Brazil next summer (or, more

15

probably, lose to Germany in extra time) but it was the template for some excellent passing football.

Stoke's style at the outset was the opposite of what Pulis served up for years. It consisted of slow, methodical build up from the back that made our efforts in last week's match appear hypertensive. It took Palace a little while to realise that by pressing the midfield and the back four – even the keeper – we could effectively shut Stoke down, and this was carried out by the three man units in the middle, Jose in particular, and up front. Stoke's early possession gradually dried up, with their best effort a header that Crouch put over. Instead Palace started to make breaks across the width of the pitch, with Ward & Moxey turning the flanks. Gayle had already found himself in space, but wasted both opportunities with a weak shot & a weak cross. Yet it was a defensive error from Shawcross from a hopeful clearance that saw Chamakh ease the defender off the ball, before coolly picking his spot & wrong-footing Begovic. Stoke's immediate response saw an excellent one-handed clawing save from Speroni, but apart from that the last 15 minutes of the first half could have seen Palace increase the lead, with a fine flowing passing move ended with Moxey's cross shot slipping inches wide, while a Campaña free kick was just off target.

We wondered how long Stoke's careful passing game would last under pressure, and the answer was not long at all. However this was not a long ball bombardment but an upping of pace, and more through balls than square passes. Palace could not live with the tempo and the pressure built, with us unable to clear our lines, the cool counter-attacking of the first half crumbled away. The defence was finally sucked in by a Crouch header, leaving Adam unmarked to roll the ball home. Minutes later a poor Moxey pass under pressure saw Gabbidon hack the ball out for a throw; Speroni could have come after the first header but didn't, Puncheon failed to clear and Chamakh's attempted block was tissue-paper weak. Two-one down and an immediate response from Olly was to withdraw Chamakh and Campaña, both of whom appeared to have run out of steam. Whether it was the addition of Williams & Garvan, or Stoke's choice or inability to keep up the fast pace, but Palace gradually started to regain momentum; Stoke's only other real opportunity saw Nzonzi smash a shot against the far post. Instead the home team reverted to some form of type with a series of niggly, cynical fouls. Williams started to run with the ball and, with the introduction of Phillips, Palace eked out some chances. Phillips wastefully shot wide; Puncheon nearly sneaked an effort under Begovic, while a Van Basten type volley from Gayle flashed wide. Our final chance came when Williams was bundled over on the edge of the box but Jedinak's free kick thumped into the wall. At the end Palace's performance should have earned a point but for the 15-minute period where we were totally bossed out of the match. Almost without exception everyone would have been marked with 8 at half-time.

Mark's marks

Speroni – 7
Ward – 7
Moxey – 8
Gabbidon – 6
Delaney – 7
Dikgacoi – 7
Jedinak – 8
Campaña – 7
Puncheon – 7
Gayle – 6
Chamakh – 7
Williams – 7
Garvan – 6
Phillips – 6

The Poor Relation

The League Cup, has always been a poor relation to the F.A. Cup, but it used to have a certain charm. The two-legged nature, gave smaller teams, both the opportunity to spring a home surprise, and the added advantage of a guaranteed payday, as well. In recent years, this charm has I admit drifted away. The almost certain knowledge, that teams will not play their first eleven, has made the first few rounds, pretty much, a reserve competition. As someone, who tries to get to as many under 21's matches as possible, this should still make it appealing. However, having calculated my expected spend for the year, and not knowing how many days off I will need to take, to accommodate Monday matches, I decided to miss this match. No disrespect to Bristol, but I have been there a few times, and the last trip in the play-offs, was, to put it mildly, very disappointing. Funnily enough, had I known we were going to lose, I might have gone. This is not because I am some kind of masochist, who likes to witness my team getting beaten, but because if all goes well, at the end of the season, I will have just missed this game. It will really grate, that I didn't really complete the whole season. That is the trouble with setting notional commitments or goals, once you start something, it's hard to back track.

I once had this argument with an ex-girlfriend, about holidays in the cricket season, and come to think of it, the football season. She didn't understand, that once I say, I'm going to be available to play; then, I am actually going to be available. Saying no, to this League Cup game, was like saying, that I would only be available to play cricket occasionally. I could miss future League Cup matches, without feeling pangs of reservation. In reflection, I will have to rethink this policy. Not only, did it not save my eighteen year relationship, but possibly more importantly, (only joking EVJ) it resulted in, me missing that Darren Ambrose goal, in our historic victory, at Old Trafford, two years ago. However, the unfortunate truth is, sometimes, even for die-hard regular supporters, money does have to be a consideration. Even with very cheap ticket prices, you still have to add travel and time off work.

Mum, doesn't have to worry about, the last of these problems, and her ticket was even cheaper, so I left her to go, on her own. The only downside, of this money saving decision is that; much like not playing cricket, but still having to phone the result through, or update the website, Mum, no longer drives in the dark. As a consequence, I still had to get up at stupid o'clock, to pick her up from the ground and be vaguely awake for work, later that morning. Her views on the game when asked at the end of the season are below.

"Oh I can't remember specific games like that,"

Obviously, with that incredibly insightful summary of our performance, I am going to have to do this, all on my own, and rely very heavily, on my own notes. Thankfully, I have Mark, to fill you in on the gory details, of our cup exit.

Marks Match Report

It appears to be the trend that Premier League managers use the League Cup these days to examine the depth of their squad. Olly - last night proved it is desperately shallow! A ramshackle outfit fell flat on their faces against limited but deserved winners in our old bête-noire's Bristol City on our seemingly annual trip to the West Country.

The Palace starting XI showed a full eleven changes from that which started at the Britannia. Alexander made his debut in goal; Ramage partnered Marange in central defence; Jerome Williams came in at left back; and Alex Wynter played on the right side of the defence. Midfield consisted of a relatively experienced line-up of O'Keefe in the holding role with Jonny Williams, Garvan, Dobbie and Grandin. Wilbraham resumed the role of sole striker. The formation can best be described as "fluid", which may be a kind way of saying no-one really knew what they were doing; such a formation only works when everyone is keyed in to the changes, and with this motley crew there was no chance of that. Grandin popped up on both flanks & in support of Wilbraham, who also slipped out to the right at times. Jonny was, as usual, popping up everywhere, while Dobbie & Garvan slipped in & out. In fact midfield was the really big disappointment - an area where there was no excuse for lack of experience but one that Palace never really grabbed control of. There was also an alarming lack of width, with Grandin & Williams often found on the inside, and it was asking a lot of inexperienced full backs to overlap at the right times.

City were no great shakes, but set the tone with an early effort from Emmanuel-Thomas that Garvan cleared off the line. They won a number of corners in the first half, and only an air shot from Wagstaff prevented them grabbing a lead halfway through the first half. The defence did pretty well, with Ramage making several strong clearing headers, while Jerome Williams and particularly Wynter showing well. As already stated, midfield was the problem, with Jonny Williams doing plenty of running with the ball, but almost invariably in deep positions that carried no threat of damage. The passing was normally shoddy, with Dobbie in particular disappointing. Alexander looked like an accident waiting to happen, with several kicks that failed to reach even the halfway line, while Grandin rarely threatened to get into the game, although he did have Palace's one chance in the first half, heading well over. Garvan failed to impose himself while only O'Keefe could be said to have played anywhere near potential, and even then only in a tidy sense. Surely we couldn't play the same in the second half.

We didn't. Even though City actually lost momentum after the interval, Palace's game declined even further. Phillips had replaced Dobbie and moved up front, with Wilbraham strangely dropping deep into the shadow striker role, but the veteran failed to make an impact apart from several offside decisions and other minor misdemeanours penalised by the ref. Wilbraham was soon replaced by Appiah but the youngster also barely caused a ripple, wasting his one good chance blasting high & wide when a cross to KP might have been the better option. Strangely it was two of the better performers in the first half, Ramage & O'Keefe, who both played roles in City's two goals. O'Keefe lost the ball in a Palace attack, catching Wynter out of position, and Emmanuel-Thomas outpaced Ramage down the right; it appeared that City had lost their chance as the defence funnelled back, only for Emmanuel-Thomas to turn Ramage and smash the ball past Alexander. As Palace chased the game De Silva came on for Wynter, with O'Keefe dropping to right back, but Palace seemed to lose all shape as we tried to unlock a League One defence with surely the smallest forward line ever fielded by an over-age team (Phillips, Appiah, Jonny & De Silva). The second goal was a catalogue of errors: Garvan over hit a pass out to the right; O'Keefe, trying (& sadly succeeding) to prevent a throw-in, nodded the ball infield but slipped over in the process; Ramage was caught on the wrong side of his man (Pack?) who skated away; eventually the ball came to Wagstaff whose finish was not great but found its way inside Alexander's far post. City could perhaps have had a couple more, while Palace played a neat series on one-two's on the edge of City's box that came to nothing as no-one could find the key through ball or take a shot, although a couple of efforts from range from Jonny & De Silva at least hinted at a threat. Lack of width totally throttled our attacks. Finally, in the last minute of stoppage time, Garvan pulled the trigger

from 20 yards and a slight deflection saw the ball hit
the roof of the net.

Too little & far too late. If any of this lot are
considered for starting on Saturday then we are in
trouble. Holloway recognises the squad needs
strengthening in all areas; particularly central
defence & full back, and also with wingers with Bolasie
& Thomas crocked. However the one area where we do have
players in abundance, central midfield, saw those
concerned fail to make any claim on a first team place.

Mark's marks

Alexander - 5
Wynter - 7
Jerome Williams - 6
Ramage - 5
Marange - 6
O'Keefe - 5
Garvan - 5
Dobbie - 4
Grandin - 5
Jonny Williams - 6
Wilbraham - 5
Phillips - 5
Appiah - 5
De Silva - 6

Sunderland Home Saturday 31st August ~~3pm~~ 5.30pm

One of the problems I envisage, about writing pieces for home matches, is that for most football supporters, there is a routine around games, which remains very much unchanged. You leave the house, at pretty much the same time, travel on the same route and generally do the same thing. Whilst this familiarity is great for us, the fans, and is part of its undoubted appeal, it doesn't make for the most exciting read. Nineteen chapters, where I leave the house at 1.45pm, drive down Melfort Road, park in Bulganak Road and wander down Thornton Heath High Street, whilst quite quick to write; ctrl C, ctrl V, and repeat, is hardly Booker Prize material. However, The Premier League, is always looking for new marketing angles, so they have assisted the potential author, by trying to disrupt this routine wherever possible. For today's game, this has been by moving our kick off, to 5.30pm. As kick off times go, it is perhaps one of the least anti-social. You actually have plenty of opportunity to do stuff around the house, or in these early stages of the season, even work on the garden. The game is also over at a reasonable time, and if you are still of an age, when a few beers on a Saturday night, is not a distant memory, this can still be done with little interruption. For the travelling Sunderland supporters today, it enables a more reasonable departure time, and let's face it, there is very little difference if you get back to Wearside at midnight, or 2 am, your evening is still knackered. The only real problem I have with today's KO time, is that I am such a creature of habit. I find it difficult to exploit this extra time. By 1pm today, I was eager to go, had pretty much read every thread on the BBS, and just wanted to watch football. It's practical, it's good for TV, but all the same, it's not 3 o'clock, and that's what Saturday afternoons are really for. My younger brother, who has some mental health problems, is even more of a creature of habit than I am. In answer to the question "do you want a drink?" he will first check his watch. However, even he was surprisingly, more adaptable than I was. Maybe I am just a moaney old bugger after all. Dad decided that as the game was on the TV tonight, he would stay at home and watch in comfort. It was a particular shame that he felt that way, because the Barclays Promo team were on hand, to ask a few questions. They took a photo of Mum, my brother and me. It has just arrived by email with the following message.

For cheering from the stands,
Come rain or shine,
Thank you.
#youarefootball

Fair play to them, it's actually a nice picture, and will be a nice keepsake. If I could only find a print cartridge, that actually had any ink in it; I would print it out for Dad. Maybe all this hype and sponsorship, will have some positives after all, and the new signage on the ground, actually looks quite good in the background.

I know Mark will fill you in with all the details, but importantly, we won! An actual win in the Premiership, and we are now a third of the way, to our lowest possible target, of Derby's twelve points. It was particularly good to see Dean Moxey have a great game, and silence some of his critics. Similarly, Dwight Gayle, our big money summer signing, showed great confidence, to step up and take a penalty. He seems like a little boy lost, sometimes, but I like him. He obviously wants to score, which despite the current trend, for strikers playing in the hole, I think is the minimum criteria for someone in this position. My other lasting memory of the game, was only seen fully later, when someone Created a Gif, [3] out of another Olly jig. Whatever some people might say about our manager, he obviously loves football, and is desperate for us to do well.

Unlike some people, I don't generally dislike Paolo Di Canio, but I thought he was rather ungracious, considering the score. How he can call our third goal, anything but a tremendous strike, I will never know. I am particularly happy for Stuart O'Keefe, one of the expected casualties of the transfer window and promotion. Strikes like that, will obviously boost his confidence, and that of the fans, that our successful players from last year, still have something to offer at this level.

It was nice to get a win yesterday and looking back at the BBS, I noticed that it would have been particularly sweet, for our growing band of ex pat supporters, in the USA. It was mentioned that, for the first time, a Palace game was shown on national TV in America. Let's hope the amazing atmosphere that was created in the ground, came across over the pond, and all the world can see the passion, that our players and supporters have. It is also an incredible mark of how far we have come, from a post-midnight, five minutes on the Football League show, to live national coverage in the states, long may it continue.

Mark's match report

This match was almost as difficult to assign player ratings to as Tuesday's, but this time for all the right reasons. Palace took the good pieces of the game at Stoke, cut out a lot of the mistakes, and showed both character & skill to come back after conceding an equaliser to seize the result by continuing to play in a strong counter-attacking method. Personally I didn't think Sunderland were as poor as most pundits and their manager believed, and which unfairly diminishes the Palace performance. My real problem is finding a keyboard with an "8" or "9" key...

---

[3] A small looped video clip

Palace's display was based upon a number of qualities. First: teamwork – everyone knew their role and carried them out almost faultlessly, and worked hard to cover their colleagues; Jedi & KG were prominent in this respect. Second, playing on the counter, pace is vital, and the signings Holloway has made in Gayle & Puncheon certainly have this in abundance. Third, the work rate was exceptional, especially from the full backs, who were responsible for a lot of the width supplied in this formation; look how hard Chamakh worked in comparison to his perceived image. Finally, there was a great deal of quality to our play, with Jedi, Puncheon & Williams all technically outstanding. Being peevish, there are two areas I'd like to see us improve in. I'd like to see us more clinical on our breaks, either in terms of improved shooting, or selecting the right option in passing to a better placed colleague, as too many counters ended with a shot from 20-25 yards that missed the target. And there were a couple of times we lost strikers in the middle of our box, which cost us one goal and – if Ji Dong-Won had any bottle as a centre forward – should have cost us another. There – that's my reputation as a curmudgeon upheld.

The atmosphere at Selhurst was amongst the best occasions I can remember, with the vocal backing of a level with our loudest away days. It must raise the players' spirits and hopefully discourage both opposition squads & supporters with the sheer volume.

The formation still looked to me like 4-3-3 with quite a lot of fluidity in the line-up, with Chamakh often pulling wide and Puncheon & Gayle striking down the middle. With no out-&-out wingers there is a great deal of reliance on our full backs to join the attack, and an excellent switch of play by Jedinak found Ward in plenty of space to deliver a cross; from the resulting corner a combination of defender, KG and Gabbidon saw the ball bounce past Westwood. Don't be surprised if the "Dubious Goals" Committee disallows it retrospectively as not being of Premiership quality, but no-one at Selhurst seemed to care. Although Sunderland then appeared to dominate territorially for the rest of the first half, the best chances fell to Palace on the counter, with Puncheon twice going close, and Jedinak closer still with a curling effort that just slipped over the angle of bar & post. The middle trio of Jedinak, KG & Campaña were more than holding their own with a combination of steel & skill, while the defence was generally solid, with the exception of Ji's appalling impression of a forward, with Julian never really involved. Palace more than deserved the lead at the interval.

As at Stoke we started slowly after half-time, and for a period were unable to clear our lines and get out of our half, and I did fear a Sunderland revival if we tired, although unlike last week even during this spell Palace came close to scoring a second through medium range efforts from Jedinak, Gayle & Puncheon on the counter. Campaña came off for Williams – whether Jose was tiring as last week or Holloway was looking to exploit gaps as the game stretched (a regular ploy of his in recent matches back to the play-offs) we don't know yet. Then came the hammer blow of Fletcher's equaliser, and it involved two of our best players being just off their games for a second, showing how quickly errors can be punished at this level: Ward was outwitted by Colback on the right; and Jedi lost two yards on Fletcher; whether one of the central defenders should have picked up the striker's run from outside the box is questionable.

At this point Palace could have folded and we came under a short period of pressure. Now Palace's character showed through, but sadly Williams badly sliced a shot from an excellent position. It didn't make much difference as, with Phillips stripped to come on, good work from Chamakh down the right, another lucky rebound and great anticipation from Gayle resulted in a penalty & red card for O'Shea. We wondered if KP would stride onto the pitch to dispatch the spot kick but, showing great spirit, Gayle grabbed responsibility and – with my fearing a "Zohar" moment – put away not the greatest penalty ever seen, but one with plenty of bottle. After that Palace defended relatively easily, and could have grabbed more goals on the counter, efforts from Jedinak & KG coming closer while Westwood denied a Williams' volley. The icing on the cake was a superb strike from sub O'Keefe after hard work by Puncheon that would have defeated any keeper.

Marks marks
Speroni – 6
Ward – 8

```
Moxey — 8
Gabbidon — 7
Delaney — 7
Dikgacoi — 8
Jedinak — 8
Campaña — 7
Puncheon — 8
Gayle — 7
Chamakh — 8
Williams — 7
Wilbraham — 6
O'Keefe — 7
```

Return of the Mac

Buoyed by last weekend's victory, and with no match for 11days, how stupid is that? The poor little mites must be a bit tired after three games and need a rest. How would they manage if they were Tennis players? I thought that I would make a midweek trip down to Tooting and Mitcham, to watch the U21's. It is on the way home, and I could catch up on the progress of some of our new signings, as well as a couple from the treatment table, who it was rumoured might have a run out. I was also inspired to go, so that I could tick off what I believe is the only ground in the country, that my sister has seen Palace play on and I haven't. My sister, by the very nature of having three brothers and three sons, has no option but to follow Palace. However, since Dad took her to Mansfield, at about the age of two and lost her shoes, her trips around the country were restricted. Firstly, I would imagine, this was because Mum considered, he couldn't be trusted with her first-born's apparel. Then, as one brother after another, arrived and took her place.

She did however, see Palace, at Tooting and Mitcham in 1976, in an F.A. Cup replay, played on Monday lunchtime. Now this was not, some Bank Holiday fixture, just a normal working day. Perhaps the idea that it is just the Premier League, coming up with strange and anti-social kick off times, is a bit unfair. After all. Dad, who was almost ever present at the time, couldn't even swing time off work, for this one. To ensure a family presence at F.A. Cup matches, which I am informed, extends back to the war, the tickets were duly passed to Mum and Christine. The latter was apparently off school, with some mystery illness, that still allowed her to attend football, (No fines in those days for unauthorised absence.) Perhaps the most staggering thing about that day, was that, 9,998 other people, managed to blag the day off work, or school, and that Tooting and Mitcham's ground, could in those days, accommodate such a big gate.

Just like Wrexham previously, I was not allowed to go, thus my ground deficit to my big sister, a fact I intended to rectify. The movement from the old Sandy Lane ground, to a new fancy one, which I have now found out has a 3G pitch, (Although, quite why you need a pitch that sends quick mobile phone messages, I am not sure.) meant that I was technically, not adding the same ground as her. However, if you apply the strict criteria of the Ninety-Two Club, I have only attended about ten grounds now, well below my peak of about 80. I will therefore, continue to use my own rules. How anybody who actually follows a particular team, is ever supposed to gain entry, to this exclusive club, I'm not sure. Anyway, I'm going all Ronnie Corbett again, so I will get back to the match. Tooting and Mitcham's new ground, I have just discovered is not actually near Tooting Station, (On my way home.) as I thought, but is near Mitcham Station, (Not on my way home). However, the deviation, unlike my writing was not great, and I was there in plenty of time. The new ground is modern and practical, and I was pleased to see that the players tunnel, was in the main stand as it should be, not stuck in a corner of the pitch, as with so many modern stadium. This area, at one end of the ground, is reserved for the much more nasally aesthetic, Jerk chicken shack, which cleverly serves people, both inside the ground and on the training pitches outside. This is such a little point, but shows a degree of practical foresight, from those trying to make maximum use and value, from a community facility. I also loved the small barbecue, just cooking away on the concourse, which the owner occasionally visited, to tend or collect new supplies. I am not sure how this arrangement, would have coped with the health and safety implications of that 10,000, F.A. cup crowd, but it was homely and welcoming, and the Jamaican Patties, were cheap and tasty.

I had come armed with a camera, and without the Stoke stewards, telling me I couldn't take photographs, I merrily snapped away to my heart's content. Firstly this was from behind the goal, and later it was from a seat in the stand, the ability to move around a ground, bliss! Palace fielded in theory, a strong team, and it was pleasing to see the club captain, Paddy Macarthy, back organising the troops, at the heart of the defence, with no sign of his long-term injury. Jonathon Parr, looked a little more tentative, but put in a reasonable shift. Two of our other new signings, didn't look to me so secure, with Elliot Grandin in particular, looking disinterested. I am however, beginning to particularly like the young development player, Conner Dymond, a fiery tackling midfielder, and I wonder if he might get a chance, to bring this much needed and underrated attribute, to the first team. His penalty that gave us the 1-0 lead, at half-time, was also confidently taken.

 The second half saw no return for Jonny Parr, but it seemed this was a scheduled change. The same could not be said for Paddy Mac, who was subbed on 60 minutes. This decision, seemed to come at very short notice. Given his terrible luck with injuries, I fear that it might see the end of his Palace career, and I can't see him making the 25-man squad now. I took the slightly pessimistic step, of taking his photo, as he disappeared down the tunnel, for possibly the last time in a Palace shirt. Although I have always felt, he has some limitations, he has been a tremendous servant to the club. I wonder how many other players, over the years, have ended their careers with a club, in similar fashions. Limping off, on a non-league pitch, applauded by just a few, is far removed, from the adoration of tens of thousands, at even a small ground like Selhurst Park.

Cardiff started to become more dominant, as the game went on, with Jordan Much, running most of their play. Despite the efforts of the exciting Kai Kai down the wing, and the late introduction of Alasani, who doesn't seem to have developed, as I had hoped, Cardiff eventually came out deserved victors, 2-1. I keep hearing, that these games are not about results, but with our much-praised academy, bolstered by some first teamers, I can't help feeling we should be a bit more competitive, than it seems we are. Overall, with Paddy's injury, it was a bit of a downer evening. Despite this, I got a few nice photos, had a nice Pattie, and my sister, no longer has that one ground over me, so it wasn't all bad.

Palace Go International

This whole writing thing is going to be tricky if I can't even remember games happening. I admit that Palace v Oman is such a game. I didn't go, I didn't write anything and I'm not going to pretend otherwise. So it's over to Mark again. One of my Beta readers, James, to whom I am immensely grateful, made the observation that he couldn't really understand what this paragraph was for, or what purpose it served. To which on reflection I will reply, "exactly, my point"

Marks match report

Around 500 hardy souls along with Pete the Eagle & Steve Claridge (there's name-dropping for you!) saw a Crystal Palace XI defeat the whole of Oman last night, in what must have been better entertainment than Roy's boys on ITV1.

Annoyingly, despite advance publicity, only one of the freshest batch of recruits appeared in Cameron Jerome, which indicates that Kebe, Mariappa, Bannan, Guedioura et al are being saved for Old Trafford on Saturday. Palace fielded a 4-5-1 formation with: Alexander in goal. Taylor at right back & the returning Jonny Parr at left back with a short but stocky central defence of Marange & Blake. There was a strong central midfield three of O'Keefe, Garvan & Dobbie, with De Silva playing wide right & Jerome wide left, with Wilbraham the sole striker.

There were no squad numbers printed in the programme for the Omanis which was probably just as well as gold numbers on white shirts were indecipherable. They reminded me of a good First Division side in that they were technically sound for much of the time, but lacked any cutting edge. Once arriving at the box there were a lot of attempted short passing but little penetration until one of the passes was misjudged & intercepted. No-one seemed willing to take responsibility & shoot (sound familiar?), with most efforts coming from long range & being woefully inaccurate – I can't recall Alexander making a save. They did make some incisions down our right side but the final ball was often poor and they lacked bodies in the box.

Palace played a little quicker & a shade more direct. Most impressive was Cameron Jerome (can we sign Thomas Cameron to really muddy the waters?) who looked quick

29

and strong, but whose finishing was just out, being too soft & cute with one before lashing over a first time effort. Wilbraham worked hard and played well but is fated never to score: the keeper made one good reaction save from a close range header, and when Aaron rounded him a defender cleared the not-hard-enough shot off the line. It was good to see Jonny Parr back; he started strongly before fading and looks like he needs more match practice before returning to the first team. The central defence was seldom worried but, for the first half at least, the most disappointing performance was from Dobbie, who was not guilty of lack of effort but gave the ball away too often too easily, trying to be too clever by half.

The second half was a slight improvement on the first, being a typical friendly with very few tackles. On the hour Parr, O'Keefe (skipper for the night) and Jerome were withdrawn, perhaps indicating places on the bench at Old Trafford, being replaced by Appiah, Boateng & Parsons. Goals came from Dobbie and De Silva, both being similar efforts from the right side of the box placed across the keeper and inside the far post; De Silva had earlier struck the woodwork with an impressive effort from the edge of the box. Late subs Wynter and Karkai (?) saw a little action.

In all a gentle stroll for the second string.

Moan U Away Saturday 14th September ~~3pm~~ 12.45pm:

Bans and Bias

Here we go, a trip to Old Trafford, now this Premiership malarkey is really taking off. Before you turn off your Kindle, (Other book readers are available, but I get much more commission, if I don't make this available for them, Amazon are smart like that.) or close the book whilst muttering, "oh no, not another 'Premiership is wonderful,' kind of book, that's not what he said, in the introduction," I need to explain. For much of my adult life, Man United have been the very antithesis, of what I like about football and its fans. It annoys me having to walk around South London, or Herefordshire, and seeing more red shirts, than red and blue, or black and white. People who say they support Man United, because they win things, but have never been to Old Trafford, really annoy me, and the love fest, TV football shows to anything Man United, really, really, really annoys me. I could go on, Man U shirts in Croydon's Whitgift centre, for just one and I may well return to this subject in the New Year, but here's the rub. I conversely rather admire, the coach loads of supporters who genuinely travel from all-round the country, to Old Trafford and elsewhere for every match. I do not choose to follow a football team, that I have no geographical link with, but anybody who does that, and actually goes, deserves an acknowledgement as dedicated. Would they have still done this, if 1990 had turned out differently, and they hadn't borrowed a decent goalkeeper, to cheat their way to the F.A. Cup? (I know it wasn't really cheating, but it felt like it at the time.) Would Alex Ferguson have been sacked? I don't know. My suspicion is regrettably, a large number would still attend, and it would just be the hangers on, that would desert to some other team or at the very least, not walk around Norbury, with Rooney or Ronaldo, emblazoned across their shoulders.

I also confess, that in private, I would give a lot to have witnessed the successes they have, for just one season. I don't think I would want to, witness it every year mind, that would just be boring. I am also honest enough to guess that, if I had, I similarly would begin to expect it. Ironically, when over the last 30 years, I have wanted them to fail miserably, be relegated, or knocked out of the cup by Bishop Stortford, (Other non-league teams are available.) I am kind of wanting them to experience, the lows as well as the highs of being a football fan. So perhaps, rather than being jealous, I actually feel a little sorry for them. They will never experience what I have, following my club. This has all confused me now. If I dislike Man Utd fans, as much as I thought I did, perhaps I should want them to win everything, every year from now to eternity. As I definitely don't want that, I guess I must like them, more than I thought. Alternatively, perhaps it is just a bit of Buddhist philosophy, coming through. I just want everybody to be happy. As we know, money and success don't always bring this emotion, (More on Chelski, and United's noisy neighbours, in a few weeks.)

Sorry I got distracted

I haven't changed my opinion, in just a few short weeks, of supporting a Premiership club, (although typing that, does somehow feel good.) it's just that the trip to Stoke was pretty normal, as away trips go. Park next to the ground, pleasant enough stewards, reasonable ticket prices and a 3 o'clock kick off, on a Saturday. The trip to Old Trafford, I was sure would be a wholly different ball game, and I wasn't to be disappointed. First up, the kick off was moved to 12.45, Saturday Lunch time. I know that some people might like this time, but for me it is largely useless, even as a Sky Sports subscriber, because I am nearly always, travelling to a game. My preferred travel method, to away games, means I am never at the ground early enough to watch in a pub, and the radio reception on coaches, is pretty dismal. 3G Mobile internet, is I'm assured fine. We have toilets, tea, coffee, and DVD players, but the ability to pick up Radio 5 Live, is still surprisingly bad. Home games, I sometimes get to watch the first half and the last 10 minutes, but it's not really my priority at these times. As a supporter who attends games, home matches on a Saturday lunchtime, which I am sure we will experience, at some time this season, seriously screws with the day. If you are travelling around the country, every other weekend, the morning of a home match is when you get things done. If on the other hand, you are scheduled for an away match, in, for instance, the North West of England, then it is even more of a pain in the arse. It would be reasonably commonplace, when discussing this topic, to ask the question, "do these match planners realise, how far it is from London to Manchester?" However, I'm pretty sure that they do, and just don't give a monkey's. After all, it always gives the commentator, the opportunity to show their exceptional knowledge of British Geography. At some point, they can say "I bet those travelling fans, had an early start today." Well I can confirm, that today, we did as you anticipated, have a very early start! 5.15am if you really want to know. So thanks for nowt.

The second, much anticipated Premiership farce, was soon also to be thrust upon us, Tickets! Which I hope will not become, a theme from hell of this season, or I will just jump out of the back of this coach now. The first batch of tickets issued to us, were at the ludicrously expensive price of £46. Now if you multiply that evenly by 76,000, you get a truckload of money. In fact, one could argue, more money than is entirely necessary. You can therefore understand my feeling of immense pleasure and gratitude to Manchester United, when we received an email from the CPFC box office, saying that, by the way, the £46 tickets were pretty rubbish and if you want to have a decent view, at the Theatre of Dreams, you really needed to pay a bit more. Luckily for us, the Man United box office, kindly offered us a small number of better tickets, at the bargain basement price of £55. Now I am definitely not made of money, and have already calculated that the season will cost about £1700, in travel and tickets for away matches, so I really didn't want to pay anymore, but here's the dilemma. I did want my Mum to be able to see, and considered that if we paid the premium price, this was more likely. So with a heavy heart, I confirmed that we would like the slightly better than rubbish seats, and requested as near to the front as possible. The seats were duly confirmed, and that was the end of that! Not in the world of football tickets.

Now before I go on, I must explain that dodgy ticket allocations, are not reserved for the Premier League. Last season, Blackpool sold tickets at a pricing differential, only to then operate a sit anywhere you like policy. Unsurprisingly people chose the more expensive seats, and when some arrived late with their upgraded tickets, found none were actually available. I raised this in passing with a steward, whose response was, "oh yeah, we've had a lot of problems with that, this season." Doh! Well maybe, just maybe, you could try doing something about it then. After all, that's kind of your job. This sort of approach, has left me slightly wary of taking things on face value, and thus started an email chain with the Man United box office. If it wasn't so incompetent, from the biggest football club in England and possibly the world, it would be quite funny. I will summarise the emails here, for comedy effect, but they do exist.

Me to MUFC: "Could you please tell me, the location of row DD in the away section of block 229, because there doesn't appear to be a seating plan, on your website and I have requested tickets near the front."

MUFC to Me: "I cannot be bothered to read your email properly, but if you have a problem with your ticket, you will need to speak to CPFC box office. CPFC have been allocated the following blocks. Or you could see the seating plan on our website."

Me to MUFC: "Thank you for your kind reply. However, it doesn't answer my question. Only repeats what I told you. In addition, your website does not actually have a seating plan. I am aware that if I have a problem with my seat, I will have to discuss this with the CPFC box office. However, I don't know if I have a problem with my seat, because I can't find out where it is, you complete imbecile. (I did make up the last phrase, but would have liked to write it.) Is there any chance that you could actually answer my questions?"

MUFC to me "As you insist on receiving an answer to your question, I can confirm that, even after paying a supplement, your tickets will still be rubbish and not what you want. But, what do we care, you will still come and even if you don't, someone else will. We have your money anyway and are the biggest club in the world."

Me to CPFC box office: "My tickets for Man U seem to be further back than I expected, despite being apparent allocated first. I will send somebody down to change them. Which really negates the purpose of an away season ticket, in the first place."

I have gone on at some length, about just getting too Old Trafford, so I will try to be brief, about the actual experience. I am pretty confident, some of the points it raises, will reoccur throughout the next 9 months. Firstly, it is an impressive stadium. However much I would like too, you just can't avoid this point. There are also, a lot of fans walking around outside the ground, who appear not to know where they are going, and who definitely don't speak with a Lancashire accent. However, if I am fair, this may be more apparent just because let's face it, there are more people there, full stop. A small percentage of 80,000, is still quite a lot of people. Perhaps in their half-and-half scarves, taking photos and looking lost, that just makes them more evident. Also if I'm honest, that's what I wanted to see and report back on, so I accept I wasn't a wholly impartial observer.

Inside, many so-called impressive grounds, I am often disappointed by the ancillary facilities, which seem to be almost added as an afterthought. I am sure that the TV commentators, who describe them in this way, do not have to concern themselves with, queuing for a crap cup of tea, or warm beer or a slot in a smoke filled toilet. (Oops forgot! smoking is banned in all football grounds and doesn't happen anymore, much in the same way that standing is also not allowed.) Old Trafford doesn't disappoint, in the disappointing concourse respect, and for your £55, you have facilities, which are basically chiselled into a landing area. There are also a reasonable number of steps, so I wouldn't recommend it for the elderly. This is quite ironic, as I would imagine that these are just the people, who may choose to pay the extra, to provide a better likelihood of an acceptable view. I do accept that the view, once in your seat, is pretty good, but it does always amuse me, that clubs consider that seating, which is still behind the goal, but square on to pitch, is of a higher quality. It is consequently, more expensive, than a seat which has a slight angle. Let's face it, it's still about the most rubbish seat they have available, which is why they give it to us.

Before I let Mark explain the game in his report, I will just say that the atmosphere at the Theatre of Dreams, from the home fans, was rubbish. In fact, it was so rubbish, I was prompted to write a poem about its rubbish-ness. Ok, so I know we aren't Barcelona, or Juventus, or even Liverpool, but come on lads, make a little bit of effort. Out sung by 3000 away fans, that must be embarrassing; no ifs, no buts, dress it up however you like, but it was plain embarrassing. Palace are loud, but I think a bunch of school girls, from a posh private school, would have out sung the mighty reds, and you won. Imagine what it would be like if you lost.

Theatre of dreams, It is called.
Perhaps cuz they're never awake
If you follow man U, you can sleep
Knowing three points u will take
With seventy thousand you'd think
They might just, a little noise make
But were Palace we've taken piss
And exposed their whole ethos, as fake.

34

We sang and we cheered on our team.
Not once did we stop for a break
But tomorrow their Kids will all ask
Dad,
" why can't we sing for f@@k sake"

The game: well much as we expected, we lost and Ashley Young fell over a lot. I am sure that MOTD will say, he brought fouls, but I personally think he cheats. If he tried that crap on the Purley Way, on a Sunday, he would never make it back to his Bentley, or if he did, would find it missing vital parts. Cheating is cheating, whichever way you dress it up. I don't trust myself to write anymore, right now. It's a long way home and I have an audio book to listen too. (Bill Bryson: a short history of private life.)

P.S Same old Man U, always cheating.

Marks Match Report

A battling performance at the home of the champions, undone by two refereeing decisions, sounds like a heroic story and bad luck, but it's not as simple as that. It may be an unpopular view to take but guts and work rate were undone mostly by our own errors against an unimpressive United. I'm not decrying our efforts, and I'm as proud as any Palace fan at the effort, and as fed up with the refereeing, but we did help our own demise – and that's not a shot at KG. This is all without having seen one iota of TV coverage so it may really be out-of-date...

Palace, as they had against Tottenham, showed two failings that could torpedo plans for a second Premier League season. We gave the ball away far too often, and especially in areas of the pitch that constituted severe danger, and most concessions were made when not under pressure. Simple balls were routinely played to opponents: Puncheon, Delaney, Gabbidon and to a lesser extent Campaña were all guilty of this on more than one occasion, but shockingly the main culprit was the normally unimpeachable Jedinak; at times his standard of passing lapsed back to the start of his Palace career, a fault we thought had been eradicated from his game. The penalty, and KG's red card, came directly from a misdirected pass across the pitch halfway inside our half.

This failure was compounded by an apparent lack of
ambition to hit United at pace. Playing on the counter
it is essential that opportunities to strike are seized
whilst the opposition is stretched & caught with
players, preferably defensive midfielders or full backs
(or, if really lucky, a central defender!) up field &
out of position. Instead the man in possession would
often check back, play the ball sideways or backwards,
allowing United's defence to filter back and regain
their defensive structure. The desire to maintain
formation often choked off our attacking options, and
was made worse by our routinely then giving the ball
back to United through careless use of the ball or a
short passing move that ended up blind alleys. The lack
of movement ahead, from all bar Chamakh, didn't help
either.

What particularly galls me is that this United team
appears to be a shadow of those sides of the last 2
years. Rooney in particular had a wretched afternoon,
typically managing one sole brilliant piece of play for
the goal that made sure of the points. With more care &
attention on the ball, and with a greater willing to
look to play quick balls behind their defence – Gayle
looked sharp enough to profit from them today – we
could have gained a result. Instead De Gea won't need
to wash his kit tomorrow morning.

Palace lined up in what looked like a 4-3-2-1
formation, with Mariappa making his debut for the
absent Ward. After a reasonable start Palace found
themselves pinned back in their own half for much of
the first 5 minutes, a result of both poor ball
retention and tactics. United's 4-4-2 gave us some real
problems down both flanks, with both full backs exposed
and often outnumbered; although Campaña tried hard to
help Moxey, Mariappa experienced a torrid debut up
against Young with little protection from Puncheon.
Palace tried hard to shoot themselves in both feet with
some careless passing in dangerous areas, Jedinak twice
giving the ball away when the side was going up towards
the half way line, while both Delaney & Gabbidon had
delusions of grandeur in attempting some fancy moves in
dangerous areas that could have cost us dear. Young had
already had two penalty shouts, the second resulting in
a deserved caution for simulation, while Van Persie,
denying the laws of geometry, somehow flicked a ball
wide of the near post, and then set free blasted a

volley that clipped the top of the bar when a goal
seemed certain.

Despite a lot of possession and territorial advantage,
United could not break through, and frustration must
have been building up before half-time, especially as
Gayle finally found himself on the end of good passes,
missing the first with a shot dragged wide, while
embarrassing Ferdinand later when zooming around the
veteran defender – we were all certain his dink over De
Gea was going in. Then Jedinak tried a stupid ball
across the face of the defence, the ball was seized by
Young who went down as three defenders converged on him
in the penalty box arc. From my viewpoint I couldn't
tell if there was contact or not, but it looked outside
the box; the referee certainly looked to his linesman,
and I'm sure the latter didn't signal for a penalty,
but it was given after a delay anyway. KG was shown a
red card, a logical decision if (a big IF) the penalty
was deserved, and Van Persie showed no mercy.

No changes at the start of the second half, and you
could understand Palace's caution in pushing forward,
but surely taking a free kick well inside United's half
and playing it all the way back to Speroni was taking
it too far. We still managed to give the ball back to
them on a regular basis, and gradually the other new
lads – Guédioura, Jerome & Kébé – were introduced as
the team tired, but none managed to make a difference.
Palace visits up our end of the pitch became rarer,
while United increasingly found room on the flanks.
They were particularly finding space behind Mariappa,
and only some brave defensive blocks from Delaney &
Gabbidon, and some unorthodox keeping from Speroni,
kept us just in the game. The killer blow, completely
out of keeping with Rooney's performance, came when
Guédioura was apparently fouled well inside United's
half, then Palace conceded concession again, and
eventually conceded a free kick with which Shrek gave
Julian no chance. As Moxey tired our left flank was now
being turned on a regular basis, but somehow we kept
them at arms' length. At least Zaha didn't come on to
wreak havoc on a tired & undermanned defence.

Mark's marks
Speroni – 7
Mariappa – 5
Moxey – 6

Delaney – 6
Gabbidon – 7
Jedinak – 5
Dikgacoi – 7
Campaña – 6
Puncheon – 5
Gayle – 6
Chamakh – 7
Guédioura - 6
Jerome – 5
Kébé – 5

Swansea home ~~Saturday 21st September 3pm~~
Sunday 22nd September 1.30pm

Never on a Sunday

I was interested to read whilst typing up these notes, that whilst the popularity of football has arguably never been greater, those actually playing the game have declined. Now whilst this may be partly due, to an increasing propensity to sit in front of F.I.F.A two thousand and whatever, I am now also aware of the problems, for people who want to watch and play. A few seasons ago, I decided that I still wanted to watch, but also wanted to play myself. Competitive football options, are limited for the only marginally competent, forty something footballer. The Southern Vets League, is quite substantial with four divisions at a variety of standards, but plays on a Saturday afternoon. In addition, it is based mostly around Kent, so I spent far too much time in Millwall and Charlton country. The ultra-competitive and aggressive nature of my team, was also starting to grate, as was their inability to actually turn up on time. Fortunately, I discovered my old boys club, have a vets team that play on a Sunday morning, giving me the opportunity to extend my footballing career, into Stanley Mathews territory, and still watch the professional game. Last season in the Championship, this resulted in only one clash. This was however, caused by an international vets tournament in Dulwich, and not Sky TV. After a surprisingly successful Friday evening and with the clear opportunity of progressing to the final, three of our team made the tricky decision to miss the final group game and watch Palace V Peterborough instead. As only a draw was needed, I was confident in my teammates ability to cope without us and was hopeful that we would make it back to the ground, for the final. After watching Palace, secured there Play-off place, which ultimately ended in today's fixture, in the Premiership, I rushed back to Dulwich, thanks to the 68 bus, only to find that my teammates had been thrashed. This resulted in a straight, third and fourth play-offs, which was already underway. Although I was happy to watch, and look forward to Brighton and Wembley, the team had not been able secure another goalkeeper, and after the obligatory change on pitch side, best boxers worn in preparation, I was back between the sticks.

I can sense that this year, there could be more conflicts and mad dashing about. As pretty much a super vets team, (super, as in even older, and not as in, smashing marvellous.) we are strictly old school in many respects. We play without linesmen, give three cheers at the end of the game and start our season in the traditional month of September, not during the cricket season. Thus, even though Palace have now played, more games than our points total would indicate, Alleyn's OB F.C. Vets, were due to start our season today. 10.30 KO against

39

Wickham Park. With the anticipated influx of young whippersnappers, (Anybody younger than Kevin Phillips may apply.) I didn't want to risk de-selection. In an ideal world, playing a morning game and getting to a lunchtime kick off, would not be a challenge, but like many of my age, I no longer operated in such wonderful isolation. Whilst many of my contemporaries, are fitting there social lives around ballet and flute lessons, for their children, I am combining mine, with ferrying my parents around. This is partly in repayment for the years of transporting me, and partly as we share a car, which is normally a sensible money saving strategy, but on other occasions, a right pain in the arse. Today it was the later.

This pain in the arse-ness, was compounded by the fact that my new vets team, seem to have a similar lackadaisical approach to kick off times, as my previous team. Unlike the Southern Veterans League, which just allowed a minimum delay to start times, resulting in starting games with ten, nine or in one case eight players. The friendly nature of old boys' football, means that a 10.30 start, can in reality drag itself back to well past 11. 10 minutes into the second half, the clock on the pavilion chimed midday, I downed gloves and was off. When I arrived home, at 12.15, there was far less urgency from my family than I was expecting. This was explained by the fact that apparently, today's game kicks off at one thirty, and not one, as I had thought. I really am going to need to concentrate more, about these minor little details. So we all made it on time and managed to secure a space in the Sainsbury's car park, with little drama. That being said, I will definitely need to improve my flexibility, as climbing across a car and out of the passenger door, is not as easy as it was in my youth, the car park is definitely busier this season. This ageing process was also brought home as I took the familiar route of least resistance, to my seat in the Upper Holmesdale. I have found, over the years, that an empty row and a clamber over seats, is often less inconveniencing to other fans, than a squeeze past people. Unfortunately, what was once a sprightly hurdle, is now a disaster, waiting to happen. However, much like chatting up two attractive twenty somethings, to try and blag a Lily Allen after-show invite, despite all indications from my body and those around me, my brain just fails to accept the ageing process,

By the end of the game, I was feeling that it might just have been better to stay down the club and drink beer. For the first time so far this season, I felt totally down about the whole game. We were totally outclassed in all departments; I was expecting to feel like this occasionally as the season progressed, but after Ollie's jig at home to Sunderland maybe I had got over confident. They say that it is this hope that kills and I felt I had had the stuffing knocked out of me, However much I say that I don't like the Premier League, I like my team more and hate them being beaten. The prospects of a trip to a surprisingly high flying Southampton, next week, now feels rather unappealing. The prospects of Lily herself calling me and sending that invite, also seems more likely than an easy path to seventeenth place.

Marks Match Report

In the first four Premier League matches Palace had not been outclassed. Spurs & Manchester United were controlled but not inspired, while Stoke were no better than us and Sunderland demonstrably worse. Yet today was as comprehensive a 2-0 stuffing one could imagine.

Swansea were expected to be a good footballing side, and so they proved with some snappy passing moves. Yet there was far more to their game than this technical ascendancy. Movement off the ball gave the man in possession so many alternatives; in contrast Palace tended to be static and too often funnelled infield denying width and allowing the defence to close us down. I didn't expect us to be out-worked: Swansea closed us down all over the pitch, pressing hard and making it even more difficult for our players to make effective passes. This was a team that had played away in Valencia on Thursday evening, yet the only team that looked increasingly jaded was Palace, who singularly failed to press Swansea in return. The writing was on the wall in the first minute when Michu found acres of space in the hole between the midfield and the defence, and was granted the freedom of Selhurst for much of the first half as Delaney & Jedinak both let him drift into space without either taking responsibility for picking him up.

Perhaps some of the confusion can be put down to the changes made by Holloway. With KG suspended there had to be one change in midfield, but Olly made three, with Campaña & Gayle dropping to the bench and home debuts for Bannan, Guédioura and Jerome. For a front six that had played well at Stoke and against Sunderland, and not been too shabby at Old Trafford, it was a surprising number of changes; it looked 4-2-3-1 with Guédioura joining Jedi in the holding roles, while Puncheon played down the right, Jerome down the left, with Bannan in the hole. Jerome never struck up an understanding with Chamakh when pushing on, while Bannan found himself dropping deeper to see any of the ball. In terms of technical proficiency almost every Palace player lagged behind his opposite number with poor ball control, decision making & passing dragging our game down.

Palace took an awfully long time to even gain a toehold in the match, going a goal down in the first minute courtesy of the aforementioned Michu, as he started the move through Routledge, Shelvey and a bit of luck before firing an effort through Speroni. With the Palace defence at odds, the next few minutes were harrowing, as an unmarked header from a far post corner cannoned back off the post, and then Moxey coolly blocked another effort on the line. Confidence drained from our team as Swansea pressed on, with Palace seldom able to string together a move, let alone a meaningful attack. Swansea were not above the cynical foul halting any possible threat, and it was from one well-worked free kick routine that Guédioura actually fired an effort on target, even if Worm had no trouble catching the shot. It seemed we had avoided the match-killing strike when Speroni made a superb save from Angel Rangel, but the seeds of our destruction were sewed in stoppage time when Delaney went down with what looked like a knee injury.

With no defender on the bench, and without KG as an optional right back that might have allowed Mariappa to move in the middle, there was no real option but for Jedinak to drop back, with Campaña coming on. How valuable might a Ramage, Ward, Parr or McCarthy might have been... As it was it effectively doomed us on two counts: Jedinak lacked the positional play of a natural defender, and was soon caught out by an angled through ball for their second goal; and it removed the most effective defensive midfield player from his natural habitat. Swansea didn't strike quite as quickly as in the first half, but it didn't take long for Michu to turn Jedinak, and although Vazquez saw his first effort saved by Julian, he set up Dyer for a second. After that Swansea rather toyed with Palace: Michu spoiled his display by scuffing a couple of glorious chances; Shelvey, who on the ball looks a little clumsy, belied that with some effective play and control. Palace were reduced to late forlorn & desperate efforts that pushed the shot count up to apparent respectability, but Worm never had to dirty his knees. The disappointing Jerome was replaced by Gayle, who at least showed some signs of understanding with Chamakh, as we actually saw someone move beyond the Moroccan to receive a flick on, while Thomas made an ineffective debut for Bannan. In all it was a rout in all but the scoreline.

Mark's marks

Speroni – 6
Mariappa – 5
Moxey – 6
Delaney – 4
Gabbidon – 5
Jedinak – 5
Guédioura – 5
Puncheon – 4
Jerome – 4
Bannan – 6
Chamakh – 5
Campaña – 6
Gayle – 5
Thomas – 5

Cars, Clutches and Crashes

As I have mentioned earlier, Dad has decided not to go away this season, but I did say at the start of the campaign, that I would try to get him to some away matches in the car. Southampton seemed the first good chance. The fact that my nephews, were travelling across from Bournemouth I'm sure added to the attraction, for Dad. Given the saga with ticket locations at Old Trafford, I got into work early the day Southampton were released, and phoned on the dot of nine. I was particularly pleased that, it was the clubs disability representative who answered. My party consisted of Mum (79), Dad (84), Niece (16), three nephews (11, 18 and 21) and me. I was confident that once I explained the age differential, she would be able to provide appropriate tickets. I ordered six tickets, to go along with the one away season ticket that we already had, and was disappointed that they didn't appear to be near the front. I did ask if this was the closest to the front available and after a brief check, she confirmed that it was the best available. Not knowing in advance the detailed lay out of every Premier League ground, it was difficult to question this statement at the time. The expensive nature of phone calls to the box office, eventually led to me running out of credit on my phone, marginally before I ran out of patience.

This started another exchange of emails, which was now becoming, too regular an occurrence. Once I had established our exact location in the ground, I set about trying to change my tickets, as the Southampton box office had indicated that I could. I emailed the Palace box office, and was told that there was nothing better, at the moment. Although I did receive an apology, that the original member of staff, who I must remind you, was the clubs disability coordinator, hadn't been able to help more satisfactorily. I was also told that as soon as a new block was opened up, the club would let me know and the tickets could be changed. So I waited... And waited.

Then I waited. I used the opportunity, to contact Southampton's own disability coordinator. He was a very helpful man, but as Dad doesn't have a blue badge, I was unable to secure parking at the ground, even if I paid. He did however explain that as long as I was able to arrive one and a half hours before the game, I would be able to drop my party outside the ground, then go and find somewhere to park. Getting my Dad into the ground was now proving just as difficult as finding him a seat, from which he might be able to see. The ultra modern, family friendly, all inclusive, Premier League, was proving less like this, in reality. On the flip side, it has all given me an idea for a new novel.

Now I would like to think that I am a reasonably patient man, but in the end I just pitched up at the club, with my six tickets in hand. As if by magic, six front row tickets suddenly became available and were exchanged. Now I am charitable enough to believe, that this was coincidental good timing, and I was obviously just about to receive an email informing me of this availability. However, one of the joys of the BBS is information, and am pretty certain that at least one block had come and gone. (with its associated front row seats.) As a result it is difficult to convincingly convey, this possibility, with any conviction.

Whatever the reason, I had my desired tickets. I could swap with Mum, and go up the back with her first allocation away season ticket tickets, and everybody would be happy. Now time to relax and hope we can get another much needed victory.

Life is never that simple is it. A text has just come in from one of my nephews that he can't now get the time off work.
I now find myself with one too many Southampton tickets. Fortunately, John, my vets team manager, , didn't get a ticket, but can now go. It will mean that he has to have my ticket as it is the only full price one that is in London. I will have to rely on my remaining nephews, getting out of bed on time, and getting the other adult ticket to the ground. Once in St Mary's, I hope we are all on the same concourse and can just swap seats around. Fortunately, it's only a quick jaunt down the M3 to Southampton, and should be no drama, two hours tops.

I picked my niece up this morning just after 10 am, it was ridiculously early really, but I have the 1.30pm deadline to consider. It will also be nice for Dad, to spend a bit more time, with his grandchildren. Coming at the journey from a different angle, made me decide to head due south, and whizz round the M25, to hit the M3. Heading due south was not a problem, but before I had even exited the slip road onto the M25, I could see that whizzing anywhere, on this motorway, was not going to be an option. I had heard about an M25 crash on the radio, but with so much time in the bank, I figured it would be better to deal with the slow traffic, rather than explore a convoluted route via Brighton. (After all, why go there, now we don't have too.)

So, just off the slip road, which just invited a reversing manoeuvre, we waited, which seemed to be, a feature of this fixture. Initially, this was with an occasional crawl forward, but generally, it was just another wait. In addition to the long periods of inactivity, I also had the sense, the car was not performing well. Every crawl and break, needed me to over rev the car, thus allowing me to break sharply, engage the clutch before boosting the rev count again. This didn't make for the smoothest ride, but most of the passengers didn't notice as… well I'm not going into details, as this would risk a clip round the ear, by the owner of the car. I was actually quite glad when we eventually stopped completely, and I could turn off the engine. Hopefully, the crash would be cleared soon, and I would be able to accelerate the car up to a steady speed, and cruise my way to the south coast, with the minimum of breaking. After about an hour, the M25 looked like a pedestrianised zone, as people wandered along the carriageway, chatting and finding suitable toilet facilities. It is in such circumstances as these, that the British stoicism and sense of propriety is often best judged. An unofficial male and female toilet was quickly established, (Gentlemen to the last; the ladies on the hard shoulder, with the men in the little woodland, on the theoretical fast lane of the slip road.)

People chatted with strangers, although anybody in red and blue, is never a stranger, wherever you may meet. Due to the early hour and short journey ahead, there was no panic and I was able to phone a few people, including coach one, to advise that the A3 or M3, was definitely the best route out of London. Fortunately, all were either passed the blockage, or navigating around. We however did not have this luxury. The benefits of 3G mobile internet, was a luxury that we never had in the heady days of the 1970s, when our coach seemed to break down with alarming regularity, as did on one occasion the players' coach. For a young lad, this was particularly exciting, as we picked them up on the hard shoulder and they just piled in, three to a seat, on our coach. You can't imagine Mr Rooney et al, doing that now. They would just email a local limo, to pick them up. Although I am not, smart phoned up, I was grateful for the news from others, and a global warning was posted on the BBS, by those with the necessary gadgetry. Mum, Dad, and Rhiann, sat in the car eating Haribo and listening to radio 5, or in Rhiann's case 1D on her iPod. The general message was a 1-hour wait, which still gave us time to get to the game, but would make my car-parking situation a bit dicey. The ticket exchange, was also looking less relaxed than had been planned. When by twelve, there was no sign of movement, and ambulances, as well as police cars, were still passing, all of the Palace fans, were beginning to look more nervous.

The consensus was 1 pm; we needed to be moving by one, at the latest.

Chatting to other drivers, I found that it wasn't just Palace fans, that were nervously discussing journey times and distances. One Arsenal fan, on his way to Swansea for the 5.30 kick off, had six of his friend's tickets. He, like us, figured 1 pm would be ok. This conversation, whilst standing in the middle of the M25, (Please any children reading, do not try this, as it is normally very dangerous.) also provided a moment of light relief. The Arsenal fan mentioned earlier, was actually from Brighton, and confessed that he had been at the Play-off matches, in May. The suggestion, much repeated on the BBS, that Brighton's remarkable upsurge in gates, was down to Chelsea fans going, when Chelsea were away, was not in specifics proved correct as the team was wrong, but it was in general concept. I managed to keep the smile to a minimum, as this information was relayed, but only out of general politeness to any football fan, stuck in a traffic jam, when they should be halfway to some away match.

As 1 pm came and went, there was still the prospect of a late arrival. When the traffic started to move at about 1.20, I was happy that some football would be seen, and I would be able to count the match towards my, hoped for, 38 game full house. The over rev break hard routine continued, as we made very slow progress, and eventually passed the sight of the crash at 2.30pm. The fact that we were required to bypass the accident, by heading off the motorway, and re-joining on the other side of the junction, caused a puzzlement, that I have still yet to fully resolve. Why, if the accident was beyond this slip road, had we not been able to do this 4 hour ago? If we had, we would now be safely in our much negotiated, front row seats. Instead, I spoke the unthinkable. "I'm not sure it's worth heading on, any further," Surprisingly, there were no dissenting voices, or even looks, just an acceptance that, sometimes life is a bitch like that. I have been amazed, at various points in my life, especially during periods of my own stupidity, that my parents can maintain this attitude, and it is a credit to my niece and her parents, that she is similarly accepting. I was the only one, who was evidently pissed off. Perhaps, if I could have looked inside their brains, as I could mine, I would not only have found, more content generally, but also a little voice jumping up and down, in a hissy fit, like there was in mine So, after 4 and a half hours in the car, we had made it to nearly Reigate, glancing wistfully at the fast moving M25 ahead, I continued up the slip road, round the roundabout and back in the direction of home, the journey took less than 45 minutes. Barbara from the BBS, had apparently been just behind the crash, and was one of the first to get moving again. As she arrived just after kick off, and we took well over an hour, to get to where she had been, I know that our decision was correct. Most importantly, I returned my parents, and my niece, back to their respective homes, safe and well. The occupants of the vehicles involved in the crash, were not so fortunate. However irritated I was about the journey, and the result, this is a perspective, that it is important to remember. So it would be another year, before I could again attempt the whole season, and it was especially ironic, that this should happen in the week when I eventually brought an away season ticket, but it could have been worse. Back in the 80s, Dad fell over in the stand at St Andrews (It's all these bloody Saints.) and broke his arm. As he sat in a Birmingham A & E department, Palace struck six times, to record their highest away win in living memory. No such fate awaited Southampton, and I doubt Dad, will get as many copies of this game, on DVD as Christmas Presents, as we have videos of the 6-0. Marks report of the game, will I'm sure enlighten

Marks Match Report

Southampton's 2-0 win looks comfortable, but in truth Palace did not play that much worse than the Saints, but whereas their mistakes went relatively unpunished, Palace found that errors can be really costly. Once again we suffered a sudden collapse after half-time which left us chasing the game, something the current first team is ill-equipped to complete successfully, and once again an opposition goalkeeper had not a save to make. Although the work rate was upped from the Swansea match, our ball retention was again poor, and sadly it was two players we consider key, Jedinak & KG, who were most often at fault.

Holloway made four changes: Ward returned for the injured Delaney; KG rejoined Jedinak in the midfield holding pair; Kébé replaced the unavailable Puncheon to

47

make his debut; and Gayle came back in place of Jerome. At first it looked like a now familiar 4-2-3-1 with Bannan flanked by Kébé on the right and Gayle on the left, although the latter two often switched. Southampton started the steadier and nearly opened the scoring following some dithering by Speroni only for Ward to clear off the line. Southampton probably shaded possession in the first half, and managed plenty of crosses into the box, but despite the odd moment of panic Palace's defence coped with them. Lambert made two chances, one a free kick that Speroni shovelled to one side as it threatened to dip under his body, then at the end of a fine passing move flashed a shot just over.

Palace looked dangerous on the break, being more confident than at Old Trafford, with Kébé impressing and KG strong in midfield, but didn't create much. The best chance came when Chamakh burst into the box but instead of shooting tried to run across Boruc then went to ground. From 100+ yards away I couldn't say if there was contact or not, but the ref instantly signalled for a free kick and booked Chamakh for simulation. Chamakh sulked for a fair while afterwards; he was also involved in a "frank exchange of views" with Moxey when the left back complained about the striker's efforts defending a corner that led the referee to lecture them both, and at the start of the second half he ignored the training cones to continue a conversation with the official.

At half-time there must have been a chance that the pressure was building on Southampton, without a home win since March. Instead Palace failed to clear an early attack down the left, despite opportunities to do so, and Jedinak let the ball run away from him on the edge of the box; Osvaldo's shot was good but it seemed that Julian got something on the ball. One down almost instantly became two, as KG gave away a needless free kick on the right, with the Saints' player surrounded by four defenders; Lambert's dead ball finish was exemplary, striking the inside of the near post – no keeper will save those. The confidence drained out of Palace: Kébé was anonymous and was soon replaced by Thomas, while KG & Jedinak started to make mistakes. Holloway switched things around with Jerome coming on for Bannan and Thomas for Gayle but it made little difference. Jerome did manage to work an opening down the right but Chamakh stepped over the ball for a better placed team mate; eight yards out there wasn't one.

Holloway switched to 4-4-2 with veteran Phillips on for Kébé, who had been anonymous after the interval but Palace couldn't even muster a shot on target, Moxey's effort being blocked well before Boruc could dirty his kit. Southampton tried to exploit Palace's stretched midfield cover, and missed a couple of chances, with Rodriguez finally netting but from an offside position. Palace's attacking efforts were summed up by a stoppage time shot from Jerome that went well over. In the end Palace could not raise the game when behind.

Mark's marks

Speroni - 5
Ward - 7
Moxey - 7
Mariappa - 7
Gabbidon - 7
Jedinak - 5
Dikgacoi - 6
Kébé - 6
Gayle - 5
Bannan - 6
Chamakh - 5
Thomas - 5
Jerome - 5
Phillips - 5

Liverpool Away the Butlins Barclays Bus

If you have watched any TV programmes, about old holiday camps, but have never yourself experienced them, you could be forgiven for believing, your day was compulsorily mapped out, from beginning to end. If however, like my family and me you have attended such camps annually, for 50 years, you will know that there is considerably more choice, to opt in, or out. No one comes knocking on your door, dragging you kicking and screaming to a quiz, or a fun and games session. Similarly, you can always leave the organised activity and do your own thing. Unfortunately, on a coach, travelling to Liverpool, this last option is not physically possible, although mentally disappearing is still a viable option. I guess that originally, these holiday camps were slightly more regimented. Over the years, the Red, and Blue coats, (Palace get everywhere) will have learnt how to strike a happy balance, but these things do all take time to perfect. As the inaugural beneficiaries, of the Barclays away day bus concept, I was enthusiastically optimistic, for the trip up to Merseyside, and it was certainly an interesting experience. Perfecting the concept, will however, like a holiday camp, take a bit longer, although I hope for future recipients, not another 50 years

The inception of the Barclays, "You are football. " advertising campaign, has produce, what I think, are some really nice adverts, and the addition of the idea that they would fund some supporters to travel to away games, was all quite positive, even for an old sceptic like myself. The first challenge for the club, must have been to select the lucky winners of the golden ticket. One of the advantages of being a small club, is that the box office staffs are far more likely to be aware of who is a regular traveller, and thus should receive little luxuries such as, free first class travel.

The coach for the selected few, was scheduled to leave at 8am, half an hour before the remaining coaches, but as most of the regular occupants of coach one arrive an hour before the scheduled departure time, this made little if any difference. The first thing that we noticed, was that my half expected executive coaches, from our normal coach company were not there to greet us, but instead we found two standard coaches from an entirely different company. This may seem like a small thing, but we have developed a very good relationship with our driver Pete over the last few years, and have a confidence that he will get us to where we need to be, when we need to be there, or bust a gut trying. The second unexpected development was that we weren't allowed onto the coach, it looked like this was to be a very structured day. Two gazebos had been set up to serve coffee and a bacon baps, but this weren't yet ready so we just hung around. There was a rumour, that Ian Wright was around and about, but nothing concrete. By the time that the coffee had brewed, and the bacon had fried, time was pushing on and the remaining normal coaches, with their familiar livery and driver, had loaded and departed. It seemed that considerable time had been set aside for photos and interviews. At 8 o'clock in the morning, and prepared for a 10 hour coach journey, I had not really taken a great deal of interest in my appearance, and more to the point, had not realised this either. The interview that followed, and was posted on #you are football, did not therefore, do much to change, my singleton status. (However, it all seems to have worked out for Bridget Jones, so maybe there is hope yet.) I did try to put across, a slightly less than enamoured view of the Premier League, but as you can imagine, this did not appear in the finished film, I have therefore experienced, in a very fleeting way, what managers, players, and owners must on a regular basis. I know that the camera doesn't lie, but it doesn't always show the whole panorama either. I was however, able to reinforce the benefits of a small club, as discuss previously. It was only after this interview, when I looked around at the assembled, bacon munching crew, that I realised, there weren't actually, quite as many familiar faces as I would have expected. I believe, there were in fact, a few members of the club staff. This in itself is not a problem, as they are as much a part of the club, as we are, but at least 1, away season ticket holder who travels regularly on coach one, was not there, and had apparently, not been on the invite list. But as I said at the start, this was a new venture and mistakes can happen, but I did feel a little bit bad, for extolling this particular virtue of small clubs, and I hope Liz will forgive me.

Eventually we were allowed onto the coach, but the normal seating plan was definitely scuppered. Mandy and her wheelchair, were banished to the back of the bus, and everybody was shuffled back to make way for cameramen, photographers, interviewers and a couple of general event organisers. (Can you believe that Microsoft word, is actually trying to change "cameraman" to "camera operative". P.C has gone crazy; they will be introducing female linesmen soon, and calling them assistant referees, or something stupid like that.) In addition, two seats had been reserved for a special guest, although no seat had been reserved for the coach's official club steward. After a bit of reorganisation, to accommodate Charlie, we were off, armed with a little goody bag of sandwiches and snacks. This in itself, was another great idea, but given that Mum and much of the coach, take enough food and cakes, to require an extra inflation of the tyres, it is one part of the day, which would have been useful to know in advance. Despite these extra provisions and my bacon bap, there is still always room, just after departure, for one of Janet's, legendary, just out of the oven, sausage rolls. We left Selhurst, well behind schedule, but full bellies, and the arrival on the coach, of the previously rumoured, Mr Wright and his guest, hid any irritation.

I expected Ian to sit at the front of the coach, do his bit, whatever that was going to be, then turn around and face the front again. However, I found him to be very engaging, funny and approachable. I was lucky, that being only a couple of seats away, I could talk to him directly. We were able to compare hats. Mine obviously being far superior in design, if, I would imagine, considerably cheaper in cost. Ian then took part in a question and answer session, in which he admitted to being nervous about coming, as he was unsure what his greeting would be like. He explained the way that he left the club, and how in those days, he had very little input in the decision. He also detailed, with good grace and humour, the abuse that he and is Mum had received, although it was obvious that this was not the way he felt at the time. At the other end of his Palace career, he also told us about turning up at the wrong Crystal Palace, on his first day of training, something that I am sure has been repeated, by many a travelling supporter. After the allotted time, one of the organisers interrupted the proceedings, so that Ian could read out a quiz. However, once it was pointed out that, anyone could read a quiz, but only Ian could explain further his aversion to the number Nine, [viii] he was allowed to continue, answering questions. After about two hours on the road we made an unexpectedly early stop. This allowed Ian to make the switch to coach two and presumably, go through it all again. We had the quiz and watched a video, before our more normal stop, further on route. The late departure and unexpected earlier stop, meant that we were far later arriving at the break that some of us would have ideally wanted. Our normal driver and coach steward, would probably have decided at this point to have a shorter stop, especially as all the passengers were well catered for with refreshments, but schedules are schedules, and a forty five minute stop was advised.

If you are not a football supporter, it must be very difficult to lay on this kind of event, because you don't really understand the priorities, of the people you are trying to entertain. Presumably, they were given guidance on the activities from a higher being. However, it appeared that for all the nice aspects of the day, it was never really explained that the number one priority, was to get to Liverpool on time. As 1:30 P.M came and went, Charlie the clubs steward received a phone call asking where he was and why he hadn't got the spare tickets back to the Liverpool box Office. For him this must have been particularly galling, as although nominally in charge of the coach, it seemed he had very little control, over what it did, and when. As a result, we again had to drop him off, as close to the ground as possible, so he could sprint to the box office with a bag full of tickets. (You see, it's not just me, that has problems in this regard.)

We could perhaps in retrospect, have stayed an extra hour in the services, as I am sure Mark will explain. In short, watching only the second half, would have been far more encouraging. One little tip I have, for future Barclays Tour Bus planners is to watch the game, or at the very least, know the score when you welcome people back onto the bus. Although, in one case, very attractive; your smiley faced, "did you enjoy the game?" is perhaps not the best greeting, when, unless you have masochistic tendencies, it is highly unlikely that anybody actually did.

The return journey from games, normally involves a brief chat about the game, and for many listening to the 5:30 match on the radio. For me I try to sleep or write. Pauline knits and listens to the radio, but then she is a lady so can multi-task. The tour bus organisers, must have been given instructions to keep us entertained the whole journey. This included an instruction about what radio station to listen too. Iaan, Wright, Wright, Wright. Was apparently going to give a "shout out" to us on his radio show and we WERE going to listen to it whether we wanted to or not. I do have some sympathy with the Barclays Blue Coats, as they were obviously receiving instructions via the wonders of mobile phonics, but in their circumstances I might just have pressed the, 'flight mode' button and told my boss, "sod Off, they don't want to listen to it." However it is a bit like the TV remote in my house, he who pays the piper, calls the tune.

I guess that, I might seem a bit like a grumpy old fan, which given the subtitle of this book, shouldn't be a complete surprise, but, the day was overall, a successful event. We got to Liverpool in time for the game, just, had a Q&A with a Palace legend, a quiz, a video, sandwiches, bacon baps and I was interviewed on both journeys for the website. We even had an unscheduled mystery tour, back up the M6, when the coach driver started to head north again, until it was pointed out that, were in fact now going home, which was in London. The quiz was obviously won by Alex and Mark, who are the font of all Palace knowledge. Although, they still haven't been able to explain why, we didn't have a match on the last day of the Wrexham (4-2) season, (answers to MIKETHETIE2010 on the BBS). The shout out on the radio, by Wrighty, was listened too, despite our protests, and he gave a special mention to Pauline's knitting exploits. We even got back to Selhurst, not much later that we would normally have done. However, unlike a normal long trip, when I have slept and feel pretty relaxed, I was quite frankly knackered. As with my current holidays, I am no longer quite as interactive as I used to be. However, I do fully accept that this is perhaps, says more about me, than it does about them.

Marks Match Report

Palace ran into two on-form strikers who formed one of the most dangerous partnerships I've seen, nearly suffered an embarrassing rout, yet coming out on Anfield I was strangely encouraged by what I'd seen. There was a willingness to hit on the break that had not been seen at Old Trafford, and when the team could have collapsed at 3-0 down they showed the guts and determination we will need in plenty this season.

Holloway made four changes to the line-up: Delaney returned from injury for Gabbidon; O'Keefe made his first Premier League start for KG; the now available Puncheon replaced Bannan; while Jerome replaced Gayle. Not sure why Bannan & KG weren't in the squad and our lack of defensive cover saw teenage giant & Klitschko lookalike Ryan Inniss on the bench. On paper it looked like a straightforward (& now old fashioned) 4-4-2 but that's not what it looked like on the pitch. Chamakh was playing down the left most of the game; Kébé down the right was often joined by O'Keefe; while Puncheon looked like he was playing a central role alongside Jedinak. To be frank it looked like a lot of square pegs in round holes. Liverpool played three at the back with attacking wing-backs and it was immediately

noticeable how much room they were allowed,
particularly down our right side.

The first half could have been a car crash as Liverpool
started sharply and were soon making opportunities,
although if Jerome had been able to reach an early
cross who knows what might have happened. Once again
our passing was below standard, particularly from
Puncheon and Jedinak, while Gerrard was allowed a lot
of space – I don't think he broke sweat once in 90
minutes. Our more attacking outlook was leaving holes
that Liverpool sliced through. Both the first goals
came from our right, with Ward outnumbered and Mariappa
often pulled wide. Suarez, given time in the box,
stumbled and deceived both defenders & keeper when
scoring from a prone position; then Sturridge turned
Delaney inside out before scoring a fine goal. With
less than 20 minutes played it didn't look good.

Weird then that Palace then had a good spell, with Kébé
spurning one good opportunity then nearly profiting
from an unwitting deflection, while Puncheon blazed
over. Liverpool were still making chances and it took
some exceptional defending, particularly from Delaney,
and a couple of good saves from Julian to keep us just
in the game. I almost completely missed the penalty
incident as it was off the ball – at, like many, my
seat at Anfield did not actually allow me to see the
goalmouth! Ion replay it is soft in all ways: very
little contact, possibly outside the box; but a stupid
offence from Moxey that would have gained nothing.
Gerrard's penalty was soon followed by Moses missing
from a yard out. Hadn't it been 3-0 at the interval in
'89?

Holloway made changes at half-time that immediately
improved the play, with Gayle on for Jerome and Campaña
for Kébé. The passing improved and we managed to keep
the ball and spend more time in Liverpool's half.
Matters became even better when Bolasie came on and
most of our best work was down our left. Admittedly
Liverpool did ease off with the match all but won, even
though they could have scored another two or three,
Sturridge managing to hit the inside of the post, while
once again Delaney was outstanding with late
interceptions. Palace didn't manage many chances, Gayle
shooting over, but Bolasie earned a free kick down by
the corner flag, and Campaña's excellent near post

delivery was matched by Gayle's glancing header. Palace had restored some pride and the three substitutes had all given us encouragement. Kudos to Olly for the changes, but would also ask what the thinking was behind the initial deployment. Despite the score line the defenders generally played well individually, and we won't run into Suarez & Sturridge too often.

Speroni – 7
Ward – 6
Moxey – 6
Mariappa – 6
Delaney – 7
Jedinak – 6
Puncheon – 5
O'Keefe – 5
Chamakh – 5
Kébé – 6
Jerome – 5
Campaña – 7
Gayle – 7
Bolasie – 7

I need a laugh

After four defeats on the bounce, five, if you include the U21's against Cardiff, I needed some serious cheering up, and Brighton can normally be guaranteed to bring a smile to my face. YouTube clips of Play-off games, are always available, but when the opportunity arises to experience that feeling, live, it should never be turned down. Consequently, a Monday night trip to Selhurst Park, to watch the Eagles, do whatever it is they do, to seagulls, seemed appealing.

Considering the number of fans, that had scrabbled for tickets to recent games at the Amex, and the uncertainty as to when we would next play our main rivals, there were very few people approaching Selhurst, this evening. Despite this, as with the earlier Millwall match, there was a separate entrance designated for Brighton fans, although I confess I saw none. As I approached the turnstiles, I was quite staggered to see that all supporters were being search, and there was a minibus full of police, sitting in the otherwise desolate car park. Honestly, no word of a lie, we were frisked to enter an U21s match. The world of football policing has truly gone mad. It reminded me of a school match, which I played back in 1984. Alleyn's, (private school posh boys) v William Penn, (not private school posh boys). On this occasion a local bobby turned up, just in case, but wasn't able to prevent all my goalkeeping stuff, being stolen out of my goal, while I was actually playing. In fairness to him, his presence that day, was on the back of the Brixton riots, and he just watched the match, then went home. I raised the ridiculous search with the steward, who just shrugged and said that the police had heard stuff, on social media. Now I appreciate, the police have sometimes a difficult and unpopular job to do, but if they want to reinforce the view that their handling of Palace/Brighton matches, has been well over the top, then today has to be a classic. Why they didn't go the whole hog, and put up their ridiculous steel barrier, used last season, is a mystery. I wondered if this was the same police 'intelligence', that prevented Lazio supporters, attending a preseason friendly. I couldn't help thinking, there was a bunch of Palace and Brighton fans, sitting at home, having a right laugh at the expense of the Met Police. Possibly, sending messages too each other, via Twitter like, "let's all meet up at the u21's, for a good punch up" before sending personal direct messages to each other, with the real meet and greet time. It all sounds very familiar to the police intelligence, that sent officers to one London train station, whilst groups of Palace and Brighton fans, were merrily beating seven bells out of each other, at another station just down the road. I am not attempting to glamourise this behaviour, one bit, but if it weren't such a show of, incompetence resource mismanagement, it would be quite funny. A riot in Croydon, or a burglary at my house and they are short of staff, an under twenty-one's match, at a football ground, "right boys, there's overtime available Monday night, who's in."

Onto the match, and although Ollie has now stated that he is beginning to understand the rivalry, it appeared for much of what was, a proper U21s side, the message hadn't got through. It was quite a lack lustre performance, very similar to the first team's, recent outings, and Brighton scored two goals in the first half, due to poor defending. In the second half, we introduce Conner Dymond and Nabil Guedioura, the younger brother of our new first team signing, and all of a sudden, we looked more enthusiastic and competitive. Nabil's brace, was certainly excitedly celebrated, and but for the last minute intervention of the woodwork, we could have won. I'm not sure whether I was pleased by this comeback, or frustrated that we didn't play with the same urgency, in the first half. I always find this, a difficult call.

One of the other really positive aspects of the evening, was seeing the injured Jonny Williams in the stand, looking well. He always comes across as such a nice lad, and despite his international recognition, he has not become a Bertie big bollox. He is often seen at these matches, watching his old, age group teammates.

The evening did end on a bit of a sour note when a fight broke out in the car park. Ah ha, I here you thinking, so the Met were right after all. However, you would be wrong; the fight did not confirm the success of intelligentsia because it was between two local youths. Whilst a fight taking place, over an extended period of time, across a small gateway that you want to use, is in itself a disturbing scene, it is more disturbing, when it takes place within spitting distance of a van full of police officers, twiddling their thumbs and counting their overtime. In frustration, I went to tell them what was going on, only to find I had been beaten to it, by other concerned supporters. In retrospect, this was probably good, as I am sure I would have been less than complimentary, about their lack of observance and action. If they are gonna be there, and presumably charge the club for the privilege, then doing something in the event of disorder, is surely the minimum requirement. Or maybe, I just expect too much?

Fulham Home ~~Saturday 19th October 3pm~~ Monday 21st October 8pm.

Today, I was supposed to be writing about the Fulham game. By delaying 48 hours, I have had to completely change my train of thought. I will however, briefly touch on Monday night, yes Monday night. What's that all about?

Fulham they are rubbish, aren't they. We'll beat them at Selhurst, under floodlights!!!
Bolasie, was back in the team, and Campana, who everybody has been screaming for Ollie to pick, was starting as well. A bit of a surprise that, O'Keefe made the team, but I'm pleased, because he gets stuck in, which I think we need. I arrived early, and tracked down Caroline and Mandy in the disabled section. I needed to do this, so that I could get the West Brom tickets, to be exchanged at the box office tomorrow. They have now been moved, to a new disabled area, because the old one was blocked by the monstrous Sky studio, plonked in front of them prior to the first game, meaning they couldn't see half the pitch.

Dad, didn't come tonight, for whatever reason, but I think he's earnt the right, to pick and choose. As the game was pretty much sold out, I managed to find someone else, who looked over 65, (Sorry Tom, just a little joke.) to use his seat.

The game itself, was another weird one, we came out of the blocks well, and the ground was rocking. An early goal certainly helped and the players seemed confident. Fulham, looked every bit as bad, as we thought they might. Then bosh! I've seen that goal, about fifty times, and it simple gets better and better. The final revelation, that it was his weaker foot, brought this whole Premier League thing into perspective. Fortunately, the players seemed to accept it was a bit freaky, and continued to take the game to Fulham. The crowd also, kept their faith and ramped up the noise. Then just before half-time, bosh again, as sweet a half volley, as you would hope to see, top corner. This is just getting stupid now. How can we dominate a game for 45 minutes, and be 2-1 down at half-time. Delaney tried to raise the crowd up, as he left the pitch, but the shock and disappointment of the crowd, must have been reflected elsewhere. The second half, just wasn't the same.

Despite some fans claiming later, that the team played without heart, in the second half, I just don't see that myself. In any case, what happened off the pitch, was no different. It is easy for us, to sit in the stands and demand 100% commitment from the players, even at 4-1 down, but let's be honest, the crowd in the second half, was shit. When the Fulham fans, not renowned for their loud vocal away support, start taunting us with, "where's your famous atmosphere," something is missing.

Personally, I didn't want to be promoted; fans of the big clubs, won't understand that. I knew that it would be a miserable season, on the pitch, but I thought we would have fun, off it. No expectation, just a love for this club, my club. Ok, the money, that would be great, it would allow us to build for the future, and if the owners were sensible, secure it. All the other stuff, is just crap. Give me Barnsley away, on a Tuesday night in February, over a 12.45 kick off on a Saturday, at Old Trafford, any day. If we could have just taken, half the money, but stayed where we were, that would have been ideal, in my opinion. Anyway, I've gone off on one. Suddenly, all this expectation had appeared, it was Fulham, after all; little old Fulham. What seemed to have slipped from people's minds, was that this wasn't the Fulham of the 80's, this was little old Fulham, full of players that would have walked into our team. Sendoros, Berbatov, Sidwell, Duff and Tarabat, didn't even make their team, for Christ sake. Yet all of a sudden, they were going to be a pushover.

That sense of entitlement, seemed to galvanise a small, but vocal element amongst the fans, to boo, (and worse) as the team left the field. Without the benefit of TV cameras, my final memory of that night, was Ollie insisting that his players went over to the Holmesdale, and applauded them, as he continued to do, as he walked towards the tunnel. I feel as a collective force, we let the players, the club, ourselves and Ollie down. Maybe, like baby in Dirty Dancing, when told she had let her father down, we may bleat that, "you let me down too," but you cannot control other people, only yourself. If we as fans want to get all sanctimonious, we have to ask, did we do enough ourselves. Did we sing, until we were horse? Did we clap, until our hands were sore? Did we stay to the very end, to show the players, what real passion and pride was about? If anybody can answer all of those questions positively, then great, I applaud you. I can't. I was totally demoralised and disheartened. I was sad and a bit resentful. Part of me, was angry with people who I didn't even know, other fans, referees, some players, Dougie Freedman, even God and the masters at UEFA. If I felt like that, just sitting in the Holmesdale, isn't it natural, that some players and the manager, may have felt like that as well. Ah yes, I hear you say, but those players are being paid handsomely for their efforts, and that is true. But passion, commitment and effort don't have anything to do with money. Technical ability, I would expect that, and professionalism as well, but passion? If that were the main criteria, for being a Premier League footballer, my Dad would have made over 500 appearances by now, and at eighty-four would be playing centre midfield.

Rant partly over, the two Fulham goals were just plain brilliant, and up until that point, we had equipped ourselves well. Perhaps that is the thing about the Premier League, we were not quite prepared for. You can be organised, and work hard, but if opponents can bring out that spark of genius, then it is very difficult to do anything about it. I even wonder, if that was the dawning realisation, that hit the players, about the same time that it hit me. If that is the case, I understand why they might have, appeared to lose a little bit of fight and spirit.

Despite the disappointing league position, and result, the gallows humour of the Fulham fans, did still make me laugh, rather than make me angry.

We lose every week.
We lose every week.
How shit must you be?
We lose every week.

 The fact that I was able to smile, rather than to drive to Putney, and put bombs in all their basement cinemas, at least means I haven't lost my sense of humour.

Marks Match Report

What had been touted by Ian Holloway as a "Must Not Lose" match, and some supporters had even assigned the early label of "Must Win", saw Palace plunge from a decent start to a bewildering and shattering defeat, broken by one moment of sheer brilliance and some pretty ordinary defending. Fulham administered the thrashing that had escaped both Liverpool & Swansea, highlighting the deficiencies in the squad. Nothing we did not know of before, but our noses were firmly rubbed in the fact. The way the confidence & fight drained away was the real worrisome observation.

The Palace starting XI was that which finished the previous match at Anfield, and I don't believe there was anyone who would criticise this decision. The attacking trio of Jerome, Kébé and (perhaps a little surprising given his greater reputation) Chamakh were ditched for Gayle's pace, Bolasie's trickery and the potential class of Campaña in a regular 4-2-3-1. Perhaps Puncheon was lucky to retain his place, and O'Keefe was selected ahead of KG, but there had to be an attempt at continuity.

Palace started well and, as against Sunderland, scored early from a scramble following a corner. The initial clearance was neatly played back to Bolasie by Campaña, but the ball ballooned into the area as the cross was partially blocked; Stekelenburg stayed on his line, allowing Mariappa to get the leap on Hangeland and score quite easily. Although Fulham saw a lot of the ball, it tended to be deep within their own half, and this time Palace pressed the central defenders & keeper; passes went back & forth in areas that could not hurt, and the occasional error gave glimpses of chances. However Palace never really threatened except from shots from the edge of the penalty area or outside, and Stekelenburg was never really extended again.

Ironically, given Fulham's patient, laboured passing efforts, it was from a ball played back to front that Kasami scored one of the best goals I've ever seen at Selhurst. Mariappa allowed him a yard of space, and in a flash the ball was whipped over Speroni and into the far corner. No blame attached to either defender or keeper but it was a body blow. The next 25 minutes were pretty undistinguished. Bolasie threatened on both flanks while Campaña faded; Palace's passing game started to fray at the edges, with Gayle rarely seeing a sniff of the ball, while Fulham didn't look likely to score unless lightning struck twice.

The key moment of the match came right on half-time. Bolasie tried to dribble the ball away from danger when a good thump into row Z would have been far better in hindsight; losing possession he was adjudged to have brought down an attacker. The free kick was blocked by the wall but before he could be closed down Sidwell had the perfect opportunity to volley the ball into the corner of the net vacated by Julian who had gone the other way following the initial shot. There was no way we should have gone in behind – neither side had done enough to lead, but the momentum gained by Fulham would prove crucial.

A strong start was called for after some inspiring words and tactical genius from Olly; Campaña was withdrawn for Thomas as the young Spaniard appeared spent. Yet, as against Swansea & Southampton the roof soon crashed in, and it started with an appalling error from our lodestone Speroni. A weak kick was seized upon by Darren Bent and only a reflex save, similar to that Julian pulled off against Barnes at the Amex, saw the ball deflected inches wide. Danger averted, everyone thought, but a train of events had been set in motion that would destroy Palace's chances. Two corners with quite some similarities. In the build up to both there were confrontations between attackers & Palace defenders, particularly involving Delaney with Berbatov and sub Amorebieta; whether these scenes ruined the defence's concentration we won't know, but when Ruiz found two great deliveries we were sunk. Mariappa was beaten in the air by Berbatov – hardly the Nat Lofthouse of our age – and the ball was guided into the

far corner. Then, despite my vocal instructions to
"******* concentrate this time" the ponderous Swiss
Senderos was left unmarked at the far post – probably
Jedinak's man – and Speroni could not keep out the
volley, the ball squirming over the line with Julian
claiming he'd been pulled back, but I didn't see
anything of that. There wasn't a man on the far post at
either corner when the ball went in, although Moxey was
in the vicinity for the second.

What was disappointing was how thoroughly the stuffing
had been knocked out of the team with the third goal.
Fight disappeared and the crowd went flat. The rest of
the game saw Holloway throw on attackers in Chamakh &
Phillips and moving to what looked like 4-4-2, but
performances dipped drastically. Midfield was Fulham's
which was no surprise given how deep Jedinak & O'Keefe
dropped – at the start of one attack both central
midfielders were deeper behind the last defender. There
was little service to the forwards and meaningful
Palace attacks became even rarer. There was a scramble
involving Delaney, a Gayle effort that was cut short by
offside, a Thomas cross clawed away by the keeper, and
a late drive by Moxey who, along with Ward, showed at
least some spirit to the end. Fulham knocked the ball
around and only an athletic save from Speroni prevented
a fifth.

Speroni – 5
Ward – 6
Moxey – 6
Mariappa – 5
Delaney – 5
Jedinak – 5
O'Keefe – 6
Campaña – 4
Bolasie – 6
Puncheon – 5
Gayle – 5
Thomas – 6
Chamakh -5
Phillips – 5

It Shouldn't Have Ended Like This [ix][x]

23rd October 16:28

Ian Holloway has left his position, as manager of Crystal Palace by mutual consent, after less than a year in charge, at Selhurst Park.

23rd October 17:30

Crystal Palace F.C. holds a press conference, at which both Ian Holloway and Steve Parish, are in attendance.

I have just watched the press conference, and I am very sad. Football isn't supposed to have that kind of effect on people. Ollie looked and sounded, so tired and downhearted. He came across, as an honest and honourable man, who had been trying to do his best, for Crystal Palace, its owners, its players and its fans. Most in their hearts, would have known this, but sometimes the pressure in life, comes from those, who have no real right to impose it. From before the start of this season, the press had it in their mind, that we would be relegated. Recently, some have almost revelled in our league position, but if they knew we were so rubbish, surely we were doing as well, as they had themselves predicted. To suggest that, we should somehow be doing better, seemed contradictory. Everybody involved in the club, knew that it would be a difficult season, and most accepted this; it didn't mean we weren't going to try to stay up, but sacrificing the long-term future of the club to do this, wasn't going to happen again. It is however understandable, that this constant drip, drip of criticism, would get anybody down. Both Ollie, and Steve Parish, admitted mistakes were made in the summer, but the truth was, we just weren't ready. Although I am very sad, that Ollie has felt that he currently isn't the man for the job, there is also a part of me, that is very proud of my club. They have shown, there are proper ways to go about your business, which are often missing, in the modern game. For those reading this book, who have gleaned there information about Ian Holloways resignation, from newspapers, who have a dubious record for truth or accuracy, I would urge you to watch the press conference, in full. You may still then, choose to believe the stories of arguments and disagreements, that is your prerogative, but you will at least be making that judgement, (wrongly in my opinion,) armed with the full story, and not just the snippets and misdirection's, some newspapers publish.

Had I not rejoined the BBS, a few weeks ago, to discuss tickets with the Co-Chairman, (A truly remarkable service, that most other fans, would find difficult to even contemplate.) I would almost certainly, have joined this week, to offer support to Ian. I had put my name to a thread on the boards, in response to a comment, that no one had posted any positives about him. These were my thoughts yesterday, and I regret that it wasn't enough, but the events of today, have not changed my opinion. I reproduce it in full, as it was posted. (With added punctuation, for those who notice that kind of thing.)

"I'm in because he cares and I care.
I'm In because he is a family man and this is a family club.
IIB I don't want the club, to piss away large quantities of money, paying off a manager when there is nobody better.
IIB He tells it like it is, however much that upsets some people.
IIB His press conferences show emotion and can be funny, unlike Dougie Freedman, who never said anything of any consequence, whatsoever.
IIB he understands and accepts his own failings, and mistakes. Unlike DF, who became defensive and IMO objectionable, when his tactics or decisions were questioned.
IIB he is not DF, who took the money and ran.
IIB He had the tactical ability, to keep an average team in the Play-off places, and then beat 2 teams with far greater resources.
IIB He will never accept a 1 -0 defeat, as ok, and then say we looked like a good attacking force, despite not having had a shot for 79 minutes. He will try to recover the game.
IIB whilst he is our manager, I will never consider not renewing my season ticket, because we are so boring. Please see my previous point.
IIB some of the new plastic fans, that we have acquired, want him gone. We are not Chelsea or Middlesbrough or Newcastle. We are Palace, we do things our way; we do things the right way.
IIB We have played Moan U, Liverpool, and Spurs, and competed for large part of the game.
IIB He like me, knows that there are more important things in life, than football.
And finally IIB, under a previous regime we probably wouldn't have lost 4-1, at home, because after going 1-0, we would have brought on 3 defenders, stuck 10 men behind the ball, and never ventured into Fulham's half, for the remaining 83 minutes. We might have sneaked a point, but I would have been bored out of my skull.

So you want positives, you got them."

The other bad thing, about today, is that some people, are already talking about Tony Pulis, as the favourite to get the job. I texted my opinions on this, to my nephew, but they are not printable, although paraphrased, they were something like, "PLEASE GOD, NO!"

At the risk of repeating myself, please watch the press conference, it may just make you reappraise you view, on this crazy, irrational, stupid world, that is Premiership football.

.

Part 2: Post Holloway & Millen Magic

Arsenal Home Saturday 26th October 3pm 12.45pm

So we move on, with a nice easy one, today, Arsenal at home, with Keith Millen, in temporary charge. The bookies are offering 9-1, on us to win, and I intended to have a little flutter, but never made it. In hindsight, although I'm trying not to use any of that, this saved me a few bob. It's amazing what you can get accomplished, on the morning of a 3 o'clock kick off, and more to the point, what a rush it is, to get things done by 12:45. Two of my nephews are travelling up from Bournemouth, for the game today, and it's a 6am start, for them. We have just enrolled the youngest, Adam, into Pete's club, previously the Junior Eagles and in my day, the Palace Guard, and they are doing some really great things, to encourage the young fan base. One of the events that they run, are regular ground tours, on the day of matches. I received an email from the club yesterday, to say that there was one this morning, nothing like a bit of advance notice. Adam, doesn't actually know about Pete's club yet, as it is a surprise for his birthday, so this seemed like a great start and I booked the tour straight away. James, his older brother, could be his accompanying adult, and I would get brownie points, from both of them, reeesult. Life is however, never quite that simple. James, my oldest nephew, alternatively known as, "sick-note," decided he was too ill to travel Friday, and now they are coming up Saturday morning. OK, so they didn't know about the tour, but it is so frustrating sometimes. They are due in at Norbury, at 9.45am, and the tour starts ten. Subject to South West Trains, it will be a rush, but we might just about make it.

South West Trains, for once came good, and I actually managed to drop them off early, then get back home for a sit down.

The major question today, once I got everybody to where they needed to be, was what to wear? I know that there are fans, that almost religiously have the same clothes, home and away, but I'm not one of those. In fact, I have been endeavouring to wear, a different hat each home game, until we win. This is a new challenge post Sunderland, as I can't remember, what hat I wore that day. I appreciate, that this indicates poor record keeping. I will endeavour, not to repeat this shoddy note taking, in the future. In the words of Ronnie Corbett, "anyway I digress," I had considered, that my 1980's flat cap, would be a brave choice and on remembering the bag of nearly new Palace paraphernalia, decided that I would go for the full 80's approach. I informed my niece of this by text, but she did find the reference to, a search for leg warmers, confusing and slightly disturbing, in equal measure. Oh dear, I think I am definitely getting old. The kids from fame look, fortunately incomplete, (funnily, I did come across the legwarmers, Sunday night, such a relief that they were hidden, or I would have felt compelled to wear them.) I put Mum, Dad and Andrew, into the car, and we were off. Caroline from the coach, who is equally as short as Mum, and sits with us at away games, phoned on the way. It wasn't a great surprise to hear, that she had forgotten to bring her Norwich ticket. These once again, needed to be exchanged, for something closer to the front, and I was hoping Mum could take them all to the box office, together. Will this ticket saga ever end? As expected, Selhurst was busy, and I received a few curious glances from younger Palace fans. Thank God, my legs weren't being warmed. I also have, serious doubts about this hat. Back to the football, a much-changed team, that the caretaker manager has selected, let's hope the crowd, live up to their own billing, as the best in the league.

We did and the team seemed to respond well. We didn't have a great deal of possession, but there wasn't, a great threat from the Gooners either, and not a peep from their fans, "Top the league, you still don't sing. Top the league you still don't sing."

Quick fag at half-time, then a visit to Caroline and Mandy, in the disabled section, which is more difficult than it may seem. The stewards, always require me to explain, why I want to go in there. "Doh, to visit my friends! Disabled people do have them," I got back in my seat, just in time to see an Arsenal player fall over, in the box. Penalty, 1-0, bollocks. From my position, it didn't look like he touched him, (Ok, so now I know he did, but a trailing leg, not the crazy mindless challenge, that MOTD would lead you to believe.)

Still nothing, from the Arse fans, what needs to happen, for them to motivate their team, or is it like the theatre, to them. I've paid, now entertain me.

After about 10 seconds, the whole ground was back on message, and I think after my criticisms about Monday, the fans couldn't have done anymore. Maybe it wasn't us, but the players seemed to respond, and what I particularly enjoyed seeing, was a more of a hard-nosed approach. I liked the way we got in their faces, and I shouted, and made this very clear, in my vocal outbursts. We may go down, but we must do it with a bit of fight. My particular favourite, was Capt. Jedi, waiting for the ref to turn his back, then shoving one of the Arsenal players, unceremoniously into the advertising hoardings. This is a game. We are now nine matches into it, and we understand the rules. Beautiful game my arse! If the ref doesn't see it, it didn't happen and even if he did, if you shout in his face enough, and the crowd express their opinion, vocally enough, it will all be OK. So occasionally, he will see it, but what are a few yellow cards between friends.

MOTD will just say, he took one for the team. All this talk of Tony Pulis, and my principles are shot to pieces. I'd love us to play nice flowing football, with integrity, but it's a bit like CND, bloody useless, unless everyone else joins in, and that isn't going to happen, because they are all busy, chasing the wonga. (Subliminal product placement, there really must be a job at Grovenor Place, with my name on it)

Oh yes the game; corner to Arsenal, quick break, Chamakh through on goal, Foul by Arteta. Surely he's gotta go? Yeeees! Our first bit of good fortune, "Cheerio, cheerio, cheerio. Cheerio, cheerio, cheerio". Not that he leaves very quickly, you've got to have a chat with the ref first, haven't you, then ponce about a bit, giving your armband to somebody, before trudging slowly towards the tunnel. Just get off and take your punishment like a man. You know Arsene, will defend you with an, "I did not witness, this so-called foul, you must be mistaken." (Please insert your own, mock French accent, as appropriate.)

Two, wonder saves from Chezni later, and the look on Jedi's face, said it all. How are we ever going to get any more points? The final goal, on the counter from Arsenal, just about summed up the season, so far. With 83 minutes gone, game over. Then something strange happened, 3,000 Arsenal fans suddenly appeared from nowhere. They can't have been there before, surely we would have heard them, but they all went away happy, which was nice for them. We also went away happy, because the team had done their best, and largely speaking, that is all we ask for. Not trophies, not Champions League, not even, if most of us are honest, avoiding relegation. Just a good honest performance. I sound a bit like my Mum now, after one of my many childhood defeats, "oh well you did your best," but sometimes, that genuinely is all you can do.

Marks Match Report

Football is a cruel game, Palace being denied a deserved point after a spirited display against a team most of us feared might really twist the knife in our self-inflicted wound. It was a display that showed the character that had been missing from some recent performances, and whether that is an indictment of Ian Holloway or certain players I leave up to you. I would like to think that it was fuelled by the odd guilty conscience over a decent man falling on his sword. At times the atmosphere reminded me of old fashioned F.A. Cup ties, with Palace playing the role of plucky underdog against Wenger's giants (in reputation, if not physical prowess).

Millen made six changes to the starting XI which lined up in a familiar 4-2-3-1 formation although it appeared to be more of a defensive measure in packing the midfield; that would later be shown to be incorrect. The defence saw one change with Gabbidon replacing Mariappa, while KG returned in a holding midfield role in place of O'Keefe. The front four were all changed with Thomas on the left and Bannan on the right, Guédioura in the hole and Chamakh up front against his old team.

However the first 10 minutes were much as feared with Arsenal monopolising the ball as Palace showed too much respect and backed off. Still their pressure only resulted in a Giroud header over, even if Szczesny didn't touch the ball until those 10 minutes had elapsed. Events started to change when Flamini left the field injured. At first his replacement Gnabry linked well down the right with Sagna, where most of Arsenal's best attacks originated, but Palace signalled a first real attacking intent with a good run from Thomas resulting in Bannan heading well over. Ozil chose to cross when well placed, while Gabbidon & Speroni nearly produced an opening for the Gunners. At that stage if anyone had claimed Palace would end in the ascendancy I'd have looked for the drug testers, but first Chamakh then Guédioura tested Szczesny from the edge of the box, both chances earned through tigerish closing down of Arsenal deep in their own half. Jedinak was winning plenty of headers, especially at set pieces from beyond the far post, and one saw a curling effort from Bannan that nearly found Delaney running in. Cazorla & Ramsay had a couple of decent chances but Palace missed two golden chances late on: KG badly missed a far post header with Szczesny nowhere; then Chamakh almost comically misjudged his leap when unmarked in the middle of the goalmouth. Arsenal were struggling to break down the massed ranks of red & blue shirts that showed a commitment similar to that in the play-offs. There was time for Delaney to rashly foul Gnabry in what looked from my unfamiliar viewpoint behind Mr. Wenger like it was inside the box.

The Palace team left to a standing ovation, and the talk was that if we could keep it tight... instead a idiotic challenge from Guédioura on Gnabry inside a minute of the second half conceded the most obvious of penalties that I thought Speroni got close to but in fact was blasted well past him by Arteta. Arsenal again seized the initiative with Gnabry being denied by a mixture of Delaney, Speroni, top-spin and perhaps the post, but Giroud badly missed a header after Sagna again escaped down our left. The first stirrings of recovery came when Moxey linked well with Guédioura to make an opening down the left. The impression it might just be our day came when a long ball from Jedi saw Chamakh go down after a tussle with Arteta, Mr. Foy dismissing the Gunner as he was indubitably the last man; however I thought Chamakh was lucky, as much a sinner as sinned against.

As Arsenal dropped a little deeper Palace started to press and it took two brilliant saves inside a few seconds from Szczesny to deny an equaliser. The Pole tipped a Ward (left-footed) pile driver onto the bar after a good one-two with KG, then from the resulting corner a Jedinak volley was clawed away, the save being even more remarkable as the keeper was out of position following a punched clearance. Bolasie had already come on for Thomas and looked threatening, then Millen rang the changes, taking off the impressive duo of Guédioura (already seizing up with cramp) and Bannan, switching to 4-4-2 with Kébé and Gayle coming on. However I feel this attacking switch not only interrupted a swelling rhythm but actually made matters more difficult, as both central midfielders, Jedi & KG, still sat deep, with the result that there was no-one to supply the wingers, who hardly became involved. Arsenal looked far more dangerous now with 10 men, Monreal embarrassing Ward & Gabbidon. More long balls started to be directed towards our forwards & wingers, and it was from one such delivery from Jedinak that was cut out that Arsenal inflicted the killing blow: with Delaney & Ward aught out of position Gabbidon was isolated against Ramsay, who created an easy chance for Giroud. With both KG & Delaney visibly struggling with knocks the game wound down quietly. The team still deserved their second standing ovation at full time – and when did that last happen to a team losing 2-0 at home? - given the effort, but with a little luck & perhaps a little less tinkering it could have been so much difference.

Speroni – 6
Ward – 7
Moxey – 7
Delaney – 7
Gabbidon – 7
Dikgacoi – 6

Jedinak – 7
Guédioura – 7
Bannan – 7
Thomas – 7
Chamakh – 6
Bolasie – 6
Kébé – 5
Gayle – 5

Taking the Home End

During the much-maligned, Centenary Football Tournament, at the old Wembley stadium, (you remember the one, it had the history and you only got to play there, for England or in a cup FINAL.) long after the section of the ground allocated to the mighty Leeds, had been vacated, by all but a handful of their supporters, a small and intrepid section of the Palace contingent, decided that it would be amusing to climb into their section. Once in situ, commencing a rousing chorus of, "we took the Leeds, we took the Leeds, we took, we took, we took the Leeds". Unknown to this young band of cockney geezers, this feat had been achieved by three fans, some fifteen years previously.

Back in the season of fedoras and giant killing, I found myself at Elland Road, about to watch a crushing of the 'mighty Leeds', yes I know I have already described them, like this once before already, but if you were born after about 1980, it probably needed repeating. So I did. For some reason, that still really escapes me to this day, we were given tickets in the main stand, and this prospect, whilst cheap, was still quite daunting. Its dauntingness, didn't get any less, after we had scored. The oldest, and not on this occasion, wisest, of our trio, decided to taunt the leaving Yorkshire men, with a single handed version of, "Just because you're losing, just because you're losing," (the 1970's equivalent of, is there a fire drill.) and I did wonder if I would make my 11th birthday. So I do have some form in infiltrating the home fans.

It was probably about this time, that after a long slug up the M1, and sitting outside Barnsley, on a coach for over an hour, (Coach 1 occupants in those days, were apparently too dangerous, to be let loose in Barnsley, itself.) I found myself in a car park outside Oakwell, trying to find out where we could stand, to watch the match. The police officers response of, "Oh, anywhere you like," seemed to epitomise, the disjointed approach to policing football at that time. It did also afford, the same trio as infiltrated the main stand at Elland Road, the opportunity to watch the match, from our favoured position, on the halfway line. I can't recall a similar rendition, from our previously vocal leader, perhaps he had learnt from the scowls at Leeds, that it was not sensible. More likely, it was because, on this occasion they weren't leaving in masses, due to the fact that, like supporters of lots of small teams, they didn't consider that a game against Palace, was a minor inconvenience.

My most recent attempt to be rebellious, was for the last match at Coventry's old Highfield Road. Having an address in the West Midlands, secured my ticket for yet another crunch game, but meant that, I was going to have to sit quietly, win, lose, or draw. A ruptured Achilles, meant that I was hardly likely to be bouncing about anyway, as long as I could keep my composure, I should be all right. Palace score and as usual, all decorum goes out the window, it's just impossible not to.

For the briefest of moments, I expected that it was all gonna go, belly up, but at least I could say that I had been there. It was at that moment, I realised just how many Palace fans were in that stand, no one came to throw us out, no one stabbed me, and I'm not even sure, anybody even gave me a dirty look. In fact, after hobbling a mile in the wrong direction, in search of my car, A Coventry supporter gave me a lift back to it. Of course, that was in the days before the game became family entertainment, and everything needed to be changed, to encourage a better class of supporter. Now that that has been achieved, obviously no one would think twice, about sitting in a different section of the ground, NOT! We have on several occasions, had spare tickets in the Holmesdale, and matching friends, who support the opposition club. Have we welcomed them and offered them the ticket, not on your nelly. The hassle that they would get, would make it unpleasant for everybody. But that's not just Palace, is it? My boss is a season ticket holder at Fulham, and has already offered me his tickets, for that final game of our visit to the Promised Land, next May. Have I accepted the offer in the generous way that it was made, no I haven't. I am wary that the attitude of those around, will be the same at the Cottage, as it would be at pretty much, every Premiership and Championship ground, So much for the, "family friendly" Premier League.

My final and perhaps, most impressive infiltration of the home section, of a ground, did not actually involve Palace at all, but returns me to after a convoluted route, the reason for the title of this chapter, and for its chronological presence here, in the week before our trip to the Baggies.

In the late 1980's, I was at university on the south coast, where I met up with, a motley crew of football supporters. 1 Mansfield, 1 Leeds, 1 Leicester and one Wolves. The prospect and the cost, of us all trudging off in our separate directions on a Saturday, or Tuesday night, was never really very appealing, so we settled on travelling, as a little group to watch the Wolves. They were, as they are now, in a steep decline, but with top flight support and 1970's mentality. This all made for, what would be described by the Americans as, shock and awe, as 3,4 or sometimes 5000 black country residents, descended on such unlikely places as Southend, Aldershot, Reading, Bournemouth and Exeter. Not forgetting two trips too Wembley, for the Freight Rover trophy final, and Steve Bull's England debut. The latter, for anybody who wasn't amongst the sparse 35,000 crowd, has to be one of the most single-minded, England supports ever seen. Has 50% of an England crowd, ever shown such disregard for the events on the pitch, but cheered a substitute with such emotion, just for running up and down the touchline.

Anyway, that is not where I was going. I was going to Exeter or as we so like to call it at the time, Executeeere. We were about to take the home section, twice in one day. Due to it being a Bank Holiday, the F.A. being paranoid and Exeter being scared witless of marauding West Midlander's, the match had been declared all ticket. My little group of friends and my oldest brother, had acquired tickets from another college friend, and we set off to Devon, with official sanction to take the home end, although we didn't on this occasion, actually want to. We were hopeful, that we would be able to get in the Wolves end somehow. This actually turned out to be relatively straightforward. We asked a steward, and he said yes.

Having been to Exeter, in the Freight Rover trophy the previous season, with about fifty Wolves fans, (and nowhere to sleep, but that's another story) I was very interested as to how the growing mass, of Bank's Mild swilling, gold and black, was going to fit in the very small away section. The solution was unconventional, and must have caused considerable annoyance to the home faithful. Exeter, just kicked their own fans out and gave Wolves the home end. So, having got tickets in the home end and then transferred to the away end, I actually found myself, back where I started.

Now there is some scientific law, that some clever bloke invented, about equal and opposite reactions. Now I am not sure, if what happened this week, was part of that law, but it did seem a rather, "What goes around, comes around." moment, if, on a smaller and soberer scale. Palace, had drawn Exeter, in the F.A. Development Cup, and the game was due to be played at Selhurst Park. I have always enjoyed these junior cup matches, since the heady days of Sansom, Gilbert, Nicholas, and the mass punch ups, of the 70's, so I headed down the ground directly from work. I met Mark and Alex from the coach, who as well as being, Palace quiz champions are incredibly nice people, and great company. We found a seat, as near to the centre spot as possible and settled in. After the obligatory search for a team sheet, I was very pleased to see that, we were fielding a very strong side, with five players from our 25-man Premier League squad. It was surely a great opportunity for these players and our most promising youngsters, to have a comfortable win. In particular, I was hoping that Cameron Jerome, could get some confidence in front of goal. It soon became obvious, (should have known by the colour of the scarves, I suppose) that we were in an unofficial away section, or perhaps Exeter had taken the home end, in retaliation for my own behaviour back in 1986. Perhaps ever since that day, they have felt honour bound, to sit on mass in home sections around the country, to regain some lost dignity. Either way their company was enjoyable. We were soon made aware of the fact that they had recently beaten Cardiff, a team who had done the same to us, back in September, at Tooting.

Perhaps after all, this might be a closer game than I expected.

Sadly, despite the score line it wasn't.

How we managed, to make it so close, really escapes me. To be honest, Exeter battered us, in every aspect. Kebe, and Jerome. C., were in my opinion pretty disgraceful. With Keith Millen looking on, I thought that they would both try to impress, but from what I could see, they weren't really that bothered. Campana did show some touches, that showed promise, but he is obviously far from either full fitness, and or the finished article. In the end it was three genuine development players, coming on as subs, that managed to inject a degree of urgency, that a knock out cup deserved, but it was too little too late. Exeter came out 3-2 winners, which was no more than they deserved. If it hadn't been for the company, of the two coach loads of Exeter supporters, (perhaps we need reassess our self-assigned, best fans in the country designation.) and my friends from the coach, it would have been a thoroughly depressing evening. I posted to this effect on the BBS when I got home. I think that this post, sums up reasonably succinctly how I felt, and the opinion of Kebe and Cameron Jerome, was almost universally agreed with.

"Just spent the evening at Selhurst, watching the u21's.
Watched the game amongst a very large contingent of Exeter supporters, and had some intelligent conversation about football.
They played us off the park and thoroughly deserved to win.
We congratulated their supporters at the end of the game.
Not a copper in sight.
No stupid EPL anthem
The most energetic and skilful team won, irrespective of league or salary.
Players who didn't compete, and didn't put the work in, looked silly and embarrassed themselves, and this was noted by everybody there. (Hopefully, Keith Millen included.)

If you want to watch, an honest game of football, far removed from the over hyped world, in which we now live, get down to the next U21's match. Ok so we lost, I'm getting used to that and our performance to be quite honest was poor, lacking any energy, but I loved it "

A bit of a break

A quiet two weeks what with the international break. Not.

I was actually offered a ticket for England v Montenegro, but the football budget this year, is looking like it's going to be pretty busted, so I declined. In any case, I was a bit busy updating the tickets spreadsheet and trying to resolve West Brom away. As well as trying to organise away tickets for me and Mum, I also made the mistake of agreeing to coordinate, home tickets, for my 3 nephews and two cousins. In the past, this would just involve, booking them, paying for them, and collecting the money off the recipient. Now, with A games, B games, Juniors, students and two Super Six tickets, its all got a bit complex, to fit the right person with right ticket. Fortunately, the cousins and nephews are of different generations, which affects the sort of matches that they want to see. Like a lot of the younger fans, my nephews are excited about witnessing us playing some of the bigger teams. It is easy to be dismissive about this, but in fairness to them, in two cases it is half their lives ago, that we were last here, and in one case he would have been three, so his excitement is understandable. My cousins are older than me, their approach is therefore slightly more stoical, they are predominantly interested in games they think, we might not get stuffed in. By putting the different requirements together, I am hopeful that I can provide practical and financial solutions, but it all takes a bit of planning,

Whilst home tickets for everyone else, is going well, away tickets for me, are still causing stress, I've explained before, about the whole away season ticket thing, West Brom tickets arrived, row DD, is that at the front, the back, or out in the car park, a quick Google will tell me; as if. Now how difficult can it be, to make available, a full seating plan of the stadium. Fortunately, the nice people at WBA sent it to me by email. Armed with the new information, I sent Mum and Dad down to Selhurst, to change what are, it again turns out, crap seats.

The box office claimed they were unable to change them, because WBA have insisted on a strict selling order. OK, so block order I understand, but row-by-row order, that is just plain stupid. In the words of Mel smith, whilst dressed as a gorilla, "mad, I was livid".

The ticket email train continues, and the CPFC box offices final two comments to my parents, "Maybe row DD, was the best available at the time." and, "Away season tickets, never guaranteed you front row seats." prompted me to stop pussyfooting about and personal messaging the Co-Chairman, Steve Browett, directly. His response was almost immediate, how lucky we are the owners of our club, are proper fans as well. Steve B in particular, even often forgoes the luxury of the director's box and joins us in the away end. As a result, he understands the problems and the joys. Ping! Email back. Not a solution as such, but at least I know he is on the case. Email to the box office, ping! Email back from Mandy Myers, she's trying to sort it.

Another email from Mandy! "WBA box office, needs to consult with their Stadium Manager." Email to CPFC box office, thanking her for her efforts. Ping! Email back, "compewter says no," or to be more accurate WBA Stadium Manager says no, he will not allow our box office, to open a new block yet, so that I can have seats, that will actually allow my Mum to see. Ticket exchange eventually sorted and a trip to Selhurst later, front row secured.

WBA Away

10:15 departure, which should mean a good night's sleep. Unfortunately the toothache, that came on 4 weeks ago, on the way back from Liverpool hasn't really gone away and consequently, I have slept very little. Oh well, let's hope the Nurophen holds out. I have at least made the provision of buying an emergency filling kit, just in case.

The major talking point on the coach today, was the potential new manager, or if I am strictly accurate, Chris Coleman's legs and bottom. I feel at this point, I should note that, I personally offered no opinion on the subject, as I felt that I was less qualified to comment, than some of my female companions.

5:55pm, I know that you might believe by now, that I have little, if any enthusiasm for the Premier League and largely this would be true. However, tonight as I sit on the coach on the M40, travelling back to South London, the small miniscule part of my brain, that really wants to stay up, has been sucked away. After ten matches, I think I understand how Ollie looked, at his leaving press conference. Drained! On arriving at the match today with our much treasured and renegotiated, front row tickets, I found that I had little enthusiasm for singing or clapping. Maybe it was our position, so low that we were unable to see the goal line, or corner flag at our end, because of the compulsory electronic advertising boards. After all of those emails! Well at least nobody was going to stand in front of Mum, today. Maybe I am too sensitive, and worry too much, but I still couldn't settle. Ok, so I was alright, because I knew the score and had failed to accept being Fobbed off, by people whose jobs it was, too sell me tickets I could use. But, what about everybody else? What about the two little girls, 7 rows back, who couldn't see, because the family next to me, stood from the very start. What about my friends from the coach, who could not stand comfortably for 90 minutes. The one spare seat next to me, and my seat could be used for somebody who needed it more. How could I sit and watch the game, knowing that loads of fans, who had paid their hard earned money to travel to the Hawthorns, would be staring at somebody else's back. I had read enough threads on the BBS, to know that the, 'I'm all right Jack' mentality was growing in popularity, but I did genuinely think that, people with children of their own, might be considerate to others at this Crystal Palace, family friendly, different mentality club. I spent much of the first half, looking around, to see if I could identify people who might want to swap. However, with everybody standing, it is hard to identify, also with only one seat spare, plus mine, I couldn't offer it to everybody.

"THIS ISN'T MY JOB!" I know that, I need to understand that. I can't put all of the world's ills right. A few years back, I tried to do this and it seriously screwed with my brain. I thought I'd learnt to be a bit more selfish, but old habits die-hard. If I can't control the frustration, at problems I can't solve, then I might need to stop coming. But I love football; I love people and want to help, where I can. Ironically, on the journey home tonight, it was suggested by Janet, that we try to set up an away travel group, to liaise with the club over certain things. It's not a bad idea, but the further comment that, I could be spokesman, I'm really not sure I'm up to that. It's difficult to explain to people, who have not experienced how these things can take over your life, why, but I know that I can't do that kind of thing again, without risking mental health meltdown. The audio book of choice today for the journey back to London, Steve Job's autobiography. Now that should help to remind me that, a little mental instability, isn't always a bad thing.

It wasn't just me, who was having a rather confused day. Mandy from the coach, who I may have mentioned earlier is blind, (Life is far too short, to read back and check, if I haven't, well at least you know now.) had arranged in advance, to have a headphone set provided, so that she could follow the match commentary. This was duly delivered, but unfortunately, it was the commentary for the Aston Villa match. Even by Mandy's standards of unimpressness, she was unimpressed and had to rely on her carer, to fill her in on the match details, but Fulham, being a Fulham supporter, I'm not sure knows enough about football, to give any real insight. (Sorry, that was just a cheap joke, and after the result three weeks ago, is really quite unjustified.)

I won't normally comment on Mark's match report, but I will today; Puncheon 4, god you must have been feeling generous.

Marks Match Report

Another disappointment in a match of little quality in difficult conditions, where West Brom proved themselves to be just as good – actually, that should read "just as mediocre" – as Palace, but were able to seize on a couple of opportunities offered while, continuing this season's theme, failed miserably to do so. Albion had a young lad who actually knows what those white things holding the string are for. Surprisingly Palace shaded the statistical battle in terms of (marginal) possession and efforts on goal but a match which could have gained a valuable result slipped away with a whimper. The season is starting to represent a "tribute" to the team of 80/81, a.k.a. the Year of Four Managers.

Millen selected the same starting XI that had performed well against Arsenal, so there was no immediate return for Bolasie, and they again lined up in a 4-2-3-1 formation. The match was patchy & disjointed, not helped by the wind, and while Palace started tentatively, it did not take long for us to make a couple of half chances. Chamakh, a most frustrating player, actually looked like striking up a decent relationship with Guédioura; perhaps the surprise value of winning a couple of early headers created openings, one of which saw Guédioura force a save from Myhill. However that promising start was soon ruptured when Guédioura was forced off after a seemingly innocuous coming together with the keeper which didn't even rate being classed as a collision. Puncheon came on and played a lot of the game as if blinkered, rarely seeing colleagues in space outside him. Chamakh had one good opportunity on the edge of the box, but was reluctant to use his right foot and instead veered left straight into two defenders.

WBA made an attacking substitution when full back Jones was injured, bringing on Berahino, perhaps seeing this as a game they really needed to win, and the youngster was to score with Albion's first effort on goal. Annoyingly it came in the last scheduled minute before half-time when Chamakh, not for the first time, lost possession cheaply and a counter down our right found Ward out of position; Gabbidon was dragged out to close down Sessegnon – I thought from my lofty vantage point he could actually have got to the ball first – but failed to cut out the cross; Delaney was marking space in the middle, not a player, and Moxey had to leave his own man to try (& Fail) to close down Berahino. I thought the lad has mis-hit his shot and was lucky to find the corner of the net, but in fact on replay it was an excellent finish.

The second half was not that much better than the first, although Palace started to press West Brom back. Unfortunately we were playing without much width; Bannan is not a natural right winger, while Thomas was ineffectual down the left. Although both full backs tried hard to compensate we rarely got behind their defence. Jedinak, probably our best player, was winning plenty of balls in midfield and, together with KG, both playing more advanced than in the first half, but moves tended to break down when they reached Puncheon or Chamakh, although a slightly fortunate combination of the two actually led to Puncheon forcing another smart save from Myhill. West Brom were not quiescent in this period and missed two good chances, with Brunt somehow missing from ten yards and then a combination of

Speroni & Moxey blocked one direct thrust. Sad to relate it was Jedinak who missed Palace's best chance, sending a free header from a corner just wide of the near post.

Millen rang the changes, but the withdrawal of Bannan instead of the ineffectual Puncheon or a defensive midfielder (e.g. KG) could only be justified by injury or fatigue as Barry was one of the livelier performers. Bolasie arrived but saw little of the ball. The last throw of the dice was Gayle for KG, which left us with a 4-4-2 set up but a weak centre with Puncheon partnering Jedi, and our relative control of midfield slipped away. Again our best performer Jedinak played a major role in the killer goal, being beaten – flattened – by McAuley who powered in a corner. Palace finished with some little sparkle, Bolasie and Puncheon having efforts off target, but the feeling was we could play until Doomsday without scoring.

Speroni – 6
Ward – 6
Moxey – 6
Delaney – 6
Gabbidon – 6
Jedinak – 6
Dikgacoi – 6
Bannan – 6
Thomas – 5
Guédioura – 7
Chamakh – 5
Puncheon – 4
Bolasie – 6
Gayle – 5

Everton home Saturday 9th November ~~3pm Yeeha~~ Oops 3.15pm

"I said to the lads, we're going to war on Saturday. I said, if I'm going to war, who is going with me?"

Keith Millen Friday November 8th 2014

Ok, so today is pretty important. We need something, because I've run out of hats. Now you would have thought, with all the Palace hats, we must have brought over the years, I would be able to go a whole season without a victory, let alone the six games, since we last tasted that feeling. Unfortunately, our house is not the most organised. I think it is down to the sheer weight of stuff, in it. Having moved several times in the last few years, and most recently from a two bedrooms house, back to my old room at Mum and Dad's, I have had the need, if not the total necessity, to down size. Mum and Dad on the other hand, have lived in their house for fifty-five years and prior to my return, had seen the occupants' list decline from a peak of eight, to just them. Replacing the human occupants has been relatively easy, and stuff, now fills the spaces that were once people. Although in a recent period of unemployment, I was reasonably successful at organising and cataloguing the programme collection, Which is missing just 300 programmes, back to WWII, and has almost as many duplicates, (All sensible enquiries, will be considered.) I have as yet not tackled everything else Palace, that litters our house. This is partly due to the fact, that I am now gainfully employed again, and partly due to the fact that, I have no idea, what to do with sixty years of newspaper cuttings.

It is therefore quite fortunate, that Mum is an elephant. In case you are thinking, this is a disrespectful way to describe someone, who has welcomed a forty something prodigal son, back into her home. I am not suggesting that Mum, is in need of a few less cream cakes, it is simply that she remembers everything: birthdays, addresses, scores, players and where things are put, or were put, twenty years ago, so could possibly still be there. My attempt to reorganise the loft, (If, putting the previously mentioned clippings, in a trunk and shutting the door, is reorganising.) and cupboard under the stairs, (How much Tupperware, can one family ever seriously need.) has affected this skill slightly, but the location of a bag of assorted Palace clothing, was still within her capabilities.(Dads, Wardrobe) A claret tie, circa 1950, an almost brand new, Wright and Bright era home shirt, and an assortment of unused scarves badges, ties and t-shirts, all lurked in the bag, along with, and here I get back to my original point, several hats. The whole lucky hat, lucky shorts, socks pants thing has never really affected me. I wear what is most accessible, and if I'm honest, cleanest, when I wake up. Perhaps it is the style over substance world, that is the Premier League, infecting me, or more likely attending matches with two style conscious teenage nieces. Whatever the reason, I have started to pay a bit more attention to how I look. Unfortunately, my nieces' presence, was missing on the day of our trip to Anfield, and I have now been pointed in the direction of the YouTube video, of my interview. The video of that day, is as a consequence somewhat unflattering, "Oh Sian, where we're you, when I needed you most." Today, I knew that I would have to subject myself to the genuinely caring, but strikingly honest, appraisals that teenage girls can give, so I want to look presentable.

Back to the hats: I liked my bespoke Primark trilby with its evil sash, but for home games, it seems less appropriate. The jesters hat, with its jangly bells, really annoys me after about five minutes, and isn't compatible with the now almost permanent toothache. Without ever-increasing doses of Nurophen, this now transforms itself into a migraine, and I might need to borrow, DorkingEagles son P.'s ear protectors, soon. After the Swansea match, I decided on a bit of a whim really, that I would wear a different hat too home matches, until we won again and then stick with that. The thin white cotton one, with an eagle on the side came and went, as did a blue woolly number and the floppy cap. The last available hat was today's red padded baseball cap. This was partially successful, (you know how tricky things are, when a 0-0 home draw is success,) but I want more. OMG, I'm turning into a Moan u fan, expectation, expectation, expectation. I NEED to find my fedora, and fast. (Last seen: on a coach back from Chester, December 1976. Description: blue with red ribbon. If found please contact: PO Box Holmesdale upper, BLK Q, Row 7 Seat 126) The international break gives me a bit of time to search.

The roads around Selhurst today, we're a nightmare. I'm not sure that TFL, the Highways Agency, and Railtrack, have got used to us being in the Premier League yet, or do they just try to cause maximum inconvenience. Palace is not the easiest ground to get to at the best of times, but if you close the local station, close one of the main roads in, and allow the Holmesdale Road to collapse, then it's always going to be a nightmare. Add into the mix a major car crash, in Croydon, taking out the trams, and an ever-increasing search for sparklers and anything that might go bang, at the turnstiles, you are very probably going to have a delayed kick off. Thus at the new revised time of 3:15pm, our tribute to the armed forces began and was very well observed. I did however, have one little problem with the minutes silence; Pete and Alice. It is very difficult, to be quite as respectful as I would have liked, when you keep catching a view of two grown adults, dressed as eagles out of the corner of you eye. They like everybody else, were heads bowed low observing a period of reflection, but they just looked so funny. I wonder how Jacksonville Jaguars mascot, would have coped. If you haven't seen him, I suggest you Google him. His pretending to Pee in the goal last season, and booting water bottles down the touchline, was one of the funniest moments I have seen at a football match. That is assuming you don't include, a 3/4 empty Amex last May (How long could I really be expected to write, without mentioning that glorious day and having a little chuckle, it's a football fans book after all.)

Marks Match Report

There are nil-nil draws and then there are nil-nil draws... This one of the better of the breed, but victory eluded Palace through a mixture of lack of quality in the box and that tangible lack of good fortune. Napoleon favoured lucky generals: I'd settle for a forward who knocks the odd one in with his knee or arse. The spirit b& endeavour shown by the Palace team deserved more than their first clean sheet of the season. To be honest that filled me with more hope in that even if we aren't able to hang on in this league, if we carry on like this we will build a team to bring us back.

The only change Millen made to the starting Xi was enforced, in that Bolasie replaced the injured Guédioura. This resulted in a shuffling of the midfield pack, with Bannan playing in a central role in what was a strange hybrid 4-3-3 with two attacking wingers but a more solid defensive unit down the middle. Palace started slowly with Everton seeing much of the ball, mostly through Gareth Barry; if Palace did miss one tactical trick it was in not closing him down enough during the match. Chances were few & far between with Osman shooting wide when played in down our right; this was to be a weak flank for much of the first half, with Bolasie occasionally switching off in defensive mode and allowing Baines far too much liberty. Speroni made one good save when it seemed he saw a Mirallas shot late & turned it scruffily round the post. Thomas was surprisingly more effective than the skilful Bolasie, while Chamakh worked damned hard and was unlucky in just being unable to control the ball in some tight situations.

Gradually Palace started to win some decent possession, mostly from deep, and fashioned some chances, mostly through a combination of Thomas & Moxey down the left. One deep cross saw KG catch the defence asleep at the far post, but the ball seemed to come off the top of his nonce, not the brow, and looped upwards. Then Thomas fashioned a shooting chance that saw the ball arc towards the top corner before an excellent save from Howard prevented the goal. From the resulting corner a neat reverse ball found Bannan with time to measure his cross; a line of no less than four Palace players thundered down on the unprotected Howard, only

for Chamakh to ruin his day's hard work by somehow
screwing his header wide. KG also nearly got on the end
of a fine driven cross from Moxey only to be beaten to
the punch by Howard, whose participation had been in
doubt after he had smacked his head against the coach
wing-mirror when disembarking. At half-time we wondered
when Everton would make us pay for these missed
opportunities.

O'Keefe was a combative replacement for KG at half-time
(injury?) and conceded a free kick with his first
intervention. The battle in the middle hotted up.
Jedinak was once again superb, Bannan never stopped
running & tackling, while O'Keefe buzzed around.
Bolasie started to receive a little more of the ball
and a superb through ball found Thomas galloping clear;
he seemed to be more concerned about the possibility of
being flagged for offside and, although Howard appeared
to make the chance easier by coming halfway then
stopping, Thomas's lob finished in the side netting. It
was to be Palace's last clear-cut chance. Thomas
gradually faded as a threat, eventually succumbing to
cramp, while Bolasie threatened spasmodically and often
gave the ball away. Chamakh, another whose contribution
lessened after the break, was withdrawn for the
muscular Jerome, who found some space down both flanks
but seldom had a colleague in the box to cross to. In
fact Palace's most interesting attack was led by both
full backs who ended up being the most advanced
players.

With about 20 minutes left Palace seemed palpably to be
running out of steam and Everton saw more of the ball
in our territory. Delaney had kept Lukaku quiet but was
still turned once or twice, but the whole team worked
like Trojans to close down any threats. Bannan had
already indicated that he was ready to be withdrawn
when Thomas went down, to be replaced by Puncheon. Now
most Everton attacks came down our left where a
combination of hard work from Moxey, Thomas & Bannan
somehow kept them out. Their best chance came from a
similar situation to Fulham's fourth goal, when
Jagielka was found unmarked at the far post; his header
back across goal either glanced the bar or was flicked
off the line by Moxey. A late Baines free kick could
have been dangerous, and at the end it took a series of
brilliant late interceptions from Gabbidon and some old
fashioned bravery by Moxey to claim a point, with

Delaney going spare at Julian for not coming off his
line.

Speroni – 6
Ward – 7
Moxey – 8
Delaney – 8
Gabbidon – 8
Dikgacoi – 7
Jedinak – 8
Bannan – 7
Bolasie – 6
Thomas – 7
Chamakh – 7
O'Keefe – 7
Jerome – 6
Puncheon – 5

Saturday 23rd November Hull Away 3pm

Well that little break passed quickly enough. Now I'm really looking forward to this one. I must admit, that when I looked at the fixtures back in the summer, this was the match I considered missing. That is meant in no disrespect to Hull, but it's a bloody long way, for a team that we played just last year. On the flip side, it is also a match that, if we aspire to stay at the party, we need to get something from. The club Co-Chairman Steve Browett, understands this, and posted on this subject this week. For once, this has seen him, and not me, a little frustrated about away tickets. As I type this on Wednesday, we have sold just 872 for the trip to the KC, whilst selling out Chelsea in just 2 days. More on which as we approach our trip to West London.

There was an article in *The Evening Standard* tonight, about us, which really annoyed me, and taught me a valuable lesson about the internet and the BBS. After a difficult day at work, in which one of my favourite work colleagues, handed in their resignation, I was already in a bad mood, when I picked up the article. It was not really any worse, or better, than much of what has been written about us before, but despite this, I found it immensely patronising. Whatever facts, or half-truths it contained, seemed to have been spun in such a way, as to make my club and its owners, look incompetent and stupid. In the business world, a month to appoint a senior manager wouldn't be that long, but somehow in football, a considered long-term approach, is seen as unnecessary delay. As with so much of English football, the phrase due diligence is largely unused. It is particularly galling that, some of the same voices that are critical of the delay, in appointing a new manager, similarly criticised the signings that were made in the summer, because the club didn't fully research all aspects of the player profiles. The surprising point however, was that some on the BBS agreed with the article. I was called an idiot, a twat and some other insults, disguised as rhyming slang, for suggesting that we should tweet the journalist, and offer our opinion on the article. One of the most disappointing and illuminating aspects of the exchanges, was not that some other fans disagreed with my view about the article, but that that they considered my call to arms, was a call to abuse. I didn't suggest that, nor did I do it myself. I was really just calling for a right to reply, which thanks to Twitter and the internet as a whole, we can now easily exercise. I was pleased that of his own volition, our Chairman Steve Parish, took this opportunity. He wrote in a number of tweets, that it was a shoddy piece of journalism, filled with conjecture and half-truth. Although I am new to Twitter, and sometimes struggle to follow conversations, I believe that *The ES* journo, subsequently offered to interview Steve Parish, for his side of the story, to which he replied that, "it was a bit late for that now, as you have already rubbished the club, and its owners." Having started to follow, the press coverage of football a bit closer this year, I am amazed at the way stories, or no stories, appear almost as fact. It makes me more reticent now, to undertake my huge project of a history of the club, through contemporary eyes, I.E. without the benefit of hindsight, and only using documents written at the time, and now stored, in that trunk in the loft. I still believe that this would be an interesting and informative project, but would it suffer similarly from factual inaccuracies, caused by this type of journalism? Who knows, but I think I am still going to do it, one day.

So as well as learning, that not everyone on the internet will agree with you all the time, and that some will be personally abusive, if they don't. I also learnt, not to start new threads on the BBS, after a bad day at the office, unless I count to ten first, let's make that one hundred.

The trip to Hull itself, was pretty uneventful. We arrived at the ground at seven thirty, departed at eight thirty. A quick stop just outside Peterborough, for coffee, fag, leak and nose through the magazine's in Smith's, where Mark can always be found reading running Magazines. Then, back on the coach, arriving just after two. Not wanting to be stung again, by service station cigarette prices and having run out, I wandered down to the shops, to stock up. I do like the location of the KC stadium, and can see that if we ever returned to Crystal Palace Park, this is what it might be like for us. Walking in through the main park entrance, does give a sense of arriving. It also gave the Hull fans, a central focus point to position there protest, of which I have to admit, I had forgotten. It is so easy to get wrapped up, in the affairs of your own club, that even I sometimes forget the bigger picture. The banner that was displayed at the entrance, struck a perfect cord with me. It simply said, "We are a club not a brand" with the word club underlined. I wanted to support the cause in some way, so I accepted a, "No to Hull tigers" badge, and duly pinned it to my coat, where it remains.

The notion that multi-millionaires, whatever their nationality, can buy parts of this countries heritage, and try to alter its very essence, is unpleasant. Without researching their whole history, I would guess that HULL CITY we're formed to represent the city of Hull. It's why they exist; it is what they are for. Like Palace and many other clubs, outside half a dozen, the fan base is drawn from the city, or from people who have a link historically with the place. When I tell people that I support Crystal Palace, they quite rightly assume I'm from South London, or was once from South London, or at the very least have family based in South London. When I meet other Palace fans, wherever I am in the world, we can talk about a shared identity. It isn't as the Hull fans identified, about a brand that is easier to sell in Asia, or any other part of the world. Hull City are Hull City and that is that. So I wore the badge, not because I have any affinity with Hull, other than being rather partial to the Housemartins, but because I have an affinity with football supporters. It appears that, I was not alone in this solidarity with the Hull supporters. During the first half of a tactically interesting, but hardly spectacular game, several Hull City supporters unfurled a banner, and paraded it up and down in front of the stand, directly opposite the directors box and dug outs. It said nothing abusive, just, "Hull City A.F.C." On setting out for possibly the fifth trip, a small group of stewards tried to remove the banner, and stop the fans from protesting. At which point, a much larger group of Hull fans, leaped to their comrades' aid. Something in my warped nostalgic mind, imagined Wolfie Smith, in his beret, running onto the pitch and shouting, "Power to the people," at the top of his voice. The Palace fans, pretty much on mass, applauded the protest and were applauded back in return. Fortunately for the stewards attempting to stifle good old honest defiance, a senior steward arrived to intervene and withdrew his troops, who were considerably outnumbered and turning a peaceful protest, into a potential hostile and angry encounter. Mark will talk you through the match, but I was again annoyed about a Palace red card. Bolasie doesn't appear to me, to be a dirty player and he was trying to rectify a mistake, by winning the ball back. This is what I want to see my players do. As Ian Holloway suggested, when earning himself a touchline ban, which may have ultimately contributed to his downfall, I'm not sure we are getting a fair deal, when it comes to refereeing decision.

It is easy to think, that if I say that I really enjoyed my trip to Hull, you might believe it was because we won, and there is no doubt that this does add an unexpected positive to the day, but this is really only half the story. I particularly liked the win, because it was witnessed by only a hard core of Palace fans, that had witnessed so many defeats, in the past. The new fans, who think that North London, is a long way to go for a game, but go anyway, because it is Arsenal or Spurs, largely weren't there. As they weren't there, when one of our youth team players, secured our Championship survival three years previously. For the team to dig in and win, when reduced to ten men, showed a great team spirit. I'm pleased for Keith Millen as well; he has taken up the reigns admirably, and obviously is a Palace man. I hope that the new manager, doesn't chuck the baby out with the bath water, which is often the way it works these days.

There were two added bonuses of the day. Firstly, we were allowed out at half-time for a fag, which made the trip to the shops worthwhile, and is an increasing rarity these days, despite the obvious demand. It is such a simple process, open the exit doors and provide a few stewards, who would otherwise be patrolling the toilets, looking for all traces of smoke. Let everybody have a fag in peace, and then close the exit doors again. No stress, no bad feeling, no smoking in the toilets.

The second bonus of the day was a betting success. The loss of a Ladbrokes at Selhurst, has quite frankly saved me a few quid over the last 18 months, because I like to bet on things that no one else would, i.e. I am the bookies best friend. Prior to Dougie Freedman as manager, I used to regularly back our centre backs as first goal scorers, but that became, even for me, a rather stupid bet. Our centre backs in those days, being unlikely to even get in the opponents half, for a corner. Today at Hull, there was a bookie in the away fans concourse, and I liked the idea of a nonspecific, Palace victory by one goal. We were frankly on recent showings, unlikely to score more than one goal, but the bet had a bit more flexibility than a straight 1-0 correct score. OK in hindsight, I might have won a bit more, with that bet, but at 9/2, I was still able to pay for the Starbucks coffees, on the way home, just.

Marks Match Report

Not many of us on the train up expected that... especially not when Palace were reduced to 10 men. As ever, what was probably a poor game was viewed very differently from the stands, where Palace displayed strength of character, no little skill, and an unexpected tactical flexibility that reflects great credit on Keith Millen, the coaching staff and the squad. And if the end was reminiscent of the Coppell "Circle the wagons" tactic, at least this time the restless natives were repulsed to give us our first Premier League away win since Dowie was manager, AJ was scoring effortlessly, and our keeper wore PJ's!

There was one enforced change from the team against Everton, with Gayle replacing the injured Thomas in a 4-3-3 formation, playing on the left. What was noticeable was that none of the three central midfielders played a strict holding role; all three were given license to push forward and support the attack, as long as one of them stayed back, and that tactic seemed to work quite well through the whole match – Jedinak, in particular, was quick to join breaks in contrast to most of this season. It did take Palace a few minutes to realise that Koren had slipped into that unseen dimension between defence & midfield, much as Michu had done so successfully for Swansea, but that door was swiftly bolted shut.

The first half, while enthralling, seldom produced any real threats on goal from either team. Hull had plenty of the ball and had the edge in territory, and while they forced plenty of corners, the defence, led by Delaney & Gabbidon, held firm. On the break Gayle & Bolasie looked dangerous on the break, although the latter was too often guilty of playing as if blinkered, seldom seeing more than the next man to try to beat. It should be noted that both wide men, contrary to past displays, worked hard in defensive roles too. Two moments of note occurred. An early aerial clash saw Chamakh receive lengthy treatment on the sidelines before attempting his best Thomas Brolin impression: twice the head bandage was dislodged, if not as spectacularly as the Swede's, and the second time saw him permanently withdrawn for Cameron Jerome. And there was a lengthy & vocal protest by the Hull City fans against the nomenclature "Tigers" which, for once, saw the supporters stare down the stewards & police and make their point. Not a great surprise that it didn't make the Match of the Day slot.

The second half didn't show a great improvement. Jerome was impressing with some muscular runs and managed to win a fair share of balls in the air, perhaps helped when McShane was withdrawn, necessitating the switch of Figueroa from full back to central defence. Hull finally managed to penetrate Palace's smothering rearguard only for Sagbo to be closed down smartly by Speroni who blocked the shot from about two yards away. Palace broke smartly and nearly fashioned a goal on the break, only an excellent last-ditch challenge denying Gayle. Again Palace carried a latent threat on the break, with Jerome & Bolasie well supported by Gayle, Bannan & Jedinak, the first three all having sight of goal but either shooting wide or not strongly enough.

The game seemed to have changed in Hull's favour when Bolasie was dismissed. My view was that, having cocked up an excellent move by taking too many touches & losing control on the edge of Hull's box, Yannick was too desperate to retrieve the ball, and lunged in a little too zealously. It's only guesswork but I don't believe there was any intent to harm Livermore, only a desire to make amends, and in my opinion at the time I thought it was a definite foul & worth a yellow card. It was not helped by the fact that Hull had made all three substitutions at that stage, and it did appear they would be reduced to 10 men, and I wonder if the referee was tempted to even things up with a red card. As it was Livermore recovered and Palace now had about 15 minutes to cling onto a point with a man's disadvantage.

Perhaps fortunately Palace had little time to reorganise and drop deep, for with minutes they fashioned an excellent team goal. The impressive Jerome led a break, linked well with Gayle, taking a return pass in the left side of Hull's box; I expected a shot but instead he sidestepped to create a better angle for a pull back that fund Bannan in space – he could hardly miss & didn't. Pandemonium erupted as Barry celebrated a few yards in front of the away supporters. After that it was a typical backs to the wall effort, as Hull

91

forced plenty of corners. Julian, as he had all game, was error-free under the high ball while Gabbidon & Delaney rebuffed almost everything else. In the gathering gloom Hull had one last effort, which saw Moxey clear a corner off the line, only for Rosenior to thump in a reply that cannoned away off the post. Salvation followed shortly after and we could celebrate Palace's first away top flight victory this decade – let's hope that, unlike then last decade, it doesn't remain singular.

Speroni – 7
Ward – 6
Moxey – 7
Delaney – 8
Gabbidon – 8
Dikgacoi – 6
Jedinak – 8
Bannan – 8
Gayle – 7
Bolasie – 7
Chamakh – 6
Jerome – 7
O'Keefe – 6
Puncheon – 6

Saturday 30th November Norwich away 3pm

I was really looking forward to the trip to Norwich, a match we could win and not too far to travel. The team news, suggested an attacking approach to the game, and with Joniesta back in the running for a starting place, we were hoping for something to cheer. I had managed to change my tickets, a few weeks ago, for something a little closer to the front, (Where have you heard that before.) and felt optimistic that a good view for Mum and me, would be assured. However, as soon as the game started my confidence of this evaporated. One of the problems with seats on the side of the pitch for away supporters, is that tickets at the front don't necessarily ensure a good view of the pitch. You become not just aware of people standing directly in front of you, but also to the side of you. CPFC2010 have been working very hard to ensure that families and those that wish to sit, are allocated seats nearest to the front. Unfortunately, the selling order imposed by most clubs, means that this can't be done for the whole section, only on a block-by-block basis. Consequently, once a block is sold, the box office has to start all over again. It then becomes more and more difficult, to allocate the right people to most appropriate seat location. It is a ridiculous system, showing what utter contempt there is for travelling supporters. To be honest, the arrival in Norwich hadn't got off to the greatest of starts, even as we pulled into the car park near the ground. In reality, it was not really that near to the ground, and the word car park, is a loose term, for an area of mashed up tarmac. Mandy, as I have mentioned previously travels to nearly all the matches. Amongst many other identifying features, she is blind and in a wheelchair. Now you would have thought, with either of these credentials, she would qualify us for a parking birth next to the ground, but not at Norwich. Even if we couldn't park permanently, next to the ground, a simple drop off, you would expect would be a basic. Again not at Norwich. Even with the fancy stadium and huge car park, next door, no such concession is made. In fact on the contrary, we were met by a female police officer, who whilst smiley and polite, had a slightly, (I'm being kind here.) condescending air. Mandy is herself, quite well known for being quite forthright, in protection of her..., I was going to write rights, but let's be honest, she is quite forthright in pretty much everything. Consequently, the liaison officer's condescension, was given right back with interest, when she stated, "I don't have to try and help at all you know". Well actually yes! I think you do. It's kind of you job! Liaison officer might give the clue. Now I would partly understand the attitude, if Mandy just pitched up at away games and then expected to receive assistance. This is far from the truth, and much effort is made by both Mandy and Caroline, to arrange things in advance, although this is met with varying degrees of success. The second little irritation was that the proposal for collecting Mandy after the game, involved her waiting at the ground, whilst everybody else walked back up a steep hill to the coach park. We were informed, that we could then wait for the roads to clear, drive back past the ground, load Mandy and get on our way home. As well as delaying our departure considerably, the hill up to the 'coach park' is steep and there are other supporters on coach one, who although they might not be worthy of a blue badge, find such a walk difficult. The likes of Bob in his late 80's, travel with the official coach, partly to make these transfers more manageable, and Mum at the spritely young age of seventy-nine, has little legs, bad knees and needs a puffer when climbing hills. I therefore had a great degree of sympathy with Mandy, and was close to laughing out loud, when she thanked the officers in a way that was so over the top, everybody, perhaps with exception of the recipient, knew it was packed full of disdain and sarcasm.

Once we had unloaded Mandy, and negotiated the rutted concrete, I couldn't help myself from trying to have a rational conversation with the officer. I should have learnt by now, that this is a largely futile process, and eventually reminded her again, as a parting shot that; it was basically her job to resolve these problems, and not just to smile and welcome everybody to the Narwich. Once we have eventually walked down to the ground, we met up with an old family friend, who is a Canary. Once again proof, that contrary to popular beliefs, football supporters of different clubs, do not always punch each other on contact. We planned to go and have a coffee in the local supermarket, but found that it was already completely rammed with other supporters, with the same idea. So we headed back up to the ground. Fortunately, the concessions around Carrow Road, are really quite impressive, as you would expect from a club with the Chairman who is Delia Smith. For all of my misgivings so far, about my day, I was pleased to be able to try a white hot chocolate, at a very reasonable price. Not something that I'd ever had before. Once again, breaking the preconception that, all football fans think about is lager.

Unfortunately, this is where the day's positive note, ended for me. It became apparent that, the whole block to my left hand side, intended to stand from the very front row. Although we were in row three, and I could see the goal directly in front of us, any action that was taking place in the remaining two thirds of the pitch, closest to us, was completely obscured. As I had a gangway seat, I was able to communicate with the two police officers, sitting at the front of the gangway facing the crowd. I asked them if they intended to try to enforce standard ground regulations. To which they effectively replied, "it's not our problem it's the stewards." So I duly attempted to ask the stewards, to impose their ground regulations. The response to this was that, they were not allowed to leave their station, and I would need to contact the senior steward. Once again, following instructions that I'd been given, I tried contacting the mysterious senior steward, with no success. In frustration, I took matters into my own hands, walked in front of the block next to me, and asked, as politely as my irritation would allow, if people in the front rows, would sit down. The response as you can imagine, was not universally favourable, but I had tried. Eventually, a senior steward, who looked like he could do with a seat himself, did appear. He walked along the front of the offending block, whispering very quietly at people, to sit down. Again, as you can imagine, this did not produce the desired effect.

Now perhaps I am oversensitive, but this lack of consideration and the lack of any attempt by officials, and the police, to enforce regulations, that allow all who've paid consider amounts of money to see, really wound me up. As a result I ended up in an argument, with another Palace supporter. Whilst I understand, in the cold

94

light of the day his prospective, that I had not asked him to change seats, which he would have gladly done. I feel he had missed the point. It wasn't about me. I can stand and I actually quite like to stand, but there are others who don't want to, or cannot physically. Changing seats with me or my mother, would not have resolved this. It is about the collective consideration of others. As for the game, I lost interest. I didn't want to be there, surrounded by these inconsiderate b@@@@@ds, whose attitude I do not share. Part of the fun of going to football, is this collective identity. We all want the same things, and we are happy when others are happy, or sad when others are sad. Today, this wasn't the case. The attitude of the police officers, was also quite infuriating. It was later suggested by one of them, that I should try to calm down slightly. This was even though my anger and annoyance, was caused by his inaction. He had made something, that apparently is not his problem, into his problem.

Mark will tell you about the game. I will tell you about the white chocolate, because to me that was the only positive of the day. In the end, I helped Mandy's carer, push her up the hill and across a rutted car park, at the end of the game. The liaison officer was nowhere to be seen. When I got home, I posted a message on the BBS. I produce it in full.

Standing in the front row again

To all the selfish Palace fans, that get tickets in the front rows and stand up, or refuse to sit down, when asked to do so. Thanks for ruining my day again, I have spent much of this season, trying to arrange tickets for my mother and friend, so that they can actually see at away matches and even when I do this, we find we cannot see.
The club is trying very very hard, to accommodate the wishes of both standers and sitters, but this is next to impossible if people choose to stand in the front row. If a supporter of a club, doesn't give a S@@@ about other supporters of the same club. How can we expect the opposition clubs, or the stewards, or the police, or the Football Association, to give a s@@t either.
I am not sure why it should really be my responsibility, to try and get some kind of moral perspective into these people, but unlike some, my nature is that I do care about other people, I care not just for myself. I could and would happily stand at a match, but and this is the really really important part here. I don't if I am sitting in the front row, because it would be selfish in the extreme. Sometimes if you are part of something, you need to do what you wouldn't ideally like, for the good of everybody.

I know some will come back and say, most people were standing today and it is only a minority that want to sit. But that is in my opinion, total rubbish. There are a large number of people who will stand, if they have to, but don't want to.

If we were half the set of fans, that some like to think we are, we would not only cheer our team through thick and thin, but we would also as in any progressive society, look after the welfare of the weaker, less able and in this case shorter members of the group.

95

Until we learn as a collective to do this, we are no better than the rest of the glory boy fans around the country, with their half-and-half scarves and cardboard clappers. Ok we might sing a bit louder, and can never be accused of being glory hunters, but if we are not considerate of each other, we are nothing; no group identity, no collective camaraderie and I hate it.

PS interestingly at Hull, when it was just old school, hard core Palace, was there a problem, no there wasn't. I think that tells you all you need to know."

Encouragingly enough, the thread did not get entirely the negative reaction, that I thought it might. Except for the guy who posted, "are you a dickhead," to which I replied, "are you?" (Ok, so I know this wasn't very grown up, but it's the internet and he started it Miss.)

The main point from the thread, that now runs to 288 posts, is that people want a choice and the clubs just aren't giving it, because they pretend it's not a problem. I think this partly because they don't care, and partly because if they accept there is a problem, then they accept that they are breaking Premier League rules, and their own ground regulations.

I decided that I would go for all football clubs, Achilles heel, Money. I have therefore written to Norwich, asking for a full refund under the sale of goods act. I'm not convinced that I have a pray, but I had to write as a matter of principle. I did everything that I could at the time; police, stewards and direct action, so I feel that I have a right to ask.

I have also sent a message to the Chairman, and initial feedback is that the club are going to try to sort it out. Fingers crossed. I'm just glad, Dad didn't try to come today. This was the second match that I had earmarked for him, but he opted out.

Marks Match Report

The Pulis era started with an undeserved defeat at Norwich, a team which performed no better than ours. Actually Palace's performance was very similar to that at Hull last week. The problem, which the new manager is not really in a position to address just yet, was that we lacked any real cutting edge as we have done all season.

I'll lay my cards on the table: I'm not a fan of the type of football propagated by Tony Pulis at Stoke, but

let's see what he can manage with a different set of
players - after all, Neil Warnock joined us with a
reputation as a long ball merchant wedded to 4-4-2, and
Dave Bassett with an even stronger claim to being a
high priest of direct play, yet both developed Palace
teams playing highly attractive football. So, like many
of us, I'll be interested in how the playing style will
develop over the coming months.

He started with a shift to a 4-4-1-1 formation with
Chamakh playing behind Jerome, with Puncheon on the
right and Bannan on the left. It is undeniable that, in
the first half particularly, the ball was played out
far more quickly from the back, often directly with the
long diagonal ball into the space behind the full
backs, but it was rarely without purpose, with the
usual exception of clearances from the central
defenders. What was noticeable was that both Jedinak &
KG played a little higher up the pitch; Jedi was seldom
seen dropping deep to pick up the ball from the
defence, which has been a staple of our tactics for the
last 18 months. In the second half Palace upped the
tempo at times and there were some good passages of
play which, inevitably, ended up being snuffed out by
the excellent Bassong & Bennett at the heart of
Norwich's defence. But there was no imminent sign of an
aerial bombardment. It was different to what we've seen
but nothing that will shock the denizens of SE25. One
small interesting point was that Gabbidon did not go
forward for corners, but Ward went up in his place.

Where Palace did struggle was against Norwich's two
second-choice wingers. Moxey, in particular, suffered
against Redmond (who had such an excellent game for
Birmingham at Selhurst on Good Friday) but also against
Hoolahan when the two attackers switched flank. Ward
also found it hard going defending the right and gifted
Norwich a corner in the first minute that saw a Bassong
header just off target. More luckily a free kick from
our left flank somehow ended up thumping the underside
of the bar and bouncing down pretty much on the line:
with Speroni grounded it looked odds on a goal but
somehow the defence smuggled the ball clear. Redmond
again turned our left flank and only a sharp save by
Julian prevented us going behind. Howson was the
creative force in midfield that neither Jedi nor KG
could completely shut down.

It was typically irritating that Norwich would score during our best spell in the first half. KG had at least had a shot easily saved by Ruddy, while a cross shot from Puncheon appeared to be blocked by the keeper. Then Moxey & Bannan managed to lose the ball in an attacking position deep in City's half; Redmond took advantage of the lack of any real cover although Moxey nearly caught him; the cross seemed to have run beyond the immediate threat, but the ball was returned into the box to give Hooper a chance very similar to Bannan's at Hull – Speroni had no real chance. Palace nearly struck back immediately, Bannan's drive striking Olsson's head before pinging off the underside of the bar.

The second half saw Palace have long periods of possession, but the problem was the lack of numbers getting into the box. Jerome was often pushed wide, while the same happened to Chamakh who was less diligent in pushing on, while Puncheon & Bannan tried switching wings. Norwich appeared happy to play on the counter and I can't recall any serious goal threat from them after half-time. While both full backs were prepared to overlap, Bannan faded late on while Puncheon's reflex action on receiving the ball of turning away to shield the ball often broke any attacking momentum, he seemingly reluctant to take on his man on the outside. Jedinak began to wrest control of the middle from Howson – something that Hughton tried to address by withdrawing Hoolahan late on for the more prosaic skills of Bradley Johnson – but chances were rare: Delaney's header (to Palace fans deflecting off a defender's shoulder) over; Kébé's turn and impressive shot just wide from the edge of the box; and a late cross that somehow reached Jerome only for his effort to bounce slowly into Ruddy's hands. In fact the closest we came was when a dangerous cross from Moxey was sliced over his bar by the otherwise outstanding Bassong. Norwich were happy to run down the clock as Palace's subs (Williams, Kébé' & Gayle) made little real impact.

Speroni – 7
Ward – 6
Moxey – 5
Gabbidon – 7
Delaney – 7
Dikgacoi – 5

Jedinak — 7
Puncheon — 5
Bannan — 6
Chamakh — 6
Jerome — 6
Williams — 5
Kébé' — 6
Gayle — 5

The King is Dead, Long Live the King

Sometimes in life, it is good to sit and reflect, before making rash decisions. This is not a comment, on my ranting and raving last week, but more a general observation, which the footballing world would be good to consider.

I would like to suggest, that I have been following this advice, before passing comment on our new manager, but that wouldn't be entirely true. I had simply become, so involved in my own little corner of Palace, that I forgot to mention it. It is not that, like every other Palace fan, I haven't been following the process with interest, but nor had I become embroiled in the mass panic, of the press and some fans. In the business world, appointing a new senior member of staff, can take months of interviews, call backs and due diligence tests. Then the new employee, will have to work out notice periods, and it all takes time. In footballing circles, this type of prudent methodical process, is almost seen as a sign of weakness, or if *The Evening Standard* is to be believed, incompetence. However, I think that it is a sign of strength. It does also allow people to think, and even at times change their mind, sometimes several times. As well as the recruitment team, fans also have time to sit and think about, what they want from the new manager. They don't necessarily have the power, to do anything about it, and they might not be in possession of the full, accurate, facts, but there is still valuable thinking time. After the unexpected resignation of Ian Holloway, one of the first names that was banded about was T Pulis, and I made no secret at the time, of my disapproval. For some with the same thought patterns, this was partly an issue of style. Ian Holloway, had promised something that I wanted to buy into, but in the end, even for him, there was a practical necessity, that had to be implemented. We hadn't witness the gay abandon of his Blackpool team, that I had considered so refreshing, even if it was ultimately unsuccessful. The thought of a Pulis style team, whatever that may be, didn't marry well, with that high and mighty concept. Whilst I did share those reservations, I was also concerned by the money that he had spent, which was considerably higher, once you look at the figures, than you might consider. Also in my mind, the team that he had assembled, was decidedly average in quality, as well as at times, having a reputation for being a bit grim to watch, and overly physical. The more I thought about this, over the weeks before his appointment, the more I concluded the fit for Palace, might not be so bad. To put the record straight, in the days before he was officially unveiled, I had contacted the same nephew, who I had screamed, "NO!" at, saying, "OK, Tony Pulis, why not? Bring it on!" The major reasons for this change of heart were twofold. Firstly, we didn't have lots of money, and I was convinced that the owners, would not be giving him a blank cheque book. So that was not an issue, and if he had been able to ensure Stoke's survival in the Premier League, with what I thought was an average squad, why could he not do the same, with our average squad. The second reason, was more about the type of football I wanted to watch. Now I have been a passionate admirer of Barcelona, and the perceived tippy tappy football. However, what I have also admired about them, was the physical dimension to their game. Their willingness to get stuck in when needed, is I believe often overlooked.

I suppose if I am honest, I think we are probably going to be relegated, and I don't mind, I honestly don't. However, on the way out the door, I would really like to have a couple of, "up yours!" moments. Now, if that had come in a Hollowayesque 5-4 victory, with seven attackers on the pitch, great. Alternatively, I would be equally happy, with Dammo and Jedi, crunching a few prima donnas into the advertising hoardings, preferably when the referee isn't looking. I have seen enough already this season, to believe that we won't get given anything, so whatever we get, we will have to take ourselves. If we take it, kicking and screaming, I really don't mind. I just don't want any team coming to Selhurst, and their players or fans, taking the piss. It is back to the concept of the fans display, on day one against Spurs. Come to our place if you like, but you won't enjoy it, and any points you get, you will know you have earnt. I don't want my team to be dirty, or deliberately malicious, but equally I don't want to go down without a fight.

Tonight under floodlights at Selhurst, is a great opportunity to start that fight, and being on BTsport, it is a great opportunity to show those that, in the words of Tony Pulis in his programme notes, "have written us off." I also agree with him, that if we can pull of a miracle, "it makes it even better." Dad decided to stay at home tonight and watch the game on the TV, which concerns me a bit, but at least he can watch it. Apart from the usual Fanatics activity, Selhurst was a little subdued tonight, but the players put in a dogged performance and a win was a fair result. It wasn't quite the blood and gusto that I have been hoping for, but Ravel Morrison's punch on Joel Ward, after the final whistle, suggested that there were perhaps some shenanigans going on. Sat in the safety of the Holmesdale, you are not always party too everything. West Ham certainly didn't like their trip to South London, which is basically good. One comedian on the BBS, suggested that Joel might just have pointed out to Ravel, that Zaha was better than he was, following their on-field bust up, during the recent under 21's England match. My personal take on it, is that Joel suggested, it was a bit soft to be wearing gloves. (I was originally going to write Girly or Gay, but I am trying to appeal to all sections of the community. I am also aware that Joel Ward, would never say either of those things, under fear of a Sine Dine ban or whatever the punishment is.) The punch, unlike any of the references just mentioned, only earnt Morrison a yellow card. Presumably, this is because Joel told the ref, "its fine he punches like a girl anyway," Whatever the justification for the yellow card, Morrison will now miss the next game, due to reaching five yellows. The wroth of Allardyce for this, will I am sure, be a far greater punishment, and I can't wait to see what happens at Upton Park, later in the year. A whole away end display, with a Little Morrison at one end and a super large Ward at the other, with the words, "He's coming to get you." might be quite amusing.

The punch reminded me, of rugby match I played in many moons ago, when one of the opposition punched our seventeen year old flanker, square in the jaw. The said colt, just rolled his not unsubstantial neck and looked at the opponent, with a big smile. The opponent, took the wise decision to take no further part in the game, and we didn't have a return fixture. Ravel may wish the same was the case for Palace and West Ham, and a tight hamstring might be advisable to fake come April.

Without the need once home, to read many negative posts from the doom and gloom merchants, I chose instead, to read the match programme, which I have been neglecting lately. It is a good read, and this was confirmed in its own pages, as it had just won an award. However, a bit like the Sunday Times, which I also think is a good read, when am I going to find the time to read it all, and to be honest, do I really want to pay that much. It's great for the occasional fan, but you are talking 150 quid for all thirty-eight, and a small storage facility to keep them. There was a good piece by Steve Parish, echoing some of my thoughts, on the panic over the time for TP's appointment, and a very funny piece as always by Kevin Day. However, the article that caught my attention, was the development result against QPR. They had apparently, come back from three down, to win 4-3, which sounded as if it was an amazing game. Sod's law, the team seems to be improving, just at the same time that the matches, all seem to be during the working day.

Marks Match Report

Well, it wasn't pretty, and for much of the first half BT must have been thinking about asking politely for a refund on grounds of quality control, but somehow Palace held out for a morale-boosting win. The atmosphere at Selhurst, strangely flat for much of the first half - bar the Fanatics' corner - rose after Chamakh's goal and helped drag the team over the finishing line. Two of the most pragmatic managers in English football were never going to produce a free flowing epic but the tension and sheer "backs to the wall" defending created its own brand of excitement & entertainment.

Pulis retained the same team and 4-4-1-1 formation from Norwich and, in the first half alone, this dictated a more direct style of play: direct, not long ball. When playing only four in midfield, unless you are graced with exceptional wingers or a creative central playmaker, you are forced into bypassing the middle as often as possible, especially when, as last night, the opposition packs five across the field. What these tactics do not dictate, and cannot be laid at the feet

of the manager, is the atrocious standard of passing
when the ball was kept on the ground. Too many times
Palace presented the ball to West Ham; fortunately they
either kept giving it straight back or putting it out
of play, with Downing the chief offender.

The first half hour ranked amongst the worst I've seen
at Selhurst. Jerome seldom got change out of Tomkins in
the air, and when he did Chamakh and the two wingers
were not close enough in support to build any attacking
momentum. The only real chance came early on when
Puncheon shot straight at Jaaskelainen. It was West Ham
who, despite their own stodgy and inaccurate passing,
who started to make chances. They had a fondness for
crossing from the right to Carlton Cole beyond the far
post to knock the ball back into the middle, and twice
these almost reaped dividends, only a brave combined
block by Delaney & Gabbidon, then a typical Downing
lack of control preventing them taking the lead. Worse
culprits were Diamé with a close range header over the
bar, then Nolan somehow limply chipped into Speroni's
hands when played in by a clever free kick.

For Palace, Bannan was having a good game, although
spoiled by giving away possession a couple of times,
but KG and Jedinak were more often guilty of the same,
while Puncheon, as at Norwich, quickly faded after a
reasonable start. With midfield malfunctioning, and
Tomkins & Collins shackling the forwards, it was
difficult to see how a breakthrough could be fashioned.
Summing up the game, the goal was a mixture of error
and a flash of technical excellence. Palace's first
corner was played low at the near post, perhaps as
planned, but not well executed by Bannan as Ward
struggled to play the ball back to the Scot; the second
cross was excellent, and, as against Everton, Chamakh
was presented with a free header about 8 yards out; he
should have buried it but failed to gain a solid
connection, the ball sliding off at an angle deceiving
Jaaskelainen and fortunately slipping between two
defenders on the line. The confidence that gave
Marouane was evident from a little flick he carried out
perfectly a minute or so later, but the real test was
whether Palace could hold onto the lead until half-
time, where we so miserably failed against Fulham. That
we did weather a brief Hammers' flurry gave everyone a
lift.

The game had to improve in the second half, especially with West Ham having to show a bit more attacking intent, and it did. In fact the first 10 minutes were too perhaps too open for Palace fans as the game was stretched, and somehow Palace contrived to throw away three golden opportunities to make the match safe. First Chamakh and Jerome made openings for themselves that they were unable to seize, and Puncheon's follow-up was on target but deflected inches wide (onto the post) by a defender. From the resulting corner Bannan was again on target, but KG's header was too high from a good position. Then Jerome broke clear but failed to beat the keeper, a sign of a striker who hasn't scored for over 20 games.

Would we regret blowing those opportunities? Palace tightened up, with the defence showing a solidity that was built by Millen & reinforced by Pulis. Although Morrison always looked a danger when on the ball he actually created very little, while Diamé was wasted out on the left. One potential danger was Downing, who was continually shown inside by Moxey, despite the fact that the winger is left-footed; fortunately the ex-England man had an awful night, and the number of misplaced passes towards the overlapping O'Brien summed up West Ham's shambolic play. So well did the defence stand up – aided by Jedinak & KG, and later O'Keefe – that Julian was strangely under employed, his own good save being low down to his left as a Downing free kick beat the wall. He was beaten by O'Brien but the whistle had already gone for some shirt-pulling at the far post. With the extra space behind West Ham as they pushed forward Palace looked dangerous on the break, with one disallowed effort themselves, a shot by KG that was aimed straight at Jaaskelainen, and at the end sub Kébé fashioned a good opportunity for himself only for his shot to loop over. West Ham ended up playing real long ball stuff up to Collins but were caught offside often enough to break their rhythm, and the final whistle was seen out anxiously but safely, to be followed by a brief contretemps involving Moxey, Ward, Tomkins and Morrison, the last-named being lucky to see yellow & not red for a hand to Ward's face.

Speroni – 6
Ward – 7
Moxey – 6
Delaney – 8

```
Gabbidon - 7
Jedinak - 6
Dikgacoi - 5
Bannan - 7
Puncheon - 5
Chamakh - 6
Jerome - 5
Kébé - 6
O'Keefe - 6
Williams - 5
```

Saturday 7th December 3pm

Today, I managed to catch two matches. Firstly was a trip to Dulwich, to watch the Independent Schools Cup, quarterfinal. My old school, Alleyn's, were hosting Eton. Despite a convincing victory, I was slightly disappointed, that the opponents weren't adorned in top hats, with an active contingent of supporters on the touchline shouting, "Rah, rah, rah, were going to smash the oiks." Perhaps, I like most people, can be guilty of unleashing stereotypes, which bear no resemblance to reality, well I'm only human. Alternatively, I have just spent too much of my life, watching reruns of The Young Ones. (ser. 2 Ep 1 8th May 1984, if anyone's interested.) As well as the vast amount of new buildings, at the school, our main pitch has been rotated, 90 degrees, and is no longer where it used to be. This to me just seemed wrong, and if I feel like this about my old school pitch, heaven knows how I would feel, if Selhurst was rotated or moved. I am sure that, there are far more important practical issues, for the owners to consider, when planning any ground redevelopment, but I can see that the nostalgics amongst us, will all have an opinion to offer. Rather them than me!

Satisfied with the day so far, I got home in time to see my nephews, who were up for the game, and head off to Selhurst. A last minute change of hats followed, as I rejected the annoying jangly jester hat, for the 1980's red white and blue floppy cap. This wasn't on this occasion, a style or noise statement, but a practical solution to what I thought was going to be a cold afternoon. The added height of the jesters hat, isn't best suited for a hood, and I considered that this was going to be necessary. As it turned out, the clear skies, (The ones in the air, not the ones who reorganise our weekends.) didn't produce the much anticipated cold snap. Even Dad, who suffers from the cold, didn't complain too much and his hand warmers remained unactivated.

The same team as Tuesday, was in some ways encouraging, as Tony Pulis obviously feels we have a competitive unit. If I'm honest, I would have liked Joniesta in for Puncheon, who I'm not really warming too, and it is always better to see an academy player. In the end, it was a comfortable victory and Tony obviously knows, more than I do. Two on the bounce now, yep that's right, little old Palace, MOTD's genius prediction for relegation, with the lowest ever points total, had won two consecutive matches. It was only December, and we were already ahead of that total. Added to this, the fact that Chamakh, who Sir Gary Lineker said, only last week, was rubbish, worked his socks off and scored. That's two goals in two matches, and more goals from open play, than Spur's £26 million Soldado. Oh! I am so looking forward to seeing MOTD tonight. Eat humble pie Messer's Lineker and Hansen. In fact, my whole antipathy to the Premier League has changed recently. I now desperately want to stay up, just to see the look of exasperation, on the faces of the pundits, who wrote us off, before we even kicked a ball. The only slight disappointment for me, will be that Ollie isn't in charge to reap the praise. This is not meant to be, in anyway, critical of Tony P. He has obviously galvanised the team a bit, and tweaked certain thing, but I am not convinced we are playing a great deal better, than we were before. Just little breaks in our favour, here and there, have meant we got, the results that we deserved. People often forget the fact that, we had played six of the top seven teams in our first ten matches. My view always was, that there was a bit of an unnecessary panic. Not that this was coming from the owners, the manager or the majority of fans. Ironically, it was coming from the press, who in any case didn't want us at the big Premiership party. We are just not fashionable enough and trying to operate on a sound financial footing. Perhaps they just don't want us, rocking the gravy boat. Imagine if a team like Palace, with fans as owners, operating within their means, could stay in the league. How much would that hurt the advocates of this crazy and unsustainable circus, that football has become? I will report on how the coverage went later, if I remember. They will probably just say, Cardiff were rubbish and West Ham were out of sorts. This will be far easier for them to swallow, than offering any compliments to us. A couple of little things post-game, that deserve comment. One of the exit gates at the Holmesdale end of the ground was locked closed again, forcing the crowd to funnel through one exit. This is difficult for Dad, as he isn't particularly confident on his feet, in crowds any more. When we asked the stewards, (The crowd generally, not me being a pain in the backside again,) if they could open the other gate, we were told no, it was for health and safety. Would that be the same health and safety, that thought penning fans into small areas of a ground, with side fences was safe? The health and safety, that bans electronic cigarettes, from football grounds, or the health and safety, that has this year dictated, a young girl playing Mary in a nativity procession, must where a crash helmet, when she rides the donkey. It certainly wasn't the health and safety, that made any sense, to those whose safety it was supposed to ensure. We struggled through, by chaperoning Dad as if he was a major celebrity, and got him safely back to the car, despite; not because of, the H&S provisions.

 Since our rise to the dizzy heights of the Premiership, and the increasing difficulty of Dad to walk too far, I have been parking in the Sainsbury's car park, at the ground. This is great before the game, but getting out is a bit of a mare. Thornton Heath High Street, even if you can get to it, is bedlam. The police also seem to consider, that blocking one of just two lanes, out of the car park, with transit vans, is sound traffic management policy. The resulting congestion, has seen me try various different routes to get home. At the end of the game today, I thought I would try, the longer, but hopefully quicker route, by turning right rather than left, (I have to move into the right hand lane anyway, due to said transit vans.) I had heard the seemingly normal message to the Cardiff fans, about the location of their coaches, but not given it much consideration. It was only as I passed Park Road, and progressed up Whitehorse Lane, that I appreciated why an announcement of this kind was needed. I would guess that, there was somewhere approaching thirty coaches, reaching up almost as far as the top of the hill. I'm interested to find out, exactly where they all came from, and why coach travel is so popular with this team. Some of the comments, I have seen about coach travel, from our fans, have been very dismissive and in some cases, a little patronising. The suggestion is often made, that they are boring and for old folks. Having been travelling by coach for nearly 40 years, on and off, this isn't the way I see it. It obviously isn't the way Cardiff fans do either. My guess is, that their fans are drawn from all over South Wales, and as such, a bit like Norwich supporters, they may well travel on the coach, for both home and away games. That is my task for tonight. I will quickly visit the forums, and ask if anybody knows.

I have avoided the BBS for a few days, because it was annoying me. I should have stayed away. "Was Holloway the weak link?" was a new thread, that I noticed. For a football discussion board, this is quite a reasonable discussion. Unfortunately, some of our BBS members, would find it difficult to have a reasonable discussion, about the colour of snow, without resorting to insane personal abuse.

My only contribution to the subject was the following.

"Just because, some people are not clever enough, to understand what somebody says, doesn't make the person who said it, a clown.
Just because, something is said with a sense of humour, doesn't make the point less valid.
Just because, you try to live life with honesty and integrity, doesn't make you a quitter, or weak."

Unfortunately, the people who I was really directing these comments at, sits firmly into sentence one. I never found out my answer, to the question about the Cardiff travel arrangements, and despite the victory, went to bed a little disheartened. by some football supporters.

Marks Match Report

Wow! A hard working but not workmanlike display from Palace today emphasising the work put in by Millen & then Pulis in the inside of the players' heads. Attitude & commitment won the points today together with a generous dash of confidence. Cardiff were second-best - for the first 45 minutes they were pretty much third-rate and as poor in their own way as the hapless Hammers - and despite seeing more of the ball didn't seem likely to claw their way back.

Pulis, to some surprise, elected to field the same XI as started on Tuesday, with mutterings about the continued worth of Puncheon & KG in particular counting for nothing, and lined up in the same 4-4-1-1 with Chamakh just behind Jerome, while Cardiff went for a 4-1-4-1.

How different the game could have been had Julian not made what from 120 yards away looked like a superb save to keep out Campbell's far post header. A goal then could have dealt a serious blow to the team's self-confidence, let alone those of us on the sidelines. Yet Palace came forward and Jerome seemed to fluff two excellent chances, being unable to work an effort on goal when twice clear; as we were bemoaning his lack of finishing ability the much-maligned Puncheon did magnificent work in making space to put in a perfect cross, where Jerome redeemed himself with a firm header past Marshall. We had seen how a single goal restored Chamakh's self-belief and the fans' confidence on Tuesday; now Cameron had his first goal in 20+ appearances since his last.

Palace found the easiest way to create chances was to press deep on Cardiff's defence as the latter tried to play the ball out from deep. This had been the cause of both Jerome's early chances and continued to look likely to cost the Welshmen. Jerome & Chamakh hunted down Turner in particular, and for most of the first half Cardiff were reduced to long balls from the back aimed at the diminutive (by comparison) & isolated Campbell, a tactic that was meat & drink for Delaney & Gabbidon. They rarely threatened Julian's goal before the interval.

Palace, on the other hand, looked ready to kill the game off. Jedinak & KG were both having fine games, and while Puncheon again faded comparatively after a bright start, Bannan was once again an outlet on either flank; Jerome caught the defence flat-footed more than once on through balls from Jedinak & KG. A reshuffle was enforced when Moxey departed early with an injury, with Mariappa coming in at right back and Ward switching to the left, where he was to have one of his best performances for the club. Bannan, KG & Puncheon all had shots wide, Jedinak put a header over, while Ward nearly waltzed straight down the middle only for his shot to be blocked.

Surely Cardiff couldn't be as poor in the second half? They restarted at a high tempo and Palace were penned back for a short period. However they soon strangled Cardiff's midfield once again and Julian was not called upon to make a save. Instead Palace pressed on looked the more likely to score again, a couple of chances being passed up before Chamakh seized upon a poor clearance and shot with a confidence reborn across Marshall and inside the far post. KG, Jerome, Delaney & Bannan all had chances to increase the lead, with one scramble having the Whitehorse Lane joyously celebrating a goal that wasn't! [Anyone care to enlighten us on that?] Cardiff's chances were rare; both Odemwingie & Mutch had free headers at close range that they put over, and Julian's one difficult moment was a save low down at his left hand post. Once again Cardiff tried hard to work a more direct style, their midfield being held back by Palace's hard work, but gained no return. In the end they were well beaten.

Speroni - 7
Ward - 8
Moxey - 6
Delaney - 8
Gabbidon - 7
Jedinak - 7
Dikgacoi - 8
Puncheon - 6
Bannan - 8
Chamakh - 8
Jerome - 7
Mariappa - 7
O'Keefe - 6

[Sorry - seem to have worn out the key between 7 and 9 - gives the lie that my keyboard is in base 7!]

Keynesian Economics

For once, the problem with tickets is not mine. Mandy in the box office, has done a great job, despite I believe, some interference from her counterparts in West London, and we have second row upper tier, a pretty much ideal spot. The problem on this occasion is the decision by the club to reduce the restrictions on purchasing eligibility, and to not seek additional tickets. Obviously, with the whole allocation selling out in two days, this now seems like a bad idea, hindsight is a wonderful thing. However, the reasoning behind the decision was sound, but shows the perils of listening to, some sections of the fan base. It also reveals aspects of the money driven Premier League, which are not fully understood by the supporters. I have read the league rules on away ticket allocation, several times, and admit to still not fully comprehending them all, but there are several key differences from the Championship. Firstly, the away club, who sell the tickets don't get a commission and so make nothing; zero, zilch, from the administration of the ticket selling process, for their away support. Like most things Premier League, this of course benefits the clubs with the biggest grounds and the highest ticket prices, as these clubs would have to pay more out, than they would receive. Not only are no costs covered, but also in addition, if the away club requests extra tickets above a standard allocation, which is surprisingly not the Premier League's advertised maximum allocation, then doesn't sell them, the away club has to pay for them all. (Not always, but to avoid, this they have to be returned them almost before they have received them, so for all effective purposes, this statement is true). As a consequence of this, Palace in an attempt to accommodate as many of their fans as possible, at Old Trafford, had been left with a not insubstantial bill. If you do the maths, just 100 tickets unsold, at £50 each is £50,000 that you have to give to the Glazers. (With a name so close, you would have thought they might have come to us first, thank the stars for Big Al.) Now to Man United, this is just a youth team players weekly wage, but to a club like Palace, who are trying to live within their means, it is a significant sum. It is also a particular irony that if the expensive ticket price puts fans off travelling, their club will be less inclined to take their full allocation. This gives some clubs, the bonus of being able to sell the tickets to home supporters or tourist, who they really want in the first place. If on the other hand, the away club doesn't realise the problem in time, they will end up paying the full, over the top price, anyway. From the big clubs perspective, it is a win, win situation. Mindful of this, the Palace owners had listened to comments posted on the BBS, and voiced in other quarters, that the £55 that Russian Oligarch F.C. was charging, would put off many supporters. Thus, the decision, not to apply loyalty points and other restrictions. It was a sensible approach, which ensured a good turnout, but reduced the risk to the club. Then in double quick time, whoosh; they were all gone and some fans were left without. It was very unfortunate and if I had been one of the unlucky ones, I would have been equally annoyed. My away season ticket ensures that this will never happen and takes some of the panic away. This has been criticised in some quarters as elitist, but his is I think, missing the point. Away season ticket holders, are not being asked to pay up front for the season, and can queue jump if they have money. We just commit to going, and when the tickets come out, the money disappears from my account, about as quickly as the Stamford Bridge tickets, left the website.

The speed at which the tickets were sold, also presents a difficult dilemma, for those calling for lower ticket prices for football, and away supporters in particular. How is it possible to argue that prices are too high, when the grounds are full every week? In fact, I read an article some months ago, that argued that for some clubs, particularly Manchester United, the price is in fact too low, which is why secondary ticket sites, both official and unofficial, can operate so effectively. The model of, very high and very low prices was used at the Olympics, and whilst I'm not sure it was entirely effective, I was able to pick up various tickets at very reasonable prices. The problem for me is that there are two types of supporters, the regular and the occasional. For the regular traveller, the tickets are definitely too high, as I'm sure my accumulated bill at the end of the season, will show, but for those attending a few games a season. the price is not necessarily a significant deterrent. The bigger clubs are not stupid. They realise this and know that they will be the recipients of most of these, occasional trips. As a result, they can charge a premium, and the smaller clubs are left with an increasingly wide income gap. There has been an initiative this year, where each club has been given £200,000, to support away fans, and it will be interesting how this is used, by clubs. My fear is, it will be used on one-off high profile activities, appealing to these occasional away travellers, rather than the regular traveller. The Barclays Bus, did give us a much appreciated freebie, but if you weren't part of the lucky 100 you missed out, which even at its most basic, meant at least 100 away season ticket holders alone, saw no benefit from this initiative.

Anyway, I was all right Jack, so I set off for the short trip to West London, at what was the ludicrously early time of 8am. This was not because I intended a huge bender, or because the box office had miscalculated the time to drive the coach to Chelsea, believing that, it was in fact an outpost of Eastern Europe. I actually work just around the corner, for a Plumbing and Heating Company, and wanted to catch up. Our new service management software implementation, had somehow ended up on my desk, and this has resulted in a backlog of my own accounts work. After a few hours, once again doing other peoples jobs, (I fear that I am not really developing, the much needed skill of saying, "No, it's not my job or my responsibility," in my working life, either.) Eventually I gave up, and decided to go down to Fulham Broadway, to find an away fans pub. Having drunk around the area after work, I knew this would be an expensive addition to the day, but it would also be fun. Having not really done my research, I asked a police officer, that's what my Mum always taught me to do. His response of, "Try Earls Court." was a bit of a surprise, as it is a couple of stops on the tube, but the Maccyd`s needed soaking up. If I didn't find something to do, for two hours, I was either going to go back to work, or back to the hog roast in the market, that I had passed whilst eating my big mac. It had looked and smelt very appealing. Obviously, no simple greasy spoon burger, for all the soon to be arriving tourists, and Kensington residents. They even had applesauce for Christ sake, and it wasn't even Sunday lunch, how posh is that. I bet the Chelski don't like that on their doorstep, it must affect the prawn sandwich sales. In fact, I'm surprised they haven't tried for a football banning order, or compulsory purchase, accusing the stallholder of exploiting or damaging, their brand. Anyway, I avoided either temptation and jumped on the tube, heading for Earl's court. Once there, I found no audible signs of Palace fans, and was beginning to wonder if the BBS comments that, "part time fans, were going to be in ascendance today." was correct after all. Eventually, I found a small group of Palace fans, outside a pub, where I had a pint and a chat. It is always good to talk to other fans, but after travelling with a similar age group, and mentality of people, so regularly, I sometime find it hard to switch on, to a different train of thought. Football fans, despite the authorities' attitude, are a diverse bunch, so I only had the one, before heading back to Fulham Broadway. This proved to be a good decision, as my phone started to bleep, as soon as I came back into signal. I had a missed call from Mum, which I returned. "Are you nearly here yet?" I initially thought this was translated as, "don't drink too much in the pub." (She knows me too well, and sometimes it's like being a teenager again.) In fairness, this was not on this occasion,[4] the reason for the call. On the contrary, her call was to my benefit, as despite my earlier premature excitement, tickets were again an issue. This was not because of, a burly six-footer in front of her, swearing like a trooper, but because she had realised, she had my ticket. We normally check these things, quite thoroughly, but with what is often just a hand written C, or the tearing off, of one end, rather than the other, it is easy to get wrong. When we travel together, it's not a problem, but today it was. In defence of Chelsea, (Remember this; it probably won't happen again.) I was so caught up in the, bloody fifty-five quid for a ticket, mind-set, I didn't think that Chelsea had offered any concessions. I therefore, took less trouble than normal, to check. Whilst Mum, could obviously get in with my adult, '55 bloody quid for a ticket,' ticket, I am not sure I could yet pass as 65. Not even 48 years of Palace, dodgy women and dodgy Kebabs, can age you that much. Another ticket swap was therefore instigated, and this time, it was my incompetence and not intransigent box office policies, that caused it. How did we ever manage without mobile phones? Oh yes I remember now, we just pitched up and paid what was due, at a staffed turnstile. Happy days.

Despite my earlier fears and those expressed on the forums, both before and after the game, I personally thought the crowd was rocking as usual. The stewards, despite initial reservations, that they would be the annoying person, stood up in front of Mum, were very efficient at their job, but at the same time not totally authoritarian. I have looked again, at the YouTube videos of the crowd, and haven't been able to see, the large section supposedly, "sat down and not singing." In fact, I am not sure that it is even possible, to **SEE,** people not singing. Although I am sure that, the vocal minority on the BBS, would just swear and tell me to F@@k off, for pointing this out. It is true, that there was a section of people, sat in front and to the left of me, who I did not recognise. Then again, more and more I realise, that I don't recognise many people, who travel, all over the place, and I certainly don't know their names. In fact, I'm not sure; I would even recognise

[4] See Everton and Newcastle away

members of the Holmesdale Fanatics. They are always behind me, and I am normally in my seat, before them. So not recognising somebody is not always the best, definitive guide to loyalty and frequency of attendance. What I did notice however, was that they seemed as enthusiastic about Palace, as the next man, woman or transgender person, (don't expect me to be P.C. every time; I have a word count to keep too.) I also noticed, or perhaps more importantly didn't notice, that they sat in their seat. Everybody around me; small man, very small Mum, and child, could see; what was a very good, if ultimately fruitless performance. As well as, the great efforts put in by the whole team, not even I, can exclude Cameron Jerome from this particular attribute today. It was especially gratifying, to see Jose Mourinho, leave his dug out at the end of the game, and before anything else, turn to our corner of the ground and applaud us. I know my Mum will disagree, but I like the guy. I think he is funny, and actually quite honest, once you get past the games, and the irony and sarcasm. I thought it was a classy thing to do, especially after we had taunted him with, "you're not special, anymore." after our equaliser. It would have been nice, if Torres, had done the same, but perhaps, "fifty mill; you're having a laugh." was a chant, that he may have found had more truth to it, and was therefore more difficult to shrug off, with a smile. I hope Mark's match report, will give you the full feel, of how close we were to a point. I also hope, that the belief the second half display should engender, can be replicated from the start in future games. I am sure that, if we could just create a mentality that says, we are as good as these guys, right from the start, we would quickly accumulate points.

Getting home was a bit of a nightmare. In fact, getting back to the pork bap stall, was a nightmare, and then when I got there, he had run out of crackling, which if I am honest, I wanted more than the pork. The problem with attracting supporters, from all over London and the Home Counties, is that you have to get them home again. This is always going to be tricky at, for instance, Wembley, because of the nature of the games. Standing in the rain for an hour, after England lost with a whimper to Croatia, was never going to improve people's mood, but Stamford Bridge? Clubs can build all the fancy stadium they like, but without the infrastructure to get fans away, you create a bad end to the day. Does your average, once a season supporter, want to queue for 45 minutes, just to get into the tube station? I'm not sure. Does it present an opportunity for bad feeling and aggression? Very probably. Fortunately it didn't come too anything today, because Palace fans, are not generally like that. Except that is, for the one lone supporter, trying to get to the pork man, by navigating past the blockage, only to find out that the delay had saved his teeth, but denied that salty crunch.

Local fans walk, much like kids that go to local schools walk, or they bloody well should. (I think I'm turning into Ben Elton.) If you change this dynamic, by changing your catchment, as in Chelsea, or moving your ground out of town, as in Brighton, you make access or exit, a not wholly satisfying experience. (Although by the time I left the Amex, on my last two visits, the transport system was pretty clear.)

Marks Match Report

If not Palace's best performance of the season, then certainly their finest 45 minutes given the standard of opposition. The last time I visited the Bridge was last century, when I walked out with the score at 4-1 (& missed three goals for my pains). This time there was no danger of my precipitate departure as Palace fought hard & long. Chelsea may have had the edge in quality and in the stats, but Palace seem to have acquired resilience under Millen & now Pulis that might see us through.

Mariappa for the injured Moxey was the only change to Palace's starting XI, although the formation was definitely 4-5-1 as Chamakh dropped deep into midfield. The problem with this was it often left Cameron Jerome isolated up front, and apart from an early run that fizzled out due to lack of support & options, too often the direct ball was picked off by Terry & Luiz. Chelsea started slowly and were initially as uninspiring as United had been at Old Trafford, but they gradually began to monopolise possession. The clever movement of the likes of Mata and Hazard started to find space and angles in behind the midfield shield. Mariappa was severely embarrassed by one of those pesky little continental midfielders and looked exactly what he was, a centre back playing out of position on the right. It didn't take Chelsea too long to open the scoring after a couple of sighters; Willian found space on the edge of the box and fired in a shot before he was closed down; Speroni pushed the ball onto the post but Torres was too quick and seized upon the rebound to slot home.

At this stage Palace's game plan looked like unravelling, with KG departing injured & replaced by the inexperienced O'Keefe. The game nearly slipped completely away when Ivanovic burst in on our left and his cross shot slipped inches past the far post. At this stage it was impossible to see how Palace would ever post a threat on goal. The midfield wasn't playing badly, with Chamakh surprisingly effective in a deeper role than usual, but apart from a Jerome shot on the break easily snaffled by Cech there didn't seem to be any way of penetrating Chelsea's box through a lack of numbers. Ironically it was a long ball that was slightly over hit that led to the goal, forcing Cech to head out for a throw. Palace moved bodies up and although the ball was lost initially, Jedinak won it back and the ball transferred the width of the pitch from right to left; Puncheon – having a very effective game – played Ward in on the overlap. And his excellent cross was turned in by Chamakh from about 12 yards out. That instilled some confidence into the team and the passing started to have some snap, before Chelsea struck back; Ramires this time found space on the edge of the box and left an unsighted Speroni helpless. It was crucial that Palace at least held onto half-time with no worse than a one goal deficit and at least we managed that with Speroni rescuing Mariappa and smothering a late effort.

Mourinho's old Chelsea team would have remorselessly choked the life out of this match. His new lot are far more effervescent and started the second half as though they wanted to bury us early under an avalanche of goals. Only some smart / desperate defending kept them at bay, although the left flank was turned by Willian, and when the ball came to the undermanned far post only a rare failure to control the ball by Hazard prevented a worse fate. Yet this Chelsea side are also far more fragile, and the near miss seemed to pep Palace up, and from that point the game became a helter-skelter end-to-end match that almost rivalled that piped onto the concourses pre-match. And it wasn't achieved through muscular direct tactics, but some snappy passing and movement that saw Palace cut through Chelsea on the break as often as there cultured approach play did to us.

At this point Bannan, who had a worthy if unexceptional game, was replaced by the more mercurial talents of Bolasie, who went straight to the right flank, and Palace started to make serious chances. Jerome had an early shot over before Puncheon at least forced a save from Cech. O'Keefe & Jedinak were biting into tackles and playing neat through balls; Chamakh was often the effective link man; while Puncheon and Bolasie exploited the pretty Chelsea midfielders' distaste for defensive duties. Puncheon delivered a beautiful cross that Bolasie should really have done better with, while Delaney had the first of three headers, the first forcing a save from Cech while the later two were off-target. Chelsea too had chances but the game was in question far later than most had suspected. Another fine move saw O'Keefe burst into the box to be denied three times in about a second by Cech and some frantic defending. Apart from Delaney's third header it was Palace's last & best chance, as Chelsea looked stronger in the last 5-10 minutes and only a quite brilliant lose-range double save by Speroni kept us going until the end. The players & manager deserve the plaudits for the performance that probably deserved more than nil points.

Speroni - 7
Mariappa - 6
Ward - 8
Delaney - 7
Gabbidon - 7
Dikgacoi - 6
Jedinak - 8
Puncheon - 7
Bannan - 6
Chamakh - 8
Jerome - 6
O'Keefe - 8
Bolasie - 7
Gayle - 5

Geordies in Toon

Sometimes, as a football supporter, it is easy to notice a little thing, and build it into something much bigger. You are completely unaware, that nobody else noticed or even cared about that little detail, a player's odd boots, or whispered behind the hands, muttering of the coaching staff. In some ways that is the whole basis of this book, which now I think of it, is a slight worry in terms of potential sales. However, on other occasions, everybody notices what you do, and the story becomes part of the clubs folklore. Jose Mourinho's acknowledgement, and subsequent comments about our fans, is possibly one such incident, as all four of the articles that I generally read in the programme, made mention of it today, and it was also picked up by the TV pundits. Presumably, the latter was to avoid having to talk about, how close the team came to matching Chelski, on the pitch, and the fact that, despite being dead certs for relegation, we could if we pick up a result today, be out of the bottom three, on Christmas Day. (Now that would be a special gift from Santa.)

As well as the praise for our support, there was also an implied criticism of the Chelsea fans, lack of vocal support. Which has also been voiced, against many of the larger clubs and new grounds. Since I started using the BBS more extensively, I have noticed the way that fans communities, are much more interconnected than I had expected. Fans of different clubs often visit the Palace forums, to comment on discussions and to offer praise or criticism. Although it would not be accurate to say, these visits are always universally well received, they do often express an alternative viewpoint. This week, one such view was expressed by a Chelsea supporter, who felt the need to defend the clubs support. His perspective was that a lot of old school fans, now mostly concentrate on away matches, and equally find the lack of atmosphere at home matches, disappointing. Whilst I understand his view on this, I am a little sceptical as to how a group of old school fans, would actually get away tickets, if they are not regular home fans. What I think is a more likely scenario, is that these fans are spread out around Stamford Bridge, in a disconnected way. CPFC2010's policy, of allowing a vocal group of supporters to be positioned together, helps to avoid this scenario. These are all little things, that our owners understand, and are often undervalued.

Picking up points today, will need all of the efforts of the players, and our fans will need to be in top voice. Despite my prediction, that Newcastle might struggle this year, they are flying high. We also have our own difficulties, in that we are two midfielders short. The buzz in the bar before the game, was partly people trying to shake the rain off their clothes, and partly discussions about how five defenders, were going to fit into four places. I wondered if as a curve ball, Damien Delaney might move into central midfield, to provide a tenacious presence, but Tony Pulis decided that it was Joel Ward, who would undertake this role. He has been brilliant at full back, so far this season, and to me, it made some sense, that he would be able to cope with the added responsibility. Others disagreed, feeling that we shouldn't be moving a player, from a position where he is playing so well, when we have other more natural midfielders available. These discussions are what make football so great. In the end, the doubters will feel that they were right, and I cannot disagree that we were completely overwhelmed. The result shows this, and Mark will give the report in the following pages. However, the experiment wasn't without validity, and I can see why the manager tried it.

The TV highlights, showed just how wet it was out on the pitch. Unlike in the old days, before roofs on terraces, you don't always fully appreciate the playing conditions, the players are experiencing. This isn't an excuse for our result today, and perhaps if anything, demands that our keeper is more commanding and communicative, than ever. The truth was, I think, that Newcastle were just too good, their league position is not a fluke. Along with the result and the rain, I was also disappointed by, the flip in the reaction of some fans to the team selection. One week Tony Pulis, like Ollie before him, is God, the next he is a "completely useless T@@T". Life isn't that black and white, some ideas don't work, some do. Discussion and personal opinion is always interesting, but irrational abuse expressed in the aftermath of a heavy defeat, is never so endearing. I will try to remember this over the coming months and chapters.

Marks Match Report

For the first time since his arrival at Selhurst Park, Tony Pulis's team selection and tactics came under question on a filthy day when Palace gave a barely adequate Newcastle team a comfortable victory in a game where we looked like having a decent shot at a point at least. The last time Palace defeated the Geordie Nation at Selhurst it had been a rare bright spot in the dire Mullery era (two years that felt like ten) as the Second Division's quality team (IIRC containing Kevin Keegan and young starlets in Beardsley & Waddle) was well beaten; this time some talented Frenchmen were given a comfortable time. Have we glimpsed the future under Pulis or was this an unfortunate one-off?

When I first heard the starting XI I guessed that the restored Moxey might be played on the left of midfield with Bannan playing inside. Instead, in the absence of the solid KG and the terrier-like O'Keefe, Pulis pushed Joel Ward into the centre of midfield. What this says of his opinion of an actual central midfield player in Campaña, or a more bold selection of Jonny Williams, can now be guessed. As a result Palace were playing two men out of position, with Mariappa still filling in at right back, and this perhaps affected the play, in addition to further upsetting the solid defensive unit Millen & Pulis had assembled. In the first half Palace lacked any real width: Bannan was ineffectual on the right with little support from Mariappa; while on the left Puncheon was functional but Moxey did not look match fit, rarely pushing forward, and at one stage given a start by Debuchy only to be overtaken by the rapid Toon full back. With a pragmatic midfield in Jedinak & Ward, who did not play badly but lacked the positional awareness required and the ability to fashion time & space for a pass, the only flashes of creativity came from the deep-lying Chamakh (& occasionally Puncheon) but Marouane's placement meant that Jerome was often operating in a vacuum. Palace's attacks were predictably long & down the middle, and while Chamakh won his fair share of flick-ons, they seldom found Jerome. In addition, being outnumbered in midfield by Newcastle's 4-5-1 formation, while the forwards tried to close down the Toon's back four, the midfield often sat off their opposite numbers, instead shifting across the pitch, allowing the ball to be transferred around safely. This became more noticeable as the game wore on, and was perhaps a side-effect of having Ward in the centre, and Newcastle dominated possession for most of the game. Also, as Swansea did, they worked hard at closing Palace down.

The game itself was pretty dull, with both side's defences proving capable of repelling most attacks. Newcastle had a little edge in quality and used the width of the pitch, while Palace's only early chance was a Krul save from a Bannan free kick that was probably less simple than it appeared. It was a sign that Palace's luck had perhaps deserted them in the way the goals came. Moxey's headed clearance from a Remy cross was directed centrally instead of wide, and Cabaye's shot took a deflection off a defender that left Julian flat-footed; annoyingly both Sissoko & Cabaye in the build up had plenty of time and were not closed down quickly enough. Palace almost seized an immediate equaliser when some persistence from Jerome on the end of a long ball forced a sharp save from Krul and sparked a series of corners that threatened, with Krul badly misjudging one and a panicked clearance being hacked off the line. We didn't know it but that was about the last time Palace really put Newcastle under pressure. Instead we had two more slices of bad luck to come. First the linesman missed Coloccini's obvious final touch for a corner & awarded a goal kick; straight from that Debuchy (?) made ground down our left, and delivered one of a number of dangerous crosses from that flank; although there wasn't an attacker in the box Gabbidon's attempted clearance flew past Speroni. The original decision didn't excuse the defending that followed but it summed up our performance.

At half-time Pulis made two substitutions but still didn't address the problem in midfield. Parr came on for his Premier League debut in place of Moxey, perhaps an admission that Dean wasn't quite ready to return, while Bolasie came on for Bannan to offer width on the right. That still left Ward in midfield, wasting a class full back; what price Campaña or Williams now when we needed more creativity? Even the option of dropping Ward back to left back, moving Parr to either left or right flank, and playing Puncheon inside, looked a more palatable alternative. Ironically, later in the game, all the wide players swapped flanks, with Parr & Puncheon moving right and Mariappa & Bolasie left. It didn't start too badly, with Bolasie looking an immediate threat, and Puncheon had a shot blocked, possibly by his own player. Later Mariappa, for about the first time, overlapped and delivered an excellent cross which Chamakh headed over. Yet we were soon reduced to more long balls that, on this soaked pitch, tended to run away from our attackers into the safe arms of Krul or the waiting Holmesdale Road stand.

Newcastle resumed midfield domination despite a lack of scoring opportunities and slowly strangled the game. Speroni had to make what looked a scrappy save from a free kick, but in fact was quite smart given how the ball moved in the air, and later foiled Cabaye in a one-on-one. By that time Jerome had blown Palace's last chance to get back into the game, blasting over a Delaney knock down, a bread-and-butter chance for a striker. Gouffran had a cross shot that smacked the face of the bar before Parr, who had impressed quietly, seemed not to expect Ameobi to be standing where he was aiming a kick and conceded a most obvious penalty. Julian got both hands to Ben Arfa's spot kick but, in line with today's theme, it wasn't enough to prevent the third goal. Delaney saw the game out by at least forcing Krul into a save with a drive from distance,

but despite a great deal of effort, Palace were well
beaten by the Toon who barely broke out of second gear.

Speroni - 6
Mariappa - 5
Moxey - 4
Delaney - 7
Gabbidon - 6
Ward - 5
Jedinak - 6
Bannan - 4
Puncheon - 5
Chamakh - 6
Jerome - 5
Parr - 7
Bolasie - 5
Gayle - 5

Good King Wenceslas

I love St Stephen's day football, which most people will know as, Boxing Day football; it is part of the tradition of the English leagues, that make it just that bit special. A local derby, big crowds, and the opportunity to shake of a monster hang over. However, about the same time that our vicar decided, that the 26th of December was a bit too close to Christmas, for celebrating St Stephen's day, as everybody was busy. The Football League, or possibly the old bill, decided that it would be a good idea to stop local derbies, and send fans up and down the country, on a non-existent transport system. When you look back at our fixtures in the 70's and 80's, it is matches against Gillingham, Aldershot, and Orient; if we really had to travel, the furthest was Ipswich or Oxford. Perhaps my love of the Boxing Day fixtures, really comes down to these local derbies, and in particular the regular matches against Brighton. It was in fact, I believe, my first away match without my Dad, in 1979, that prompted the much sung, "Hark now hear, the Palace sing, the Brighton run away, Again, and we will fight, forever more, because of Boxing Day." song, or at least if it wasn't, it was the first time that I had heard it. The fact that we lost 3-0, would in my mind, reinforce this historical context. Maybe the song, originated before that trip, but as I was never part of the battles, that normally ensued around this fixture, I didn't notice. Younger fans, may also be surprised, that this match was actually a Division 1 fixture, when Division 1 was the top division, and not the 3rd Division. This kind of mathematical inconsistency from the football authorities, may go some way to explaining, a generation of schoolchildren who cannot do basic maths.

The thought of a Boxing Day fixture, between these two rivals now, would send the Met, into free fall melt down, so it is just a distant memory, and perhaps this is why, we are now more likely to be sent much further afield. Fortunately, in the relative scheme of things, we got off lightly this year with a trip to Aston Villa, and would be back in time for a gathering, at some family friends. Learning from last season's trip to Blackpool, I now appreciate that, family gatherings at my sister in laws and the associated wine consumption, do not mix with long coach journeys. Not wishing to have to find a convenient alleyway, before boarding the coach, Christmas Day was a low alcohol affair, although, much like a low Premiership wage bill, this is a relative term.

When we made our trip to Liverpool, on the Barclays Bus, the promo folks were keen to find out, what we did on the journeys. They were particularly interested in Pauline's knitting, and this even prompted a special, Wrighty shout out, on his radio show, which we were instructed to listen too, on the way home. Now some coach activities, have more use than others, and some are just time fillers. My writing, depending on your prospective, could be seen as fitting into either category, but Pauline's knitting, is definitely a practical use of time, especially on a cold winter day. On today's relatively short trip, she was able to knit a complete hat, and wear it to the game. This particular skill would have solved my own hat problem, in an instant and maybe I should consider a new hobby. (I would prefer at this point, if you refrain from nodding in agreement, it is discouraging.) I did also learn an interesting fact today, which had never occurred to me before, and probably never occurred to you, either. How do you knit on a plane? Given that, you can't take sharp pointy things onto planes. Well for anybody who is interested, apparently they make special bamboo knitting needles, that pass through security, no problems. It's nothing if not educational, this football travel.

I couldn't face anything, even vaguely productive myself on the journey, due to the previously mentioned, low alcohol Christmas Day, and sleep was my only activity. The game itself, was played out between two poor sides, and was settled by one piece of exceptional individual skill, and for once, this wasn't achieved by the opposition. Dwight Gayle, our big summer signing, who was introduced late on; initially wandered about like a little boy lost, before producing a finish, that explained too many, why the club and Ollie, invested so much of their summer transfer budget, on an untested raw talent.

There are moments as a football fan, that make all of the journeys, and the time, and the disappointment, worthwhile. My position in the crowd, was almost perfect, and had the net not been in the way, I am almost certain, the ball would have ended up in my hands. That brief time lapse, from shot to goal, when I and the few people directly around me, knew we had scored, was magical. Yet, at the same time, intolerable. I have learnt over the years, that nothing in life or football, is ever certain, until its certain, whatever the probability. The Villa keeper, could turn into stretch Armstrong, or Steve Austin, and then I would be racked with disappointment, all over again. All you can do in this situation, is to wait, and prepare to explode, just that millisecond, before everyone else. I am not exaggerating when I say, there was something about that goal, which made me believe, I was watching a pivotal point in our season, and that I was part of a special moment, for the club. The goal itself, and the three points, that took us out of the relegation zone, were only a part of this feeling.

It is often difficult to explain, to a non-football fan, why a particular moment, has such significance, but I hope it is possible to explain to you. As football supporters, we are familiar with the interview platitudes, about fans and players all working together, for the club. I am sure that like me, many of you, have grown sceptical of the badge kissing mercenary, that is there one minute, and gone the next. In fact, Steve Browett, in his much appreciated foreword, for this book, quoted Sir Steve, (I have just genuflected[5], as is appropriate.) in this regard. It has been common to suggest, that players at some clubs, don't care, and have no passion. In fact, only 2 months ago, this was the accusation, being levelled at the Palace players, and resulted in Ollie's resignation. Yet in one moment, as I looked down at the Villa Park pitch, I knew this wasn't the case, with this current team. Genuinely, this was a shared moment of exhilaration. Our Captain Mile Jedinak, who I admit when he first arrived, I thought was technically incapable, had run his legs off, for the previous 90 minutes; yet, he grabbed Dwight Gayle, who was running around, as if he was a teenager who had drunk too much Tatrazine, and

---

[5] Verb: to bend the knee or touch one knee to the floor in reverence or worship.

physically pulled him, over to the Palace fans. The sheer joy on Dwight's face, and his own passion, had to, he knew, be shared with us. Joining the party on the pitch, was Damien Delaney, a player that just two seasons ago, was released by Ipswich Town, and who had considered switching to American football, just to make a living. The tears that he had shed, away from the limelight, but captured on TV, at Wembley, seven months ago, had left nobody in any doubt, what it had meant to him then. Yet, he was a player, that many expected to fall by the wayside, in our Premiership journey. Instead, he was beating his chest, just yards from us, in a totally unself-conscious way. Dean Moxey, the friend and colleague, who had left the pitch at Wembley to find him, and talk quietly and privately to him, was fittingly on the pitch again. There to share, another special moment. However, my own personal favourite moment, was captured by the cameras, and has since become my screen saver. Johnny Williams, who joined the club as an 8 year old, and Dwight Gayle, who still looks like an 8 year old, running towards us, almost hand in hand. as if they were in the school playground. The expressions on their faces, a pleasure to be seen. I am sure if the picture had been taken from their position, and not ours, they would have seen thousands of the same expressions, smiling back at them. It was a moment that I am sure, will stay with me for a long time, a genuine sense of a shared goal, and a shared determination to succeed. If we don't win another game all season, I know that, neither I, nor anybody else, will ever be able to say, that the players didn't care enough. I know this, because I saw it in their eyes.

After the F.A. Cup semi-final in 1990, I stood overlooking the Villa Park pitch, and smoked a big Cigar, until pretty much everybody had left. This kind of behaviour is no longer allowed, but I did have a surreptitious drag, on my electric cigarette, just for old times' sake, and I can tell you, it felt almost as good. In addition, I was reassured that, the stadium didn't spontaneously com-bust, and no one fainted, due to my exhaled water vapour. The journey home was quick and relatively subdued. A quiet contentment, is what coach one does best.

Marks Match Report

An outsider would not have expected much from this match between the two teams with the worst possession rates in the Premier League (well, that had to change somewhat today), the worst pass attempt & completion rates, the lowest number of crosses from open play, and the teams that played the highest percentages of long passes – hey, that was The Guardian! As it was Aston Villa pretty much proved they were as bad as the stats suggested despite a majority of possession, whereas Palace proved more dangerous with limited ball. I thought this might be a good chance for a result, and while I was ready to settle for a draw, there is a sheer beauty about a stunning stoppage time winner that encourages us to ignore all the figures except the final scoreline.

In the absence of the suspended Chamakh, Pulis chose a simple 4-5-1 formation with Bolasie initially on the left and Puncheon on the right, while Bannan at last found a berth in the middle along with Jedinak and – despite much groaning – Ward. The only other change saw Parr replace Moxey at left back. One of the problems with this formation was that Jerome was often isolated, and for the first 10 minutes Villa enjoyed almost continual possession without actually creating anything really dangerous. It was Palace who forced the first save from Guzan when, after switching wings, Bolasie's far post header from Puncheon's cross brought a routine save. Puncheon, Bolasie & Bannan instigated a number of decent breaks, but while Bolasie's crossing has improved, the touch of Jerome was far too heavy, while Puncheon also halted some good moves with inept play. The defence looked sound, with Mariappa showing a vast improvement at right back, while Parr was sometimes caught a little for pace. The most dangerous moment came when a Gabbidon slip in dealing with a Villa break nearly saw their strikers take advantage, but they proved as inadequate in forcing a save from Speroni. The last touch of the first half saw Mariappa head a corner off the line which was the closest Villa were to come to a goal.

If the first half had been relatively low on quality & excitement, the second half started at a faster pace and at least supplied more of the latter. Palace's five man midfield was functioning well, with both Jedinak & Ward solid while Bannan provided evidence that he is far more useful in a central role. The main threat came from Bolasie who stayed on the right wing and ripped that flank of Villa's defence apart on a regular basis. He created a chance that saw a Bannan shot clawed onto the post and out by Guzan, while Puncheon twice spoiled great chances by almost tripping on the ball and being unable to get the ball out from his feet cleanly, allowing Guzan time to block the eventual shots; a later effort from Ward clipped the roof of the net and for a second many of us thought we'd scored. Sadly Jerome was never a threat and Puncheon was soon replaced by Williams on the left, with Gayle later on for the lone striker. Palace, who had pressed Villa's midfield on the halfway line, now dropped back to a

126

line 10-15 yards outside our box and conceded a lot of territory and possession which was worrying. Agbonlahor, surprisingly used in a deep role, started to run with the ball and a couple of chances were made, the most worrying a snap shot inside the box that flew straight into Julian's grasp. As the final whistle approached there was a header that Julian acrobatically tipped over, a save that was more routine that it looked.

A point seemed to have been saved, and the Villa fans were despairing of the display and Lambert's resorting to the long ball, but then two substitutes who had hardly touched the ball sparked a break. Moxey had come on for Bannan and played in a wide left role and seized upon the ball, outpacing two Villa players before laying the ball forward for Gayle. Dwight had hardly touched the ball, so deep had the midfield dropped that not only was he even more isolated that Cameron Jerome had been, but his selfless closing down of defenders was in vain. Now he outpaced the cover then hit a splendid shot from the edge of the box that flew into the top corner. Cue pandemonium and some late ineffectual Villa pressure before the final whistle saw us gain three deserved points.

Speroni - 7
Mariappa - 6
Parr - 6
Gabbidon - 6
Delaney - 7
Ward - 7
Jedinak - 7
Bannan - 8
Puncheon - 6
Bolasie - 8
Jerome - 5
Williams - 7
Gayle - 7
Moxey - 7

£400 million v £10 million.

 At the West Ham home game, a few weeks ago, everybody entering the ground, was given a letter from the club, regarding ground regulations and remaining seated. I felt a bit guilty about this, because of the conversations on the subject, that that I had instigated, or contributed to, on the BBS. The club, appear to have taken a quite sensible, and pragmatic position on the issue, at Selhurst, but this can obviously lead to its own problems, when concessions that they make, albeit unofficial, are exploited and pushed to the limits. In the particular case at Palace, it appears that one of the problems, has been caused by the new Sky TV studio, which was a requirement of joining the league, but as yet, has not actually been used. Selhurst is not awash with space, and the only place it could go, was right in front of the disabled section, obscuring their view. As the specification for the new studio, was I believe, not accurate, and this wasn't known until it was in place, the options to do much about it, were very limited. Moving the disabled fans to other areas, then created its own problems. They were now, directly behind some sections of the crowd, who have been much more inclined to stand, than others have. Alternatively, perhaps with the ground regulation's allowing, "Standing during periods of excitement," these sections of the ground, are just more easily excited. In the upper tier of the Holmesdale, with far less excitable individuals, I wasn't aware that it was a particular problem, but on the journey up to Manchester today, Mandy and Caroline, had explained some of the problems, that as a disabled person and carer, respectively, they face on a weekly basis. The need to arrive, an hour and a half before the match, is just one such irritation. The BBS, has had a reasonably steady stream of opinion, on the subject of standing and sitting, since the letter. My own personal beef, has always quite selfishly, been about the arrangements at away matches. I was therefore pleased that, along with the letter about the home match, we were advised that a similar letter, would go out with all away tickets, purchased in the front rows. This was dully done, with tickets for today's game, being the first to include this letter. Despite some reservations expressed, that people had been given tickets in the front, without asking for them, as soon as the game started, it became obvious that the idea had been incredibly effective. I was even prompted to take a picture, to counter any future BBS arguments, about the subject. As I have always argued, the seated area, actually extended back much further, than those who had received the letter. Proving pretty categorically to me, that the desire to sit, is higher than those who NEED to sit, and all types of fan can be accommodated, given a little bit of coordination and care. My only slight disappointment, and a feature of the fuller grounds, is that we weren't able to sit with my brother and nieces, who had brought their tickets at a different time. I would have quite liked to have sat in the upper tier with them, both because of the company and the view, but having spent much time, negotiating a regular front row seat, I didn't want to risk messing the box office about, by asking for a different seating criteria, for this one match. The reasonably static nature, of travellers on the first two away coaches, also meant that, we were not able to travel with the other four members of our family. I would have gladly again, moved to a different coach to arrange this, but I know that Mum, really enjoys the company of people, that she has travelled with for years, and is a bit paranoid, that if she loses her place, she won't get it back. I'm sure that that would not happen, but I certainly did not want to start arriving even earlier for away trips, than we already do, to put my proverbial, towel on my sun lounger.

I must admit, although I am not a great fan of modern grounds, especially ones that have been paid for by local councils, and virtually given to overseas multi-millionaires, The Etihad is very impressive, and affords a great view even from virtually pitch side. The concourse facilities are also impressively spacious as well as having nice touches, to make away fans feel welcome. The showing of the Play-off match, against Brighton, before the game, certainly put everyone in good moods. Unfortunately, the same cannot be said of the pitch side stewards. It was noticeable that, in every other section of the ground, pitch side stewards only sat in front of gangways, but in front of the away section, they seemed to be almost every 10 yards. So we had finally cracked our own fans, obscuring our view, but were now having to negotiate with the stewards, which in my experience, is often a tortuous process, and equally as futile as negotiating with the Norfolk police. Now I fully accept that, had I been having the discussion with the female steward, that the two ladies sat at the end of my row were, (Not my mother or Caroline, I hasten to add.) I would probably not have used the language, or the tone, that they did, but there was a definite chicken and egg scenario. If the steward hadn't been obscuring their view, then they would have had no reason to confront her, and quite possibly, although by no means definitely, they would not have sworn quite so much at her. In retaliation, she would then not have had to threaten to chuck them out. Fortunately, one of the senior stewards saw what was developing, and changed this particular steward's position. The new steward, looked a little nervous, as he took his seat, as two South London women, (Probably from New Addington, harsh but fair.) in full flow, can even I thought, be quite scary. In fairness, he made quite a good fist of reducing his not insubstantial frame, to the least noticeable size, and stayed almost motionless for the remainder of the game. Unfortunately, once this kind of irritation starts, the smallest obstruction to your view, is then seen as a major obstacle. The Etihad does have little pits around the pitch, for the photographers to sit in, which is again a good and intelligent addition to the ground. Unfortunately, the runners that continually visit to collect memory cards, do not seem to be aware of the views, of the paying public. Once or twice, they almost received the same treatment as the now relocated steward and Caroline joined in, but obviously without the swearing bit. In a small ground, where every possible seat, represents a considerable percentage of those available, I can almost understand, why these pitch side seats are important, but at the larger grounds, I feel that, they should be taken out. If all of the seats started a foot higher, many problems would be resolved.

Off the pitch, the other highlight of the afternoon involved Sean Scannell, who left the club several years ago, but who had been with us, since being a very young boy. Presumably without a game himself, he made the trip to Manchester, and took up a position in the stands, with the Palace faithful. Subsequently, his name was sung with appropriate gusto, by all who knew what was going on, and I guess, a few at the back of the Lower tier, who didn't. It is a sign of the special affection, even ex-players have for certain clubs, that he would do this, much in the same way that one of the Chairman, can often be seen in the concourse at away games, mingling with fans and enjoying a pint. It is also a sign of how my youngest niece is growing, into a young woman, with the associated self-consciousness, you would expect from a newly designated teenager. Several years ago, Sean Scannell held her hand, as she made her mascot debut, and he had become her favourite and most adored Palace player. The signed photo, which I am sure, is now a little embarrassing for her, still hangs in the living room. I believe that a few tears were also shed, when his career took him to more northern pastures. As a quite confident child, I am sure that 4 years ago, she would have been out of the blocks like Usain Bolt, just to say "Hi". Today, she didn't move, and I'm sure that, if I had been close enough to ask her, rather than relying on texting her, she would have said something profound like, 'oh well, what's gone is gone,' whilst casting Gooey eyes, towards Joel Ward.

 Out on the pitch, our fears of a cricket score, were not being realised, and the team as Mark will tell you, were performing in a way that we could only have dreamt about. The natives were even getting a bit restless, and there were periods of the game, when we really should have made our advantage tell. However, in the end, it wasn't to be another point towards safety, and Dzeko, a member of their squad assembled at approximately £400 million, scored to send our motley crew, of just £10 Million, home with a harsh defeat. It was telling that we were all initially disappointed, as we got back on the coach, but we were able to raise a smile, at Manuel Pellegrini's after-match press conference. He suggested that, it was difficult to play against a team, that came and put ten men behind the ball. I will finish my piece today, with the fact that made this observation, so amusing and then say no more. Man of the Match - Manchester City goalkeeper Joe Hart

Marks Match Report

I understand that a well known Mancunian, Mr. Pellegrini, complained that Palace packed 10 men behind the ball at the Etihad today. Well, yes, we did – when defending, especially in the first half. However the fact that City's announced Man of the Match was custodian Joe Hart might give the initiated a clue that it wasn't all out defence. Tony Pulis had a game plan and it damned well nearly came off! Fears of an avalanche of City goals slowly receded (the common opinion amongst Palace fans was 5 might be on the cards) and we managed to conceded that number less than the North London "giants". We ended up going toe-to-toe with the billionaires in the second half and with a little better luck & finishing may well have come away with a point or more...

It was a warm welcome at the Etihad where everyone we met was friendly & helpful, and the efforts made at the stadium for the supporters are in stark contrast to the cold manner of City's despised neighbours. However the City faithful do appear to be lapsing into the United ways of expecting to be entertained and were as quiet as the librarians at Old Trafford; perhaps they were waiting for the 6 or 7 goal thrashing to be administered. The seat wasn't great, low down to the side of the goal that looked likely to make viewing difficult for at least 45 minutes given expectations, although a nice big screen did help (even if highlights tended to be of the sky blue nature). Pulis sprang a slight surprise by keeping with the same XI that had started at Villa in a flat 4-5-1. City, as expected, dominated possession for the first 25-30 minutes with Palace rarely exiting our half. I thought the midfield was dropping too deep, sitting about 30 yards out, which allowed the excellent Silva lots of space to work his magic. The whole Palace team was pressed into defending, of particular note were Puncheon's efforts on the right where with Mariappa they tried hard to hold the line, and an excellent tackle from Bolasie of all people on the left. City tried hard to work the flanks and did find some dangerous crosses, Parr having a hard time against Jesus Navas, while the rest of the team threw themselves in the way of shots so successfully that Speroni only had to make one real save in the first half hour when nearly betrayed by a deflection off Delaney.

Jerome had been almost totally isolated so deep were the midfield five positioned, and Palace's first real attack came when Bolasie forced a simple save from Hart. Parr made a break and his cross resulted in a nasty collision between Hart & Jerome; although the keeper received a shiner of a black eye (& the sympathy vote) Jerome was unable to continue – in hindsight it might have helped if he'd "accidentally" trod on Hart's hand or foot at the same time! This change actually strengthened the Palace team as Chamakh offered more in terms of movement & control. It was City who pressed as half-time approached, with plenty more shots blocked or deflected as the Palace box started to resemble the Alamo, and Speroni made one athletic tip over from a

Fernandinho header. The half-time stats showed a frankly unbelievable 70/30 split in favour of City: we guessed that Palace's 30% included the time spent treating Hart & Jerome, with the balance made up by the amount of time Julian was taking over his goal kicks!

City fans would have been bemused at the start of the second half by the Palace fans' praise for Sean Scannell, who was watching on from the upper tier, but their team started in much the same way by monopolising possession. However it appeared that Palace were playing a higher line and soon some strange events came to pass – Palace actually attacked! Puncheon, who had a fine game, had a shot turned wide by Hart, and from the ensuing corner Chamakh put a close range header just over. Stung by this City were forced into a double substitution, but such are the paucity of resources at the Etihad they had to throw on a couple of YTS unknowns in Nasri & Negredo; must be down to their last $50bn...

The changes did not have any immediate effect, and Palace actually had a spell of real pressure. Puncheon curled a shot wide, then cleverly played in Bannan whose run was halted by an excellent tackle; within a minute Jedinak's curler from the right was tipped over by Hart, only for Bolasie to deliver a weak corner. A goal then might have seen City under pressure. It is typical Palace that City, having had such possession, would score during our best period, and a break down our right found us short of numbers in the middle. The initial cross was not cleared, and when the ball was returned Dzeko had dropped off the six-yard box, and was followed neither by Gabbidon or Delaney (the latter was mostly his marker in the game) or picked up by the midfield tracking back; his finish gave Julian no chance. Palace's response was to go straight back down the other end, Ward forcing another excellent save from Hart, only to miss a far post header from the resulting corner that really should have been our equaliser. Despite the introduction of Williams & Gayle, Palace never got as close again, Chamakh once robbing possession only to be denied by a perfectly-timed tackle from Kompany. City kept hold of the ball and were not above the odd cynical foul to break up Palace's limited supply, and might have snatched a second in the dying minutes only for Dzeko to send a header fractionally too high. At the end the entire

132

Palace team deserved the applause they received for
their hard work.

Speroni - 7
Mariappa - 7
Parr - 7
Delaney - 7
Gabbidon - 8
Jedinak - 8
Ward - 7
Bannan - 7
Puncheon - 8
Bolasie - 6
Jerome - 5
Chamakh - 6
Williams - 6
Gayle - 5

Fly Like an Eagle

I have often felt that, the frequency of minutes silences, or as they are more often these days, minute's applauses, have become uncontrollable. However, the tribute to our ex-Chairman Ron Noades, who died over Christmas, is not such an occasion. Sat as I am under a leaking roof, with no clear view of a large section of the pitch, because I have needed to move my seat, so my young nephew can sit with the family, it is quite difficult to avoid, what might seem like an implied criticism, of the man who was Chairman of the club, when the Holmesdale Stand was built. The two are a genuine unintended coincidence of no longer being able buy additional tickets, near to ours. However, I do not want to appear a hypocrite, because people who know me well, will be aware that I was never, as a young man, Ron Noades' biggest fan. Though some may disagree, I think I have matured a bit with age, (Or perhaps, become more pragmatic,) and I guess that some of my objections at the time, seem quite inconsequential, considering the changes that have come to football, over the intervening years. I remember once, challenging him over the club changing of the kit, every couple of years, which I thought as an ideological young man, was exploitative and unnecessary. I still largely feel the same now, but can raise a private smile, that this is now two kits every season, and every club does it. I think that, even though I didn't always agree with him, he did have the vision to see, what was coming. There is also no doubt that, he oversaw the most successful period in the clubs history, and for this alone, I stood and applauded with no sense of reservation. The fact that his wife and family were in the crowd, also perhaps showed, that he did have affection for the club, that I underestimated. The other point that I think is worth making, which I have consistently heard from other fans, is that whatever your view point, correspondence to him would always be answered. Although at Palace we are lucky and this openness has been continued, by the current quartet, I am sure this is not the case, at many clubs. Whatever the individual experiences of Mr Noades, the loss of any member of the extended Palace family, is always sad.

Prior to the tribute, I was also concerned another member of the CPFC family, was having difficulties, which might affect their health and well-being. The wind, which had affected Dads journey up to the ground, was causing Kayla the Eagle, considerable difficulties. Although I am definitely not an expert on Eagles, I did always assume that flying, was one of their strong points. Although it was windy, I did not think that the winds were strong enough, to affect a powerful Bird of Prey.

My position high up in the corner of the Holmesdale Stand, gave an uninterrupted view of the Arthur Waite Stand Roof, even if it did not give the same view of the actual pitch. This allowed me to follow with concern, the situation that was unfolding, on top of the obviously slippery surface. Kayla, after one of her regular swoops across the pitch, had found herself blown off course, onto the stand roof; from where she was now having difficulty, taking off again. It appeared that the surface gave no purchase, and every time she attempted to fly, she was blown backwards, before she could get airborne. There were a few cables on the top of the stand, and these combined with the streamers from her feet, initially gave the impression that she had become entangled, somehow. I looked down towards her handlers, but couldn't see them, as they often move around, and I did wonder, if they were aware of her plight. With each attempt to take off, she got closer and closer to the edge, and was finally blow over the back of the stand, disappearing from view. As I have probably indicated in earlier chapters, I am by nature a bit of a worrier, and was convinced for a little while, that I ought to tell somebody, what I had seen. I didn't want to find out later, that she had been injured, and everybody had thought, somebody else had told the handlers, where she was. I managed to resist this impulse to interfere, but was relieved when she appeared safe on her handlers arm, just after the match had started, safe and well. Given that an Eagle was having difficulty flying, and the electronic scoreboard, (On a day when I needed it, to see a section of the pitch.) ceased to function. It was no surprise that two teams, near the foot of the table, failed to produce a match of free flowing, passing football. However, there was a resilience about the Palace, even if we failed to take all three points, against an eventually ten men opposition. We were ourselves lucky to finish the game with ten men, after Chamakh struck out at a Norwich player, but after some of the decisions so far this season, it was about flipping time, that we got one in our favour. The subsequent, unsuccessful attempts to wind him up, so that he picked up the red card, he had deserved the first time, were very cynical, and not really, what I would have expected from Norwich. It was also ironic that Captain Jedi, picked up his own yellow card, for suggesting a Norwich player should get one. I don't actually disagree with this guidance to referees, as with a lot of other guidance, but it often appears that they pick and choose, when to follow it. They also seem to, fail to follow the principles, (presumably unsporting behaviour) behind it. Surely, it is just as unsporting, and I would imagine irritating, to have your hair continually ruffled. The four man officiating team, should spot this kind of winding up, some of them don't do a fat lot else. Although, as Mr fourth official, doesn't seem to be able to stop a watch, it is perhaps too high an expectation, that he might be able spot, blatant antagonism. Before I pass over to Mark, for his usual detail analysis, I must comment on the fact that we didn't shoot enough, and when we did, we didn't test the goalkeeper, who must have dreaded every shot in his direction. Professional football clubs, invest much time and energy, planning tactical approaches for every game and opposition, but sometimes a bit of common sense must surely make you adapt. It was very wet, it was very windy; just shoot for Christ sake, the goalkeeper will hate it. I know I play in goal. Take my word for it. Just shoot. Of course, there are always exceptions, if you are Cameron Jerome, it's probably best to pass to someone else, because to be frank, you couldn't 'hit a barn door with a cannon.' Alternatively, as we used to say on a Sunday, "my granny could have scored that, and she's dead." I used to think that scoring goals, or at least looking like you might score a goal, was the No 1 criteria for a striker, (The clues in the name.) but I'm sure some clever pundit, will tell me that this view point, is old hat. To this I will reply, I've worn a few old hats this season, and I actually quite like them.

Marks Match Report

Palace lacked the quality to seize the three points today on a pitch that under the sheeting rain slowly became stickier but never approached unplayable. There always seemed likely to be a goal scoring opportunity coming up at any time given the filthy conditions, but both sides too often failed to deliver effective final passes or crosses, and neither goalkeeper had a great deal to do, although Ruddy was flapping at quite a few corners in the second half.

Palace switched to a 4-4-1-1 formation with KG returning in central midfield, allowing Ward to return to left back in place of Parr, while Bannan made way for Chamakh who played just behind Jerome. This was a surprise as both players omitted had played well against both Villa & City, and while it did mean Ward returned to his second-best position to be replaced by a proper midfielder, it also robbed the middle of the pitch of almost all creativity, with the more prosaic skills of Jedi & KG preferred in the heavy conditions. As it was KG would only last to half-time, but instead of calling upon Bannan, Pulis chose the more defensive option of switching Ward again. As a result there were more long balls played from the back than recently, although Norwich did not prove as efficient at dealing with these as Newcastle, while Chamakh, Bolasie & Puncheon were relied upon to open up the defence. And why were we so unwilling to shoot from the edge of the box? The number of chances we passed up was amazing, especially in these conditions – we're not going to run into Joe Hart every week!

Palace started slightly the better and made inroads down the right where Puncheon was linking well with Mariappa; it was Puncheon who had Palace's best early chance but totally mistimed a far post volley; Jedinak then placed a free kick just over. With a greasy pitch and Palace playing a higher pressing line than at the Etihad there was always the prospect of profiting on a mistake, and while there was a lot of movement around Norwich's box the final ball was too often over hit, particularly by Bolasie. Norwich had threatened sporadically but really should have opened the scoring when Bassong headed a free kick straight at Speroni. Puncheon then set up a chance for Jerome, but it was asking a lot to volley a hard-hit cross from an acute angle beyond the far post, and Jerome's effort nearly matched the famous roof-hitting finish of Gareth Taylor.

Out of the blue - should that really be various shades of dark grey? - Norwich took the lead. Gabbidon hesitated, perhaps betrayed by the conditions, and was robbed of the ball, and Palace could not close down Johnson's shot from the edge of the box that (from the far end) seemed to zip off the post and shoot behind a static Speroni. That seemed to wake Palace up and there was a period of pressure rewarded by corners & free kicks, one of which should have seen Chamakh dismissed for raising his hands and making contact with an opponent's face in retaliation. Norwich escaped once when Jerome's header was cleared off the line, but from the ensuing corner Jedinak was sent flying across the box and referee Mike Dean awarded the penalty. Fer was booked for the foul, Jed8inak cautioned for waving an imaginary yellow card, and Puncheon coolly sent Ruddy the wrong way from the spot.

Parr replaced KG at the interval, with Ward switching into midfield, and Palace started well, with Chamakh very effective at running with the ball, and both Palace wingers making inroads having swapped flanks, but as before Puncheon's delivery was far more dangerous than that of Bolasie. Again a series of corners were won, and Jerome missed a great chance when volleying over from one of these. Ruddy was flapping at quite a few and at one stage seemed likely to fall into the net with the ball. Sadly some of our crossing, form Bolasie & Ward in particular, was woefully over hit; funnily enough the best opportunity came from Delaney's cross for Bolasie's header - if only it had been the other way around...

Palace's spell of dominance could not last and Norwich had their own spell where, if not running the game, they restricted Palace in our own attacks, the best chance coming when Hooper's shot from a tight angle bounced off Julian's knees and evaded any Canary in the middle. Palace had by now withdrawn the willing but limited Jerome for Gayle, who made a couple of good runs, but I was glad when Hughton removed the dangerous Hoolahan for the beefier arts of Elmander. The game was in the balance when Williams replaced the inconsistent Bolasie, with Puncheon switching back to the right flank, and seemed to swing Palace's way when Fer's crude challenge on Jedinak earned a second yellow card. Palace pushed hard but never really came close to a killing blow.

Speroni - 6
Mariappa - 7
Ward - 6
Gabbidon - 6
Delaney - 7
Jedinak - 7
Dikgacoi - 5
Bolasie - 6
Puncheon - 7
Chamakh - 7
Jerome - 5
Parr - 6
Gayle - 6
Williams - 6

F.A. Cup 3rd Round; 3pm Saturday 4th January 2014

As a small child, playing football with my mates, or in the garden with my brother, it would always be the F.A. Cup Final. I don't know exactly how many Cup Finals that I played in, but I am sure that it would have broken even more records than Ian Callaghan, although I am not sure that I have lifted the trophy, more times than Ashley Cole. This second memory, is because my brother is older than I am, and therefore always won, it would have been foolish as a child, to challenge this natural order of sibling behaviour. I wonder if the kids in 2014, are still pretending to be playing this competition, or if it has now been surpassed by the "Champions" League final. (Speech marks, deliberately inserted). One thing I am certain of, is the game they play most often, will not be a league game, at home to Norwich, in a Gale and Downpour. It will surely be a cup match of some sort. They are exciting. They offer the opportunity to play the most unlikely combination of teams, and even for the smaller and non-league clubs, there is a chance, just a really small one, but a chance nonetheless that the game you are playing, down the park, or in your garden, could one day happen in reality. You might not get to play in it, but you could watch it and dream.

In 1990, I had that dream fulfilled, and standing in the stand at Villa Park, smoking that ridiculously large Cigar, the tears from 1976, at Stamford Bridge, were all forgotten. Crystal Palace were going to Wembley. Fast Forward 23 years, and the cup still holds an appeal, that I can't really explain. The chance to travel to far flung places like Hartlepool, Scarborough and Plymouth, (Terry Venables you still aren't forgiven) or play against proper non-league teams, such Walton and Hersham, always brings a break and a refreshing change. A third round draw, away to West Brom, didn't really meet this criteria, and I was seriously considering not making the trip. Unfortunately, my original decision, to tick the all cup games box, on my away season ticket application, (We were already out of the League Cup, so it wasn't entirely reckless) meant that I would need to make a conscientious decision, not to go, rather than a passive non-decision. The vagaries of the ticket sales process, came to my aid, and before I could muster the courage of my convictions, ping, my inbox declared that the tickets had been purchased, and I was going like it or not. I liked it, it was a fun day out, and I think Mandy, even managed to get a commentary of the match she was present at. The stewards, probably in fear of their lives, after their ear-bashing reminder of their incompetence at the previous match, even helped push Mandy back to the coach. The usual saga of fans, left waiting for Charlie our steward to get the tickets back to their box office, didn't seem to inconvenience anybody to much, and the advance information, that we would be allowed out at half-time for a cigarette, was a little piece of customer service, which is often lacking at many grounds. Mum, even managed to negotiate the very long steep slope, up from the parking area, without stopping to use her puffer, too many times, and importantly, we won. Wemberley, Wemberley, we're the famous Crystal Palace, and were off to Wemberly.

The glamour of the F.A. Cup, still lives on in some of us, but quite whether playing for Palace, can ever be seen as glamorous for some of our players, is debatable. As we arrived back in London, after the Norwich match a few weeks ago, I had a bit of a strop on, it probably came across. As a result, I neglected to mention the high life, that playing for Palace can bring. Due to the walk and the traffic, we left Norwich late, and somehow managed to be passed by the players' coach. As we approached Stratford, their coach appeared to have pulled into a bus stop. There was a minute, when my brain, was imagining Tony, Jedi and the rest of the boys, pilling on our coach, and Charlie asking everyone to squeeze up to make room. As we got closer, my 12-year-old self was down hearted, as the player's coach pulled away from the bus stop, and continued south. It was only as we passed the layby that we realised, the reason for the temporary pause. Standing at the bus stop, boot bags in hand, were an Algerian international, and a Champions League goal scorer. Welcome to Palace Arlene and Marouane, no blacked out Bentleys here, you can get off the coach, and catch the bus, like everyone else.

Marks Match Report

Third Round Day – used to be the biggest day of the football season, a day when you could rescue your season with one decent result. (Younger readers look away while a senile old man foams at the mouth about the iniquities of modern football & how money was ruining the game.) It still has some of that magic, especially when returning home from an (on paper) difficult away draw and making the fourth round for the first time since Neil Warnock roamed the Earth. I daresay many of us travelled to the Hawthorns worried that we might see two shadow teams turning out, given recent F.A. Cup teams put out by Palace – anyone remember the tie at Derby? – or the XI put out at Ashton Gate earlier this year. And there was the issue that the league match earlier this season was possibly the worst game in terms of overall quality. At least both teams retained a strong familiar framework in the squads, and the match was a slow burner that eventually banished the memories of that miserable November afternoon.

Tony Pulis has at least treated the F.A. Cup with some respect over his time at Stoke, and although he rested a few key players, he certainly provided a strong defensive keystone, retaining Speroni, Mariappa, Delaney & Gabbidon and recalling Parr at left back. In a 4-5-1 formation that had worked so well at Villa the

width was provided by Williams & Bolasie, who swapped
wings on a regular basis, while Bannan returned to a
central role along with two more defensive partners in
KG and Hiram Boateng, while Gayle fulfilled the lonely
role as sole striker. The bench contained two old
timers in McCarthy & Dobbie, while Puncheon, Chamakh,
Moxey & O'Keefe provided experienced cover. It looked a
most un-Pulis like team, and it has to be said, even by
a doubter like me, they actually played in a role that
no Stoke fan would recognise from his time at the
Britannia. There was not much use of the long ball,
which wasn't that surprising given the personnel
involved, and there was a lot of good passing football
played, even if sometimes the execution was a little
off.

The game started at a very low level of intensity as
though both teams weren't really bothered; not quite
the low tempo of a preseason friendly, but there wasn't
a great deal of attacking play or shuddering
challenges. West Brom had quite a bit of ball without
creating anything, in part due to good work from KG,
Bannan and the inexperienced Boateng. It was Palace who
fashioned the first clear opportunity with good work
from Bolasie on the left followed by a deft lay-off
from Gayle that saw Bannan break into the box; he
rounded Foster but the angle was too acute and his shot
hit the post & rebounded to safety. Albion responded
with a Vydra effort easily saved by Speroni and the
game started to become more contested, with Palace
looking dangerous on the break with Bannan & Williams
finding cute little angles, The opening goal owed more
to error then inspiration though, as a poor bass on the
edge of West Brom's area was intercepted by Boateng,
who laid the ball through to Gayle; the keeper was
caught out of position, expecting a back pass, and
although Gayle's left foot shot wasn't clean it was in
the corner Foster couldn't reach.

Albion's response was almost instantaneous, with a
header from second phase possession after a corner
bouncing on top of Julian's bar. Palace started to drop
deeper and often defended with all 10 men behind the
ball, Gayle being perhaps 10-15 yards outside our own
penalty area. What this meant was that almost every
clearance was returned immediately; these just made
clearances even more hurried as Albion could push more
men forward and press the defenders, and West Brom had

a spell camped around our box. One particular tactic that Delaney had real trouble dealing with was long diagonal balls from left flank to right side of the area, where Shane Long won a number of knock downs that Palace somehow blocked. Late chances for Long & Vydra were saved by a scrambling Speroni and we made half-time with our lead intact.

The second half was to be a far more entertaining affair for a number of reasons. The game was stretched, with Palace at first proving capable of slicing through the WBA defence with smart counter attacks, although Bolasie often brought these to a halt with poor use of the ball. The winger also had the best chance in an unfamiliar role, having a free header from 8 yards out following a corner, only to mis-time his jump and see the ball sail over off his shoulder. West Brom also gradually brought on attacking substitutes in Amalfitano, Sinclair & Sessegnon while sacrificing defenders. One of them – I think it was Sinclair, but it could have been Amalfitano – decided they would make Jonny Parr's day a nightmare, and found a lot of success down our left flank, often getting behind our full back and getting along the goal line. Fortunately for Palace Speroni's keeping was, with the exception of one fumbled cross & one weak punch, up to the highest standards, the highlight being a one-handed diving save from Vydra, and somehow reacting late to turn a Berahino effort over. There was also plenty of last-ditch defending, with the usual suspects Delaney & Gabbidon usually finding themselves in the way of crosses & shots.

O'Keefe had been introduced for Boateng, who had faded in the second half, perhaps inhibited by a booking, while a double substitution saw Puncheon come on the right wing in place of Williams, while Chamakh acme on for Bannan. As West Brom abandoned defensive duties the game was really stretched in the final 15 minutes, end-to-end stuff with Palace somehow wasting several good opportunities through over elaboration and a seeming unwillingness to pull the trigger and shoot. Chamakh – who was excellent in holding up the ball – Puncheon, Gayle & Bolasie were all guilty of this, and on one break Gayle netted from close range only to find Bolasie had been offside when breaking the WBA back line for the cross. The last 10 minutes saw desperate defensive measures; after Julian's weak punch a lob finished on the top of the net, while one late chance somehow saw a shot deflected wide for a corner. As the game entered its last 15 seconds of stoppage time Palace broke away again, and Bolasie ignored demands he head for the corner flag, cutting inside and eventually setting up Chamakh for a simple finish with the literal last kick of the match, as referee Dowd blew for time while the celebrations started.

Speroni - 7
Mariappa - 7
Parr - 6
Delaney - 7
Gabbidon - 7
Dikgacoi - 6
Boateng - 6
Bannan - 7
Bolasie - 6
Williams - 7
Gayle - 7
O'Keefe - 6
Chamakh - 7
Puncheon - 7

Transfer window and beyond

Spurs Away

 Just when you think, we have stopped the world, and especially the TV pundits, taking the mickey out of our team, Palace sometimes have the annoying habit of doing something, that brings you back to square one. Step up to the microphone, Jason Puncheon.

 The day had started well, with a beer on the train with my brother, a G&T on the train for my sister in law, and of course, two cokes on the train for my nieces. It would, be wholly inappropriate to give my 16-year-old niece, cider, even in the presence of her parents. Victoria Station provided another opportunity, to have a drink and some food, before moving on to the tube. Unfortunately, one of the aforementioned `Cokes', had remained undrunk, so it fell upon me, as the responsible adult, to insure that this was rectified before we reached Tottenham. The result was that, I was pretty much in need of the toilet, by the time we reached Tottenham. (As any man will know, despite going twice at Victoria, at 30p a time, this is no guarantee that the urge will not re-emerge, 2 minutes into the next journey, on any moving vehicle.) As anybody who has visited Tottenham will also testify, the walk to the ground, is always longer than you thought. Combining these two circumstances, is never going to be an entirely pleasant experience. The last thing that you need in this situation, is a protest at Tottenham Town Hall, which closes the most direct route to the ground, and requires a detour around Tottenham back streets, without the prospects of an emergency MacDonald's toilet stop. On route, we passed the Palace coach steward, running hastily back in the direction of the tube station. This was a little bit of a puzzle, but when quizzed he was apparently looking for the coach. This was also a little bit worrying, because I had always assumed that the coach steward, would know where the coach he was stewarding was. In fact, I pretty much assumed that he would actually be on it, as it is quite difficult to steward a coach, whilst running through the streets of Tottenham. He agreed that this was normally the case, and reassured me that the coach had dropped Mum and the others, as planned at White Hart Lane. Unfortunately he had forgotten to take his ticket off he coach, which had now driven off, to park. Unlike many of the more provincial grounds, this wasn't actually at the ground. With the change of drivers recently, he couldn't contact them by phone, to find out where they were parking, so was reduced to running around the streets of North London. To the best of my knowledge he could still be running around the same streets, at this very moment, but as Mum returned home safely, he was either successful in locating the coach, or the passengers organised themselves and left without him. I never did ask; which shows that the pure relief at eventually finding a toilet, wiped all other considerations from my mind, or just indicates, I am an uncaring individual of the first degree. So desperate was I too have found a toilet, that when it was located, I didn't really appreciate, we were in fact, right by the ground. Had this not been the case, I would have been forced to make a very difficult decision, toilet or fag. As a smoker, I do often have this dilemma, when approaching grounds. The time directly before entering away grounds, is often the last opportunity to have a cigarette, for close on 3 hours. The need for that sense of calm tranquillity, that nicotine can induce, is often needed as a Palace supporter, and it is an important part of my routine. Mum and Caroline go in to the ground, possibly buy a coffee, and find their seats, while I stand around chuffing on as many cigarettes, as time, or my throat and lungs, will allow. The desire of clubs, to encourage fans to get to grounds early, is all very well and good, but for smokers, entering the turnstiles normally indicates a period of abstinence, that many of us seek to put off as long as possible. The fact that, I didn't have to choose between two separate forms of relief, at White Hart Lane, was not due to stadium design, by a club with the foresight to provide the facilities, around the ground that supporters may want and need. On the contrary, it was due to an ever decreasing concept of a good old fashion Public convenience, which hadn't been knocked down, to provide something more profitable. This particular grey stone building, directly outside the away end at White Hart Lane, when viewed from the outside is not unique. Once you enter, it has the familiar paddling poolesque interior, and flagrant aroma. However, once you accustom your eyes to the half-light, you soon realise that it is a bit like Doctor Who's Tardis. I didn't wandered around for too long, as this always tends to elicit strange looks, in a public toilets, but it appears to extend further and further back, away from the pavement with no apparent end. It is quite simply the largest of its kind, that I have ever seen. So as a consequence, my lasting vision of my visit to Tottenham, is of one large toilet. It strikes me as no great coincidence, that the increase in the number of complaints about inappropriate urination in public places, has coincided with the closure of these facilities. One old Public Toilet on Shepherds Bush Green, is now a night club, which I recently attended. I admit to finding the concept of trying to pull, in a Public Toilet, even one with a bar and flashing lights, was disconcerting. This closure of public toilets, is neither new, nor exclusive to London. Back in my student days, we were once caught short on the way back from the pub, only to find that the public toilets on route were locked. After finding a discreet bush, we were a little shocked to also find two police officers, who took considerable pains to explain, that the behaviour of one of my friends, (The one with largest bladder.) was unacceptable. Although we were in no position to argue the case, that if the toilets weren't locked, we wouldn't have needed a bush, this was firmly our position. The reason for including this little anecdote here, is not purely to extend the toilet humour, but because, on being asked his name, the staunch and passionate Wolves supporter replied, "Steven Bull." at which point, as you do when you've had a few beers, the surrounding group found it very difficult to stifle our laughter. We were fortunate that like today, many police officers, do not appear to actually know a great deal about football, or the behaviour of football fans. They were certainly unaware that

Steve Bull, had scored 150 goals for Wolves, in the previous 3 seasons, and had just made his England debut. Yes I know in retrospect, it wasn't big or clever, but at the time it was funny, and the old school copper, with his young trainee, was a bit of a knob, so didn't really deserve the respect that we obviously should have given.

I started today's piece, by alluding to Palace creating opportunities, for the world to take the mickey out of them, and this is another reason for the toilet stories. Jason Puncheon's penalty today, was without doubt, the @@@@est penalty I have ever seen. If you haven't seen it, think Chris Waddle with less accuracy and you will be close. I know some people will have sympathy, I know he didn't mean to do it; I know that there were another 89 minutes, and ten players, but it was still rubbish. (I will resist the temptation, to use one of many more toiletry synonyms.) I genuinely believe, had he scored, we would have won, so I make no apologies, for a lack of conciliatory thoughts or words, coming from my fingers today. Maybe Mark will be more objective, in the following pages.

Marks Match Report

```
Tottenham ended the game with the points, probably
deservedly, but that appeared unlikely given the first
30 minutes of the match. Some of our passing & tackling
in that first period was of the highest order but
unfortunately Palace's red-hot start was not matched by
the quality of their crosses or the ruthlessness of
their finishing, and could not last the hard pace they
had set. While the effort & work rate could not be
faulted, over the whole 90 minutes Spurs were the
better team in areas that counted.
Palace started with one change from the team that
started against Norwich with Parr coming in at left
back, with Ward moving into midfield in place of KG, in
a 4-4-1-1 formation. Tottenham, in a very traditional &
(on paper) attacking 4-4-2, started very poorly and the
first five minutes didn't see them exit their own half.
Palace started at a strong pace, pressing hard in
midfield and picking up any number of loose balls. The
standard of passing was good - Jerome was played in
within a minute only to be caught offside, whilst
another minute hadn't passed before Puncheon's shot
drifted across Lloris's goalmouth. Puncheon on the
right and Bolasie on the left were launching attacks
down both flanks, supported by both full backs, mostly
profiting from Jedinak & Ward snapping up most
possession in the centre, and some lovely holding up &
laying off of the ball by Chamakh. Sadly neither
```

winger's crosses were anywhere near good enough, and while Parr did better on the left, Mariappa's crossing was also poor. This also affected Palace's corner taking, as we won a number in the first half taken by Bolasie or Ward, but only one caused any real danger to Spurs, with the ball hitting a stationary Lloris on the line.

It only took seven minutes to break Spurs' resistance (or so we thought). Delaney picked up an interception in our half and then strode down the middle of the pitch before laying off a good pass to Chamakh, who failed to take the chance to shoot but was bundled over in the box for a penalty. Now Puncheon's effort wasn't the worst I've ever seen from a Palace player (Peter Taylor & Pembo stand well clear in that award) but it was blazed high & wide. I thought that might give Tottenham a kick in the rear but Palace continued to make chances, mostly on the break as Spurs' careful possession play was broken up by Palace's midfield & defence; their only real output was Lennon, who was causing Parr defensive problems. Chamakh & Parr forced chances before Jerome brought a good save from Lloris again catching Spurs' defence on the turn. The latter occurred after Speroni had down well to stop and then smother a shot from distance on a pitch that had started to cut up in the warm-ups, but it did signify that Spurs were starting to grab a foothold in the match. Perhaps Palace had put so much into that first half hour that they looked a little drained, and the pressing game was less obvious. Lennon created an excellent opportunity that somehow eluded both Soldado and Adebayor inside the six-yard box, while a shot from 30 yards hit the angle of Julian's right hand post & bar, rebounded across the goalmouth behind the keeper and somehow stayed out before swerving behind for a goal kick.

Half-time seemed to come at a good time for Palace who needed some rest, but the restart was almost an exact mirror of the first 5 minutes as Palace found themselves penned into their half. After a couple of close shaves Spurs broke the deadlock by grabbing possession as Palace finally moved forward. Adebayor flicked on a long ball and Eriksen found space behind Gabbidon with Mariappa nowhere to be seen; he beat Speroni with a good finish. Jerome nearly fashioned an equaliser when set up by Parr but the angle was too

tight for a finish and too much for a pull back, but
the game started to tilt decisively away with the
introduction of Defoe, who gave an exhibition of pace
and finishing that was beyond our players. Palace held
on for a quarter of an hour before Lennon's run found
Defoe in the box, who left Parr on the deck and,
despite a desperate lunge from Delaney, smacked the
ball past Julian from about 10 yards. Palace had
already introduced Gayle & Williams, and now Guédioura
returned from injury in one last effort to salvage a
draw. In stoppage time the Algerian hit a shot that
either defeated Lloris all ends up, or the keeper was
showing supreme cool in knowing it would swerve just
wide, while finally Palace managed a couple of decent
crosses that were met by Chamakh, one just deflected
over by the keeper, the other clipping the roof of the
net.

Speroni - 6
Mariappa - 6
Parr - 6
Delaney - 8
Gabbidon - 6
Jedinak - 7
Ward - 7
Puncheon - 6
Bolasie - 7
Chamakh - 7
Jerome - 6
Gayle - 5
Williams - 6
Guédioura - 6

It's 3pm on a Saturday

There is a weird sense of normality, surrounding today's game, at 3pm on a Saturday. I have kind of been waiting for one of these, to describe our normal Saturday routine, and it has taken until mid-January, to really have the opportunity. So much has changed this season, that our normal routine, is no longer normal at all. The pre-match quiz, first instigated by Dad on the walk to the ground in the 70's, and then taken over by my niece in more recent years, has all but disappeared. No longer do we all create our own Buzzer sound, and argue over who 'pressed ' it first, reasonably safe in the knowledge, those Daddies little girls will in the event of doubt, always choose Daddy as the winner. (I'm honestly not a bitter man.) I originally thought that the absence of the quiz, was because the 80-page programme, no longer had room for a quiz page, but examining it today, in detail, I realise that the quiz is still there. Perhaps, it is just the ageing process of my nieces, that little things that were once so much fun, are no longer so important. There is a part of me that misses some of these rituals, but at the same time, they are also so much fun to be around, and so interesting to talk to, about whatever it is we talk about, that before I started to write, I had almost not realised, we had stop quizzing at all. I am sure that parents will notice these changes more acutely; often they are so gradual that they are imperceptible until you suddenly think. When was the last time we did the quiz, or when was the last time somebody asked me, "what do you think the gate will be today?" The changes brought about by the Premier League, have perhaps been the catalyst that makes you change a routine, or a subconscious act of superstition. However, routines can be nice and are part of the fabric of being a football fan. I hope future generations, will still be able to create their own, more flexible traditions. Whilst I am getting all melancholy, I need to mention the response of the Stoke fans to Tony Pulis. Fans can often be, too quick to forget, the contribution that players and officials made to their club, as soon as they have moved on, but the Stoke fans, made a special point of thanking TP, in words and banners. Of course they wanted their team to win, but the need to say goodbye properly, is often underrated and they wanted this opportunity. Although I have never really liked Stoke or their fans, for irrational reasons that I can't really explain, I did respect this attitude, and they have risen in my expectations. Looking back on the trip to Liverpool earlier this year, and the story that Ian Wright told us about his departure to Arsenal, I wonder if some of the animosity towards Wrighty, might have been different, if his departure hadn't been so quick and unexplained. I appreciate that the business and football worlds, cannot always be based on sentiment, but the importance of these little things to fans, particularly the younger ones, shouldn't be underestimated by clubs and their owners.

Despite the good wishes that surrounded, the beginning of the game, I am sure that by the end, and our well deserved victory, Tony Pulis's name, was not held in such high regard in the potteries. Although in one section of South London, a few more sceptics had been won over. Even Jason Puncheon, had also gone some way to atone for last week's miss, even if I am personally less eager, to alter my opinion of the second of these individuals. I will however, still take considerable satisfaction from Match of the Day, tonight, although I doubt that the pundits, will be perceptive enough of their own contradictions, to squirm as much as I would like them too.

Marks Match Report

A hard earned but precious win was ground out by Palace, with redemption for last week's "sinner" Puncheon grabbing the only goal. For periods in the first half, and at the start of the second, it was difficult to see how Palace would break down a Stoke team that looked relatively comfortable & by a shade the most likely to score. Once Palace had broken that assumption they clung on, dropping deeper as usual just to keep us on the edge of our seats, but held on and could have grabbed a decisive second goal but for some brilliant goalkeeping from Butland.

Pulis had made only one change to the XI that had started against Tottenham, with Guédioura replacing the ineligible Jerome. It appeared at first that Chamakh would be pushed up front as the sole striker, with Adlène playing in the hole, but for most of the game Marouane was isolated up front with Palace deploying a five man midfield. In a game identified as one where three points were the realistic target why not just swap Gayle for Jerome? With Ward continuing in midfield and Mariappa filling in at right back there was no place for the creative skills of Bannan or Williams. Although the game started well with both sides looking to push on, chances were at a premium. There was an early header that flashed wide from – I thought – Chamakh (BBC say it was Ward), but Gabbidon nearly added to his own goal haul with a sliced volleyed clearance that cleared Speroni's goal; from the corner Mariappa was beaten in the air at the far post – from a slight nudge in the back – but Speroni claimed the ball bravely down amongst the flying feet. Set pieces looked to be Stoke's most dangerous weapon, and from another Wilson's header had expertly tipped round the post by Speroni – the ball bounced nicely but it was still an example of athleticism & timing. A goal then and Palace

might have struggled. As it was the early progress down
the flanks from Puncheon & Bolasie, with strong support
from Parr, gradually disappeared and they started to
struggle, unable to control midfield, and Stoke slowly
started to squeeze the life out of the game. There was
little or no creativity in midfield despite promising
touches from Chamakh & Guédioura. Stoke looked more
athletic and prepared to push men forward; Assaidi on
the left wing had Mariappa on toast while Parr was
finding life defending far more difficult than
overlapping. It was thanks to the reliable if prosaic
performances of Delaney & Gabbidon, allied with
Julian's safe hands that kept the Potters at arms'
length.

At half-time the muttering about playing men out of
position and the conservative formation & team
selection started, and it grew in volume as the start
of the second half only continued to follow the trend
of the first, with Adam shooting just wide. Why was
Bannan suddenly out of favour? Would the skills of
Williams find a position on the pitch? When would Gayle
be trusted? At some stage Palace would have to gamble
on something different. Then the whole situation was
turned on its head by some perseverance from Mariappa &
Puncheon. A break down the right seemed to have run out
of steam but good work by these two kept the ball alive
and ripped it away from Assaidi near the goal line.
Puncheon was trying to line up a shot with his left
foot but was denied space and was just, so we thought,
running blindly across the face of the penalty area. He
must have seen a gap we hadn't ass he shot, and
although it wasn't powerful it was accurately placed in
the far corner out of Butland's reach.

Now, of course, the situation was set up perfectly for
Pulis's formation. The difficult bit was grabbing the
lead, now they had to hold onto it. Irritatingly they
started to drop deep instead of pressing Stoke high up
the pitch. The time & space this allowed Adam was
dangerous, and his rasping shot must have been no more
than a foot wide of Speroni's left post. O'Keefe was
introduced in place of Guédioura, who had suffered
cramp; we didn't need Barry or Jonny now and Stuart's
spikier approach was perfectly suited to the role. In
replay Stoke's substitutions left them with a midfield
three that Pulis would never have fielded: Adam,
Ireland & Nzonzi; while the dangerous Assaidi was

withdrawn to our (& undoubtedly Mariappa's) relief. They huffed and puffed but found Gabbidon & Delaney in obdurate mood, and their tackles started to show a frustrated & angry edge. Instead the game stretched in the last ten minutes and Palace could have scored several times on the break: Ward, Puncheon & O'Keefe were denied from short range by a remarkable triple save from Butland; substitute Wilbraham forced another save, then, after a long break by Parr, shot just wide first time when he had more time to steady himself; finally after another break Wilbraham & Jedinak set up Puncheon from close range, only for another brilliant piece of keeping from Butland to keep the game alive. Stoke were still pressing when the final whistle went and Palace climbed above the dotted line.

Speroni - 7
Mariappa - 6
Parr - 6
Delaney - 8
Gabbidon - 7
Ward - 7
Jedinak - 6
Bolasie - 6
Puncheon - 8
Guédioura - 6
Chamakh - 7
O'Keefe - 6
Wilbraham - 7
Moxey - 6

Fickle Fans and Cup Exits

As referred to last week, we football fans, can be a fickle lot, changing our point of view, just as quickly as an embarrassed TV pundit. The derision that greeted Puncheon two weeks ago, has been matched in equal measure, by the praise that has been heaped on him, this week. Although, I hope I am a little more consistent in my views, I admit, I did have a fickle moment with regard to today's game. I hate MK Dons, as I think they pretty much represent, everything that is wrong with British football, that isn't covered by Man U. If you want a team in the Football League, in a town where one doesn't currently exist, you should in my opinion, either start one from scratch, or take an existing team from the locality, and invest money into that. Either way, you should have to work your way up through the leagues, as A.F.C. Wimbledon has done. The concept of moving an existing team, away from its traditional fan base, and positioning them in a completely different place, is to me, so fundamentally wrong. The F.A. should never have allowed it to happen. Consequently, I have never as far as I am aware, wanted them to win a single game. There does however, always become a point, where personal expedience overcomes this more general principle, and this was the case approaching today's match.

We were drawn away, against the winners of the Wigan and MK Dons replay, and to be quite frank, the thought of a long trip to Lancashire, in the fourth round of the cup, didn't really appeal. The chance to secure a new ground, a short, direct train ride away, was much more to my liking. There was also an opinion on the BBS, suggesting a big away allocation would be given, and Palace could take 5000 plus to Stadium MK. The away support to Wigan, would inevitably be smaller, and the travel costs bigger. Thus, I found myself, listening out for the replay result, with added personal interest, and wishing for a Dons victory. Needless to say, it didn't happen, and I found myself at the ground this morning, at 7 a.m. with a long day ahead. Cup draws often cause excitement and personally I always want either: something glamorous, something different, something close or something where a win is expected. Wigan away did not fulfil any of these normal criteria. In the end despite torrential rain and a deserved defeat, it was a good day out.

The journey up to Wigan, allowed me to wind up Mandy, about the potential signing of a new goalkeeper, which has been circulating in the press, and on the forums. Mandy, for anybody who doesn't know her, is Julian Speroni's most ardent fan. Any criticism directed at him, however justified, can normally be guaranteed to provoke a very firm response. As a consequence, I take every opportunity to Mandy bait. As normal, she won the argument and succeeded in freaking me out, at the same time. For those of us, with unimpeded senses, Mandy's ability to know where we are on our journeys, by assessing time travelled and more remarkably, changing road surface, is quite remarkable. What however I didn't quite appreciate, was how finely honed some of her other senses were. After the game, we inevitably returned to the subject of goalkeepers, due to what I have seen Mark describe as, "A Solid and Brave performance" by Julian. I

153

have no personal beef with Jules, and he has without doubt, been a fine servant to the club, however, I have often questioned his ability to deal with crosses. Consequently, when Mandy was extolling his virtues, some of which were in fairness to me, unlikely to be picked up by a man, I was jokingly flapping my arms about, behind her back. Without any hesitation, she stopped mid-sentence a told me, in no uncertain terms. that I could, "Stop that flapping, as well." This caught me slightly off guard, as even if she could see, I was directly behind her wheelchair. I am still not sure, whether her correct interpretation of what I was doing, was due to an expectation of what I was likely to be doing, or to a heightened ability to perceive air movements, and small sounds. Whichever it was, it was very impressive. If anybody is in any doubt, as to why a blind person would travel the lengths of the country, to support her team, then I hope that this little story, will enable you to understand, in a very small way, how much can be experienced. If a few, fake ball grabs by one person, can provide so much information, then the noise and movement of thousands, must multiply this effect. Add in a commentary by radio, (Sometimes even of the correct game.) or feed, or in person, then the experience is obviously very rewarding. An alternative viewpoint might be, that it is just the chance to spend, a few hours in my company, although this seems highly unlikely.

As we got closer to Wigan, we did start to voice concern, that the game might not actually take place, as the rain and the wind, even from inside the confines of a coach, was evidently strong and heavy. The thought of turning around and travelling home again, without a match, was even less appealing than the concept of the trip in the first place. It was definitely a case of, no news is good news, and we were extremely grateful for Mandy's presence when we pulled into the ground. With advanced warning that the, 'red and blue chariot' was on board, the stewards directed Stuart our driver, to the closest possible parking slot to the away entrance. By all accounts, this was in fact only marginally closer that the official car park, but it showed a genuine attention to the experience of all away fans. With the veracity of the rain, even a few less steps in it, would be appreciated by everyone. Considering the weather conditions, we had made very quick progress and were early, so I decided that I would get Mum into the ground, and then head off in search of a local pub. This in itself was actually going to be a difficult exercise. (The getting Mum into the ground part, there's always a pub nearby, unless Tesco's and Enterprise Inn's, have been working there magic up north, as well.) I am sure that Mum, very quickly appreciated how Kayla the Eagle must have felt, a few weeks back. Stuart's umbrella, lent to Caroline, lasted I would calculate, about one and a half seconds, before it inverted itself, buckled and became more akin to a weird medieval weapon. Mum was only able to progress forwards, with a steadying shove from me, and we were grateful for the sanctuary of the stadium wall. The Wigan stewards, not content with parking us next to the ground, were again on hand to suggest refuge from the wind and rain, as we waited for the stadium to open. They were even kind enough, to find an alternative entrance for Mum, which involved fewer steps. All of this was unrequested, but just provided. I then headed off, over the car park, to the Red Robin. On my return, fortunately not as wet as I would have expected, I was asked by Jon why I hadn't been into the marquee bar, attached to the away end and specifically provided for away supporter. The answer was research, i.e. I didn't do any. Although this would be a sensible addition to any ground, it is such a rarity that I hadn't even considered it. As mentioned previously, my nicotine requirement, normally prevents early entrance to grounds, and the use of their concourse facilities. So a bar attached, but allowing exit and re-entry is perfect, I shall know better next time. One of the nicest aspects of the day, was the notice on the tickets, that it was unreserved seating. Not only had this saved a lot of faffing, before the game, but it also meant that on arrival, Mum had found herself a seat, that was unlikely to be obstructed. However, as had become the norm, to do this, she had moved very close to the front, very low down. On looking around at the relatively small turn out, this seemed slightly unnecessary today, and I set about finding something a little higher. I soon spotted DorkingEagle, who can normally be relied upon to find a good spot, and we moved to sit next to him with Janet, John, and a few others, from the coach. The siting of disabled facilities, within the main body of the stand, not only provides a much better position and atmosphere for them, but also a section of seats, midway up a stand, that is unlikely to be obstructed. When Selhurst is eventually redeveloped, I hope that this is the approach we take. As I have said on the forums and in this book several times, my choice to sit during games, is not really a preference, but a necessity for Mum; I saw an opportunity to leave her safely seated and move up the back. I am now, a bit long in the tooth, for packing in a central mass of bodies, but I could hover on the outskirts, have a sing, a shout, probably swear a bit and yet not upset anybody. Everybody's happy. I was even able, to move myself away from a small group of quite obnoxious fans; definitely not all London accented, who were very drunk and not really watching the game, at all. No scene needed to be made, no confrontation, I just moved away, just like in the old days. Football has such a diverse following, that this ability to move around is invaluable, and unreserved tickets for games such as this, are a sensible approach.

Although as I have already said, we lost, and I would have liked a good cup run, it was a good day. We got away quickly, which is an added bonus, especially after a defeat and were home in good time. In my notes on the match, I did mention a couple of penalties, that we could have had, but I don't want to appear as if its sour grapes, so I will let Mark fill you in. My one other note is that Cameron Jerome is ..... (Please refer to previous entry on Tottenham away, and a certain penalty miss.) I am not quite sure why I have formed a dislike of him, it is in my opinion, as irrational as that shown by many towards Dean Moxey, but I just have. Normally, I am a great fan of somebody with limited ability, who tries hard, and although I sometimes feel that his effort, is selectively used, I can't really say that he doesn't try. I suppose that a striker, is a slightly different beast to many other positions, the minimum criteria being that, he can, or at least attempts to, strike. I am not sure that either of these attributes, is part of his armoury. I am also annoyed by, players getting offside on a regular basis, and being built like boxers, but being crumpled to the ground at the slightest touch. Arron Wilbraham, never really elicited the same feelings, and I am not sure that I really think, CJ has been a vast improvement. Maybe the fast approaching transfer window, will provide some extra firepower.

Marks Match Report

Palace bowed out of the F.A. Cup yesterday in a game that while low on overall quality was not short of incident or controversy, which is pretty much all you can ask of a cup tie. It also left us at the hands of the only "shock" of the fourth round so far, as 5Live and TalkSport kept reminding us on the long drive home. And at least the sudden torrential rainstorm a couple of hours before kick off that led to the postponement at nearby Accrington held off, so it was only a strong wind that the players had to deal with, although conditions alone could not account for the low home turnout, especially for the holders, in comparison to a surprisingly large (& loud) Palace following. Wigan, despite some crude & cynical challenges, and the "aid" of an inept & inconsistent referee, deserved their win overall, and until the last 30 minutes seemed to be the only side with a genuine appetite for the game.

I've expressed my feelings on the devaluation of the F.A. Cup over recent seasons, so I was pleasantly surprised by how strong a team Tony Pulis put out, given the proximity of a perceived "vital" league match against Hull on Tuesday. Bannan came in on the wing for Bolasie while Jerome returned as the sole striker with Chamakh dropping into the hole in a 4-4-1-1 formation. O'Keefe joined Guédioura in central midfield while perhaps the most unexpected appearance was some unknown called Paddy McCarthy in the place of Gabbidon. Must be our first deadline signing... Unusually the Wigan team left us in the position whereby the Championship side was stronger on paper than their Premier League opponents.

It was the absence of Jedinak & Ward in midfield that really shaped this match, as Palace never really established a hold in midfield, which might put my comments about a lack of creativity against Stoke with those two as a partnership in context - perhaps Mr. Pulis does know more about the game! O'Keefe, while willing, was lightweight while Guédioura proved incapable of either winning, retaining or passing the ball. Sad to say the best midfielder was Ben Watson, who played deep and was never picked up by either of our central two or by Chamakh, who might have been the most natural choice on paper & position to do so. Even worse was that Wigan's two wingers McLean & McManaman were ripping us apart on the flanks, Parr in particular having a very sorry afternoon.

In general much of Palace's play was inept: the first touches was usually poor, there was a lack of movement & anticipation, while Wigan seemed a lot hungrier and were almost without exception first to a loose ball. This malaise extended to everyone with the exception of Speroni and the two central defenders, and occasionally Bannan. Yet it was Palace who nearly struck first, Jerome's snap shot bringing a fine save from Al Habsi, who was also straight in the line of an effort from O'Keefe. However Palace just could not fashion anything from midfield and turned the ball over on a regular basis, while the defence was creaking at the hinges all through the first half. Parr was having an awful match, McManaman running past him at will, and so nearly presented Watson with a gift goal through a stupid weak pass inside our own box. Speroni had to make one brave catch and one diving collection at the feet of Wigan attackers, while Delaney & McCarthy were very busy. It was down our right flank that Wigan finally broke the deadlock, McLean on a break being allowed to run by Mariappa, and his pulled back cross was met with a fine finish by Watson from the edge of the box into the top corner; Speroni had no chance but no-one had picked up the ginger one's run from deep. Palace had no one to match Watson's play or that of Espinoza and didn't look likely to drag their way back into the game, Chamakh appearing mostly uninterested & Jerome just inadequate; only some luck and marginally off-target finishing prevented the game being over by half-time.

Parr had already departed on a stretcher following what looked like a hard aerial challenge from McManaman which limited room for manoeuvre with the substitutes at half-time, and whatever was said at half-time appeared to make no difference as Wigan continued to move serenely onward. Puncheon was getting more involved & O'Keefe at least made Al Habsi make another regulation save from the edge of the box. Then Palace started to wake up. A Bannan near post corner appeared woefully hit low but Watson on the near post missed it only for it to luckily bounce off an unprepared Al Habsi; from the rebound Puncheon's volley drew a much better & intended tip over from the keeper; and from the corner that followed Jerome had an air shot from 8 yards out, which summed up his game. It was really not until Pulis withdrew his ineffectual nominal "strike" force and replaced them with two players with something to prove in Wilbraham & Gayle that Palace came alive. It also helped that they played as a pair up front, in close support for each other. Within seconds another seemingly under hit Bannan corner (was it a cunning plan?) was flicked on by Gayle and prodded home in a tangle of limbs – I thought McCarthy got the final touch at first but everyone congratulated the much-maligned Wilbraham for his second ever Palace goal.

Game on and Palace now looked the most likely side. With Gayle Palace now had a striker who was prepared to run on beyond the man making the flick on and his pace worried the Latics' defence, as he so nearly made it two in a couple of minutes with a shot from a similar position to his match-winning effort at Villa Park, just it was lower and Al Habsi again made an outstanding save. Sad to say though it was Palace's weaknesses in midfield and at full back that cost us the game. Guédioura again lost the ball to allow Wigan to catch us on the turn; Espinoza's pass found the gap between McCarthy & Mariappa, and the latter's challenge on McLean was ineffectual (to be fair Adrian was carrying a knock on the ankle). Somehow McLean's shot bobbled and beat Julian at his near post, taking an age to go in. Palace rallied with Puncheon to the fore, but two late and decent shouts for penalties for a tug on Gayle & a little nudge on Wilbraham were refused. Wigan nearly sealed it only for Speroni to perhaps redeem himself saving a two-on-one situation, but Palace's last chances went when Puncheon delayed his shot allowing the block, and Wilbraham could not convert a late cross.

I am not normally one to rail at officials (okay, stretching your credulity there, I think) but the performance of Mr. Jones and team was spectacularly poor. The two late shouts for penalties I can live with, although the first should have been seen by the linesman on our left who was equally & lamentably as bad. How they both awarded a free kick for the challenge that saw Parr depart on a stretcher after about 8 minutes of treatment but felt it was not worthy of a card is beyond me, especially as the only caution to date had been a very early one to Jerome for a vicious dive / show of dissent! More annoying was the number of cynical fouls committed by Wigan that were

penalised but not deemed worthy of further action. A
tackle from behind is supposedly a straight yellow; a
"professional" foul to take down a player who has
beaten you is equally a heinous; yet a combination of
the two doesn't see the merest hint of yellow while
talking back is..? Wigan were allowed to break up the
second half when Palace finally came into the game with
a series of these fouls that went unpunished until late
on, while the amount of time wasting allowed was
equally incredible. And Mr. Jones is a Premier League
official..?

Speroni - 6
Parr - 4
Mariappa - 4
McCarthy - 6
Delaney - 6
O'Keefe - 5
Guédioura - 4
Bannan - 6
Puncheon - 6
Chamakh - 5
Jerome - 4
Moxey - 5
Wilbraham - 7
Gayle - 7

Hull City home Tuesday 8pm

It's finally happened; I have nothing much to say. It's been a busy few weeks, and with the delights of the transfer window deadline, just a few days away and a word limit gradually approaching, I will keep things very simple.

You can't by success and changing your name won't help much either!

Despite spending, what I consider a ludicrous sum of money, on two strikers, Hull couldn't break down our defence, and we secured a Premiership double. Kevin Day, in his programme notes today, touched on what I am beginning to feel about this whole Premiership business. All of a sudden, I've started to care just a little bit more, and the crowd's reaction at the end of game, suggests that others feel the same. Six points against one team, that's more than half of the total points, we were supposed to get in the whole season.

I almost wanted to start Singing to Steve Bruce, "Sacked in the morning." but last time we did that, to an ex Man U player, our manager told us off like naughty school boys[6], so I resisted the temptation. Although, because Steve Bruce is an ex Man U player, he would like so many before him, walk into another highly paid job, and be given an almost infinitesimal budget, to work with. That being said, he probably wouldn't even wait to be sacked, just jump ship for a bigger payday, or a so-called bigger club, such is his loyalty. In the words of Kevin Keagan, "I would so love it if we beat them, I would so love that." and we did. The only shame is, he does actually produce teams, that play quite nice football. BUT, and here is the big one, just like Swansea at the minute, playing nice football, doesn't necessarily win you matches, nor does stamping on Damien Delaney, or your keeper, wildly kicking out at opponents. I think that both of these offences, actually said more about the effect our team is starting to have on opponents, than in depth match analysis. We are really starting to get up peoples noses. Perhaps the big Holmesdale display, from the first match of the season, is now starting to come into play.

Let the games really begin.

PS: Message to Hull keeper, if you are going to get sent off, for kicking an opponent, at least contact with him properly, or you look a bit stupid when you're walking; OFF, OFF, OFF.

---

[6] Stoke away, first game of the season

Marks Match Report

A crucial win for Palace last night on a wet & windy night when grit & determination were required against a Hull side who for long periods in the second half penned us back. We were our own architects of potential disaster though as the quality of our passing diminished as the match went on, and were perhaps lucky that Hull's new multi-million strike force had no opportunity to gel.

Palace made one change to the XI that had started the previous league match against Stoke with Moxey replacing the battered Parr, and started quite brightly: after an inventive free kick routine nearly opened up Hull's right side, from the ensuing corner the ball travelled across the six-yard box, with Jedinak somehow contriving not to get a touch. Hull concentrated upon keeping possession, knocking the ball around at the back where there was always a spare man with their three central defenders & wing-backs, although the effort put in to close them down by the front four, Jerome in particular, should be noted; perhaps they put too much in as this would gradually ease off later in the match. Hull's threat was never quite fulfilled, with Jelavic getting in front of Gabbidon but failing to make effective contract from close in, while a Davies header was saved quite easily. There were also a couple of shouts for penalties involving Long & Jelavic that were turned down; from 100 yards away they looked to have some merit.

Palace broke the deadlock early, fine work on the right by Bolasie saw an excellent cross met by Puncheon, whose header was blocked by Chamakh; the rebound was fired across the goal into the corner. Hull's response was an unpunished stamp by Jelavic on Delaney, who after treatment retaliated with a silly foul punished with a yellow card. It has to be said that the referee Mr. East was inconsistent all night, with the challenge on Delaney and a later clattering of Speroni going unpunished yet allowing McGregor to get away with an initial foul on Jerome by booking the Palace man.

161

Palace were playing some decent attacking football but the shots were coming from outside the box, the best a free kick from Jedinak that was touched over by McGregor. Hull put in plenty of crosses but seldom found an attacker, the closest they came to an equaliser being a Huddlestone free kick in stoppage time that must have moved in the air as Julian inelegantly clawed the ball away.

Statistics show that the most dangerous time for Palace in terms of conceding goals is the first 15 minutes of the second half, and this proved the most difficult time again. Palace's passing seemed to break down completely, with the ball being served up regularly to a Tiger. The midfield seemed to drop deeper and Hull's defenders were not closed down in their own half as they had been during the first 45 minutes. Jelavic was having some success in the air against Gabbidon, and after one early weak header into Julian's arms it was his knockdown that saw Livermore shoot over from the edge of the box when he really should have scored. Later two successive atrocious short passes from Jedinak & Moxey again opened up our own defence only for Boyd's shot to be saved, Long putting the rebound into the side netting from an offside position. Rosenior then missed from close range after Palace's left side was opened up again, Moxey often finding himself outnumbered as Palace failed to come to terms with Hull's attacking wing-backs.

Pulis then made what seemed a strange substitution, replacing Bolasie with McCarthy as Palace also switched to a back three. Despite leaving Palace unbalanced in midfield this did help prevent Jelavic & Long coming into play as often as they had, and Paddy didn't seem at all rusty after his inordinately long lay-off. Palace were pretty much playing on the break now and Chamakh found himself in the clear from a good Jerome pass, only to take too much time over the shot & fail to beat McGregor. Hull now switched formations going 4-4-2, which Pulis then matched by withdrawing Gabbidon for O'Keefe. The visitors continued to enjoy the majority of possession and Long escaped McCarthy only to put his header over. As the game entered stoppage time O'Keefe fouled McGregor by the corner flag, only for the keeper to make a weak attempt at a hack on the Palace man, earning himself a red card. Even down to 10

men the final chance fell to Hull, but Quinn's shot
slipped inches past the far post with Speroni rooted to
the spot. The celebrations at the final whistle
betrayed how important those on & off the pitch thought
this result would be.

Speroni - 7
Mariappa - 6
Moxey - 5
Gabbidon - 6
Delaney -7
Jedinak - 5
Ward - 6
Bolasie - 7
Puncheon - 8
Chamakh - 6
Jerome - 6
McCarthy - 7
O'Keefe - 6
Wilbraham - 6

Transfers and Pizza

I have a confession. I did something bad, which I promised myself I wouldn't. It was peer pressure really, or that's my excuse. Sometimes it is just so hard to stick to your principles, when everyone around you is behaving stupidly.

What did I do? I didn't run on the pitch, like the fan on Tuesday, nor did I let of a pyrotechnic, in the seated area at Anfield. No, my sin, was to get caught up in the made up, completely nonsensical business, that is the transfer window. Fortunately, I stopped short of driving to Beckenham, and standing outside the training ground looking stupid, although I confess I did think about it. (Well, I had nothing else on.) Instead, I sat at home with Mum and Dad, Sky Sports, Twitter and Holmesdale radio. The latter had some technical difficulties, which left me somewhat more interested in, the style over substance of Sky, than is strictly justified. Perhaps the funniest part of the evening, and what sums up Sky news the most to me, was one announcement of breaking news. The Stoke chief executive, could apparently, be seen pumping his fists and celebrating, could this be the signing of the new wonder boy, Iam Overpricetovich. We all sat and waited, Palace fans in particular slightly concerned, in case we might have been gazumped at the last minute, on our marquee signing. Cut back to the studio. Cut back to various other training grounds, where equally nothing is happening. Cut back to Stoke. "We can now reveal, why the Stoke CEO was so excited," hold breath, pause for effect; The Pizza had arrived. No word of a lie, 'Sky sources' didn't mention that one, did they. This was probably because, it hadn't appeared on Twitter first. The strangest thing about this announcement, was that there was no apparent embarrassment, on the behalf of the reporter or the studio presenters. Whilst I accept that, from the viewer's perspective, it was funny, this wasn't because it was some master comedy moment, dreamt up by the Monty Python team. It was funny because it showed up the evening, and the Sky reporting, for what it was; conjecture, guess work and stating the bloody obvious. "Tom Ince has just arrived at CPFC, training ground. Could he possibly be considering a move to South London?" No you numpties, he just heard that the Pizza was about to be delivered, and was a bit peckish. Of course he's thinking about it. It doesn't mean it's happening, it just means it's a possibility.

When I was out of work, I applied for about 500 jobs. They looked at me, I looked at them; they rejected my kind offer to work for them. This is the real world. Can you imagine that, in the media obsessed Premier League world, they would need a permanent station, dedicated to it. Oh my god, I have done it now, "Sky sources tell us, that Sky are in negotiations with the Premier League, to gain access to all HR processes, at all the Premier League and Football League clubs. Yes, we do know that, the Football League has nothing to do with us really, but 'Whatever', we have the money so sod off. We can do what we like"

For Palace, it proved to be a late, but effective transfer window and with the exception of not getting Zaha back, because David Moyes apparently didn't want him to come back to London, it was good business. (You could try picking him then David, then he wouldn't have time, to come back to Croydon so regularly, and maybe, just maybe, he would settle in to your club a bit better.) Although, perhaps agent Wilf, will be able to damage Cardiff, as much as he would have helped us. From a nostalgic perspective, it was also disappointing that Andy Johnson's, return to South London was blocked at the last minute. He made be ten years older, and have had injury problems, but he knows where the goal is. If nothing else he could have just demonstrated this, minor detail to Cameron Jerome. He could also teach Ashley Young a thing or two about winning penalties, You just run quickly at people until they trip you. Despite what some might feel, no need for AJ to cheat, because people, did trip him up.

Transfer windows, as well as being a good promotional activity for Sky, also seems to activate supporters into heated debate, or maybe it's just a Palace thing. For some, it is an opportunity to look enthusiastically to the future, whilst some will just take the chance, to have a moan about the past. The summer transfer window, was quite widely criticised, and with nothing much happening in the early part of the evening, this was again being discussed on the forums. I personally don't think, it was as bad as many do, most of the players brought have contributed something, and I would be surprised if any of those being critical now, would have been complaining about signing Jimmy Kebe at the time. Only Kebe, Grandin and Marange were not of any real value, and sometimes it just doesn't work out for a player. It was also at the time, important that we got bodies on board, nobody knew what was going to happen, at the end of the window. Perhaps, the fact that we didn't need these signings, was actually a positive indication, of how we were able to acquire better players later on. By Premiership standards, they didn't cost much, so nothing was really lost. At least this transfer window, has been pretty much accepted as a success, although a goal scorer would have been nice, but hopefully Glen Murray will be back from injury and that will be, effectively like a new signing.

Although we have taken advantage of the system of loans, both in and out, I am not a fan. I might well expand on the reasons why, over the next few months, but basically, I feel that it distorts the market. Would the twenty players, currently on loan from Chelsea, have been offered the contracts that they were, if the Russians knew that they wouldn't be able to offset that cost by lending them all out. The big clubs, would also struggle to maintain, their current hovering approach to young player acquisitions, if they couldn't lend them all out again, and then claim credit for their development, which they have quite frankly had no part in. On the reverse end of the scheme, Watfords attempt to borrow promotion, makes a farce of the game.

On the plus side, we have borrowed Tom Ince, (At a price, that makes a pay day loan, look cheap) but to do this, we have had to buy Jason Puncheon, I will leave you to imagine, my views on this particular deal.

Arsenal ~~Saturday 1st February 3pm~~. Sunday 2nd February 4pm

As with all of the London matches, I was using public transport again, travelling to the Emirates, with my brother and niece. We had arranged to meet Graham and Mel, who despite living in Brighton, and being Arsenal supporters, are still long standing family friends, and great company. It has been quite interesting, that unlike games outside the capital, many Palace fans, have chosen to congregate away from the ground, that they are visiting; have a few beers and then travel the last part of the journey. Victoria seems to be a venue of choice, and there were a fair few Palace fans, already in place as we passed through, on our way to the White Lion, in Covent Garden. Despite meeting early, by the time we had navigated the tourists, (Good preparation, for an evening at the Emirates.) been served, and moped up the beer that I tipped over my niece, it was closing in on kick off. The last of these events, could be seen as a cunning plan, to avoid drinking too much, and falling foul of the whole Spurs, Public convenience saga, again, but in reality, was just over excitement. (I don't get out much.)

The approach to the Emirates, for someone who hasn't been there before, is I accept, impressive, and once inside the ground, the view is similar. However, at the risk of repeating myself, I do feel that if clubs want to encourage people to arrive early, they should provide better concourse facilities, and a smoking area. The positioning of the away supporters, straddling the corner flag, does also creates a slightly strange atmosphere. For the Palace fans, this was particularly off-putting, because the Holmesdale Fanatics were not up the back of us, as usual, but set off to the side, along the touchline. Whilst this did affect our ability to keep the singing coordinated, with them, as the sound filtered down through us, it did conveniently enable us to see what they were up to. As they are normally behind me, or at home matches, obscured by the upper tier of the Holmesdale Stand, this is not something that I am familiar with, and does make for some entertaining viewing, at times when the game is a little slow. What I notice, was that the large majority of them, were actually watching the game. They were linked armed, and bouncing, but definitely watching the game. Quite often when you look at away fans, there are a significant number addressing not the pitch and the players, but the opposition fans! I have often found this rather peculiar, especially if you have travelled several hundred miles for the privilege. But the Fanatics were definitely watching, and despite the outcome, we once again were able to create a great atmosphere. I am aware that, it is very easy to believe your own hype, when it comes to atmosphere at games, but I have watched a couple of YouTube videos, taken from well outside the Palace section, and there is no doubt that we did create, pretty much, all the noise that was generated in the ground. Even after the two Arsenal goals, there was only a brief period of, "Ars-en-al, Ars-en-al" and then it was back to, "We Love you. We love you" from the away fans. It is difficult to quite understand, why grounds so big and impressive, are so devoid of atmosphere. I know that fans of the big clubs, will claim that it is an urban myth, but it really isn't.

At the end of the match, I was surprised and frustrated, by the time that it took to actually get out of the ground. I know that in the event of an emergency, we could all spill onto the pitch, even so, this is a new 21st century stadium. There is nothing more frustrating, than watching your team lose, and then having to wait 20 minutes, before you can actually get out of the ground and start heading home. More importantly for me, I WANTED A FAG. The queues at Highbury and Islington Station, doubled this annoyance, and so I asked a friendly copper, how far it was to Archway. The correct answer and not the answer he gave me, is, "a bloody long way," but I somehow ended up, back on the same train to Norbury as my brother and niece, who had just shuffled along. If I hadn't called into a friendly off license, I might claim this was part of an ongoing fitness strategy, but the truth is, as you have probably gathered by now, I am actually just very impatient. My niece, gave a good impression of being pleased to see me, as I stumbled down the train in the direction of her mobile, but sometimes I think there is a fine line between funny, entertaining, uncle, and slightly embarrassing uncle.

Marks reports will as usual enlighten you, as to the good and bad points, of the team and individuals, but in my view, we did alright, against a team that by beating us, went top of the league.

"Top the league, you still don't sing, top the league you still don't sing "etc. etc.

Marks Match Report

Despite much hard work and effort Palace were sadly unable to make a dent in Arsenal's title ambitions in what was yet another hard working display at one of the big clubs but lacking that little edge of quality or luck in overturning what must have been some seriously skewed possession stats. In retrospect it was a relatively untroubled afternoon for the Gunners, with Szczesny having but one save to make, yet their domination of midfield left Speroni strangely underemployed for most of the afternoon as well.

Pulis made two changes to the team that had defeated Hull and both were, on paper, eminently sensible: Parr replaced Moxey at left back, having recovered from concussion and after Dean's less than stellar Tuesday outing; while KG came in for Mariappa, allowing Ward to drop back to right back. It made sense against Arsenal to put square pegs in square holes and no-one was really playing out of position. The 4-4-1-1 formation sat very deep in the first half, very rarely venturing anywhere near the opposition's penalty area, and the first 10 minutes were much like they had been in the match at Selhurst with Arsenal dominating possession.

Actually the first 45 minutes at the Emirates was a perfect replica of the game at the Etihad: Palace defending deep about 35 yards from goal, the bus firmly parked with hand brake engaged, while Arsenal's pretty football found precious little openings against a brave defence. Speroni was only called into action three times: an early block of Monreal's shot; a fine diving save to turn Koscielny's header past the post; and a brave save at the feet of Sagna. Delaney & Gabbidon made countless interceptions & challenges, aided by KG, while both full backs kept penetration of the flanks to a minimum. What was a problem was the lack of accuracy of Palace's passing: with Arsenal enjoying so much of the ball it was imperative not to gift it back to them so cheaply once we had it. Palace only threatened sporadic break-outs, with both Bolasie & Puncheon making runs but rarely finding support or an accurate cross. Chamakh had an early run from deep but a heavy touch saw him beaten to the ball by Szczesny, while a near post effort by Jerome was the closest to a chance on target.

If the first half was a repeat of City then the start of the second drew less flattering comparisons, as once again Palace conceded straight after the interval. Oxlade-Chamberlain, playing in an unfamiliar deep-lying midfield role, escaped Chamakh's attention and his run took him goal side of Ward, his finish giving Speroni no chance. Palace almost responded immediately, with a fine run by Puncheon down the left saw Bolasie's header find Jerome, who drew a smart save from Szczesny. Palace now pushed higher up the pitch and enjoyed more time in the Gunners' half, but this did leave gaps between the midfield and defence, while there was little end product from either winger. Bannan came on for the hard working but isolated Jerome, which added a little more skill to the midfield battle, but the killer bow came with less than 20 minutes to go, when KG gave the ball away in midfield; once again Oxlade-Chamberlain found space behind Ward and although his finish was strong Julian got a big hand to it & will be disappointed not to have saved it. Gayle came on for Chamakh but Palace's responses were long range efforts from Bolasie, Ward, Jedinak & Parr that never threatened the goal. Arsenal were content to keep trying to pass the ball into the net and ran down the game fairly comfortably.

```
Speroni - 6
Ward - 6
Parr - 7
Gabbidon - 8
Dikgacoi - 6
Jedinak - 6
Bolasie - 5
Puncheon - 6
Chamakh - 6
Jerome - 5
Bannan - 6
Gayle - 5
```

West Brom Home Saturday 8th February

One of the mysteries of the transfer window, despite the hours of TV and radio coverage, is the rules. Prior to last week's fixture at Arsenal, we signed some players, loaned out some players, loaned in some players, and converted one loan player to a permanent deal. It was a bit confusing, as some of our loan-outs played last week, where as our loan-ins didn't, add to this that there appear to be, different rules for the Premiership and the Championship, and the fans are left wondering what is going on. The BBS is a useful information point, as somebody with too much time on their hands, can often point people in the direction of the regulations, rules and often it appears, exceptions to the rules. If you then add the further complication of work permits, are these applied for, before the transfer goes through, or after, and if it is after, what happens if the work permit is refused. You start to understand, why occasionally, clubs get it wrong and apparently play ineligible players. International clearance is another great mystery. I once played for a team on the Welsh borders, whose first and second teams played Welsh football, and the third XI played in the Herefordshire League. This was a complete nightmare, as if a player was dropped or promoted, we technically had to get international clearance. (I think we eventually negotiated some special dispensation.)

The consequence of all this, was that for today's game against West Brom, we had three new signing available for the squad, which added to the anticipation of what was otherwise, for me, a pretty uninspiring fixture. We have already played West Brom, twice this year, and I struggled to get excited the first two times. I think that this might be, a relic of my exile to Herefordshire, which I have just mentioned. During this 10 year period, I didn't get to many games, as my own playing and coaching commitments, made this difficult. However, I did always try to get to the Hawthorns, as this was my most local venue, local in Herefordshire, being a very relative term. I have just discovered that Herefordshire, is so remote and inconsequential, that my spell checker doesn't even recognise it, as a place, and keeps underlining it, with a red wavy line. I also played Cricket in the Birmingham League, so spent every other Saturday, in the summer, travelling around the West Midlands. I think that these things, have combined to give me a Meuh factor, when it comes to West Brom.

One of the joys of being a football fan, is the ability to act in a largely irrational fashion, and West Brom for some reason, brings out this irrationality. With no good reason, I don't like them very much, and you might actually be beginning to think, I am a moany old git who hates everyone. This in my non-football life, is very far from the truth, but I concede that with regards to football, it might be true. I have just finished Danny Bakers autobiography, and I think that the acknowledgement of this irrationality, was one of the reasons why his 606 radio show, was so enjoyable, and why nobody else has really been able to replicate his presenting style. These two conflicting emotions,(Meuh and Dislike)mean that while I can't really get excited about the game, I do really want to win, not just because it is important, but also because I want to beat the Baggies.

The game also presents me, with a difficult issue of etiquette. Is it OK, to cheer and clap somebody, whilst simultaneously booing their Dad. Tom Ince is a great addition to our squad, but Paul, now I don't like him either,(He played for Man U, I am nothing, if not consistent) with a bit of luck, he won't be there, or at least they won't show him on the big screen, that way I can avoid, this tricky situation.

All in all, it turned into a great day, Ince and Ledley both scored, and Murray made a substitute appearance, receiving a magnificent reception from the crowd, as you would expect for a player, who almost single handedly, scored the goals that ensured our promotion. If he is as fit and healthy as he looks, this will give an amazing boost to the squad, and the fans.

15th in the league, at the beginning of February, now no one expected that, did they, least of all me.

Marks Match Report

A crucial win today for a Palace team reinforced by recent signings and the return from injury of one of last season's heroes, but one that took a lot more hard work than seemed necessary. West Brom barely showed up for the first half and put on one of the worst 45 minutes I've seen this season, but Palace once again left something in the dressing room at half-time and conceded straight after the interval. With Palace suddenly edgy and wobbling a little, and with Albion showing a sudden appetite for the fight, the whole game turned on one crucial minute just past the hour mark.

When the initial team selection was announced with three debutants there was some discussion over the formation. Three centre backs with Puncheon & Bolasie as wing-backs? Instead Palace lined up 4-4-1-1: Scott Dann replaced Gabbidon in the centre of defence; Ledley - who has more than a passing similarity to Delaney - started at left back, finally giving Pulis an entire back four of giants; KG partnered Jedi in the middle with, perhaps surprisingly given their performances last week, both Bolasie & Puncheon retaining their posts on the wings; the slight Tom Ince played in the hole behind the more advanced Chamakh.

After a decent start from Palace the first real chance fell to WBA as Anichebe outpaced Dann in the inside-left channel but shot straight at Speroni. Then Palace started to play with some real purpose, some good moves

171

threatening a breakthrough, a fine far post header from a difficult angle by Bolasie drew a running save from Foster, while a corner was cleared from the line after a series of rebounds. Ince was already looking to be a skilful player with a fine touch & turn of pace, already striking up an interesting partnership with Chamakh, and he marked his debut with a goal following a fine piece of refereeing from Chris Foy. Chamakh slipped a through ball to Bolasie, who was bundled to the ground; the ball ran free to Ince as Foy played advantage, and as Foster advanced Ince coolly lifted the ball over the keeper and into the net.

The following period of play saw Palace's new look team play some attractive football, looking to use both flanks while Chamakh dropped off the central defenders to hold the ball up. One advantage of having Ledley & Dann in the team was that Palace suddenly had a real aerial threat from set pieces: Those two plus Delaney, sometimes Ward, and add to that the far from negligible threat of KG, Jedinak & Chamakh. This undoubtedly played a part in the second goal when Palace won a corner down the right. Ince's delivery was perfect as the defence, perhaps distracted by the myriad of threats, totally failed to pick up Ledley, and he thumped in an unchallenged header inside the near post from about 8 yards out. Although Palace did not mount another real threat on goal before half-time, they remained in control of the game as Albion's deteriorated, with some truly execrable passing; they did find the crowd on a regular basis. All the stuffing appeared to be knocked out of them, they lacked any creativity & appeared as forlorn as Palace did that second half against Fulham.

I have no idea what is said to the Palace team at half-time but once again they managed to leave something in the dressing room, conceding not just within the first 15 minutes, but in virtually the first minute. Albion introduced Scott Sinclair and the unlisted #50 (Bifouma?) and the change was immediate, with virtually a training ground move down our right, Bifouma trading passes with Anichebe before slamming a low shot from a narrow angle. Speroni seemed to have everything covered but it somehow went straight past him at his near post. With that the nature of the game switched dramatically, West Brom suddenly infused with hope, with the two subs & Anichebe really upping their games, while Palace suddenly looked nervous and their game started to break down. The passing in particular deteriorated, even from short range, with Jedinak in particular doing well to win the ball only to immediately give it straight back with an inadequate pass. We also appeared to drop deeper, only closing Albion down 10-15 yards in our half when previously we had pressed them around the halfway line. There were several occasions when panicky clearances went straight to opponents just beyond the penalty area, while Palace were lucky that some rebounds off our own players didn't fall for Albion. During this period Palace did break out with Chamakh & Ince prominent, and another low near post corner nearly saw a Delaney flick find the net. Albion responded with a rasping shot from Morrison that was pushed over by Speroni, who was to make amends in the immediate future.

The turning point in the match came when, after another concession of the ball by KG & Jedinak, another attempted clearance cannoned off someone and fell to the feet of one of three WBA attackers looking suspiciously offside but only 10 yards out. One of them (Mulumbu?) got off a shot only for Speroni, who was initially moving the wrong way, to sprawl to his left and first stop then fall onto the ball. The importance of this moment was reinforced when, within a minute, a fine through ball (ashamed to say in the moment I didn't see who played it!) saw Chamakh clear of the last two defenders. It seemed a slight lack of control carried him a little wide & allowed the defenders to close but as he entered the penalty area he was clattered by Foster; Foy ruled the keeper had not played the ball (from our perfect position at the back of the Whitehorse we had no idea but were quite prepared to accept this eminently sensible decision) but did not show a card of either colour to the keeper – perhaps he thought it was too tight a decision and the defenders had tracked back enough. Either way, it was interesting to see Chamakh & not Puncheon take the penalty, but more importantly it was delirium when Marouane sent Foster the wrong way and rolled the ball into the right hand corner.

The last 25 minutes or so saw Palace regain some equilibrium and, with some better service from Bolasie, they might have increased the lead. There were also some heavy tackles from Albion as they tried to force their way back into the game a second time, and while Palace's defence occasionally creaked, Speroni was rarely called into serious action. It was interesting to see Pulis's use of the subs' bench. First saw the return of Murray to a thunderous reception in place of Puncheon, with Ince moving to the left and Chamakh back into the hole, and Glenn didn't look rusty. Then Parr came on for Bolasie and moved to left back, allowing Ledley to reinforce the midfield. Finally Jerome Thomas replaced Chamakh who had worked damned hard & taken some hard punishment. Every move tightened the team and showed not just a good tactical brain but also how important it was for our transfer window signings to be able to hit the road running, which all three did.

Speroni - 7
Ward - 6
Ledley - 7
Dann - 7
Delaney - 7
Dikgacoi - 6
Jedinak - 6
Puncheon - 6
Bolasie - 6
Ince - 7
Chamakh - 8
Murray - 7
Parr - 6
Thomas - 6

You're only supposed to blow the Bl@@dy doors off

I felt strangely confident, about yesterday's game. I was not expecting a resounding victory, but at least the chance for a battling draw, was a real possibility. It was also an away midweek match, which whilst needing a day off work, and a very tired Thursday, is always fun. Originally, I was expecting a small turn out, but the generous decision by the owners, to provide free transport, fuelled the numbers up to an impressive 1300. Whilst not affecting me directly, the cancellation of the tube strike, was also going to be a bonus, for those travelling by train.

In the end, seven coaches,(Or nine, if you go by the numbers on the actual tickets.) left Selhurst just before 1pm. As always, despite the best efforts of the stewards, or at least those that turned up, early enough to be of any use, it was all a bit of a shambles. The complete lack of capability of the box office, to sell 350 coach tickets, with the correct numbers on them, reinforces the inflexibility of the current ticketing software. Our regular stewards, Charlie and Graham, are familiar with sorting out these difficulties, but when we have additional coaches, the stewards seem to be appointed on a pretty ad hoc basis, and it is perhaps not fair, to be too critical of them, for not being totally expert. We are however lucky that the coach drivers, are very competent and unlike the Barclays Bus drivers, always seem to know where they are going. Today, as well as the usual Kings Ferry coaches, we also used Worthing Coaches and Lucketts.

Whilst we were waiting, in a dry and clear Executive car park, and watching the assembled supporters, move from coach to coach, trying to work out which one they should be on, I received a text from my nephew, suggesting we should keep an eye on the radio, as there was a suggestion, the game might not go ahead. At the time, this seemed quite peculiar, but I did pass it on to stewards and drivers. When we were all on board, and waiting for the last few stragglers to arrive, a young fan approached our steward Charlie, asking if he could still get a place on the coach. There were definitely seats available, on at least one of the coaches, but Charlie quite rightly, sent him up to the booking office, to officially book a place. He returned disappointed a few minutes later, having been told it was too late. This seem pretty intransigent from the box office, but they must have had their reasons, although I'm not sure I understand what these would have been. The coaches were still there, the tickets were still there, and a Palace fan wanted to spend 10 hours on a coach, to support their team. At the end of the day, perhaps this young fan would have thanked the box office, but it was disappointing to see him walking away, rather disconsolate, as we started our convoy out of the ground.

Despite normally leaving the ground as a group, it is almost inevitable, that at some point during the journey, we will be separated. For the steward on coach two, the ability to find a quick route, to wherever we are going, seems to be an almost compulsive quest. In fairness, he is usually successful in beating us, to at least the agreed stop. This is probably by avoiding central London, which unlike in the 70's, no longer involves a regular Saturday night trip, past the Playboy club. This was always a popular part of the journey, in the days when most of the coach was male, and the abbreviation P.C. had not been invented, but now seems a time consuming strategy. Today most of the coaches, stopped on the M6 toll at Norton Cane, which was pretty crap, as it was being refurbished and there was not a bunny girl in sight.

Whilst waiting, we started to here news that one of the M6 bridges was closed, due to high winds. The various drivers and stewards, implemented a plan and an alternative route, and we set off as quickly as possible, when the coaches were loaded. Whilst it was intended that we would stay together, I think that there was also an unstated agreement, that drivers would just do their best to get to Everton, by whichever route seemed safest. We had not long been back on the motorway, when we got word that the planned route was now blocked. Unfortunately, we had passed one of the turn offs, that would have given a further alternative, but coach 2 hadn't. A new plan was needed for us, whilst coach two could turn off earlier and work their way around the blockage.

The next few hours were a mixture of frustration, irritation, and above all that overriding hope, which Palace fans seem to have in abundance. Time ticked and we didn't move, and then moved very cautiously. I have said before, how amazingly perceptive Mandy is, when it comes to road conditions and noises, but on this occasion, for the first time that I can remember, she seemed quite disconcerted. It is one thing, driving down small country roads, with the wind and trees crashing against the side of the coach, when you can see what is happening, but it must be a completely different experience, when these unpredictable noises and vibrations, come completely unexpectedly. As the hours clocked by, we began to hear information of other fans trapped in traffic, all over the West Midlands and Cheshire. Games were being called off, both south and north of our destination, but there was no news from Everton, so we continued heading north, hopeful that we would eventually see some football. Calls were made to Everton, to see if there was any possibility of the kick off being delayed, but the feedback that we got was pretty much, "no, tough, the game goes ahead as planned" whilst this wasn't helpful, it did at least show that the game was going ahead. At around 7pm, we had reached just south of Chester, friends and family were texting and calling, to say that they were in the ground, and whilst it was windy, it was all ok. The players had even been out, doing there warm up. My cousins, Alan and Frank, had earmarked this match at the beginning of the seasons, and were in the ground after a day out in Liverpool, so although we knew we were going to be late, I reckoned that we would be there, midway through the first half. Coach 2 was even closer to the ground, and looked like they may even make kick off.

Bang. 7.15pm Match Postponed.

I appreciate that the weather, is out of the control of even Sky TV, but Bollocks. We had sat in this bloody coach for 6 hours, and now were about to turn around and drive all the way back again, just 30 minutes before kick off. To say that this was frustrating, is an understatement. I don't think that any of the travelling Palace support, would really complain about the game being off. If there are serious safety concerns, but what really annoyed people, was the timing. How can my nephew, who lives in Bournemouth, text me at 1pm saying that the game might be off, and yet it takes 6 hours, to actually call it off. During that time, over 1000 supporters are making their way to the game, in dangerous conditions, and now they have to turn around, and travel back through those dangerous conditions. For an exercise in risk management and safety, this seems pretty absurd. The word coming through, on various different weather feeds, is also that the worst is almost over, and inside the ground is fine. By 10 pm, many of the blockages will have cleared, instead it's a big, "sod you." from the police, councils and football authorities.

The trouble is also that we have now got into a position, where it is very difficult to turn around. This has not been helped by the fact that, there are lots of cars coming in the other direction, on this B Road, and we have to drive with our dipped headlights, Shiiiiiiiiiiiit. That was seriously close. The diver flicked the full beam on, and there was a big F-off, tree across the road. Cue a very sharp piece of braking, and a gratefulness to the seat belts, that we had all been reminded to put on.

The only positive at this point, was that when we stopped, on a B road by a barn conversion industrial estate, a few miles from Chester, to avoid an imminent collision with said, F-off tree, I was able to get off the coach and have a cigarette. It was needed. The police, who seemed to arrive remarkably quickly, were keen that we should turn around, but as other coaches arrived behind us, this seemed to be a pretty unfeasible manoeuvre.

We are now back on the motorway heading home, it is 9.30pm and I have just heard from coach 3, that they are still heading north. They were stuck on the motorway, and had not been able to get to a junction, which allowed them to turn around. In a black humour sort of way, this is quite amusing. They have travelled for 8 hours, and can't even start to make their way home. Other fans are stuck on various parts of the rail network, and are unlikely to be getting home at all tonight. In these circumstances, all you have to hold onto are the small mercies, we will be back earlier than we had originally planned, and the big mercies, that we will at least get back, safely. Our drivers must take great credit for this, and we owe them a debt of gratitude, for quick feet and reactions, without which, we would at best be in a hospital in Cheshire, and at worst.. Well I don't want to go there, and let's hope none of our travelling support did either.

There are two types of supporters, that travel on the coach, the sandwich brigade and the burger brigade. The former is largely self-sufficient, and with the exception of a short stop, to stretch the legs, grab a coffee, and smoke as many cigarettes as is humanly possible, we are quite happy to stop only briefly. Anywhere that allows the fulfilment of these three criteria, is fine. The burger brigade are much lighter travellers, who without the incumbency of a large cooler bag, packed with sandwiches, sausage rolls and cakes, like to have an extended stop to eat. Generally, the two groups can coexist quite happily, but there was a bit of a disagreement today, about where to stop on the way home. Norton Canon where we had stopped on the way out, and formulated our route plan, was the scheduled break, and as soon as we pulled in, those up the front, jumped off as quickly as possible, to avoid the queues. By the time that the people wanting to eat, had expressed that this was a pretty crap place, it was too late to get everybody back, and move on to a service station, that was actually open. I guess it was just expressions of grumpiness, following a wasted journey, but although I was well stocked with sandwiches myself, I did see their point of view. The drivers knew about the part closure of the services, so it was a bit silly, for them to stop here again. That being said, after the journey that they had safely negotiated, on our behalf; I don't think it was fair to criticise too much.

After such a long trip, you would imagine that Pauline, would have managed to knit a size XXXXL jumper. The very expensive, and specialist wool, that she was using today, looked very impressive. Unfortunately, when we got back to the car park, at Selhurst, just after 1am, she dropped it on the way back to her car. Despite inquiries next day, it had disappeared, so if you see anybody walking round Selhurst, in a half-finished cashmere jumper, ask them where they got it and we can try to reunite it, with its owner and creator.

Marks Match Report

Was one of about 50 Palace fans to make it into Goodison. Had £5 on each keeper to score first...

Mikes Match addendum

Not even Mark can find a great deal interesting to say about this match but I can reveal that the team was scheduled to be.

Speroni
Ward
Dann
Delaney
Parr
Puncheon
Kg
Jedi
Ince
Ledley
Chamakh

I have just also got hold of a copy of the programme which in years to come will be one of those collectors'

178

items, that if you know what you're looking for, you can pick up at a car boot for 50p, and is worth a great deal more. As I have said before, I don't really read programmes any more, but I was pleased to see that two of my all-time favourite Palace players, were featured. Alan Whittle pictured in younger days than I remember, but still with trademark bags under his eyes, I knew had played for Everton, but the other, Kenny Sansom, I didn't realise, had ever played for the Toffees. You learn something every day, even when there is no actual football to watch.

Man U, Masks and Money Madness

The Buddhist philosophy of peace, love, and happiness to all, that started unintentionally, to corrupt my thinking about Man United, when I was writing about our trip to Old Trafford, back in September, is far from my thoughts, as I reflect on yesterday's defeat. There is quite a lot of animosity, between the supporters of the two clubs; considering we have spent much of the last two decades, mixing in different circles and are not geographically close, to an outsider this can be a bit of a mystery. I do not intend to open the reasons, up to scrutiny, because for many they will be so historic as to be almost irrelevant. In the case of the most serious incident, I am also not significantly aware of the details, to be able to do justice to the reasons why, one of our supporters, Paul Nixon attended a match and never returned home. Others however, seem to keep these events, at the forefront of their minds. There was much indignation, prior to the game, that Man United fans, were reportedly going to be attending the match, in Cantonna masks. I have to confess, that I had even forgotten, how these two incidents were linked. Whilst I can understand, why it is a sensitive subject, I am not sure that many who thought about wearing these masks, had this in mind. Whatever the situation, it appears that the club, intended to take action to prevent them, hopefully this might have prevented some historic bad feeling, coming to the surface. Despite this action by the club, and the considerable efforts to prevent Man United supporters from buying tickets, in the Palace areas, there was still an underlying tension in ground.

There are often two ways, to raise awareness of your club to a wider audience, one is positive and the other is negative, and unfortunately it is often easier to do the latter, than the former. As yesterday's game was live on TV, at 5.30 pm, the Holmesdale Fanatics chose the game, to put on another tremendous display in the Holmesdale standard. The banners reading, *"Together our spirit is unbreakable"* epitomised much of what the club has achieved, over the last few years. The slight rawness of the banners, without the more common corporate manufactured finish, and the fact that the display was once again, made for and paid for, by the fans, is difficult to replicate. The feedback from TV viewers, from around the world, was that it was impressive, and even before the game Robbie Salvage, who is not normally one of the clubs biggest fans, reportedly stated on Football Focus that we were, the best fans in the league.

Unfortunately, much of this good work, was undone by a small number of Palace fans, who threw things at Wayne Rooney. I will not in any way condone the throwing of coins or lighters at a player. Coins in particular, have been shown to have the potential when thrown from a distance, to cause serious injury, even if this was not the intention. I am not sure that, small plastic lighters, have ever had the same effect, but we all know the rules, and for this reason alone, it is not something I would do. Knowing that you will be caught and banned from the ground, should be enough reason to temper your hostility, to any opposition player. All that being said, and even taking away any history between Manchester

United and ourselves, there was one reason why, this week, had I been near that corner flag, I might also have been inclined to vent my spleen, in Wayne Rooney's direction. This was after all, the first match after he had signed a new contract, worth a reported £300,000 a week. Yes, that's what I said, and you read the figures correctly. Wayne Rooney, will earn more in a week, than I will in the next 10 years. It is quite frankly obscene, and I am getting angrier by the minute, as I type. There has been considerable discussion about it this week, in the press and on club forums around the country. Nobody can really justify it, and nobody can explain it. He has been rewarded, for threatening to walk away from the club, with a bigger salary. Yet at the same time, fans are being asked to pay, higher and higher prices, for tickets. Did Jimmy Hill, really want this, when he organised the removal of the maximum wage, in 1961.

On a rational basis, I know that it is not Rooney's fault, that he has been offered the money, and if it was offered to me, it would be very difficult to say, "No thanks, pay me half that, and reduce the season ticket price at Old Trafford by 50%. I can just about manage on 7 million pounds a season, and Coleen will have to economise a bit." Despite this, I cannot help but feel, something has to be said and done. Perhaps screaming at Rooney, like a wild animal is not the best way to do it, but if you are a low paid 19 year old, who has to scrimp and save, to find the £55, to go to an away game at Man U, I guess this might seem like the only way, that anyone will take notice. The real culprits in all of this, are the footballing authorities, that have allowed this wage spiral and the TV companies, that have encouraged it. If they want to throw their money away, in this irrational, unsustainable way, then I guess it is theirs to do what they like with, but the supporters should not be asked to pay for Coleen Rooney's, new Business or Dress.

Whilst not accepting that throwing things at players is right, I wonder sometimes, if the legal and football authorities, ought to at least take into consideration, why it might have happened. I would consider myself a staunch capitalist, but even I can see, that this salary is immoral. The problem doesn't stop at Man U, who it could be argued, can actually afford to pay this salary and so it is reasonable. The problem filters down to smaller clubs, like us, where good players are prised away, with the promise of Salaries that we can never compete with. They are then often left to rot in the reserves, or loaned out to other clubs, who happen to have almost incestuous relationships, with the money kings. It also creates an atmosphere of complicity, as no one wants to disagree with the top teams, or propose controls, because what chance do they then have, of getting one of these players on loan.

If you look at two of our own former youth players as examples. Wilf was signed by today's visitors, but they obviously don't want him. Simplistically we could sign him back again, as could anybody else, but he is now on a salary at least 100% higher than when he left, and will quite reasonably, not want to take a pay cut. Even a loan deal, would similarly cost more, than many would consider, he is worth, at present. All this time, No one gets to see, one of the most exciting talents in English football. In the event that a club decides that they do want to buy or borrow him, at this wage, the knock on effects don't stop there. If I am a team mate, I will then want to go to the manager and say, " hang on a minute, you're paying that bloke Zaha, 35K a week, I want a pay rise." And thus the spiral continues. I know that the pundits will say that it is great that smaller clubs get to see these great players, but we didn't need the loan system to see, Kenny Sansom or Ian Wright, nor did Scunthorpe need it to see Kevin Keegan. Clubs just took the radical step of scouting these players, signing them, developing them, before allowing them to leave at the appropriate time and fee, when the buying club actually wanted to play them. I referred to two examples, but I have decided not to get started on John Bostock[xi], as I am not sure that my keyboard is sturdy enough to cope with the pounding.

I have gone off on one a bit, but the finances of the Premiership teams, despite the billions of TV money, show that the majority cannot even sustain these Salaries, which makes them doubly irresponsible. I would like to scream at the owners, of these clubs, and the Premier League, but unfortunately, they are not so accessible. They don't come down, towards our most vocal section of support, to take a corner. They hide away, in there ivory towers, so in the meantime, the players will always cop it, as symptom of anger, even if they are not the cause.

The Palace crowd today was mostly full of passion and very vocal, but in addition to the abuse directed at WR, they also exposed the fine lines between humour and abuse. Some of the chanting, in relation to one of the players that was prized away from Palace, as mentioned in the last paragraph, was particularly questionable. It is always difficult to strike this balance, and finding things to sing for 90 minutes, without repetition, must be a tricky business. 10 years ago, we would have resulted to long periods of, "red and blue army," but the Fanatics do like to vary things about. One chant today, suggesting that Wilf Zaha, could have intimate relations with whomever he wanted, was in my opinion quite funny, as it was more about supporting him. The other, which suggested that the recipient of these amorous advances, might have a low moral compass, was on the contrary quite unpleasant and I chose not to join in, as did a lot of the ground. Despite the popular opinion, that crowds of football supporters have a low moral compass themselves, the volume of a particular chant, can often reflect the approval or otherwise, of the subject matter, as much as it does, the ease of tune and knowledge of the words. I was pleased that the bulk of the crowd, shared my view, that referring to David Moyes daughter directly, in this way was not acceptable. As for the game, well much like the reverse fixture, we lost; they fell over a lot and got a penalty. Deja Vue.

Marks Match Report

```
Sorry to strike an unpopular note, but I don't believe
that Palace deserved anything out of tonight's game. We
just didn't work hard enough, too often sitting too
deep to pressure United's midfield and, almost
```

incredibly, failing to put in enough challenges in the middle to disrupt the opposition. We needed to be in their face, closing them down early and hitting them with challenges instead of standing off. Allow Rooney & Mata time & space and they will make you suffer, but Palace achieved the difficult feat of making Michael Carrick look half decent. It was a performance totally out of keeping with Pulis's philosophy. In the end it was a comfortable win for a less than spectacular United side and the match was effectively over after the first goal.

Palace lined up in a familiar 4-2-3-1 formation but with a couple of key changes in personnel & positions. Parr was brought in at left back to strengthen the defence against United's long list of inadequate wingers [still bemused over how – excluding Januzaj – this motley crew kept Wilf out] which allowed Ledley to replace KG in the middle. The real surprise was Murray starting up front after Pulis's declarations the striker was some weeks away from a start; Chamakh moved into the hole with Ince & Puncheon switching between wings with Bolasie relegated to the bench.

Palace started well and Murray could well have earned a penalty in the first few minutes when manhandled by Vidic. Glenn's return highlighted the difference in having a sole striker who was strong enough to win the ball and bring others into play. Vidic was also to have a long-running battle with Jedinak from corners, with the Palace skipper seeking to block De Gea; the referee spoke to them often but did sod all. However it was soon evident that Palace, as they had against Arsenal, were sitting far too deep, with Jedinak & Ledley holding a line about 35-40 yards out, while all 10 outfield players were packing the area to defend corners. Mata was being given lots of room to pull the strings, while Rooney drifted into that difficult space between the defenders & the midfield shield. The regular out ball was a sweeping ball to Januzaj on the left while Carrick and old man Ferdinand were allowed time & space to bring the ball forward unchallenged. Pulis tried to urge them to hold a higher line and for the last 15 minutes of the first half they did, looking a more cohesive unit.

Palace did have some chances, with Ince supplying a couple of excellent crosses from the left. De Gea made a fine save when, of all people, Parr turned up at the far post and his effort took a ricochet before being turned around the post. But the best chance came from another Ince cross but an unmarked Chamakh failed miserable from 10 yards out, his header being almost straight down & bouncing comfortably into the keeper's hands. But play was increasingly concentrated down the Holmesdale Road end: Januzaj had a goal disallowed for handball; Vidic put an easy header over from close range after Delaney had cleared Rooney's cross-shot from under the bar; but the worst was Fellaini's miss with the goal gaping right on half-time.

Palace's torpor returned after half-time; they really should sack the tea-lady! After an early Murray flick that dropped kindly for De Gea, Palace started dropping deep again, and both Rooney & Mata started playing right up on the edge of our box, often only numbers and luck preventing a killer final ball. But it could not last, with Chamakh committing a forward's challenge on Evra: from my perspective it was a definite foul just inside the box and a clear penalty, which Van Persie put away clinically.

Could Palace raise their game? Sadly the answer was no as we continued to sit off and refuse to commit to challenges in the middle, compounded by a number of poor passes wasting precious & limited possession, with Puncheon & Jedinak being prime offenders. The second goal also game from a move down our right, with Evra's great run and pull back being finished with class by the freshly enriched Rooney Palace made changes in personnel but not formation, with Jerome replacing a tiring Murray and having one decent effort saved by De Gea and another weak header from what seemed a simpler chance. Van Persie nearly scored a third with a break and shot that thumped the crossbar while Palace struggled with little useful ball. In the end it was a tepid & timid performance that earned exactly what was gained – nothing.

Speroni – 6
Ward – 6
Parr – 7
Delaney – 6
Dann – 6
Jedinak – 5
Ledley – 6

Puncheon – 4
Ince – 5
Chamakh – 5
Murray – 7
Jerome – 5
Bolasie – 6
Gayle – 5

Swansea Away ~~Saturday 1st March 3pm~~ Sunday 2nd March 4.30pm

It is often easy, in the parochial word of football, to paint your own supporters in a favourable light, and those of others more negatively. As I read through my notes about last week, and prepared for the match away at Swansea; I realised that the opposition this weekend, was in some ways a good example of this, and how perhaps at times we should move on. Back In 1980, a Swansea supporter David Williams, attended an F.A. cup match against Crystal Palace, and similar to Paul Nixon never returned home. Yet despite this, there is not as far as I am aware, the long-term animosity, between the two sets of supporters. I recently found an interesting article on the incident[xii], which confirmed that a Palace fan, was eventually found guilty of murdering David, and sentenced to life imprisonment, eventually killing himself 10 years later. Which in its own way, is another tragedy.

Perhaps a bit like the difference between Bradford and Hillsborough, some of this simmering bad feeling, is due to the perception of no one being punished, or having taken responsibility, in one case. Whatever the reasons, our trip to the Liberty Stadium, far from being a tense trip, had been made a family friendly affair, with kids for a quid and a special area set aside for, "families." (You of course cannot have, an area set aside for sitting, because everybody already sits, at ALL Premier League matches.)

This all meant that, the usual palaver over suitable tickets for Mum, wasn't necessary and I could relax in the days leading up to the game. The only slight, negative aspect of the day, was the mode of transport. As I have said several times, I am generally happy to travel by coach, unless a more appealing option comes about. For the majority of the season, discussions have been taking place with one of the quieter owners, to make his steam train available, to travel to one of the matches. A number of potential matches had been earmarked, one of which was, I believe, Swansea. Sources had suggested,(Reliable sources, not Sky sources) the carriages were going to be pulled by conventional train, to Bristol, then by steam the rest of the journey. It was a brilliant idea. Unfortunately, even more than a regular train trip, events like this, take a lot of planning. Without knowing the exact date and time of the fixture, until the last minute, it was seemingly impossible, to arrange properly. This is just another example, of how supporters and clubs, trying to be innovative, are thwarted by the football authorities and TV companies. On the plus side, the rearranged time did give us an extra hour in bed.

The whole kids for a quid idea, has also opened up the subject of tickets again. In particular, the way home teams, sell tickets to away teams. Due to the numbers, that Palace anticipated would take advantage of the offer, the club requested to take their full allowable allocation, but with a week to go, it was looking like there would be a considerable number unsold. According to one of the owners, posting on the BBS, we would then have to pay for them, at full adult price. This would have left the club considerably out of pocket. Palace would not apparently, have enforced this payment method and would have sold the tickets, on a sale or return basis. It was however suggested by some fans, that if all of the tickets were, "sold " to children, then Swansea would receive just £1000 instead of £35,000. The club could obviously not arrange this directly, by just allocating tickets at random to junior members, so the fans organised it for themselves. I along with a large number of supporters, brought tickets for nephews, nieces, children, grandchildren, friend's children and quite possibly, that lad down the street. As a result, we saved the club a considerable amount of money. It all seemed like, a rather ridiculous situation, and possibly some people who might have liked to go, at the last minute couldn't, because all the tickets were, "sold" when we all knew they weren't. However, it was great that the Palace fan base, once again stepped in to help the club financially. This facet of the Crystal Palace support, as I am sure, is similar at many smaller clubs, is not just a recent phenomenon. Palace in my lifetime have had, The Lifeline club, The Trust, The ambassadors and who can forget the efforts of fans such as Joyce "the Voice" True, selling lottery tickets. The tradition at Palace also goes back much further, and my first visits to Selhurst, sitting on my Dad's lap in the main stand, were thanks to, the security on a loan of £100 to the club in the 1960's. Which not surprisingly, the club paid off, as soon as promotion was secured in 1969.

Discussions on this whole issue of away ticket prices, have also been active in the national press this week, with Newcastle in particular, trying to arrange reciprocal pricing agreements, with other clubs. This in theory is a great idea, but as one of the owners highlighted, it is not as simple as it may at first appear. If a club like Newcastle, normally give away supporters very poor seats, behind the goal, about a mile from the action, and want to reduce the price by £5 to say £20, but in return want other clubs, who give away supporters prime pitch side tickets, to also charge £20, then it's not really a like for like reciprocal arrangement. Whilst I am a great advocate of cheaper away tickets, when you have these things pointed out, it does make you realise that ideology is one thing, and practical implementation is another.

After an almost, Saturday 3 o'clock kick off, last week, it is back to concept of Sunday football. For as long as I can remember, Sunday league football has been denigrated by much of the footballing establishment and players. If you ever got involved in a discussion about football, and were asked who you played for, and admitted they x or y F.C. were, "A Sunday league team," you would normally add the word 'just,' in front of the sentence. The person you were talking to, would then know that you realised, Sunday football was not, "proper" football, but just a bit of a kick around with your mates. If the other footballers present, also played Sunday league, then the conversation could continue, but if he was a Saturday footballer, the conversation might well end at that point, with something like, "Oh, OK". It mattered little, if the Saturday football was Alleyn's old boys 6th XI, or that the Sunday team that you played for, contained an assortment of ex pro and current semi-pro Ryman's League players. The important thing was the day that you played. It was relatively easy in my youth, to miss Palace matches on the basis that, I played myself. No one would ever question this excuse, it was valid, it had a certain kudos. The alternative excuses of, a visit to your girlfriend's parents, or a wedding invitation, would not be quite so universally accepted. It is therefore slightly ironic, that so much of the supposed, best league in the world, now takes place on a Sunday. I cannot but help wonder, if a young and relatively unknown Premiership footballer, has ever turned down an outing, with a new set of friends, on a Sunday, by explaining that it's because he is playing football, only to be met with a little derision, and a retort of, "Oh ok, Sunday league! We all play proper football, on a Saturday"

Now I'm sure, that there will be some economists reading this, who will look knowingly and say, "oh yes but it is the TV companies that fund the game and they want to show matches on a Sunday." I do understand this, and would just about accept the movement of two fixtures a week to a Sunday, for this reason. However, the movement of this Sundays match, away to Swansea has little to do with the broadcasting of the match, to armchair Sky soccer, supercalifragilistic Sunday fans. No, Palace fans, have to travel to South Wales for a kick off at 4.30, because of the Europa League. The involvement in this largely irrelevant competition, of the team that finishes in 6th place in the league, or the team that wins the League Cup, or a team that wins the fair play league, or anybody else they really want in it, but missed out on all other possible criteria, results in a Thursday Europa cup match, against teams from other countries, who have likewise ascended to these dizzy heights. Thursdays, as anybody who has been in a local league, end of season backlog will tell you, is not a great night for playing football, if you have a game two days later, on a Saturday. But unlike the mere mortals, who are just told to, get on with it, highly paid Premiership footballers, are incapable of this physical exertion, even with the addition of first class business travel, and must rest there poor tired £100,000 a week muscles. This results in all teams in the Europa League, being able to switch their matches to a Sunday. Of course, these decisions aren't made in advance, and take place only when clubs have secured there place, in each round. To add to the confusion, even when a match is played on a Sunday, and not scheduled for UK TV broadcasting, the clubs involved cannot pick their own kick off time. It must fit into a slot, so that the Premier League, can screw even more money out of football fans, elsewhere in the world. It's not as if, they don't have enough, already.

There are a number of specific and personal ironies as far as I am concerned about the movement of this match. Having explained earlier how Sunday football, for most of my playing days has been derided, I have now reached the stage in my own playing career, when I am less worried about these things, and more worried about just being able to bend, over far enough to tie up my laces. I actually wonder, if there could be a market for slip on football boots. This might sound fanciful, but the idea of white and orange boots, would once upon a time, seem equally fanciful.

As a result of the passing of time and the desire to watch Palace, I am now no longer playing Saturday football. I have joined the ranks of Sunday veterans' football and very enjoyable it is too. I may well return to this subject latter, but for now all you need to know, is that we kick off very fluidly sometime between

10.30 and 11.30 on a Sunday morning. To say that this season has been slightly disjointed, would be an understatement, as the previous seven games have all been cancelled due to waterlogged pitches. For those who might now advocate a winter break, we had it over December, and then it started raining, so we are now up to nearly 3 months without a game. For those of you who may still be in there athletic prime, this enforced break would be difficult to manage physically, but for those near the end of, long and largely uninspiring footballing journeys, these periods of inactivity are almost akin to hamstring suicide. Now here is the irony, this week is looking like it might be dry, or at least not noahesk. So what happens, Swansea play Napoli on a Thursday, lose, don't pick up any injuries, don't have a delayed flight and consequently, we have to travel to South Wales on a Sunday. Thus meaning that I am unable to play again this weekend, and the hamstrings will continue to get tighter and tighter.

Since starting to right this chapter I have now found out that my vets team in fact have no match scheduled for this weekend, but in the true spirit of this book, I will leave the passage unaltered, the principle still applies and quite frankly I can't be bothered to start all over again.

The day its self has started with a bit of a panic, Dad wasn't feeling so well, and as the whole family is either travelling to, or already in South Wales, we needed to make suitable arrangements, to check up on him. Calls were made, keys exchanged and pulses were taken. Once we were satisfied that all was in order, we set off for the 10.15 departure. I have often joked with my Mum, about how this actually turns into a 9.15 departure, but I was today grateful for this over cautionary approach. Once at the ground, I realised that I had forgotten headphones, to listen to the next instalment of Terry Pratchett and Neil Gaimons, Good Omen. Added to this, having cleaned a lap tray, to put my new laptop on, I had left this at home as well. Consequently, once I dropped Mum off, it was a quick trip back home and back again. By 10.23am we were on the road, minus a few of our regulars, who for one reason or another were unable to make today's game. Could the reason be, a Sunday afternoon kick off?
Anyway, on to the important business, today's sandwiches are, smoked salmon and organic mayonnaise.

We arrived at the ground at 3pm, in the pouring rain, so apart from a quick fag, we stayed on the coach and listened to the end of the League Cup final. Normally this would be a game that had little interest, but such are the complex permutations, now that we are in the Premier League, that it did have some direct affect. Despite my diatribe about the Europa League, I am a hypocrite. The fair play league, as mentioned previously is still an outside possibility as a backdoor route into Europe, for Palace. We currently lie in 6th place. Now with only one team potentially qualifying, 6th place may seem like a long way off the pace. However, the complex nature of everything that is E.U.F.A. means that we are actually in second place, as four of the five teams above us, will almost definitely qualify for some European competition, in their own right, leaving just us and Everton in the hunt. Now as I understand the complex rules, unlike in the F.A. cup, the League

Cup runners up, don't take the place of the winners, if the winners have already qualified. In this scenario, the League Cup place, will then pass to the next position in the Premier League, which doesn't currently qualify. As it stands now, this could be Everton. Therefore, a victory for Man City, could well push us into effective first place, in the fair play league.

Now that you have read through that paragraph five times and googled, 'Europa league qualification criteria' I move onto England's standings. I managed to find out how England were doing in the European standings, only to discover that the Premier League has now slipped to fifth place, and so even if we do qualify from an English perspective, we now need to rely on results in the Norwegian and Lithuanian top flight. Maybe we can send a contingent to Lithuania, to influence things, aka Eric Cantona incident. I am now desperately in need of some Valium, or maybe just another cigarette

Once in the ground, it was pleasing to find out, that Swansea had taken the sort of step, that is generally unknown in the Premier League. As the wind was blowing the rain directly into the Palace contingent, and specifically onto the first few rows that had been designated for `families,` i.e. sitters, the stewards had made a decision to dispense with the advertised seating plan, and allow people to sit where they liked. In addition, they made the sterile section, between home and away supporters available, instead of the wet front rows. Consequently, I was able to find a seat near DorkingEagle and his family, who can normally be guaranteed to have researched the best location. I was also able to locate my brother and his family, and they found a seat behind us. The front row above any gangway is pretty much always a great seat, and today was no exception. Once again, it was noticeable how when left to their own devices, fans will naturally gravitate to their preferred location, both standers and sitters, can then be easily and satisfactorily accommodated.

Despite the concerns about the atmosphere created if people sit, once again Palace were in good voice.

Of all the grounds, that I have been to so far this season, the Liberty is my favourite. The middle walkway gives the illusion of a two-tier stand, whilst keeping it tight and atmospheric. The disabled fans can also stay directly within our section, and are not shuffled off to a small corner, or mixed in with the opposition. I know that it is small, by Premier League standards, but I hope that if we do eventually redevelop Selhurst, or even build a new ground, this is the type of model we follow.

Still out of the relegation places coming into March, can we really pull this off?

Marks Match Report

The definitive game of two halves yesterday as a fighting second half performance from Palace dragged a point from what seemed an inevitable Swansea win in wet South Wales, and for the first time we viewed the template of Pulis's Stoke tactics overlaid on a Palace team: high tempo, pressing hard on the halfway line, and early direct delivery to the strikers or wingers. I doubt the Palace team would be able to play this type of game for a whole 90 minutes at this stage in Pulis's reign, but would love to see the same pace and attacking intent deployed at home some time.

Palace lined up in a strict 4-5-1 formation: Jedinak, KG & Ledley formed a flat middle three flanked by Bolasie on the left & Ince on the right; there was no-one in the hole which left Chamakh isolated up front. Actually he would have been lonely anyway as the first half was the perfect example of the importance in maintaining possession. It was almost a masochist's dream as Swansea's football was both beautiful & foreboding to withhold, their short passing & movement off the ball repeated from their display at Selhurst earlier this season, without a doubt the best footballing team I've seen this year. After Palace lost 9-0 at Anfield the old Eagle Eye ran a story about Steve Coppell replacing the entire outfield 10 with dustbins as they possessed far greater mobility. Here Swansea just passed the ball around our static midfield & defence, the De Guzman goal being the zenith when an unusually long pass sparked a move that saw Palace's centre completely scythed apart, the scorer finding himself clear in front of Speroni for a simple finish. We were particularly vulnerable down both flanks, with Routledge keeping Ward honest on the right while the left side was sliced & diced by the excellent Dyer with Ben Davies in support.

In contrast Palace's football was lumpen and matched the leaden skies. There were a couple of neat flicks from Ince but little else, while Bolasie appeared to be the only Palace player with the ability to make things happen on his own, but wasted an early chance set up by Parr with a cross that was over hit by about 20 yards. Yannick aside everyone else was moving in treacle, with a soft Chamakh header being the only minor threat posed to Vorm's goal. Too often the ball was given back cheaply to Swansea and the pass & move cycle renewed afresh, while we conceded plenty of free kicks in dangerous areas. The only question seemed to be how many they would score, but through a combination of good luck and desperate defending Palace somehow limited it to one; it would have been two if another fine move that unhinged our left side had been finished from 6 yards out by Bony, instead Julian produced one of his reaction close range saves to keep us in the game. Palace's woes increased when Chamakh limped off to be replaced by Cameron Jerome and Pulis, sensing we needed a little more threat up front, pushed Ince into the hole, moved Ledley to the left side of midfield & switched Bolasie to the right wing, but it made little difference. With the exception of the fore-mentioned Bolasie & the ever-dependable Speroni the rest of the team were immobile obstacles before the Swans' play. How does one threaten an equaliser without the ball?

The skies at half-time turned a most threatening greyish brown with a hint of maroon; given the already torrential rain we wondered what storm was going to strike. It was obvious that Palace had to make a change before the match was irrevocably lost, and Murray appeared at the start for Ince whose involvement had been marginal, except for providing a non-Cardiff opportunity for the locals to abuse. Switching to a 4-4-2 with two holding midfielders, two wide men & a couple of reasonable hefty strikers, this was old school Pulis: the ball was going to be sent long and the forecast matched the skies - it was not going to be pretty. The midfield line, which had been deep as usual, was pushed up to the halfway line, and the tempo of the game increased notable. It was a gamble – we would either batter our way back into the match or get cut to ribbons on the counter as Swansea exploited the space behind the midfield, but a change was definitely needed before we subsided to a limp defeat. How often Jerome & Murray have played together in practice is questionable and it took them some time to strike up any sort of partnership, but given that Palace's midfield – with the notable exception of Bolasie – was still incapable of making a difference that didn't seem to matter. Swansea appeared content to sit on their laurels, time wasting from a long way out (pot & kettle here!), withdrawing the dangerous Bony – perhaps Pulis was looking to capitalise on tiredness following their Neapolitan sojourn on Thursday spiced by a wet pitch?

While Murray was proving adept at winning & holding up
the ball the real threat came down the right with
Bolasie, who did to Swansea what they had inflicted
upon Jonny Parr, ripping apart Angel Rangel on several
occasions, but too often his crossing was poor or luck
continued to desert us. There were few chances, a half-
hit clever volley from Murray and a looping header from
Jerome that both dropped easily into Vorm's hands.

Pulis had one final card to play, Withdrawing Parr for
Jerome Thomas to push up on the left with Ledley
dropping into the full back position. With Swansea
withdrawing the quietly impressive central defender
Williams after what looked a blow to the mouth but was
later reported to be illness, Palace started to claw
their way back. Jerome & Murray started to look like
they had not just been introduced while KG broke out of
the midfield torpor with some strong challenges and
runs. In the end it was Murray who fashioned the
equaliser on his own, chasing a lost cause and inducing
panic in Swansea's defence, somehow robbing Vorm of the
ball before being brought down by Chico Flores. With
Mike Dean 40+ yards back I expected a non-decision or
even a foul awarded against Murray (not because it was,
but that's the usual outcome) but the referee awarded a
penalty; his linesman was no help whether the foul was
inside the box or not, but we did have the delightful
sight of the loathed Flores receiving a late
comeuppance in a red card – Murray is now on Andy
Carroll's Christmas card list. The penalty was
emphatically put away in the top right corner by Glenn,
the first of hopefully many Premier League goals.

There was still around 10 minutes for Palace to strike
down the 10 men. Murray has a shot blocked for a corner
before Bolasie, working hard to recover a lost ball,
again found himself reaching the goal line, and his
cross fell perfectly for Thomas on the edge of the box
with the Swansea defence wrong-footed. What induced the
winger to throw himself in an obvious dive instead of
taking the easier option of shooting? Lack of
confidence? Lack of match practice? Whatever it was
Pulis is right to stamp down on it, not only from a
moral perspective but also for blowing a great chance
to grab two more points; at least Dean got this
decision perfectly right. There was just time for
Bolasie to rampage in from the right and send a shot
just over before Palace players & fans could celebrate

a point gained that seemed impossible only an hour
earlier. Kudos to the manager for changing the
formation and style of play.

Speroni - 7
Ward - 5
Parr - 4
Delaney - 6
Dann - 5
Jedinak - 5
Dikgacoi - 6
Ledley - 5
Bolasie - 7
Ince - 4
Chamakh - 5
Jerome - 6
Murray - 7
Thomas - 4

Southampton Home Saturday 8th March 3pm

I have recently taken to going into work, on the morning of a home match. Partly because I am trying to implement some new systems, which are leaving me behind with my own work, and more relevantly, I am finding that a Saturday morning, just drags so much. In my younger days I could lie in, but perhaps it is a sign of age that recently, whatever the day, I wake up at 6am. This is great for next week's trip to Sunderland, but irritating when you have to pace around the house, waiting for 1.45pm. I can't even head off early and hit the Red and Blue bar, because I have to drive Dad, so I might as well go into work. Although we have worked our way up the division, the next three games look on paper to be difficult, even if you consider the Macems league position. As a result, today seems very important, but I admit to being both nervous, and at the same time, a little nonplussed. Surprising as it might seem, I have no particular dislike for Southampton, even though they were the first football team to make me cry,(Stamford Bridge, 1976.) I am also quite impressed with what they have achieved this season, and would like them to shake up the European qualification. I just hope that it doesn't include today.

There were lots of little bits in the programme today, about the positive and negative press that we have received, after the Man U game, and the Liverpool Flares thread on the BBS has taken on a whole new lease of life. The BBS can be quite an irrational and at times unpleasant place, and it was therefore nice, that the Chairman and others were able to place some balance to the arguments. Unfortunately, there wasn't a great deal of balance to the resulting game. Even though there was only one goal in it, we were pretty much outplayed, and it was a lot less entertaining, than reading grown men row, on the pages of the internet. Let's hope next week's long trip to Sunderland, is a bit more entertaining.

Mark's match report

Palace's limitations were show up this afternoon in a dismal home defeat that featured one shot on target in the whole game, and – Jedi's risible free kick aside – not one effort on gaol at all in the second half, when Boruc could have taken a half day holiday for all the work he had to do. The manner of the winning goal was wholly in nature with the rest of the performance, coming from our corner and featuring a nightmare contribution from Jason Puncheon. Southampton had some decent footballers but hardly set the match alight, Julian being almost as unemployed as his opposite number.

195

There were three changes to the Palace XI: Moxey replaced Parr at left back; Puncheon returned against his old team on the right wing, with Bolasie switching to the left and Ledley turned up in the hole in a 4-2-3-1 formation, which was the 4th different position he'd played in within 7 days; finally Murray started in the sole striker's role.

The first half was played in unfamiliar sunshine and was a fairly level affair, with barely an effort on goal by either side in the first 30 minutes. Southampton played some pretty possession football and probably had the edge but seldom forced Julian into work apart from picking out a couple of crosses; there was one excellent save from a close range header that turned out to be offside but that was it. Both Dann & Delaney made important interceptions with foot or head. Bolasie was again proving to be Palace's main threat but Puncheon on the other flank was having a terrible game, once having a clear run down the wing only to automatically check inside and stop a move. Jedinak looked well off the pace while KG seldom looked likely to create anything. Murray was doing well off scraps of possession but Ledley's best work was in defensive duties, leaving Glenn terribly isolated. Once again Palace conceded the ball too cheaply.

The goal came just when Palace had imposed a little pressure with a second corner. The ball was cleared to the halfway line where Puncheon appeared to have any danger covered. Somehow he managed to lay the ball back short for Rodriguez to pounce, perhaps thinking of the pass to Moxey. Julian nearly rescued the situation with a tackle 30 yards out but as both players went to ground Rodriguez found the ball at his feet and rolled the ball home. It was the sort of blunder schoolboys don't get away with. Puncheon's game, already in tatters, never recovered, and Palace were suddenly playing without any cohesion. Lambert's cross-shot beat Julian but rebounded from the post as Southampton pressed for the kill. Stoppage time saw two rarities in one moment: a Palace shot on goal and from Bolasie at that, smothered by Boruc. Southampton's reply saw Julian beat away a swerving effort with the last play of the half.

Surely changes needed to be made? Who would come on for the hapless Puncheon? There was a long list of potential candidates: Jerome, Thomas, Ince, Bannan, Gayle. Yet for unfathomable reasons Pulis, so quick to make interval changes last week, left the same team to dig themselves out of the hole, although KG did try to push forward more often. Bolasie almost forced an opening, suddenly breaking free to bear down on goal until being upended by Louvren. There was a defender roughly level with the pair so referee Webb was probably justified in not sending the defender off but it was a tight call; Jedinak took the free kick and nearly found the Whitehorse Lane executive boxes; we didn't know it but that was to be our only effort on goal for the rest of the game.

Palace put in a lot of effort but Puncheon's wretched game continued, while Ledley lacked the creative spark to help Murray, despite putting in hard work. Bolasie threatened and even managed some good crosses, but Louvren & Fonte dealt capably with these deliveries. Finally Ince came on the right for the hapless Puncheon, while Jerome replaced KG and pushed up alongside Murray, but it didn't improve matters much, Jerome finding himself offside on a regular basis. Thomas came on late for Bolasie and managed some dangerous deliveries but none that found a Palace head. We huffed & puffed but the Saints' brick house wasn't blown down. A chance missed to pull away from the bottom three, and Pulis's delay in changing the team around should be the subject of hearty debate. Do we need a more creative player like Bannan in a midfield three, or start with a second striker, at home?

Speroni - 6
Ward - 6
Moxey - 6
Dann - 7
Delaney - 6
Jedinak - 4
Dikgacoi - 4
Ledley - 6
Puncheon - 3
Bolasie - 7
Murray - 6
Ince - 5
Jerome - 5
Thomas - 6

Och Eye the Noo

6.15am start today, on the first leg of my north eastern adventure. I think most fans would consider, it is quite ridiculous, to have Palace away at Newcastle and Sunderland, two weeks running. The late notification of the two games, due to Sky not confirming the televised choices, made planning accommodation and travel very difficult for travelling supporters, and very expensive. I had decided some months ago, that as long as the Newcastle match wasn't moved to Monday, I would take the opportunity, to have a get away from it all break, in the Highlands of Scotland. I would travel up to Sunderland and back from Newcastle, on the supporters coach, and in between take the train. As a result, it was an even earlier start today, as I needed to confirm that I had everything I needed, and as of this moment in time, I am not sure if I have achieved this, only time will tell. I couldn't decide initially, whether to take my bike or my guitar, and in the end decided on neither. Even after this decision, it could hardly be said that I was travelling light. Despite the added legroom, created by Mandy`s wheelchair, I was still glad of the coaches boot. The trip itself up to Sunderland, was uneventful. We got off on time, and had a short stop at Leicester Foss. Even after half a season, I have still not remembered that Costa express mocha, does not need extra Sugar once it has been correctly stirred. Even for my sweet tooth, the last mouthful or two are far too sickly and always end up in the bin, and have probably contributed to the previously mentioned, rotting teeth.

The line-up today, looked on the face of it, more adventurous than some recent weeks, although there is surprise in some quarters, that the manager seems to shuffle the same players around, rather than play players in their natural position. I was however pleased, that the services of our two summer loans signings, were deemed surplus to requirements, as I am still struggling to find any real affection for either. The Stadium of Light is very attractive and the facilities below stairs, so to speak, are some of the best I have experienced so far.

As I sit at Newcastle station tonight, reflecting on one of the most boring football encounters, that I have witnessed for a long time, I am pleased that I have made the trip worthwhile, by choosing to spend a week on my own on a Scottish Island, possibly not speaking to a soul. At this moment in time, this seems like the height of, adrenalin rushing excitement. Everything is relative after all. Two seasons ago, when Dougie Freedman, presided over some of the most boring football I had ever seen, I almost didn't renew my season ticket. I honestly felt that, if this was what we would have to watch, to stay in the Championship, I would happily be relegated. I am beginning to feel this again now. I know that some people, will be happy travelling back to London with a further point in the bag, against fellow relegation rivals. Such is the financial incentive to be in the Premier League, that I can see why this may be attractive. If the club can reinvest the money, to secure a new or improved ground, and secure our financial future, I can live with this. However, it does feel a little like selling your soul to the devil. Football is predominantly about scoring goals, to do that you need to shoot, or at least get close enough to the oppositions goal, that a ball blown by a freak gust of wind, might travel into their goal. Travelling from one end of the country to the other, to see neither of these occurrences, is not what draws me, to sit on coaches for hours at a time. Perhaps sitting alone on an Orkney beach for a week, will provide me with a new definition of excitement, and I can learn to accept survival football.

Marks Match Report

It was, according to Tony Pulis, a "must not lose" match yesterday; certainly it was a game neither side appeared equipped to win. While the swirling wind and a poor pitch hampered some of the play it cannot excuse the overall poverty of it. Palace departed the happier of the two teams, maintain their lead over Sunderland, but questions about the ability to score and the central midfield are starting to pile up: it has been over four & a half matches since we managed a goal that wasn't a penalty, and don't be fooled by the match stats as Mannone in the home goal didn't have anything other than comfortable saves to make.

The Palace line-up was interesting given that neither specialist left back made it into the XVI. Mariappa, who has barely been glimpsed under the new regime, came in at right back, with Ward switching to the left side. Ledley played on the left side of midfield but not in an advanced role; perhaps he was stationed there to help cut down the threat from Adam Johnson. Bolasie was in a more familiar advanced role on the right, while Ince switched to the hole behind Murray, the position where he had such an impact on his debut.

Palace hardly put a decent move together in the first 20 minutes with Sunderland seeing a lot of the ball in our half. Worryingly we gave away far too many cheap free kicks in areas where crosses could rain down into the box, especially with both full backs seeing yellow cards early on. The referee, while consistent in his cautioning of players, was less so in his decisions on what constituted a foul challenge, with both Bolasie & Murray seemingly cut down from behind on several occasions but not winning the free kick. Palace's midfield wasn't helping matters either, both KG & Jedinak frittering possession away cheaply with some awful short range passing. Sunderland's best early chance came when Jedinak & Mariappa somehow conspired to set up a Mackem chance that went across the goal; Sunderland were finding a lot of space behind Mariappa (a tactic United used at Old Trafford so long ago) and Bolasie was having to do an awful lot of diligently tracking back. Fortunately Sunderland's crossing was mostly below par, and on the odd occasion when they did find a forward the header was off-target, Julian having one early shot straight down his throat as the only save in the first half. Actually the best cross into Palace's box came from a wildly mis-hit volleyed clearance from Ince that ballooned to Borini at the far post only for an athletic volley to go well wide. Palace were also slow to pick up on the Black Cats' short corner routine.

Up front Palace hardly registered, not surprising given the dearth of creativity in the middle & the propensity for Jedi & KG to give the ball away. Ince was once again lightweight, easily knocked off the ball and lacking a bit of bite in the challenge; he spoiled one good break with a poor pass. Murray, isolated and not getting anything from the ref, was hardly in the game. When Palace did have a chance of imposing a little pressure from a set piece Bolasie took a quick free kick straight to the opposition. Towards the end of the half Palace did manage one decent passing move down the left only for Ledley to stub his tow when shooting from the edge of the box. The game was summed up when Palace's best chance came when Mannone slipped clearing under pressure only to find Ince's 30-yard effort comfortably returned to him.

Sunderland upped the tempo immediately after half-time with sub Altidore bringing a sharp save from Julian although an offside decision made it a moot point. He did better later on for real when turning aside another Altidore effort. In return Ince & Murray worked an opening for Bolasie down the right but the shot lacked power and was easily gathered by Mannone; Yannick soon returned the favour for Murray with a good cross but Glenn was unable to get a decent connection with his head. Sunderland lacked invention, with Johnson well shackled by Ward, and their best openings tended to come when Palace gave the ball away while moving forward: Jedinak, KG and (surprisingly) Dann all committed the grievous sin of gifting the opposition the ball, and Delaney gained a yellow card in breaking up one such break. As against Southampton we nearly conceded from our corner against a swift break.

Growing desperate right back Bardsley broke into our box onto to throw himself into a ridiculous dive after brushing against a defender. Sunderland nearly grabbed the points when yet another loose ball in midfield was seized upon and Borini escaped the defence in acres on the right, only for his shot to canon off the bar, then fire narrowly over seconds later. Their last real chance game through yet another Jedinak error, bailed out by Speroni's rapid advance from his line and solid header clear. By this time Palace had made changes: Jerome came on for a lacklustre Murray; Guédioura for the disappointing Ince; and Puncheon for Bolasie. This did pep up the attack and some late chances came, with Ledley putting a decent chance wide and Puncheon's shot on target but not making Mannone work. However the best chance fell to KG after good work from Guédioura and Jerome saw the ball drop to KG 10 yards out, only for his shot to sail past the far post. It would have been totally undeserved, but then neither side had the quality to break the stalemate.

Speroni - 7
Mariappa - 6
Ward - 7
Delaney - 6
Dann - 5
Jedinak - 4
Dikgacoi - 4
Ledley - 7
Bolasie - 6
Ince - 4
Murray - 5
Jerome - 6
Guédioura - 6
Puncheon - 6

Hearts V Dundee and Palace Get Everywhere

5000 years ago, on an Island off the North Coast of Scotland, a group of Islanders decided that they would drag some really big rocks, into a field, by a Lock, arrange them in a circle, and tip them on their ends. A bit like Premier League transfer deadline day, it all sounds and looks impressive, but serves no real purpose. I am sure that, if those individuals were around to explain their actions, they would disagree, but whatever their original purposes, they did give me a valuable Palace photo opportunity this week. The advantages of visiting The Orkneys in March, is that it is too cold, wet, and windy, for anybody else to bother, and you are pretty much on your own. This is not everybody's idea of a good time, but the opportunity to sit and think about stuff, was much needed. It also provided the chance to take lots of photographs, at least one of which I am hoping will become the front cover of my Poetry anthology, "Greetings cards with attitude" which is due out next month. The trouble with letting a football supporter loose with a camera, on a 5000-year-old monument, is that at some point the desire to wrap their scarf around it, and take a photo will just become too strong. The ability to do this uninterrupted by other people, with and without the self-timer option, was one of the main advantages of this isolation, and I took full advantage. My old school hand knitted scarf, is longer than the more modern equivalent, and could be secured without effort, round even the largest standing stones. I loved my time on Orkney, and the standing stones were a particular highlight. They reminded me of the Palace. Not as grand or as well visited as the better known Stones Circles, at places like Stonehenge, but partly for this reason, more enjoyable to visit. It is just a more individual experience, and I admit that I did also get a little irrationally emotional, whilst I was there.

Part one of the Orkney adventure is now over, and I find myself once again, heading in the direction of a Palace away match, only this time, I have started my journey about 700 miles away from Selhurst. I think that as a consequence, this will turn out to be the longest distance that I have travelled to a match, and certainly the longest travelling time. I was a bit disappointed that the Palace Co-chairman, didn't in the end send a private jet to pick me up, and I have instead been forced to spend a rather rocky one and a half hours on a ferry, followed by eight and a half hours on a train. The compensation is a far nicer view from the window, than the standard M1, M6 verge that I am used too. It is particularly ironic, but not entirely inconsistent with many other holidays, that the weather outside, looking along the Dornoch Firth is spectacular. In fact, the last time that I actually saw the sun, was on this same train going in the other direction.(The Orkneys, are not a great place for getting a tan, in March.) The reader who is not a follower of obscure Crystal Palace Bulletin board threads, might wonder why I would have expected The Chairman of a Premiership football club, to send a private jet to pick me up from Orkney, and fly me to Newcastle. Well answer is, I asked him. I'm pretty certain that he doesn't even have a jet, but I asked him anyway. It was a stupid, self-important request, that didn't deserve a reply. For fans of the majority of Premier League clubs, who are highly unlikely to get even close to conversing directly with their club's Chairman, this must seem even more so, but for Palace fans this communication is common place, and quite often results in this type of request. I must point out that on this occasion, my request was deliberately intended to be absurd, to emphasise a point to other Bulletin Board Posters. Rather absurdly, it did actually result in a personal response from Steve B. He obviously understood, the point that I was trying to make. Having arrived at the BBS relatively recently, I have watched with interest, the interactions between fans, and bemusement at some public interactions with the clubs owners. It has reminded me very much of the relationship between some MP's and the electorate, and in the week of the death of Tony Benn it is perhaps appropriate to raise this issue and I will do so after I have changed trains in Inverness.

This will be brief, if we want communications with politicians or senior club officials we have to be responsible, about what we do with that communications, or they will all end up saying nothing of any consequence. I would have done a better job of this analogue, but I have to confess, that travelling to the match, just got a whole lot better than normal, due to the arrival on the train of a Hen party. Now with all due respect to Mum, Caroline, Mandy, Liz et al who normally make up my travelling companions, I could quite happily travel in this company, every week, without complaint. In the circumstances and just to prove that, whilst there is some planning involve in this book, I am trying to adapt to situations that occur, I admit to having been distracted.

Their arrival on the train, also saved me from sitting next to a mother and daughter, who had travelled down on the same train from Thurso. At 8.40am, all seemed well, but by the time we got to Inverness, the mother was by all accounts incapable of even locating her bag. Now whilst I would predict that my current company, might well have drunk a similarly large amount of alcohol by Edinburgh, I doubt that they will look or sound quite so bad, afterwards. So excuse me if at this point I switch off and look at the scenery.

The last night of my Scottish adventure, was to be spent in Edinburgh and was the only night that I hadn't pre-booked. I had met a lady from Germany last Saturday, and she had persuaded me to try staying in a back packer's hostel. This seemed on the face of it, a nice cheap way to round of my trip and the chance to meet a few people, after the relative isolation of Stromness. The first few hours in the hostel, were nice even though I was the oldest person there. I met some Aussie and US Students, and taught them how to use the hostel record player. However, realistically they were never going to ask me to join them, when they went out in the evening, and I didn't really want to spend another evening on my own. Football is always great in this regard, even if you turn up at a match, knowing nobody, and having no real information about either team, for 2 hours you are not on your own. You can oogh and Argh, along with everybody else, and even occasionally strike up a conversation. As luck would have it, Hearts were playing

Dundee, in Edinburgh, and I headed off in search of Tannerdice. On the journey to the ground, I got talking to a family member of one of the players, and this gave me a little something to look out for. He was also able to, fill me in about the tribulations of the club, which were very much akin to our own troubles in 2010. By the time, I got off the bus, in the rain again, I was really quite keen that Hearts won. Despite, or perhaps because of, what were very poor conditions, and not much better playing standards, I thoroughly enjoyed my introduction to Scottish Premier League football.

One of the problems of watching football in the English Premier League, is that at times, the standard is just too good. I know that some people reading this, and looking at our league position, might laugh at this concept, but I do think it's true. The good strikers are snuffed out by the good defenders, and the midfields can be locked into battles, which neither side really wins. The fact that pundits on television, spend so much time analysing miniscule points of position and tactics, that I don't really understand, underlines this. Generally, if the ball is passed back to your centre back, he is going to control it and pass it forward to a teammate. He is not going to slip over, or turn and chip it over his own keeper, in a mistaken belief that the said keeper, is standing on the goal line ready to receive it. The technical abilities of the players are too predictable, and the playing conditions are too good. As I watched the match, I realised that what I missed, was the unpredictability, or at the very least the anticipation of unpredictability. That excitement every time a ball is passed to a keeper, or defender, that they might, just might make a complete and utter balls up, of whatever it was they were trying to do. Similarly, there was the excitement, when a player who is generally not great does something really good. It was just a lot of fun, what watching sport should be. As indicated the standard wasn't the best, but the match was competitive.

We Palace fans, have got a little up ourselves recently, about how good, noisy, and dedicated we are. Some of this is justified, but having just travelled down from Thurso to Edinburgh, I have to give a special mention to, the sizeable contingent of Dundee fans that did their best to create an atmosphere. There travelling, and those of fans from clubs such as Inverness and Aberdeen, would make our own journeys seem like a local Derby. Leaving the ground, I set out to find a bus back into the city centre, and asked a chap of about sixty, at the bus stop, the best bus. As you do, when you have barely spoken to anybody for a week, we got chatting, and decided to walk back towards town together. The walk turned into a drink, and the discovery that despite his strong Scottish accent, and roots, he had spent much time in the 1970's, living in Tooting, South London. More importantly, he was at that time, a regular at Selhurst Park. It was actually a real shame, when he had to disappear to catch the last train, back to just north of Glasgow. I was very grateful for the company, and slept well in my hostel bed, whilst the other occupants of my shared room, partied at some club or other in town.

Newcastle Away Match Day

On the morning of the match, unlike my fellow fans travelling up from South London, and leaving at 7am, I was able to enjoy a relaxed morning, although in honesty, not much of a lie in. Once awake, I was suddenly very conscious of the other nine occupants of the room, so I grabbed the clothes I had prepared last night, headed to the bathrooms and dressed. Unfamiliar with hostel protocol and facilities, I took the easy option of a trip to Starbucks, at about the same time the faithful were leaving Selhurst, so as not to wake anybody. Edinburgh is a beautiful city, and free from people, early on a Saturday morning, you have a real opportunity to take in the buildings and views.

Unfortunately, I am not yet mobiley webbed, and I wanted to check the BBS, so I settled for drinking in, rather than finding a park bench, overlooking the castle. Although I accept that I spend too much time on the BBS, on this occasion, I needed to find out specific important information. Where were people drinking before the game? When you don't habitually drink on away trips, it can be a slightly daunting prospect, and as I was going to be laden down with bags, I didn't want to be wandering around Tyneside, trying to attach myself to stray Eagles. I was a little surprised to find, one of the other supporter on the boards, who had been discussing good places to drink, was the Co-Chairman Steve Browett. (Him with the non-existent plane.) Not only would most other Chairman, be unlikely to drink in a pub before away games, even if they went, but it must be pretty unique, for one to not only do so, but also advertise where they will be. I decided to head to the Brodega, as well. This was not because, I am some kiss arse, look who I'm drinking with sort of bloke, but because I figured, if Steve was there, the place would be crammed with Palace fans, in general. With the decision made, road map printed and coffee drunk, I had a last wonder around Edinburgh, before heading back to the hostel, to collect my bags and make my way to Waverley Station.

I have travelled from strange places to Palace matches in the past. Getting on a country bus near Peterborough, at 7am in a dress suit including CPFC cummerbund and tails, got me particularly strange looks, on the morning of the 1990 Cup Final. However, despite this familiarity with obscure journeys, it is still always a pleasant surprise, that you are not the only one, approaching a match from a particular direction. It was therefore nice to see a splattering of red and blue, at the station and to celebrate; I brought a cheeky can of cider, for the train. The journey down was without incident, football scarves can normally ensure that you are either ignored, or can strike up a conversation. Today was the latter, which helped to pass the time. Once in Toon, and having found my bearings, I was safely in the pub by 11.30. This meant I could stash my bags, and start a chat with the early arrivals. OLI28 was there and another lad from Leeds, whose user ID on the BBS, I really should have remembered, but the cider had started to kick in. It was nice to put a couple of faces, to BBS usernames and the time past quickly, and the beer went down smoothly. Around half twelve, Steve arrived with a small group of friends. Although I had never met him before, my brother had once done so in a restaurant, and told me how friendly he was. What struck me most, was how relaxed he appeared. I can only assume that his appearance in pubs, up and down the country is so commonplace, that he is allowed to just go about his business, without the constant pestering that you might expect, if Ashton or Abramovic were to try it. This put me in a little dilemma, because I did want to introduce myself. He has been very helpful over the season, in attempting to sort out the ticket situation, and I just really wanted to say thanks. On the other hand, I didn't want to walk up to one of the club owners, and just interrupt his conversation. In the end, the opportunity came in a natural, hopefully non-intrusive way. Joe,from the chippy in Dagenham, who I know quite well, was sitting on the next table to Steve's group, and I was chatting to him, when Steve came passed,(I guess even football club owners, need to use the facilities after a few beers.) By jokily criticising Steve, for not sending me a private jet, to pick me from The Orkneys, I was apple to introduce myself. His response of, " yeah I'm Rubbish aren't I." hopefully indicated that he got the joke. I was able to go on and thank him generally, for his contribution to the club, and specifically with regards to tickets, without making a big issue of anything, before continuing my chat with Joe.

After I had confirmed with Caroline, by text, that the coach was making good progress, I left the pub and made my way to the ground. Unlike some new stadium, this is virtually in the city centre, so even with my bags and a skin full of cider, it wasn't too much of a struggle. I needed to meet up with the coach, to dump my bags, as I am sure that they would have contained at least one of the myriad of items, that you are no longer allowed to take into a football ground. In addition, if what I was hearing was correct, the climb up to the seats at St James, is enough of a challenge without the addition of a 40lb dead weight. (Although, I had been before, this was not since the new stand was built)

Caroline has a reputation on the coach, of not exactly being the best time keeper in the world, and it is a standard joke in our house that on the night before a game, she will inevitably phone to ask, what time the coach is leaving. Due to the fact that most of the regular travellers on the coach, arrive 30 minutes to 1hour early, it would be unfair to say that she is ever late, because she isn't. However, hopefully she will be the first to admit that she isn't always there, at the time she was aiming for. It was therefore not a great surprise that the, "5 minutes away." text that I received, wasn't entirely accurate. The coach eventually arrived at what was a good time for the supporters, but again required Charlie the steward to run at breakneck speed, round to the box office with the spare tickets, when he should really be stewarding the coach. It's not his fault, just the antiquated ticketing procedure, of Premiership tickets. I am sure that I will sound once more, like a stuck record, when I ask, "Why are they transported round the country, like something from the 1960's?" computers and the internet were invented some years ago. It is a bit like that time, at 10.55pm on transfer deadline day, when all the clubs in England, delve around in a cupboard to find a fax machine, that still works, while somebody at the F.A. sits in a plush office in Grosvenor place, thinking that all is rather quiet. Realising only later, that the fax machine has run out of paper, or Toner, or has just been unplugged from the wall. It is all rather outdated.

Anyway, bags safely stashed in the coach boot, I was able to get back to the business of the day, by having another beer or two. I had already been questioned by a text from Caroline, about how much had been drinking, which saved my Mum asking the same question. On previous occasions when this has happened, I just text back, "mewh, mewh, mewh." or something similarly dismissive, but today I was with only a degree of poetic licence, able to say, "Blame the Chairman."

Up in the gods, I met up with Louis, from my vets team and his son, it is always nice to catch up with him and talk Palace and Alleyn Old Boys. The addition of beer always being a bonus, and I was still firmly in holiday mode. It is occasions like this, that I fully understand the beauty of football. We talked tactics, team selection, and substitution strategy; flipping between Palace and Alleyn Old Boys Vets, in a seamless way. The nature of the game, is that it is pretty much the same, regardless of whether it is professionals on £100,000 per week, semi-professionals at Dulwich Hamlet, or old codgers who could once play a bit, turning up at the old boys club on a Sunday morning.

Our seats although a long way from the pitch, were not quite as bad as I had expected, and if I am honest the view was pretty good, even if it wold have been an idea, to take the binoculars out of my Orkney luggage. Although I am sure, some officious steward, would have said, they were a health and safety risk, or damaged the NUFC brand, or some other nonsensical reason to not allow them. That being said, there wasn't actually a great deal to watch, although we did try to attack a little more than last week, which in reality wasn't a difficult achievement. At half-time, well actually a little before half-time, the bladder isn't what it used to be, I headed back to the bar and secured another beer. The concourse areas at football grounds, during the course of matches, should be pretty empty, but it is interesting just how busy they can get. On days like today and last week, when there is so little excitement on the pitch, it is perhaps unsurprising that people might prefer another beer. I adopted the one out, one in principle and had another bottle, and a look out the window at the back of the stand, across Newcastle. There was after all, no wet paint in the concourse, that could have provided alternative entertainment.

One goal, and not a great many more shots, is not a great reward for a round trip of 1520 miles, or 1060 miles as the crow flies, to see two Premier League matches. I appreciate that many visitors to Old Trafford, will travel a comparable distance for their visit, (I couldn't resist that.) but I'm sure you get my point. I am also sure that tonight, on Match of the Day, Gary Lineker will at some point, extol the virtues of the 'most exciting league in the world'. If this is true, the other leagues must be very, very boring indeed. My mood has not been enhanced by the knowledge that the only goal of those two games, came in the 94th minute of the second game, and wasn't scored by us. 30 seconds prior to this goal, 2000 place fans were screaming at a little black dot, and explaining in very easily understandable words, that he was not our favourite person, and could not see a penalty, even if it was Ashley Young, and this made the situation worse. Add the knowledge that you have a 6 hour coach journey ahead, then you can just about sum up my mood, as I got back on the coach at 5pm. The game today did have some slightly more encouraging features, than last weeks at the Stadium of Light, but a lot of our fans won't see that. They will just see the score and think Sunderland was better than Newcastle, which it wasn't, except for that one little additional number, in the point's column.

As we pulled away from Newcastle, towards the angel of the North, and the familiar view of the English motorway network, a dawning reality started to hit me, or in fact 3. Firstly, after all the anticipation and our movement out of the relegation zone, we had a terrible run to come, and could still easily go down. Secondly, if we managed to avoid relegation, there was a serious possibility, that we might have to watch more of this dross football next season. However, the most pressing realisation was that Mum doesn't drive after dark anymore, and when we get back to Selhurst, I was supposed to be driving home. You can if you like, read this entry again and do your own calculations, but it was all a bit touch and go. Headphones on, cushion in place, I need to get some serious shuteye and hope my Liver, (or is it kidneys?) and a strong coffee at the stop, do their job while I sleep.

Marks Match Report

This may be the first match report this season where I ask you: "What the **** just happened there?" It was all my fault. With seconds left I mused how often Palace had let in late goals to the Toon at Selhurst. And while all around me were still on their feet abusing the referee & linesman for a penalty shout it took a few seconds for the crowd to part and there was Cissé, unmarked eight yards out, powering a header past hero Speroni. All our hard work gone in a flash and a game which deserved a point and could have given us three was lost.

Our eerie at St. James's Park was better than before, when the top corner of the stand might as well have been in Berwick for the size of the pitch. We were high but behind the goal & could at least tell our own players apart – well, most of the time, anyway; you'd think they'd put numbers on them to help me out... Expectations were low after last week's turgid match at Sunderland: Palace's starting XI mustered about 7 goals between them this season; while Newcastle hadn't scored a goal in the six league matches Rémy had missed.

Surely the mortgage was going on a 0-0 draw! As it
turned out the game was far more open than last week
and both sides stretched the other in attack.

Pulis kept the same 4-5-1 formation but dropped Murray
& Ince to the bench with Jerome starting up front and
Puncheon on the right, although he was to swap wings a
few times with Bolasie. Ledley played in a midfield
trio that was a lot more fluid & fluent with all three
making breaks forward, and their passing was far more
precise than has been the case over recent months. They
were also pressing high up the pitch denying the
opposition midfield space. Newcastle started with a
shot that was half blocked before being saved by
Speroni, but Palace soon came into the match. The work
rate of Jerome, Puncheon & Bolasie was outstanding, and
although Yannick soon shot over when there were perhaps
better options, he was causing Newcastle's right flank
problems. Puncheon worked a cross that Jerome headed
the way he was facing so missing by about 12 yards, but
the midfield was winning ball and breaking upfield.
Shots from Cissé & Sissoko were well saved by Julian,
who was having a strange half: his shot-saving was
superb, one close range block from Gouffran being
crucial but he put one kick yards out of play &
presented the Toon with another mis-hit; suffered a
moment's confusion with Delaney that led to much
histrionics; and towards the end of the half he almost
spilled the ball at the feet of Cissé. Delaney led one
excellent break upfield which didn't bring an immediate
advantage, but crosses weren't finding our own men,
with the exception of one corner that Dann somehow
missed with his head from 8 yards out. The last kick of
the half was a Newcastle free kick that went just over.

The second half continued the tempo of the first and
Palace created three good chances early on: Puncheon
shot wildly after a good move found him space at the
edge of the box; another good move saw KG played into
the box but his first touch was poor and his finish
smothered by Krul; and finally Bolasie fired in a shot
from the left that clipped the top of the bar. Jerome's
hard running was making a lot of difference. Perhaps
this little spell forced Carver to introduce Ben Arfa
on their right, and this may have led Pulis to withdraw
Bolasie for Bannan, with Ledley switching to left flank
to help close down the man who had already threatened
to unhinge the left side defence, with Cissé again

missing chances and Tioté also denied by Speroni; the block from Cissé when the defence was split was brilliant.

Sadly Palace's attacking options started to fade with the substitutions as the tiring Jerome & Puncheon were withdrawn for Murray and Guédioura. Murray didn't have the pace that Jerome used to chase balls played over the top; Bannan didn't do enough when on the ball; and Adlène didn't do enough off it. The midfield, which had pressed fairly high for much of the match, started to drop deep and allow Newcastle space to play in our half and they did it very well, looking to play to feet and either turn the defender or lay the ball back. One shot smashed against the bar (Julian may have got a touch) and the rebound was turned across the box for Ameobi (?) to fail to turn the ball in form a few yards out. As time ticked away Palace broke and there was a shout for a penalty as Murray tried to break between two defenders, the ball to me seeming to come off the defender's shoulder rather than arm. Unfortunately my view was blocked by the protesting supporters and suddenly Ben Arfa was in space on the left and our defence had parted; Cissé, who you would have bet on missing any chance, actually couldn't & forced it past Julian from close range. No idea who was beaten on the left or where the central defenders were – Cissé looked to have so much space that he was surely offside... wasn't he..? That was the natural & wrong reaction. The blow was terminal and all the hard work went unrewarded.

Speroni – 7
Ward –¬ 6
Mariappa – 6
Delaney – 6
Dann – 7
Jedinak – 7
Dikgacoi – 7
Ledley – 7
Puncheon – 6
Bolasie – 7
Jerome – 6
Bannan – 5
Murray – 5
Guédioura – 4

Scoring Goals for Palace John Terry

There is a popular concept I was taught from an early age, that you should never laugh at other people's misfortune, but I would argue, there are exceptions to every rule. Perhaps today is one.

The first thing that struck me in the programme today, was that Chelsea were top of the league, and we weren't bottom. At the beginning of the season, the former would not have been a surprise, but the latter might have been. Given that we have achieved just two point, from our last five games, and are in fact not even in the relegation places, then the surprise is multiplied. Of course, all this could easily change today. Despite our efforts at Stamford Bridge, they really are head and tails above us. If we can come out of it, without a major drubbing that saps the confidence, then we have a sporting chance of getting enough points, from the remaining games.

Of the articles in the programme, I actually read, all four today expressed views that I largely agreed with. Alex Warner in 'View from the upper', echoed my thoughts after the last two games, that he could just about put up with the style of football that we are playing, until the end of this year, as it serves a purpose, but he wouldn't want to watch it every week. The money if used wisely, can secure the clubs future, and that is more important than our own short-term enjoyment. Tony Pulis, expressed how ridiculous it was to have us travelling to Sunderland and Newcastle in consecutive weeks, and both he and our captain Jedi, expressed how fantastic our support was on those two long trips.

Kevin Day, as always, wrote a very funny article about trying to stay polite and calm, when visitors come to your door at 4.50pm, on a Saturday, just as your team have conceded a 94th minute goal. It is perhaps one of the reasons why I travel away. I would only be glued to the radio anyway otherwise, and the only people I have to speak to, in the horrible aftermath of a last minute defeat, are those that are feeling the same way as me. I do not have to make them tea, and although I try my best, I do not have to mind my language in quite the same way, as he was required to do. (His visitor was his father in law, who as well as being a Geordie, is also a vicar)

The final article that impressed me, as it always does was, "The view from the boardroom." as well, as what is obviously a marketing necessity, to mention next year's season tickets, Steve Browett also mention our away support. Now I am sure that many other owners, if they actually wrote in the club programme, would wax lyrically about fans loyalty, amazing support, sacrifice and the whole remit of normal sanctimonious crap. However, I doubt that they would mention the kind of detail that Steve B does, making it abundantly clear that he understands the problems we face, and is actively trying to do something about it. I spoke at length last week, about meeting Steve in the pub in Newcastle, which itself says a lot about his genuine fan credentials. In his article today, he particularly mentioned, not only ticket prices, but also location of away sections, and his own desire for the introduction of safe standing. He has mentioned the whole topic of the location of away sections, at grounds, and particularly about Newcastle, on the BBS before and this resulted in him turning down, that offer of a price match from NUFC. It would have superficially been very easy to take this offer, and the good publicity that it would have created, but he knew that it would not be fair, to match the price of pitch side tickets at Selhurst, with those miles away from the action at St James's. Principles are not something that I feel a lot of club Chairman have. We are very lucky and I hope that the fans realise this, and our four owners are rewarded appropriately.

The match itself, despite my reservations expressed last week, was what does sometimes, make the league great to watch. However, it is more about what makes football fun to watch, at whatever level you watch it. I have played a bit of rugby in my youth, and generally the team with the most talent wins. You can minimise the losses, but if the opposition is better than you are, it is very difficult to do anything about it. There is something about football, which enables a well-organised and determined side, to cancel out the ability of, even a team assembled at the cost of a small African country. On these occasions, the vast majority of the football world, smiles and metaphorically punches the air. It is a collective two fingers up to the Oligarchs, who think they can buy our game. When this happens, due to an own goal by John Terry, that smile is just a bit wider. Please add to my expanding, "I don't like very much list," John Terry. There's no great logic to this new entry, either. He is a passionate sort of chap, who was captain of my country, with very limited ability.(IMHO) All of these traits, should make him near the top of the, "Players I quite admire" list, but unlike Frank Lampard, who I do quite like, he isn't. This has nothing much to do with the recent Anton Ferdinand situation, because I didn't like him before, but this has hardly dropped him down the table either. As a result, I think that this scrappy deflected goal, is up there with Geoff Thomas's quarterfinal scramble at Cambridge, as one of my all-time favourite, rubbish goals.

The almost immediate lyrical rewriting of the Beatles, Let it be, normally reserved for our thirty goal striker Glen Murray, made this game one of my favourites, for a very long time. The three points against the league leaders, that gave us a 5-point cushion from the relegation zone, was almost an added bonus.

John Terry, John Terry,
John Terry, John Terry,
Scoring goals for Palace,
John Terry.

And just in case anybody has forgotten, I work five minutes' walk from Stamford Bridge. Every time there is an evening match, I pass thousands of South Londoners, getting on the tube at Wimbledon, to cross the Thames, into the big corporate world of Chelski. Their new blue shirts, crisp as if they have just come out of the packet, and I grimace. Do you think that I wore my Palace jacket, scarf and tie to work all week? You bet your arse I did.

Marks Match Report

These are the days where you get paid back for rainy nights on wet terraces or 600-mile round trips or the threat of relegation or – worse – administration & extinction. The old stadium rocked, answering an early Blues' enquiry about our "famous atmosphere." The stats may tell a story of Chelsea dominance but out on the pitch there was a different story. A gracious (by his standards) Jose Mourinho credited both Palace's team & supporters but also wrote down what he felt his team lacked: Balls. Well, there were plenty with some to spare in Palace colours. When the team was announced with no changes to the starting XI from last week, I thought the bus would be well & truly parked. However Palace had 14 shots to our opponents' 21 and I was underwhelmed by Chelsea's performance, as they didn't start to look dangerous until we pulled the wagons back on the edge of our box; even then the chances made of the break hinted that the bus handbrake had slipped.

The first half took some time to get going, with Palace initially tentative and Chelsea seeing a lot of the ball. Palace seemed to be dropping too deep again, and while the threats of Hazard & Schürrle on the flanks promised much, most of the Chelsea play came when Luiz or Lampard brought the ball forward before being enveloped in a wall of red & blue shirts. There were a couple of scares particularly when Schürrle nearly forced home a cross from close range only to be denied by a great block from Ward. Chelsea seemed most dangerous from corners and – Pulis will love this – long throws but most deliveries were dealt with by the outstanding Delaney and his defence or by Julian's safe hands. The exception saw Torres fail to turn fast enough and the chance was blocked. Luiz tried some shots from distance that were usually missing by the length of that bus.

Chelsea, lacking invention and pace, didn't actually force a save from Speroni in the first half that I can recall, and the Palace players' confidence levels rose visibly. Mariappa, possibly our best player in the first half, often popped up in attacking positions, occasionally linking well with Puncheon and KG, and from one Jerome was flattened for what looked an obvious penalty offence, but Mr. Mason, so quick to book our two wingers for their first offences, ignored

213

the appeal. Bolasie and the hard working Jerome started
to stretch the defence on our left; Yannick had already
dragged a shot wide before, in quick succession, he was
denied by an excellent tackle inside the box, then just
failed to control a driven cross from Puncheon at the
far post. Although Jedinak disappointed with two shots
that dribbled through to Cech, the home players left at
half-time with a degree of satisfaction & hope.

The second half almost started disastrously as, from
yet another corner, the ball dropped to John Terry's
feet 12 yards out, only for him to mis-kick and spoil
the chance. It was not to be his day as Palace attacked
and Ward sent in a terrific cross from the left, a
flashing glancing header leaving Cech motionless. We
all assumed it was Ledley but apparently it was the
Hero / Leader / Legend who beat his own keeper. Nice of
him to resolve our goal scoring problems for us!

The rest of the match stretched into an eternity as
Palace were happy to drop deep and hit a defence that
lacked pace on the break. The main performer was Jerome
who was truly indefatigable but Puncheon, who had a
relatively poor first half, improved and there was some
great interplay. Yet giving Chelsea space to play
around our box invited danger, and it took a full
length save from Speroni to deny Hazard a prompt
equaliser. Palace's response was a great break led by
Jerome that ended with Puncheon placing a cross shot
just wide. It was almost a boxing match: Chelsea
countered with a Terry header that clipped the bar.

The problem for Palace was down the left side of our
defence. Ward and Bolasie, who had been diligent in
tracking back, were constantly being outnumbered &
outflanked, and only some desperate defending, with
Delaney again prominent, kept them at bay. Pulis made a
switch pushing Ledley, who had been the midfielder who
should have been helping out in the first place, out
wide, sacrificing Bolasie, and introducing O'Keefe,
whose first few touches of the ball conceded possession
far too cheaply. Speroni again rescued Palace by saving
what seemed an inevitable goal with a save from Oscar
(?), then Palace countered with a fine run by Jedinak
setting Jerome in on goal, only for his shot to strike
the foot of the near post and rebound to safety. As
Chelsea pushed and the Whitehorse Lane End held its
breath, Palace continued to strike on the counter:

214

Ledley twice put shots across the goal, while Cech
saved from Puncheon and then tipped an O'Keefe effort
over. Chelsea's last good chance came from a suicidal
back pass from O'Keefe; Torres, only 8 yards out, found
Speroni closing him down and his ineffectual lob
dropped behind the net. Although Chelsea pushed and
intimidated ball boys, Speroni and the entire Palace
team denied them another glimpse of a chance, and the
standing ovation at the end was thoroughly well
deserved.

One aside – the ball seemed to me strangely light
today, highlighted by Speroni's kicks that were caught
by the wind late on, but it did seem to be zipping all
over the place and both sides played plenty of well
over hit passes & crosses. I am on my own in thinking
this? (Can Mourinho work this into his post-game
observations?)

Speroni – 8
Ward – 8
Mariappa – 8
Delaney – 8
Dann – 7
Jedinak – 7
Dikgacoi – 7
Ledley – 7
Puncheon – 6
Bolasie – 7
Jerome – 8
O'Keefe – 5
Murray – 6
Parr – 6

Escapism

For some people, going to a football matches is an escape, a chance to let your hair down, and forget the trials and tribulations, of everyday mundane lives. 30 years ago, whilst doing one of the first Sports Studies degrees at what is now the University College of Chichester,(Some people just don't think things through do they.) I did quite a lot of studying about football hooligans. Much of the research on the phenomenon, as I recall it now, indicated that it was escapism, which resulted in the large majority of the running about, shouting, and posturing. For some, this escapism seems to become its own trap, as the escape gradually becomes the norm, until it's so intertwined with your life that it is difficult to see the separation. When the season started, I was going to choose which games I went to, but it becomes so habit forming, it is difficult not to go. When there is no football, what do you do at a weekend? It is difficult to know at exactly which point it happens, it is such a gradual absorption. Those fans of a certain generation, may remember the film about the undercover football cops, and the scene in the toilets at the police annual dinner. Supporting a football team can become a bit like that. One day you have a normal hobby, and the next it has become, just a little obsessive. There are however, some events that kick you back into the reality that; it's only a game. One such event happened this week. My Dad, the chief reason I am a Palace fan, a sports fan, and a vaguely decent human being, had a heart attack. At 85, he is no spring chicken, but even so, it caught the whole family out. Mum, who has been married to Dad, (and I assume vice versa,) for 55 years, called me at work and I set out to get to the hospital, as soon as possible. At the time of the Cardiff game, he was still an in-patient in Mayday hospital, and although he would definitely prefer to be at home, he is being well looked after, but it is a worry for us all. Now there is always a dilemma in these situations. Should we go to the game? When your Dad, has just had a heart attack, this might seem like a slightly callous consideration, but as I said, football can take over your thought processes. As it was largely his responsibility, that I turn into a Palace fan, I know he would understand. If Dad had been released on Friday, then the problem might have been greater, but the good old NHS, had at least assured that he was in safe hands. Mum, was understandably reticent, and felt that she should stay at home, undertaking visiting duties, while I went to Cardiff. Despite Dads insistence, we should both go, I am pretty sure that Mum, fully intended to put Dad first. Cue the wider family. My sister drove up from Bournemouth, so Mum and I were free to do, what we do every Saturday. The second dilemma, was how best to get Dad to hear the match. Unlike me, Dad is definitely not a techie. A radio he can use, and if I set up Palace Player before I leave, he can turn the computer speaker on. But that's about it. Mobile internet! Well that's just not going to happen. On Friday night, I dropped off a couple of old radios, and a set of headphones, as well as my Kindle fire, just in case Palace Player could be cajoled into action, from his hospital bed. I did joke with him that if it was last season, I would be more wary about giving him access to the commentary, but given recent showings, I thought that he was safe, as the likelihood of too much excitement, was very slim indeed. In the event, all my attempts to provide access to commentary were wasted, as no radio signal could be received in his ward. Another method was needed, to provide the necessary result feed. Step in the family again. My brother Ian, sat at home listening to the commentary, whilst apparently Ironing…, relaying any important messages to my sister, by text. She was then able, to keep Dad up to date. To make him feel more like he was actually at a Premiership match, I do recall that there were signs around the ward, telling people not to use mobile phones. This is obviously one of ~~Mayday Hospitals~~ Croydon University Hospital's, (its not just Hull City, that likes to rebrand,) unenforced ground regulations. Unlike guests sitting on the bed, which is a bit like E-cigarettes at Old Trafford, strictly not allowed.

 For me and particularly Mum, it was a nice break from the difficulties of the last few days. The fact that the boys secured an easy victory, was a much needed boost, and in its own way I'm sure it will aid Dads recovery.

 I have read since the match that our own Wilf, guesting for the Red and blue Birds, was rubbish. One Cardiff fan came onto the BBS to post.

 "please, please take Zaha off us, his attitude is disgusting, he doesn't know when to pass, his final ball is terrible, and only tries when he wants, can't count the amount of times he gives it away each game, he barely starts anyway, and I want that to continue"

 The funny thing is that I thought he was their best player, which either suggests that I really don't know what I am talking about,(I appreciate this is quite possible.) or that the rest of the Cardiff team show the same attributes as described above, but in greater abundance. One of the things with Wilf, is that we know what he is capable of, so I am sure that is why I was so jumpy every time he got the ball. I know he could hurt us. He also got a lot of stick from Cardiff fans for applauding us at a corner. I am not sure what some supporters expect sometimes. It was the first time that he has played against the team he first joined when he was a young boy. We sang his name and he clapped back. It must have been nice for him to be appreciated after half a season at Moan U, and then being farmed out to a team whose fans never liked him. At the same time, it is being rumoured that Olly Gunner Schoolboy, had insisted that if he scored, he should celebrate. I have never been a great believer, in players not celebrating against their old teams, most of the time it seems almost as choreographed as some of the over the top badge kissing. However, Surely the decision to celebrate or not to celebrate, comes from within the player. No manager can tell you to celebrate something you don't want too, it is a bit of a contradiction.

Marks Match Report

```
A key game that saw a determined and — as almost always
now — highly organised Palace deal a demoralising
```

defeat to a Cardiff team that ended an incoherent rabble. Julian had one serious save to make in a game that was accepted as "must win" by Solskjær. We reckoned last time Palace scored three away in the top flight was Hillsborough in 1997 (Herman Hreidarsson @ 67/1 paid for the entire trip!) and the last three goal winning margin away from home at this exalted level was a now frankly unbelievable 4-1 win at Coventry under the football genius Alan Smith topped by a Ricky Newman screamer. The Palace support was at its peak in Wales in concert with the team. Day was topped out when the aggressive driver who felt 85 mph was dawdling was last seen explaining his actions to the coppers some 15 miles later down the M4!

Palace unsurprisingly fielded an unchanged starting XI in a 4-5-1 formation while Cardiff chose a very attacking team, and for those of us plagued by nightmares of Wilf Zaha being the decisive factor, the homesick winger started for the mis-named Bluebirds. Palace actually started the brighter, with a well-worked deep corner routine finding KG in acres of space beyond the far post but the finish was poor. Palace made a lot of space down the right where Mariappa was prominent in supporting Puncheon, and the latter had a couple of shots on target that were dealt with easily by Marshall. On the left Bolasie looked dangerous but seldom delivered, lacking close support from Ward for reasons that were obvious. Cardiff's problem was soon obvious: there was no team plan and they scarcely put together a decent move in the first 20 minutes, and with only one defensive midfielder they were open to the counter. Their only real threat was from Zaha down our left where he kept Ward pinned back and three times beat Joel on his weaker left foot to put in crosses from the goal line, but delivery wasn't great and nothing was made of the opportunities.

Cardiff gradually came into the game but were unable to break down a solid yellow wall of 9 men through the middle and had limited success down the flanks. When the crosses did come in most were dealt with by the defenders: in Delaney, Dann, Mariappa & Jedinak we had plenty of height to clear the first ball, and Speroni cleared up the few that got through. There was one header that saw Speroni make an untidy sprawling save on a greasy pitch; had we known that would be Cardiff's attacking high point we would have breathed easier for

the next hour. Instead Palace struck, good interplay
between Puncheon & Ledley saw the former shoot through
a defender's legs and past a stationary keeper. Cardiff
tried to respond but couldn't raise their game.

Second half started with Cardiff seeing a lot of ball
and territory but running into an unyielding defensive
line. Zaha, who in the first half had applauded the
Palace fans who sang lustily about his wish to return
home, was withdrawn for Noone, and left as the home
fans were reminded that he was too good for them; he
had faded after a good start and had been an
increasingly peripheral influence. Meanwhile Chamakh
had returned to the team in pace of Bolasie and added
some nice touches in the hole, with Ledley moving to
the left flank. There was one moment's panic when
Speroni didn't reach a cross but Chamakh got the ball
clear; with another tall lad on the field in the
unlikely event Cardiff could actually get in position
to cross the ball their chances of getting on the end
of it were decreasing rapidly. In addition as they
pushed up there was a great deal of space for the ever-
willing Jerome, Chamakh & Puncheon to counter attack
into.

The game was really sealed by a second Palace goal:
Chamakh thumped in a header from a Puncheon free kick
which was well saved by Marshall, but the ball
rebounded onto Ledley's knee and, despite the keeper
having a second grab at it, the ball trickled over the
line. Joe's lack of celebration (I at first thought it
was Delaney) and some looks over at the linesman led to
some hesitation over whether the goal stood, but it
did, and with 20+ minutes left to play the home fans
started streaming out of the stadium. Cardiff on paper
still had a chance but the stuffing was completely
knocked out of both players and supporters, while
Palace rather insolently began playing keep ball. There
was no way the Bluebirds could batter their way through
the middle — Jedinak & KG were an outstanding shield —
and the more they huffed & puffed the greater the gaps
at the back. Puncheon's second & Palace's third was
just a boot into a dying victim, outstanding finish as
it was giving the keeper no chance; not quite a
beautiful as John Terry's effort last week but it'll
do. Team & fans celebrated the victory with a feeling
that safety was all but assured, but older hands were
recalling, with typical Palace pessimism, a celebratory

lap of honour at Selhurst in 1993 when 8 points clear
with 2 to play (unfortunately Oldham had 3 games
left...). It would still be a shock if Cardiff could
recover from this body blow.

Speroni - 7
Mariappa - 8
Ward - 7
Delaney - 7
Dann - 8
Jedinak - 8
Dikgacoi - 7
Ledley - 8
Bolasie - 6
Puncheon - 8
Jerome - 7
Chamakh - 7
Parr - 6
Murray - 6

Nothing is Ever Simple, at the Palace,

Nothing is ever simple at the Palace, even when you are sitting pretty, seven points out of the relegation zone with six games to go, and should be feeling pretty chuffed. If we win today, we could move as high as 12th, which to be honest, is a bit mind blowing. However, there is always a 'but'. The footballing but. We have known since February, that after today we have three away matches and two home matches. Six points will take us over forty points, so that is just two wins from three home matches. The little catch is that two of those three are against Man City and Liverpool. I know that we have just beaten Chelsea at home, but instead of encouraging me, in a way that worries me. Every team however bad, can normally get one shock result against the big teams in a season. If we are going to get the forty points, you normally need for survival in this league, we will need to win one of those two matches, or one of the away matches. If we lose today, the problem becomes a whole lot worse. Football fans up and down the country, will be very familiar with these statistical calculations, thanks to the wonderful world of computers; you use far less paper and mental arithmetic in working out all the options, than you used to. At least we no longer have the long division calculation of goal average, to bring in to the equation. What most fans don't have to add into the unknown's category, is the prospects of a point's deductions. It is well understood that teams going into administration, will lose ten points, but what if the club transgresses rules in another way, and have points deducted for another reason. That shouldn't be a worry, but as I said at the start, nothing in the world of Palace is ever simple.

It appears that Cardiff, are now trying to claim that the club via our Sporting Director, Ian Moody, made approaches to contacts at Cardiff, where he used to work before an acrimonious sacking, to try and find out the Cardiff team, in advance of last week's match. They have apparently sent a long dossier to the F.A. presumably to get us punished in some way. The accusation seems to centre on some obscure F.A. rule, which states that clubs should operate in good faith to each other. In a slightly ironic twist, it has been suggested that Ian Moody, was actually refused access to the Cardiff Directors box, which in my mind could be seen as a transgression of the same rule. There are many other complications to the situation, which centre on the involvement of an ex club hero, now managing at another club and a misdirected text messages. It is all a very messy situation, which has taken the gloss off, what was a very straightforward and important victory.

The F.A.'s history of dealing with various breaches of rules, is at the very best inconsistent, West Ham were not deducted points for the Tevez affair, and it now appears that Sunderland have also played an intelligible player, this season. They were also not deducted points. All logic would therefore suggest that a points deduction for asking a friend, "any idea who's playing Saturday?" would be quite ridiculous, but Palace have been on the receiving end of unfair F.A. decision previously, so we cannot be sure it won't happen again. (For those of you who are younger than about twenty, you will not know that Palace qualified for Europe in

1991, but our place was given to Liverpool at the last minute, despite the fact that everybody believed Liverpool were still banned from European competition.[xiii])

This all makes today's game, even more important than it otherwise was. The fact that many Palace fans, considered that the dossier was in fact the ranting's of a desperate, high trousered, lunatic; did result in some short-lived sarcastic humour from the Palace faithful. The same chant was the only time, that I can recall a Sporting Director being given his own song.

He spies when he wants,
He spies when he wants,
He's Ian Moody,
He spies when he wants.

I was therefore slightly nervous before the game, but after another victory, I was considerably happier.

You will see from the start time of today's game that it was again, not a 3pm kick off. I am normally the first to object, but I have no negative thoughts today whatsoever. The delayed kick off, was to coincide with a minutes silence for all those who died at Hillsboro, at the time the game was abandoned. Now I was not there, nor do I know directly, anybody who was, but I do remember exactly where I was. My ex and me, were in her parent's holiday cottage Wigtonshire, Scotland, and I had flicked on the TV before we went for a nice long walk, inevitably ending up at The Queens Arms. I sat transfixed by what I was seeing, and needless to say, the walk didn't happen for me, but did for her. It is not that my ex is uncaring or unfeeling, (Despite what some of my family might feel.) but she is not a football supporter, in fact she doesn't even like football, (OK, so it was pretty doomed from the start, I accept this now.) as a consequence, she just didn't get it. Unlike me, she didn't understand that it could have been me, or my brother, or my Dad, or my niece, or just friends who I had stood next to for my whole life, it had no resonance to her at all. As a result, she didn't understand how it affected me, to just watch the disaster that was unfolding in front of my eyes. I suppose it was like watching an earthquake, or a bomb blast in a foreign country as far as she was concerned. It was sad, she felt sorry for those affected, but it just didn't affect her, in the same way. We didn't have a row as such about it, because we didn't really row about anything, (I just normally did what I was expected to do.)but I am pretty sure she was annoyed that I didn't want to be the life and soul of the party.

Given everything that happened that day and over the next 25 years, remembering the ninety-six football supporters that went to a match, and never game home, is very important to me and I did get a little emotional at 3.07. Once the game began however, I still enjoyed the match, except for Howard Webb giving a penalty and then changing his mind, something he is not known for doing.

I think that it would therefore be appropriate at this point for you to do something similar, not change your mind about something at random, but put down this book for a minute and take a short moment to remember. If you are too young to do this, visit the Hillsboro families support group at http://WWW.HFSG.co.uk When you have done this, enjoy the last month of our incredible season.

Marks Match Report

It wasn't the best of games, with Palace working hard while Aston Villa lacked any real ambition, and the refereeing was of an even lower standard, but today could have seen Palace finally survive a season in the Premiership / Premier League. This, of course, is the Sky Sports age so we'll forget our previous seven seasons in the top flight that didn't end in relegation...

Palace, with Moody's phone possibly impounded and lacking intelligence on the Villains line-up, decided on an unchanged starting XI in the usual positions, and as the game started took up a deep & conservative stance. The possession stats for the first 15 minutes must be horribly lop-sided but Villa managed precisely nothing with all the ball, while on the rare occasions Palace gained possession their attacks had a far sharper threat. Puncheon had already tried an ambitious far post volley by the time KG departed with an injury, necessitating a swap as Chamakh went into the hole and Ledley moved alongside Jedinak in the centre. This move helped Palace's attacking ambitions but made life a little easier for Villa as Jedinak wasn't really at the races at this stage, and the visitors nearly seized an opening when, after a series of Villa corners, Clark's header was kicked clear of the far post by Jerome. After that the chances started to fall Palace's way, with Bolasie having a couple of decent efforts with boot & head while Chamakh's far post header was just wide. The best chance came when a very clever free kick routine played Bolasie in by the corner of the six-yard box; he appeared to miss his kick and slip over, but from my angle I couldn't tell if Holt had anything to do with that by nefarious means.

Having ended the first half on top it was strange to report that Palace barely started in the second half, with possession conceded far too easily, especially down the right with Mariappa, Puncheon and Jedinak guilty. Fortunately Villa lacked any cutting edge and didn't take advantage of this slow start. Jerome & Bolasie began causing problems, and when the latter fired in a shot Guzman's careless-looking save saw the ball drop to Jerome, but with the goal at his mercy he struck the underside of the bar and the ball bounced away to safety. Palace gradually took control, with

Jedinak improving and the reliable Ledley one of the better performers. The main threat continued to be from Bolasie down the left where he was well supported by Ward, and he created a couple of chances for himself. Puncheon too came back into the game and it looked like he might have engineered an opening when referee Webb looked to have awarded a penalty when a defender might have handled a Puncheon cross, only to change his mind after consulting with the (admittedly better placed) linesman. One can only assume Webb is our World Cup referee on the basis that at least h will be upsetting foreigners for the summer.

Fittingly it was the two wingers who combined for the only goal, Bolasie's cross from the goal line finding Puncheon around the far post; after taking what seemed like an age to control the ball, Jason's shot went back across Guzman and in off the far post. Bolasie departed not long after, replaced by Parr in what was a surprising decision given the pressure Yannick had exerted all game on Villa's right flank; perhaps the little limp was disappointment & diplomatic. Playing on the break Palace really should have made the game safe, the best chance came when Puncheon, with Murray & Parr free in the box, shot from a tight angle and hit the outside of the near post. That could have proven costly as Speroni, keeping commendably alert on another less than busy afternoon, made another fine save from a Weimann close range shot, diving and extending his arm to turn the ball behind. Palace started to defend deep and there was more than a hint of panic about some clearances as Villa finally found some gumption far too late in the game. It has to be said that Villa were particularly poor in both approach & execution most of the game, one cross field pass over hit by some 40 yards, and at the end their large & loud support gave their players some awful stick. But who cares!

Speroni – 7
Mariappa – 5
Ward – 7
Delaney –7
Dann – 8
Dikgacoi – 6
Jedinak – 6
Ledley – 7
Puncheon – 7
Bolasie- 8

Jerome - 6
Chamakh - 7
Murray - 6
Parr - 6

Everton Away Mark II

As well as my apparent dislike of all things Premier League, I am also ambivalent towards European football or at least the Champions League, filled as it is with very few champions of anything. Runners up, I could just about live with, but when you get teams finishing fourth in their league, in a competition with such a grandiose title, I think UEFA make themselves look a bit stupid. The Europa League, although I have previously described it as irrelevant, is in a way at least a bit more honest, until that is, you start giving the non-champions from the Champions League an entry, once they are knocked out of their own competition. It's a bit like seeding the F.A. Cup third round and if the big teams still can't get through, let them join in the F.A. trophy, all because some TV company, probably not even based in Europe, want to sell advertising space during the final. Well I'm sorry Mr TV mogul, sport isn't supposed to be like that. I guess that any euro-fanatics reading, will say well if you don't like it, just don't watch, it's obviously not as if Palace will be playing in either cup, in the immediate future. (The Fair Play title has now drifted away, possibly as our results improved, and I think the Latvian F.A. has placed an embargo, on any more cards in their league.) If it were only that simple; Firstly, (sad but true.) I live with my parents, and Dad without his weekly fix of live football, will watch just about any game, anywhere. This used to be just British games, but after making the mistake of raving about Barcelona, this now extends to European games as well. As the rent is very low, and he pays the virgin subscription, TV choice is pretty much his domain. Although I could in a desperate measure, hide the Sunday paper TV guide, and he would be pretty scuppered, as the concept of an on screen guide, has pretty much passed him by. The second and all together more relevant influence that the European football calendar has, is on the Premier League fixture programme. Now I do understand that with so many champions, in the Champion's League, and another few semi-champions, in the Europa League, it would be difficult to schedule Premier League games on the weeks where these games are planned. However, surely some common sense could come into things at some point. Several months ago, fifteen hundred Palace fans, set off to Goodison Park, and the events of that evening have already been relayed. What was not known at the time, was that very little opportunity for rescheduling of cancelled fixtures, is available. This is not because either Palace or Everton, have any involvement with either competition, but because UEFA rules prevent matches in the Premier League, in these weeks. Presumably, this is because Crystal Palace, pull in such phenomenal viewing and listening figures, on illegal streams and more conventional radio stations, that a dead rubber European fixture, would have to be played in an empty stadium, and with single figure viewing stats. Sorry Michel, but if you're that bothered about viewing figures, try having a few less match official, with their little black sticks and electronic number boards. They can then sit at home boosting the numbers. (Rescue remedy taken and breathing exercises completed, I shall continue) The result of all this, was that there were very few dates available, for this rearranged fixture and a marked lack of urgency on behalf of Everton, in choosing any of them. Given the circumstances surrounding the first match, a little consideration wouldn't have gone a miss. People had already spent time and money travelling to Liverpool once, and some attempt to allow planning would have been appreciated.

I was lucky, when the rearranged game was announced, I was sat in front of a computer and was able to pick up a train ticket to Liverpool, for just £20. This meant I didn't need to take a full day off work. The owners of the club, had already advised us that those who travelled to the first match by official coach, would get the second transport free as well. I could justify the money for a train there, to save a half days leave, but still travel back with the 'coach one ultras,' with enough sleep for work next day. Others were not so lucky, and it was quite sad how this lack of consideration by the TV companies, Everton and the Premier League, resulted in some of our own supporters turning on our owners. Some fans were making demands on them, which I found unreasonable. The argument put forward in some quarters, was that the club should pay for all supporters, to travel to the return fixture by coach, to compensate them for the costs that they incurred, first time around. Now I really don't consider that I am unreasonably sycophantic towards the owners. I hope I have been honest enough to be critical when I have seen fit, both in these pages, and on the same BBS, which was now in my mind, placing unreasonable expectations on the owners. However, on this occasion, I was prompted to point out certain things in defence of cpfc2010. They cannot I appreciate, always say exactly what they might think, even when they want to. There is a risk that this might alienate some fans, who perhaps they would personally be quite happy to alienate, and so I thought I would remind people of certain harsh realities, I hoped they would have said themselves, without the shackles of decorum. It appeared to me that every time they have tried to support the fans, by one scheme or another, some fans that miss out, openly criticise these attempts. They have been accused of elitism, and showing favouritism to this group or that group, when all they are trying to do, is to support and understand the fans, in ways that are reasonable but also practically possible. My major thrust was, I wouldn't blame them if they gave up trying to improve supporter's experiences, and behaved like other owners, by just take the easiest and most lucrative option. Although this was not the purpose, one notable 'positive rep[7]' was received, which at least made me think, I had struck a chord in at least some section of the CPFC family. It was particularly ironic that whilst some fans criticised our owners, for only offering free coach travel, to some of our supporters, Everton were refusing to refund the ticket price of anybody, who couldn't make the return fixture. This was not only for Palace fans, but also for their own supporters. Now that is something that fans should justifiably criticise and is I am not convinced actually legal. Fortunately for my two cousins, who were some of these unlucky few, who made it into Goodison originally, but couldn't make the reschedule date, cpfc2010 honoured Everton's moral obligation, and refunded them in full, even when they knew that they would be unable to reclaim the money from Everton.

---

[7] Positive and negative reputation marks can be given to other users on the BBS.

Everton Away Mark II Part B Subsection liivix

Although working on a home match day, has become quite a regular and productive occurrence, I am still not too comfortable about doing this for away midweek match. On a Saturday morning, I can come and go at work, pretty much as I please, but midweek with only a half day leave booked, I found I was looking at the watch all the time. Consequently, I didn't get a great deal done, and was glad to change into my evil sash, and get out the door. A quick tube journey got me to the station in plenty of time. To save money, I had booked on an early train from Euston via Crewe, but I was still rather surprised that there was an absence of Palace fans, at the Station. Travelling from Edinburgh to Newcastle seemed a more popular route to a Palace game, than London to Liverpool. Perhaps after all our protestations about being different, we have become like Moan U, with fans not actually travelling from our clubs home City. Alternatively, our fan base was not able to so effectively, navigate the mysteries of train ticket booking, which enabled me to pick up a £20 ticket, as opposed to a £60 ticket on the train I actually wanted to get. Whatever the reason, I was pretty much a solitary Eagle on the 1:40 pm, out of London. So instead of some friendly football banter I settled down to a bit of writing. Although, I was still greeted on the platform by a minibus of Met Police, presumably they had no under 21's matches today. With the majority of Palace fans, obviously travelling from a different station or at a different time, (They have form on this kind of intelligence gathering.) they must have been rather confused to see a loan fan, with a stupid trilby making his way to carriage E.

One of the consequences of being a bit of a techie, is that I am constantly trying to find different bits of it, which will help me write. Unfortunately, I also have two other traits that are a bit at odds with this. Firstly, I am also always keen to find a bargain. I like spending money, but I like to think that I have spent far less money accomplishing something, than other people would have done. Brands and trends are not my priority, but functionality is. This therefore makes me believe that although companies like apple, have spent billions of pounds developing integrated and syncopated IT, I don't need it. I can find something that will do the job, without selling out to the latest brands. The truth that I have now realised, is that some of these products are very popular, because they are good, reliable and convenient. Why have a phone, a camera, an EBook reader, an mp3 player, audio book reader and word processor, when you can have one product that does it all, and only needs one charger and one pocket to carry it in. As a result of this stubbornness, in the process of writing this book I have owned and used: 1 PDA, 1 cheap micro laptop (broken), 1 Asus tablet (broken.), 1 Kindle Fire, (No keyboard available and now broken.) a home PC, (Windows 7, then windows 8 and now windows 7 again.) along with numerous memory sticks. My current tech of choice is a Google Nexus, which sort of does what I want, has a keyboard attachment and hasn't died yet. Along with the cumulative cost of all these items, which now surpasses the device I actually wanted, it has also meant that I have not been as organised as I would have liked, in writing this diary. It is a particular irritant that the first entry that I made, and that acted as a catalyst to everything that followed, is lost somewhere. I know that when I wrote it, I fessed up to the fact that everything before that point, was from memory. I have even mentioned my starting point, in the introduction, so it definitely did exist, but I will now have to write it again from memory and I will admit now that I am going to pretend, I didn't lose it. All the changes in chronological order, are confusing enough for me and I'm the one writing. I have partially solved the problem of organisation, by a nifty little programme called Evernote, which does at least allow me to synchronize stuff, written on different devices. With my nexus now working OK, this shouldn't really be necessary, but just like a geek who still yearns after an Atari games console, when he has a PlayStation 4, I do still like to write on my old PDA from time to time. I can hold it in my hands, and it has a proper keyboard despite it being able to fit in my pocket. I can type lying in bed, in the bath, or in my hot tub. If it didn't still have, 2005 technology unpredictability, I would use it all the time, but it has crashed so many times, I think I have written two diaries. I have even tried to rewrite the lost Anfield trip on it once, only to have a complete melt down, when it crashed before I saved it. As I travel towards Liverpool again, this time via Crewe, I will have another go, but if the final published version had three blank pages, where the Liverpool away match should have been, at least you will know why.

My arrival and change of trains at Crewe, was similar to London with the absence of police, but with still only a small hand full of Eagles. Arriving in Liverpool at 4:10 it was still too early to go to The Ship and Mitre, so I headed down to the docks. I have only been into Liverpool itself twice. Once with a Liverpool supporter, after losing 5-0, so I try to forget that one, and once on the same Liverpool supporters' wife's hen night. (I had to choose hen or stag and I chose hen, it had its advantages at the time.) On both occasions it was dark, and I had therefore not fully appreciated what a varied and vibrant city Liverpool is. This is one of the drawbacks of official coach travel and out of town grounds; you travel up and down the country, but are still often oblivious to what places have to offer. Back in the distant past, we used to arrive in towns early and wander around places like Chesterfield, where we visited their crooked spire, you could really say you had been there.

Eventually, it was an acceptable time to hit the pub. Although I had researched that it was a real ale pub, I hadn't really appreciated what a wide range of beers they sold. A slightly "stupid southerner" moment ensued, as I asked the bar lady what cider they sold, only to be pointed in the direction of a book, containing a range of ciders and beers that would probably have bettered the annual Selhurst Park Beer Festival. I eventually settled for a cheeky strawberry based cider.

One of the nice things about travelling independently, and stopping for a drink in various pubs around the country, is having conversations with the locals as I did in Edinburgh. For some strange reason, I actually find it easier to strike up a conversation with fans of other clubs, than I do Palace fans. On reflection, I wonder if this is because I assume that Palace fans are in groups, who travel regularly together, and it is only me that is on my own. They wouldn't want me interrupting their obviously exciting, and in-joke filled conversation. On the other hand, maybe when talking to locals, I feel safe that I can chat any old nonsense. It doesn't matter, because I won't see them at next week's match, and have the embarrassment of them easing their way towards the exit. Whatever the reason, I got into a conversation with three locals in their late 50's. In London you get used to hearing lots of different ascents and accept that people from all around the country have moved here to work or study. It is perhaps a sign of my own unconscious prejudice that when I visit other cities, I half expect everybody to be from tup north, or wye eyeing me, all the time. The three men that I started speaking to, were from a range of places and supported a range of teams, from the big league. Being of a certain generation, they did understand my reservations about the Premier League as a whole. What they were slightly more surprised about, was my almost throw away comment that the Chairman will probably be in for a drink in a minute. By the time, SteveB did arrive, to back up my observation that our owners were proper fans. They appeared to have moved on to another venue, or were busily edging their way to the other end of the bar, unseen. Adjourning to the smoking area outside of the pub, (a bench on the street) I got talking to a few fans, one who I had seen regularly over many decades, but never spoken too, and one young lad who I had never noticed before. It was a nice atmosphere, and I was beginning to understand why at the original fixture, some had apparently been distinctly unbothered by the postponement, and had just stayed in situ till late in the evening, after the storms had died down. SteveB was also out on the road and talking to a small group. Despite my earlier encounter at Newcastle, I was still impressed with his relaxed demeanour, the suit was on, but the tie wasn't, and I could imagine a slightly reluctant fastening taking place, as he approached the director's box later that evening. I overheard him being asked, why his co-owner hadn't joined him for a pint in pub? It was generally agreed that SteveP and a yellow Ferrari, might not be the best fit for this real ale pub in the centre of Liverpool. SteveB went on to say that, he had tried it once, when a train was delayed in Preston on the way back from Blackpool, but it was unlikely to happen again. I tell this little anecdote not to ridicule SteveP, or even to suggest, what great circles I drink in before a game, but because it emphasises two points about football and Palace. Firstly, that two people, such as the two Steve's, with such different lifestyles and interests, can come together with the shared passion, which is football. The second point reinforces how lucky Palace supporters are, to have owners that understand the club and its fans, because they too are fans. Actually giving up their time, to travel to watch the team in the same way that we do. OK, one may drive there in a yellow Ferrari, and they may sit in the directors box, (Although I suspect SteveB does this out of duty, not choice.) but they do go. They can discuss what we can discuss, with the same passion and I would imagine on occasions, irrationality. Can anyone honestly imagine the Glazers, or Abramovich, changing trains in Preston after visiting Bloomfield Road, to watch a Championship match? As we approached kick off, I started to think about getting to the ground, and texted the coach to see how their journey was going. Caroline replied, with a message from my Mum, reminding me that I had to drive tonight and not to drink too much. My reply to Mum, via Caroline was "if she wanted to nag me, at the age of 48, she should learn to text and do it herself." After all, I had actually remembered today and was drinking Coke at the time, sometimes I feel

231

like I go to football with my Mum and not my mates. Oh yeah, now I remember, I do.

There was a steady stream of Taxis, collecting and dropping off at the pub, and I joined one of the other supporters by sharing a ride up to Goodison. He needed to get a ticket, and I wanted to dump my bag of tech in the coach. He was anxious to get to the ground early, but I reassured him that as the tickets were on the supporters coach, and it was still some distance away, there was no great rush. The queue at the box office seemed to be oblivious to this, and there were no signs or information, so fans trying to collect and buy tickets, queued, shuffled, and then wandered around a bit. By the time that the coach eventually arrived, about 7.30 PM, some fans must have been wondering if they were actually going to be able to get in, by kick off. I had spent the time, talking to a local Policeman, when I have had more time to think about what he said, I will write about it; along with the further recognition of the Hillsboro Victims that took place before the kick off.

Charlie made his customary run to the box office with a stack of tickets, and we settled into our seats. Goodison is in my opinion a fantastic, proper old school ground and I like it. However, badly we got beaten tonight, I was pretty sure the Palace faithful, under a low roof, were going to create a great atmosphere and I was going to enjoy myself.

Back in the year of the three lions on a shirt, and 30 years of hurt, my Dad, my brother, and me, had a season ticket at Wembley for the European championships. When England scored the fourth goal against the Dutch, my older brother turned to me and asked me to pinch him. Now as any younger sibling will tell you, the opportunity too, without fear of reprisals, inflict pain on an older brother, is an opportunity that is not to be passed up. I was born in 1966, so I know all about 30 years of hurt and Chinese burns and psychological torture. (I once woke in the night, shouting I can't afford it, I can't afford it, at the top of my voice, after a particularly intense game of Monopoly. I wonder if the four owners have ever had that experience after a particularly hectic transfer window.) So I admit that I did take him literally and proved to him that he was not in fact dreaming and England were beating Holland 4-0. Eighteen years on and having woken in the night many times since, shouting the same thing, with my brother now the one to supply the loan and not the one to inflict the debt. I wished he and my Dad had both been with me again tonight, to see another incredulous football result. As it was, my Mum was there beside me instead, but it was a stranger who offered me a similar opportunity, to wake him from a dreamlike state. When the second Palace goal went in, he didn't offer the opportunity to inflict pain, but asked the following question. "Can somebody please tell me, which game I'm at, because I sure as hell ain't watching Palace." The joy, jubilation and shear irrationality of what we were watching, was what makes football so special. I hugged my Mum, I hugged strangers, and a huge bloke in the front row, kept hugging everybody. He accomplished this, whilst taking photos of himself, the stewards, the players and probably his seat. For those who had made the journey in the storms previously, it was I guess, just that bit sweeter. When the final whistle went, I think all the travelling fans knew that they had witnessed something, they would be able to tell their children and grandchildren, and to be quite frank, anybody who would listen, whilst not slinking along a bar towards the exit door. The fact that I would get home at three or four in the morning and have to get up for work at six was completely and utterly irrelevant. Palace who had been predicted to go down with the lowest points ever recorded, had won away at Everton, who themselves still harboured ambitions of the Premier League title. In doing so they had amassed enough points to avoid relegation, with four games still to play, and we had battered them. The Scouser who overheard me telling my nephew this on the phone, as I walked back to the coach, took objection to this description, but I was so convinced by it, I couldn't even be bothered to argue with him and just laughed. I was certainly not going to sour the evening. Ok, so the score, 3-2, might not look like a battering, and allowing Everton a goal on 84 minutes, did make it all a little nerve raking. I would still argue that the result was never really in doubt. As I am sure the TV pundits will not say, I will on their behalf, it was in all reality, just a consolation goal. For the last hour, I suddenly wanted to be in this stupid over hyped, money obsessed league. I wanted to upset the odds, and show everybody who had written us off, we deserved the chance to be there. No disappointed Scouser was going to spoil that. If he had accepted that, we had battered them, (I repeat that in case he's reading this, and it sounds so good,) then I would have said sorry for messing up their title chase, because I actually would have liked Everton to win the league. However, it appears that even for a smaller big team, graciousness in defeat was just too much of a challenge. The stadium announcer and many other Evertonians, were far more gracious in the acceptance of our performance. Given my previous criticism of Everton, in terms of the way they dealt with this rearrange fixtures, it is nice to be able to be positive for a change. The stadium announcers, formal acknowledgement of congratulations to us, on our victory, followed by, "and we look forward to seeing you back at Goodison, next season," was very magnanimous and professional. Whilst this sent the travelling fans into song again, "We are staying up, I say we are staying up," it was a little surprising that the players themselves, seemed to have very subdued celebrations. Given what we experienced in the 90's, with Oldham's amazing run and our own capitulation, this might have been another sign of the professionalism, which has been introduced into the team. However, us fans don't have to be professional, we are allowed for this moment, to believe that mathematics is not relevant, and celebrate like we had won the cup, all the way back down the M6 to London.

Before I let Mark provide the details of the match, I will get my defence in. I know that both Cameron Jerome and Jason Puncheon score tonight, and have pretty much secured our survival. For one night only, I will accept their contribution, and will allow some on the coach and BBS to say, I told you so they are both great players. I will eat humble pie and not mention any short comings. It is not a night for rationality or negativity.

Marks Match Report

Giving everyone 0 as first game I miss all season the silly b*ggers go and turn in a performance like that! Customers & staff at "The Hollow Tooth" in Amiens wondered why this loon in a Palace top kept interrupting his meal to read text messages, shake his head & laugh uncontrollably.

 Mikes Note

 I didn't realise Mark wasn't able to go to Everton so I could have avoided the humble pie thing and just written my own report, changing goal scorers as appropriate. It would have been something like this and you will now understand why I got him in to do the match reports.

 We scored (Jason Puncheon)
 Half-Time
 We scored again (Scott Dann)
 We battered them but didn't score again for a bit
 They got a lucky goal (somebody in blue not really bothered who)
 We scored again (Camerone Jerome)
 Scouser's left ground and we felt sorry for them so after singing songs about fire drills we let them have a consolation goal (again someone in blue if you're that bothered who, Google it, I don't care).

 All Palace Players: 10

No Maths Required

It seems like almost a footballing lifetime ago, when I made my first trip of the season, into the wilds of East London. That trip to Dagenham, was largely meaningless, and at the time it was hard to believe, the trip to West Ham, in April, might be almost similarly meaningless. However, maths can have a surprising way of creeping up and biting you on the backside. So although I travelled back to East London in a relaxed mood, knowing that we still had Man City and Liverpool to play, prevented me from over exuberance. I was again joined on the journey by my brother, sister in law and nieces. Learning from previous bladder popping excursions, with this motley crew, I opted for a change of tipple. In addition to quantity advantage, the ready mixed G&T and Vodka and Coke cans, were on special offer in the local off licence, and fitted much better into my pockets. I also didn't bother trying to be a bad influence on my older niece, as I only end up having to drink hers as well, (She is such a lightweight.) adding to the bladder pressure. The quick journey up to Victoria was uneventful, but at this point Hazel, decided, having just started to commute to London for all of two weeks, she was now the expert in all things tube. This expertise included a little shortcut to the trains. The unfortunate consequence was that we came out on different ends of a busy platform. The danger in these situations is that a group of four, looking for a group of one, can become six groups of one, all looking for each other. (This is the kind of mathematical error that I fear the league table publishers have made.) In the days before mobile phones, whenever you went anywhere with your parents or friends, you would always make provisions about what would happen, in the event of separation. Now that most people are in constant communications, and toddlers have mobile phones almost before they can take themselves to the toilet, (I honestly don't have a toilet issue, it was just the first example of toddler behaviour that came to mind.) the advanced planning of days long gone, is deemed pretty unnecessary. Unfortunately, getting a phone signal at Victoria underground station, is not possible and without a plan B, somebody needed to find the missing member of our party. It was decided that I was the most logical person to carry out the search. Now there are a number of possible reasons why, I was chosen;

1. My svelte like figure enabled me to move easily along a crowded platform.
2. I was the most dispensable as a member of the remaining group.
3. I was not seen as responsible enough by my brother, to take charge of his two teenage daughters, as I would probably drag them into the nearest available pub.
4. All of the above.

Whatever the reason, I set off in search, and found Hazel, just as a train arrived onto the platform. It seemed reasonably logical to me that as we were all travelling in one direction, (The location we were going, not some kind of weirdly inappropriate fantasy.) and knew where the journey was scheduled to end, we should get on the train, and meet up at the other end of the line. Once we got above ground, we would after all, be back in the world of the mobile. Hazel as a concerned parent, did have to think about what to do, but once reassured that Ian had the girls, and I had the G&T, she took little more convincing. In any case, why would they not get on the train? As the train pulled out of Victoria, we passed three loan individuals standing on the platform. Ian looked slightly perplexed. My youngest niece looked at her neurotic best, and my oldest niece, true to character, looked completely nonplussed by her sister's irrational concerns. We did make a few futile attempts to text, but this was purely to ensure that once a signal was re-established, they would know that we were going to crack on and wait for them. Mostly we just chatted and drank. Although I did imagine briefly my brother's journey, in the presence of one daughter unable to tweet for 30 minutes, (A teenage disaster.) and one daughter, with the back of her hand against her forehead, in her best drama queen pose. This image, or possibly Hazel's Company, or just the V&C, made me smile and enjoy the journey.

The messages that arrived on both our phones, as we arrived at West Ham, informed us that the rest of the party were on their way, and that Rhiann's phone, can get a signal where ours couldn't. The splitting of party did have an unanticipated consequence; Rhiann my niece, had started up a conversation with a lady called Karen, (For all the younger readers, this is what happens when you can't tweet, and bother to take you earphones out for a nanosecond.) and was able to present me with a flyer about a boat trip to Fulham. As I was reading this, Karen introduced herself to me directly, and I confirmed I was very interested and would email her as soon as I got home. I had heard earlier in the season that the clubs Foundation, were running a boat, but I had almost forgotten about it, as the season progressed. Now I had been reminded, it definitely seemed the way to celebrate, what an Oldhamesk escape aside, I hoped would be survival. I would have loved to have had my family with me, for the trip, but regrettably accepted that their commitments at the church, made this unlikely. The chat with Karen and the reuniting with my family, made the walk down to the ground, pass a little bit quicker than usual, as it is a deceptively long walk from West Ham tube, to the ground. It will be an even longer walk, once they move to the Olympic Stadium, for unsuspecting first time visitors; and let's face it, to fill that place they will need lots of these, given they have to advertise cheap tickets in *The Evening Standard,* pretty much every week already.

Like many football supporters I am never truly satisfied, and since our victory against Everton, I now find myself looking at various other footballing scenarios, which would make my season complete. Obviously, I would like Brighton to lose the Play-off finals, with a dodgy penalty in injury time, that is a given. However, I would also like to see Orient promoted and West Ham relegated, the possibility of these two teams in the same league, after West Ham made such a big point about being a bigger club, during the Olympic Stadium fiasco, would give me great satisfaction. Perhaps today's results, will make that a little bit closer to reality.

If there is ever a moment of justice in football, our captain Colossus scoring the winning goal from the penalty spot today, was that moment. As I am sure that Mark has alluded to on many occasions, Mile has been a ferocious campaigner all season, and his conviction that it would be him, and no one else that took that penalty, whilst initially causing some consternation in the away end, showed him for the leader that he is. The celebrations at the end of the match, were far removed from the quiet professional approach to victory at Everton. This time, it was no holds barred jubilation. The picture that has become my work screen saver, taken facing the Palace supporters, epitomised the season. The players where all in a line holding hands, facing towards us, and the mutual respect was caught there in that moment. Having been present at all but one of the league games, (Bloody M25,) the most I have ever achieved, I really did feel a sense of shared achievement. It felt like my victory as much as it did the players. I didn't travel back with Ian and the Girls for no planned reason, but sometimes I can be quite a solitary individual, and enjoyed the journey back, just listening to the happy banter around me.

Marks Match Report

Palace stunned West Ham with the perfect display of counter-attacking football, teaching the so-called "Football Academy" a real lesson. Five straight top flight league wins and the dizzy heights of 43 points mean nothing short of a Vincent Tan inspired points deducting conspiracy will deny us the joys of Premier League football for a second successive season. This result was the final vindication of Tony Pulis's management reign at Selhurst Park, leaving the doubters – and that includes me – with a very healthy & satisfying portion of humble pie. The achievement of his teams – on & off field – is one of the greatest managerial feats most Palace fans can remember, probably ranking alongside Steve Coppell keeping the (first) Administration squad of the young, old, lame and bloody awful in the second flight.

Said manager made one enforced change with KG replacing the unfit Chamakh, with Ledley filling – at least nominally – the position behind the lone striker. Sam Allardyce sent out a similar formation, with two attacking wingers and the efficient Nolan as support to the giant Carroll. This resulted in two teams playing the ball down both flanks, while anything down the middle tended to be long. The difference was that whereas everything for the Hammers was aimed for

Carroll to win in the air, Palace had the option of playing the ball over the top for Jerome to run after. Neither tactic was particularly effective although Nolan was able to supply more close support to his striker than Ledley was for Jerome. Again both sides were happier using wingers and there was an early chance for Carroll whose far post header struck the outside of the stanchion. Generally though Carroll was well policed by either Delaney or Dann, who picked him up depending upon which side of the box he was.

Palace then created a little pressure, winning a succession of corners thanks mostly to the efforts of Bolasie on the left, and from one of those corners KG rose for what looked an unchallenged header that looked bound to end up in the opposite side of the goal but somehow stayed out; Dann also had a decent chance from a similar position a little later. West Ham's wingers were also having some success with Downing creating problems for Ward, but the pace of Palace's breaks were the real difference between the teams, so different from the laboured build-ups of no more than two months ago. Jedinak's storming game in the middle also helped delay any real Hammers' pressure, and it was not until nearly half an hour had gone before they exerted real pressure. Speroni had already tipped over one effort from distance, then Carroll started to win balls in the box, getting the better of Delaney on three occasions: merely seconds after blocking a shot at the foot of one post, Julian clawed a Carroll header out of the net at the other. The centre forward was to put another harder chance wide a little later. Although the home team's spurt died off before half-time the game was in the balance.

Carroll was also the leading figure at the start of the second half with three decent half chances all spurned. Slowly the match started to slip towards the visitors with Bolasie tearing McCartney apart on the left while Puncheon was gaining the upper hand on the other flank over the "liability" (cf. My Hammers' mate) Armero. Combined with Jerome's hard running and Jedinak's steel the West Ham defence appeared vulnerable, and the only surprise was that it wasn't Bolasie who unlocked it. Puncheon had a loud but not convincing appeal for a penalty turned down a few minutes before he fed Jerome who broke into the box, this time drawing a trip from Armero; referee Atkinson rightly awarded the penalty,

238

and Jedinak's finish from the spot was clinical and
unstoppable.

Although the Irons tried to muscle their way back in
the game, from that point on it really became a
question of whether Palace could add to their advantage
as counter attacks shredded the home team's cover as
Bolasie's brilliance and the skill of Puncheon was too
much for them. Unfortunately Palace decided to play
like Arsenal and were brilliant up to the edge of the
box when they decided to score the perfect goal. Jerome
was left screaming in frustration as chances were
carved out but wasted, with the two wingers, Ward &
Ledley all delaying shots or trying one little reverse
pas too many. It seems strange (& frankly hypocritical)
to moan about a Pulis team playing too much football!
West Ham's response was typical Big Sam, ditching any
pretence of following the Football Academy textbook and
going straight for Route One, withdrawing both wingers
and sticking another tall lad up front in Carlton Cole;
actually Downing & Jarvis, who had swapped wings in the
second half, had gradually faded from the game in the
second half, and Diamé looked far more dangerous on the
left than he had in midfield. Palace responded by
withdrawing our own two wingers with Parr & Ledley
shoring up the flanks and Gabbidon helping repel the
aerial assault. In the end skill at pace outwitted the
thud & blunder that stoked the home fans' ire, and the
after-match celebrations from the squad confirmed the
great teamwork & spirit that had achieved safety
against all the odds.

Speroni - 7
Ward - 7
Mariappa - 7
Delaney - 7
Dann - 7
Dikgacoi - 6
Jedinak - 8
Ledley - 6
Puncheon - 8
Bolasie - 8
Jerome - 7
Murray - 6
Gabbidon - 6
Parr - N/A

Travel and Reflection

Although my journey to Upton Park last week, did contain a small moment of drama, for one of my normal travelling companions, it provided an experience for which Chessington Zoo, (Sorry, World of Adventures, it's that re-branding thing again.) would charge a few hours of the minimum wage. In fact it prompted her to inform me that, "She had never done anything, so fast, backwards, with her legs in the air".

For the able-bodied traveller, the main problem that we have is finding a seat, or in my case finding a toilet. For Mandy, the problems are far more difficult to resolve. Firstly, she must find a carer for the journey, and if travelling by coach, she is pretty much strapped in at Selhurst and unable to move until the lift drops her off at the destination. She then has to negotiate the hit and miss approach to disabled facilities, whilst relying on the home club providing some sort of commentary, that isn't delayed by anything up to seven seconds, or of the wrong match. The coach is therefore for her, like my Mum the only real option. Even so like me, Mandy does like to travel independently for some games. Driving is sometimes an option, but after taking a one way street the wrong way, near the Emirates, one of her drivers is now reluctant to drive to London matches. (Even blue badges don't get you off this particular fine.) and Mandy is left like the rest of us relying on the vagaries of TFL`s weekend service. For the able-bodied this is often challenge enough.

I am at this point, required to make my first and hopefully last retraction, or amendment. The driver in question, has just informed me that, "it wasn't a one way street, it was a width restriction and that just makes me look stupid." and I stand corrected. I do not wish to make anybody look stupid, even when his or her name has been deliberately left out. I do however want to sell some books, and I am still not exactly sure why, or how, you get the actual ticket that they did. I figured that if I just said no entry, everybody would understand, and if I am brutally honest, I still think it was funnier that way, as well. I hope that anybody else, who may have a slightly different and less amusing, take on any of the events mentioned in this personal account of the season, will take this on board, and not require me to add lots of little footnotes, all over the place. This is primarily because I haven't actually worked out how to do this, [8] and secondly because it can rather break up the flow. Group apology now offered in advance, could I please just get on with the story.

For a blind lady in a wheelchair, the problem is multiplied several fold. Now as any regular tube traveller, with nothing else to look at on a morning commutes will testify, London Underground advertises on every tube map, which stations are wheelchair friendly, and I imagine this is invaluable for a wheelchair user. Unfortunately, this information refers to the normal standard of service and is not live. If a lift isn't working, this can make all the advanced planning, rather

---

[8] I worked it out

redundant. Arriving at Canada Water, Mandy and Fulham, (I really ought to know his actual name by now.) found that the lift wasn't working. They now had two options. One was to get back on the train and try to navigate an alternative route, with the possibility that other lifts would be broken, or undergoing maintenance. The second option was bravely, or possibly recklessly provided by Fulham, and accepted in the same vein by Mandy. Having not seen the CCTV or Youtube video, I can only describe the solution from my own imagination.

Fulham nervously backs Mandy towards the escalators with the instruction. "When I say go put your breaks on." The escalator starts to take Mandy down, Fulham rocks her backwards, A reasonable feat on the flat, the brakes are engaged and Fulham hangs on for dear life, whilst as indicated earlier, Mandy sits strapped into her seat, legs in the air. It is perhaps on these occasions, that being blind, might be considered a distinct advantage, as I am not sure I would have wanted to see what was happening, had I been in her position. As far as I am aware, this did not have to be repeated on the return journey, and any injury or disaster was averted. The CPFC chariot, adorned in its red and blue customisation, lives to wheel another day.

Disaster averted and no death or injury incurred, this little anecdote, can now take its place alongside; the Hungry horse, the broken arm and the last minute drive to Swindon in the college minibus. They can be exaggerated, developed and humourised, (without offending people) at every available opportunity, and become part of the folk lore that is in every group of supporters repertoire. There are however, some scenarios that will never be treated in this way, because they didn't have a happy ending. Two weeks ago at Goodison, I referred to one such tragedy. Partly for editorial reasons and partly because I genuinely wanted to consider my comments before writing, I held back from any elaboration. With just three games to go, I can't delay anymore. Whilst I was waiting for the coach to arrive at Everton, I got talking to a young Policeman, he was friendly and sociable and his company helped to pass the time. (Talking at length to coppers, is not a regular pastime of mine.) Probably because there was scheduled to be another tribute to those who died before the game, we got onto the thorny subject of the Hillsborough tragedy. Given the revelations that have been suspected for many years, but have only recently come out, with any official recognition, I was taken aback by his comments. The thrust of his point of view was that he did consider that the Liverpool supporters, were in some way responsible. In this way, he was implying that the extensive reports and investigations, had their own agenda and did not tell the whole story. Now this view would have shocked me if the officer was an old stager, and we were having the conversation off duty, in a pub in South London. However, we were standing outside Goodison Park in Liverpool, before a match where we were about to remember those that died, from that very City. He was in uniform and relatively young. He could not in any way have been held responsible, for what other police officers did or didn't do 25 years previously, yet he still felt that he should, or could, even in passing, make this comment. That was pretty much the end of our conversation. I didn't know quite what to say to him after this. Now I understand that the views of one police officer, like those of one fan, do not represent the whole of the organisation. Even so if these views do still prevail, even amongst the more recent intake it is very worrying. Although I cannot say that I have experienced any real negativity this season, I am aware that one section of the Palace support has had difficulties with the police and I can't really comment on how much, if any, has been self-inflicted. I fully appreciate that these problems, are not in any way comparable to the loss of life experienced 25 years ago, but when you here the comment that I did, it does make you aware that as a football supporters, you are sometimes not treated as equally, as some other sections of society. In February, the New Statesman carried an informed article on the subject titled "Everyone's equal in the eyes of the law, unless you are a football fan." [xiv] It was both interesting and disturbing.

My discomfort at this conversation, was countered by the subsequent tribute in the ground, where hundreds of schoolchildren, joined by scarves of all the clubs in the country, encircled the pitch. It was a respectful and moving act of remembrance, and showed that despite our different passions and locations, football fans are in essence all the same. The fans of Man City our visitors today, may seem to have nothing much in common with Palace, but every time I look at their multi-million pound team, league position and stadium, I remind myself of the first Manchester derby that I attended in 1985, at Main Road. They were absolutely rubbish and lost 3-0. The current order of things hasn't always been as it is now, and maybe will change again. Manchester is always also a reminder of the girl I went to see, so after all it does serve some positive purpose.

With this loose end tied up, I can now sit back and enjoy the remaining three games. Mark will probably describe City's 9 or 10 goals in detail, but for once it doesn't matter, and I don't really care. If we can by some miracle, pull out another performance similar to Chelsea, a few weeks ago, we could continue to influence the title race. I would like to help Liverpool triumph, but I'm not going to lose sleep, either way. Probably knowing us, we will put in an amazing performance, and win our sixth game on the trot. Kevin Day in his programme notes today, quoted one of his mates, "It's Palace mate that's what they do" and that rather sums it up. What exactly it is we do, is completely unpredictable and that is what makes it all worthwhile.

Oh yes and by the way, we had another new kick off time today 4.10pm, on a Sunday

Marks Match Report

A cold dose of reality washed over Palace today as we found that we weren't quite as good as we thought we were given recent results. There is no harm in losing to one of Europe's wealthiest clubs, even if their stature hasn't quite caught up with their expenditure, but in the end it was a fairly easy victory for City as they calmly kept Palace at arms' length and exploited

their advantages in pace & movement. The defeat wasn't
as dispiriting as that inflicted almost a season ago by
Swansea, and there wasn't a crushing presentment of
doom now Palace were safe, but it did seem almost as
inevitable inside five minutes as our game plan
unravelled swiftly. City are not only skilful and quick
in both thought and deed, but they also worked as hard
as us; they will also be hoping we can damage
Liverpool's title challenge next week.

Palace lined up in a 4-4-1-1 formation with Chamakh in
the hole in place of KG, but perhaps a blow was dealt
to our hopes just before kick off when the Anfield
result was made certain. City now had a real chance of
the league title instead of just a desperate hope and
it may well have buoyed up a side that has slipped
recently. It was also a shame that Yaya Toure was
passed fit to play as he was to put on an excellent
show of all-round midfield prowess. Still, if we could
keep it scoreless for as long as possible, then perhaps
City's nerves would... Damn! Palace had already escaped
a couple of occasions where Aguero had broken inside
the left hand side of our area, now Toure's deep cross
saw Dzeko slip between Dann and Mariappa, and bury a
header past Speroni.

For a time Palace were rocking. Ward was finding Milner
far more of a handful than he had most opponents this
season, while Aguero was drifting away from the central
defenders into space on the edge of the box, Delaney
often finding he was no longer marking anyone. Damien
did have one narrow escape: having spent all season
thumping the ball into the stands when in danger he
decided to play a dangerous ball back to Speroni, only
for it to be intercepted by said Aguero; only a quick
sortie from goal by Julian and some lucky defending
prevented an early second strike. There was also plenty
of dissent & finger-pointing between our keeper and
central defenders on the nature of coming for crosses
and calling for the ball, indicative of the pressure
they felt they were under.

Strange as it may seem out of this period of defensive
chaos Palace actually fashioned a decent 10 minutes
when they knocked the ball around and made penetrations
down both flanks. Sadly the final ball was too often
found wanting, or there was one or less bodies in the
box to aim for, and the sum total of our pressure was a

243

weak shot from Puncheon that dribbled into Hart's hands. The England goalie could really have taken time for a shampoo & perm for long periods of the game so underemployed he was to be. City edged back into dominance and there were notable misses from Dzeko and Kompany, the last being a header that should really have passed inside the near post instead of thumping wide. Now, if only Palace could keep it to 1-0 at half-time and then perhaps the tension would build in the second half... Damn! Toure won the ball in City's half and then exchanged a couple of passes, making a looping run that lost Ledley and outpaced Delaney on the left; although Palace managed to hold him up for a second or two on the edge of our box Yaya found time to turn and strike the ball into the far top corner – Julian was caught somewhat in no-man's-land but given the quality of the finish it ultimately made no difference to the goal.

The second half was relatively tame. City were happy to knock the ball around and strike on the break, with Milner still causing Ward issues on the left. Palace' spasmodic responses were hardly threatening the blond perm: Bolasie, who had looked so bright in the first half, now faded; Jerome ran hard but too often offside; Chamakh made some good runs but usually lost the ball in the end; while Puncheon, despite forcing Hart into the only save he had to make after the interval, was seldom on his game. Jedinak strove hard in the middle but was outclassed by Toure, while Ledley's lack of pace really told for the first time in his Palace career. City flooded midfield and when Palace did break too often the ball was turned inside, then backwards, as the defenders got back in numbers.

As the game slipped away Pulis tried some attacking changes, withdrawing Jerome & Chamakh for Gayle & Murray, and later Ince came on for Bolasie. Although Gayle held the ball up well on a couple of occasions and laid it off City blanketed their box and, despite entreaties to shoot, no one pulled the trigger. In the end City nearly grabbed a third when Dzeko's shot was saved in unusual style by Speroni's legs as our keeper dived the wrong way – I guess there was a deflection? City's fans, who were the loudest we'd had this season – well, they did have a lot to sing about both before & during the game – celebrated a routine 2-0 win while Palace's efforts when outclassed earned home applause.

244

Speroni — 6
Ward — 5
Mariappa — 6
Delaney — 5
Dann — 5
Jedinak — 6
Ledley — 5
Bolasie — 6
Puncheon — 5
Chamakh — 6
Jerome — 5
Gayle — 6
Murray — 5
Ince — 5

Tears, Tickets and Three's

When I sat on the Barclay's away day tour bus to Liverpool, back in October and came up with the idea for this diary, I had no idea what the next few months would bring. In many ways, that was the point and what made it such an interesting project. I was at the time, putting the final changes to my debut novel. Prisoners, families, dolls and judgements, had actually started at the end, so I pretty much knew what was going to happen, when writing it. There are inevitably plot twists and changes that occur, as the story develops in your head, but the end goal and basic structure didn't deviate too much, from my initial idea. I could not control or manipulate English elite level football, in the same way, (As I don't have the money, or a TV station.) and this made the idea, appealing.

It is perhaps therefore quite appropriate, that this book draws to a close, almost as it started. I made the decision to write a diary of the season, as we travelled with Ian Wright on the coach to Liverpool, and except for next week's armada to Fulham, the season ends with a home match against the same Liverpool team. For both our sets of fans, the season has exceeded all expectations. Palace are eleventh in the league, with a real chance of a top half Premier League finish, and Liverpool stand on the brink of their first Premiership title. This in itself is an amazing revelation. The red side of Liverpool, dominated so much of my early football life that it is difficult to believe that in the era of Sky Sports, stupid anthems and Monday night football, they have never triumphed, in the major English competition. Whilst I always want my team to win, I kind of also hope that Liverpool win the title, it makes for a nice, no lose situation.

One of the things that I enjoy most about football is spending time with my family, which is the way I have always done it. Firstly this was with my Granddad, Dad and Brothers, and more recently with my Mum, nieces and nephews. So when I got the call that a pre-match meet at the Moon in Norbury was planned, I couldn't think of a better way to end the home season. Much to my surprise, Dad, whose appetite hasn't been so good, since his heart attack, agreed to join us. For 5.30pm on a Bank Holiday, the pub was busy and some reorganisation of the furniture was required, to seat all eight of us. After sorting out the drinks, I informed the bar staff that we would like to eat, but was told that the chef hadn't actually arrived yet. He would be about 20 minutes. This was not a problem; we had an hour until we needed to leave. At 6.45 with food still not arrived, but apparently on its way, I made a quick call to the kebab shop next door, to purchase three plastic food trays. One toasted sandwich and some garlic bread duly transferred, we got Dad into the car, and waited for Mums chicken and chips. Mum eventually gave up, and we headed for the ground.

Not entirely surprisingly, our late arrival at the ground, and the full stadium meant that I couldn't park in the car park, and I had to drop everybody off before returning half way home, to find a parking space. For many years now, we have parked in the same road, but it is surprising how after just one season, parking at the ground, you get used to a new routine. The relatively short walk up Thornton Heath High Street, seemed a right pain in the backside. I was also aware the Holmesdale Fanatics, had arranged a final display, and I wanted to be there, to take my place, with whatever coloured paper or plastic, I was required to hold in the air. In the end, I did quite enjoy the walk and realised that after my initial annoyance, I quite miss it. I even managed to strike up a conversation with a couple of Liverpool supporters. After the Chelsea and Man City games, some of our supporters have got quite fundamentalist, about away supporters in the home areas. In an almost excessive fashion, there has been much talk about outing Scouser's, who infiltrate home areas. It is quite ironic that whilst this is taking place, there is a campaign to take over a whole section of Craven Cottage, next week, which is not officially allocated to us. The vitriol directed at fellow football supporters, trying to watch their team was quite ridiculous. If you buy tickets for a home section and then post about it on Twitter, this doesn't make you a hooligan, but it does make you a bit stupid. The two Liverpool supporters that I spoke too, also had tickets in a "home" section, but I didn't take copies of their passports, seat numbers and run to the nearest steward. They were not thugs out for a scrap, and I advised them instead, to keep their heads down and enjoy the game. I hope that they did the former, but I doubt in retrospect that they will have enjoyed the game, in its entirety. The reports that came out on the BBS after the game, did drag me in to rather heated exchanges with some of our fans. As I think I have revealed throughout the course of the season, I am not some saintly dispassionate supporter, who loves everybody. However, I think that my attitude is a long way from wanting to, or actually trying to, punch an opposition supporter for celebrating a goal, by their team. I think the latter attitude is a bit pathetic, and I hoped that as a club, our supporters were better than that. Expressing this view on the BBS, got me my 2nd 'Negative rep' of the season, and as you would expect from somebody with the attitude I was trying to argue against, the negative rep was accompanied by an insult.

I eventually made it into the ground, just in time to hold up my square of red plastic, which made up the final Holmesdale display of the season. It Proclaimed, "Fortress Selhurst." The work that has been put into these displays, over the course of the season is not to be underestimated. I had never really considered them before this season, but I am now much more appreciative. Some little things that you may wish to think about. How much time does it take to produce 8000 colour-coded sheets of card or plastic? How much would this cost? How long does it physically take to put each one on very seat? How do you find somewhere big enough, to lay out the design, and paint the large banners that accompany the larger display? Without any detailed insight, I guess the answers are; a bloody long time, a great deal of cash and with great difficulty. I know that this final display, wasn't perhaps the best in terms of artwork, compared to the machine produced, club or sponsor funded displays of other clubs, but this is in a way, has always been part of their charm, and what makes them almost unique. Add to this, the concepts behind them, and you have something a little special. I was glad that I made it in time, to play my part. That being said, Fortress Selhurst, was looking a little bit like a sand castle, made with sand too dry on a windy day, after about 60 minutes. This was not too surprising given the exertions of recent weeks, and with nothing really to play for. What happened next, will be remembered into old age, by everybody who was there to witness it.

For much of my life, "Remember Wrexham!" has been a catch all phrase, for any seemingly impossible situations with time running out. Needing to win at the Racecourse Ground by two clear goals, to have a chance of promotion on the final day of the season, when for some reason still not clear, we had no match. Palace scored two goals, in the last 4 minutes, to win 4-2. As I think I have already stated, I was not allowed to travel to Wales, as it was a school night. Yet despite this, it has still become that classic never admit defeat moment, that all supporters will have experience at least once. For the next generation of Palace fans, tonight at Selhurst Park will become, their Wrexham moment. It is perhaps fitting that it was against a club, whose own Istanbul moment will be far better remembered. The recovery from 3-0 down, to draw 3-3 might not have won us a top European competition, but it was no less remarkable, and provided the fitting farewell to Selhurst for the next few months. My only regret was that I needed to collect the car and bring it back to the ground to pick up Dad. As a result, I was not able to stay for the lap of honour. Neither was I able to see Luis Suarez leaving the pitch in tears. I don't mention this last situation to gloat, as I have already stated, I would have liked to see Liverpool win the league, but because he is such an enigma. His indiscretions are well publicised, and yet there is something about him which is completely different. His playing colleagues at Anfield, talk very highly of him and suggest he is a quiet family man. His reaction today, also showed that he is an emotional and passionate individual, who is desperate to win and takes defeat very hard. Whilst this cannot justify some of his part actions, it does also show that players are so much more than the media generated persona. As fans, we often think we know players, but I guess we never really do.

As I walked back to the car, elated by the way we had come back from an almost impossible situation; I did feel a little sorry for the Liverpool supporters that had travelled down to London expecting so much. However, as I walked back down Thornton Heath High Street, where a few hours earlier I had chatted so comfortably with some of these supporters, the atmosphere was very different. There were a number of large groups of supporters gathering in various locations. The atmosphere was certainly tense. I texted my brother and warned him to keep my nieces close. Given my comments last week, it was ironic that the Liverpool supporters, who had obviously not been at the game, could create such a tense atmosphere. The irony was doubled by the fact that there was not one police officer in sight, on the High Street, whilst a large unit of, (Or is it an overtime of) yellow jacketed officers provided an in-penetrable cordon around the visiting supporters, within the ground. I don't believe that in the end, there was much actual confrontation, but the potential was definitely there. After such a wonderful evening, it all left a slightly unpleasant taste, and I admit it caused me to again consider my conversation with the Liverpudlian Policeman.

Marks Match Report

I do dislike these end of season nothing-to-play-for
matches; even the masochistic thrill of relegation –
or, as we're Palace, probably insolvency – was missing.
Instead we end up with some kind of Istanbul tribute
gig replete with weeping Scousers... Lord alone knows
what Sky's audience made of this

This season the only time Palace have looked like
taking a really serious hiding was up at Anfield, when
the half-time score of 3-0 could – should – have been 6
or 7. Admittedly this was the Holloway era but even
then Delaney and Gabbidon were made to look pawky &
awkward in the face of Suarez & Sturridge. No great
shame as these two match pace with skill and
understanding to form the best striking force in the
Premier League, especially at a time when a sole
striker appears de rigeur. Whereas Manchester City were
willing & able to draw into a two goal lead and then
settle on cruise control while suffocating any chance
of a Palace feedback, it was evident, not least from
Rodger's pre-match bombast, that Liverpool would keep
the pedal to the metal. Only now they would come up
against the Pulis-improved hard working & organised
brand of Palace in front of a packed Selhurst which,
under lights, throbbed with an intense atmosphere. The
stage was set for a classic.

It didn't actually work out that way, or not for about
80 minutes or so anyway. Amid rumours of illness in the
camp Pulis made one change to the team dismissed by
City, KG returning to the reportedly sick Jerome, with
Chamakh on his own up front. On paper this strengthened
the defensive part of the midfield duties, but it soon
became clear that KG, Jedinak & Ledley lacked the pace
to break quickly and support Chamakh, who became very
isolated. The first 10 minutes were pretty even with
neither side creating much, but then Liverpool started
to monopolise possession and chances came. Sakho had
already missed with a header from a corner when the
clearest opportunity fell to Johnson, the full back
escaping Bolasie's attentions with an offside-beating
run only to head over when faced by a lonely Speroni.

249

Liverpool didn't have long to wait as from a corner Allen, in acres of space beyond the far post, beat Julian with a downward header. Palace's famed defensive organisation was creaking with Suarez, Sturridge & Sterling all lively in escaping markers, although the linesman's flag helped cut short any further scoring.

Palace's main thrusts had come down the flanks at this stage, although it was more a matter of unrealised threat as the crossing tended to be poor and the support for Chamakh very distant, with – at times – both Ledley & KG being pushed a little further forward to no great effect, the sole effort at that stage a half-chance for Dann at the far post from a corner. Bolasie was his usual frustrating self, plenty of skill & pace but little end product, while Puncheon was to fade after a decent start. Then Palace somehow crept back into the match as Liverpool seemed to regroup, with Puncheon's shot almost beating Mignolet, who then had to tip over a Jedinak thunderbolt. Half-time came with at least a feeling of hope – we hadn't conceded that killer second goal as against City.

That hope was quickly crushed after the interval, although at first it didn't look like that, with Ledley's mis-hit shot that floated through to the keeper, then Suarez picking up a deserved caution for yapping in the ref's ear. At first it looked like Julian had pulled off another of those match-turning saves when touching a Sturridge shot onto the post with Suarez blasting over from close range, but that thought was rapidly extinguished as Ward failed to close down a Sturridge run and the deflected shot was carried just out of Julian's reach. Before Palace could regroup Ledley lost a challenge with Suarez who, after a rapid exchange of passes took Dann out of the game, beat Speroni at his near post. With Liverpool's strikers running riot, especially across the face of the box, and clever little through balls penetrating the penalty area, it appeared only a matter of how many the Scousers would score.

Perhaps that thought sealed Liverpool's fate. City, knowing they only needed the three points, had closed the game down in the second half. Liverpool, eyeing their goal difference deficit and with perhaps their manager's declarations still foremost in their minds, kept going forward, with Johnson less a full back than an out-&-out old-time winger and forced Julian to tip over a rising shot. Perhaps their fans demands of "Attack Attack Attack!" would have been replaced with the more prosaic request to park the bus.

Palace's players in contrast seemed unwilling to shoot, the prime example being when Ledley found himself in unexpected acres of space in the opposition half, moved forward to the edge of the box then looked for someone better to pass to. No-one was willing to pull the trigger. The exception was Bolasie who was creating danger down the right only for the final ball to be lacking killer quality. Pulis made his first change with Murray on for Chamakh, and Glenn at least had a shot, although it was woefully wide; he was soon joined by Gayle for Puncheon. In response Palace's defence was working overtime blocking shots and crosses, drawing Liverpool in...

When the blow fell it came from a completely unexpected source, Delaney finding himself receiving a short free kick some 25 yards from goal; his siege gun of a shot screamed into the top corner (we missed the deflection that carried the ball beyond the keeper's reach) bringing the crowd to the boil. Coutinho nearly replied straight away, his shot again tipped over by Speroni, and from the corners that followed Palace broke. Bolasie found himself free on the right, evaded a weak effort from Sakho on the halfway line (defender really should have with hindsight taken him out) and, just when it appeared he'd held the ball too long, rolled in a cross to Gayle who had drawn back to the penalty spot, and the sub coolly finished past Mignolet.

Liverpool had been hit with two in a couple of minutes, not really having the chance to adjust to the changed realities at 3-1, and with the crowd now at fever pitch and their own nerves jangling, they seemed unable to switch into a defensive mode, bringing on Moses, still pushing on, with Julian having to remain alert to save at Suarez's feet. Palace then delivered the fatal blow to Merseyside's title chances with only 2-3 minutes left. A long diagonal ball [from Dann?] was superbly laid off by Murray to Gayle on the edge of the box and somehow escaping the defence's attention, and he rolled the ball past the advancing Mignolet. Cue chaos! Liverpool at least responded with some heart and an amazing series of pinball in the Palace box set off by

confusion between Delaney & Speroni saw the ball
ricochet across the goalmouth without a final touch,
Moses's effort being blocked. The final whistle was
treated with an enthusiasm for a point unseen since
Hillsborough in 2010 and the sight of distraught
Scousers in the stands and white-shirted internationals
draped disconsolately across the Selhurst turf. I'd
seen Stockport do this to us, thanks in part to an
injury to Palace keeper Fraser Digby, but can't recall
us recovering a three goal deficit before.

Speroni - 7
Ward - 6
Mariappa -6
Dann - 7
Delaney - 7
Dikgacoi - 5
Jedinak - 6
Ledley - 6
Puncheon - 6
Bolasie - 8
Chamakh - 5
Murray - 7
Gayle - 8
Ince - 6

And now the end is near

The last game of any football season, is always a cause for celebration; a magnificent promotion already achieved, a chance for promotion at the last moment despite unlikely odds, the feint possibility that you might avoid relegation, a relegation party when your fate was sealed weeks ago. In the case of Crystal Palace in 2014, it was to be mid-table obscurity, when all the sensible money had you relegated by Christmas. It doesn't matter; it is always just a celebration that your team, that you have invested so much time and money on, is still there. They still matter. It is against such backdrops that some of my best days as a Palace supporter have taken place. As a 13 year old boy I waited on my own, with my little Kodak camera for the likes of Ian Walsh, Kenny Samson and the team of the 80's, to emerge worse for wear from the players bar, after 52,000 people had crammed into little old Selhurst park. In 2004, I sat in silence at Highfield Road, until I realised that the main stand contained many an eagle, doing just the same. The play-offs have somewhat confused the process as they did that year. The trouble is that now you don't always know when the last game actually is. It's difficult to galvanise a right good knees up when there could be one more game or even three. The way the fixtures worked out this year, had always bent itself to the possibility of a last game, winner takes all showdown. As a result, plans were made early. Now from my experience, the best parties are nearly always the unexpected rather than the lavishly planned. Fulham away on Sunday the 11th May 2014 was no exception, but was an enjoyable end to the season. Walking towards Upton Park a few weeks back, I met Karen from the Lower Holmesdale, who had had the foresight back in October, to book a boat to the game. I had read some months back that the CPFC Study centre were running a boat, but had almost forgotten about it, but now I was spurred into action to snap up one of the last twenty places on this alternative boat. As soon as I got home, I emailed Karen to book my place. It would mean travelling separately to my Mum and my brother's family, but I had never travelled to a match by boat before, (Stromness to Thurso, not really counting.) and wasn't going to miss the chance. Preparation for a Palace day trip, always starts a bit early, (it's a coach one thing) and in this case, it started a day early with a trip to the Whitgift Centre, Croydon. I definitely needed new shorts; for a boat trip you have to have new shorts, and then consequently new deck shoes. I would also more importantly need a new camera. I have to say at this point, for any younger readers who might think what's wrong with the one on your phone, that having owned a smart phone, when they actually had proper keyboards, didn't try to run your whole life for you, or predict unsuccessfully what you were trying to type, and equally as importantly you could download just about any standard windows software for free and it would work, I have gone very retro with my phone. It now just pretty much does, what it was intended to do. The benefits of this are many fold, but the main downside is that I don't have a functional camera to hand, when I often want it. At the beginning of the season I brought myself a nice bridge camera, to compensate for this and to allow me to take some nice pictures of the season, but after a lugging it to a few games, I came to the conclusion that it was just too big for football matches. The jobs worth stewards at some grounds, also seem to believe that taking pictures at an event which I have paid handsomely for, infringes ground regulations and image rights, of already excessively funded players and clubs. So it had just become too much trouble. The fact that probably 90 percent of the crowd, have more powerful phone cameras, which they make no attempt to limit the use of, is just one more selective enforcement of ground regulations along with; e-cigarettes, standing and as I was to find out later inflatables and flags. I have digressed, but the point amongst this little rant was I wanted to take some nice pictures of the day, and didn't want to take my nice expensive camera. I confess that this was also slightly influenced by the idea that after 3 hours drinking, on a boat, it might be dropped into the Thames.

After an overnight charge, the new pocket camera was ready to go and so was I. As could almost be predicted on a Sunday when you want to travel anywhere, network rail tried to screw things up with no trains from Norbury into Victoria. When I first started travelling to watch football in the 70's, it appeared that somebody from British rail actually looked at the football fixtures, and planned additional trains and football specials, where they might be needed. In 2014 with all the technology and computer programs available, it would appear that the reverse is almost true. Luckily, for all their faults, the good old London bus can pretty much be relied upon to pick up the pieces, as can the tube, (Except when they decide to strike, but this seems to be reserved for nights when I am trying to get to Concerts, rather than football.) Therefore, it was a 9.30am departure, bus to Brixton, change at Stockwell, Northern Line to Waterloo. Leaving Waterloo for the short walk up to festival pier, the first error of my day became apparent. It was bloody cold. I think that this also led to a slightly subdue atmosphere at the pier. The passing of the first, of what I believe were five boats with almost 1000 red and blue crew, lifted the tone and we were on our way.

The trip itself took us the wrong way up the river as far as Wapping before we turned around and headed towards Putney. There is something peculiar about bridges, in much the same way as subways, which encourages grown men to start random chanting. Therefore, every bridge we passed under was an opportunity to do what Palace fans do best, a brief but resonating, 'Eagles.' This was varied from time to time, but after a rather premature piece of micky taking about John Terry, delivered about three bridges too early, it was generally decided that, 'Eagles, eagles,' was less likely to reveal our weak knowledge of London river geography. So we stuck to that. As was feared from the first sight of the Thames, it was still bloody cold, and getting colder at the front of the boat. The simple solution of switching to Brandy, instead of cider, whilst attractive, seemed a recipe for disaster at such an early hour. The only alternative, if I wanted to smoke was to cram into the deck at the rear of the boat, which was sheltered from the wind, and busy enough to offer shared body warmth.

I should at this point be able to include a variety of fantastic photographs, but for two reasons this isn't possible. Firstly, I haven't yet decided if the book as a whole will contain any photos, and secondly I made one rather critical photographic

254

mistake when I left the house. I forgot to actually put the fully charged battery, back into my newly acquired camera. An emergency call to Mum to bring the offending small square of metal with her, was unfortunately no good until we got to the ground.

Not all celebrations are loud raucous affairs and our trip up and down the river Thames to Fulham, was pitched about right for me. We had a sing, we drank some beer, but we also had the opportunity to sit and watch the bemused tourists, trying to work out who we were and where we were going. Even when they had no idea, the answers to either of these questions, they waved anyway. Speaking to some of the fans who travelled on the other boats, they seem to have had a considerably more rowdy journey. We travelled in parallel with one for a short while, and attempted a, 'we're the left side; we're the right side' with them, but at the time I know I was thinking this is all a bit sensible. I even wondered if maybe I should have chosen a different boat, but that was just a brief flirtation with, wishing for days long gone, because I really enjoyed our trip and drank just about the right amount.

 Given what I have just said about the general sensible behaviour of the passengers on the boat, I was surprised when coming in to dock a Putney Pier, to see Minibuses of 'high vis jacket' police, waiting. At least they let us land, because the boat that I believe started the idea and was organised by the Foundation, was refused permission to alight until 2.55pm. Now I understand that the police have a difficult job to do, but this makes little sense to me. What did they think that the fans were going to do for the extra hour, on board a floating bar?

 There was another reason that I had tried to remain vaguely sober. I had been invited to join my boss, a Fulham season ticket holder in a private members club directly by our landing point. This plan never materialised, because amongst all the undoubted talents, skills and expertise of the Met Police football officers, any kind of local knowledge is not one of the attributes that they require. I know that I should have been able to phone my boss, but I have also developed another rule concerning phones. This rule is that I generally do not to have numbers stored in my phone, that might cause problems if I drink to my much and either sent a text to the wrong person, or sent a message to the right person, but then subsequently wish I hadn't. So without his number and no idea where the Winchester club actually was, I went in search of my brother and his family, who I had been informed by the aforementioned new-fangled texting thing, were warmly ensconced in the Larrik Inn.

Once I had the feeling back in my legs, I was pleased to meet up with not only my brother, but also John from my vets team and his family. Football is still often seen as a male domain, but in my experience, it is often very much a family outing. As well as my regular travelling companions on coach 1, one of the nicest aspects of the season has also been widening my circle of Palace friends. Sometimes it is just a raised hand in acknowledgement, but it is still an important interaction. As I alluded to previously, I am far from a party animal and don't have a massive circle of friends of my own age. In this regard, Palace has really become an important part of my social interaction, away from work and family. The walk along the river to Craven Cottage, was longer than I realised, much like my first away trip of the season, it caught me unawares. It did however give me time to inflate the inflatable sticks, that had been carefully stored since our trip to Cardiff, for the play-offs in 2004. It also enabled me plenty of time to annoy my nieces by bashing them over the head. with the said inflatables. Unfortunately, I wasn't able to persuade my nieces to actually take possession of the said inflatables, and unlike the man walking through the park with an inflatable woman, in a Palace shirt around his shoulders, (David Mellor eat your heart out,)I didn't find a convenient way of transporting them either. The Palace fans that we passed, all seemed in good voice and spirits, although this could not be said of the Fulham fan, who called me a prat. This may or may not be an accurate description, but was none the less, an unnecessary observation. Despite my considerable intake of cider, I resisted the temptation to reply that; "although I may be a prat, I am a Premier League prat" and continued to poke my sister in law with my inflatable, (Eat your heart out Sid James.)

Fulham's away end is a bit of a mystery, split as it is between away fans and neutrals. I assumed that there would be separate entrances and some kind of barrier on the concourse, but this isn't actually the case. This makes the decision by Fulham to not allow Palace extra tickets in this area, all the more difficult to understand. It is also a little difficult to understand why after entering the ground, my inflatable sticks were confiscated by the steward. Once again, this seemed like a very selective implementation of ground regulations. Being a grumpy old git and knowing that the said sticks, had been kicking around my house for 10 years and were in effect irreplaceable, I thought I would test the resolve of the steward. Firstly, I asked if I could deflate them and put them back in my pocket. When this was not seen as acceptable, (I obviously might have sneakily blown them up again.) I then informed the steward that I would like to collect my property after the game. The original steward agreed to this and was considering how this could be accommodated, when one of the senior stewards arrived and said that this was not possible, "We don't have the facilities." By this time, I was on a bit of a role and tried to discuss the concept of theft, with the senior "I've got a high vis jacket, so I'm important" Steward. His retort was that you shouldn't have brought them with you. My reply was, "why?" which confused him a little, and I sensed that this confusion was now being tempered with a "I'm a steward, there is nobody controlling my actions, and if you want to not get thrown out with your plastic sticks, I think you should shut up" attitude. I duly obliged, because he was right, he was a steward at a football match, he was a law unto himself, and I had drunk a shed load of cider. If he wanted to confiscate my property, but not the inflatable women, (he probably thought he might have a chance with her later,) the inflatable walking frame, banana etc. etc. that did make it into Craven Cottage, then he could. Much in the same way that he could chose to enforce, or otherwise, any of the myriad of ground regulations that appear nonsensically from time to time, at football grounds.

As I watched my 10 year old inflatables, disappear into a bin, with some other dangerous weapons such as bottles of water, lemonade, balloons, and flags that were too large, I desperately needed a fag. Oh forgot, I am now inside a football ground. I am actually outside, because I can see the sky, there is no three sided building in which I am standing, but there are notices everywhere that tell me that it is illegal. I hate these signs. They are in my opinion a lie. It is not illegal. It may be against ground regulations, but that is like saying selling a bottle of Coke with a lid on is illegal, Or standing in an all seated ground is illegal, (Although I'm not sure about this one, that might actually be illegal, anyway I digress). I didn't want to have another row, so opted to find Mum, Caroline and my camera battery, (ha-ha all part of my cunning plan, to divert their attention from my camera and flares, with a few inflatable sticks, the flares bit is an exaggeration, but you get the point).

With battery located, I went in search of refreshment and consequently the lavishly decored WC facilities that are available, at every football ground. On returning to the only semi-permanent stand, Fulham have to show for 13 years in the Premier League,(I know this is not entirely their fault, but it is still a sad observation.) I had my ticket check twice again, once at the bottom of the stairs, and once at the top. This was presumably to prevent the considerable number of Palace fans, with tickets in the neutral section relocating to the official away section, and is a perfectly sensible health and safety precaution. However, once I started to descend towards my seat, I realised that I had in fact been let into the wrong entrance. What exactly the stewards were therefore actually checking, escapes me. It was obviously not for smuggled inflatables, because these were in abundance.

Despite all these precautions to enforce ground regulations and ensure that fans only occupied the correct seat, it was pretty obvious that today, no one was actually going to sit anywhere. Except that is, a small section of neutral, neutrals directly next to the official away fans. To be honest, I am a bit tired of the whole trying to find Mum a seat thing, and with a few beers on board, I admit I just couldn't be bothered today. I did suggest that she could move in with the neutrals if she could get past Checkpoint Charlie, but she decided to stay with us. She is not an old fuddy duddy, (Old yes, but not the fuddy duddy part.) and I think she, like every fan, likes to be surrounded by our noisy exuberant supporters. That being said, we weren't that noisy or exuberant today and the HF didn't seem to be around on mass, which was a bit weird.

At half-time, I risked leaving the stand and checkpoints and found John and his brother out in the concourse, overlooking the river Thames. With a beer secured, we talked and watched the rowers pass up and down. It no longer seemed so cold and the view I admit, does make Craven Cottage, something a little special. When I go to watch Cricket at the Oval, one of the nice things is that you do not always think, the sport is the be all and end all of the day. I wander around the concourse and take in all that is going on around me. A wicket may fall and the crowd cheer, but I never feel I have to watch every ball. At football, things are generally different. Today with nothing to play for, (unless you include the £750,000 per place in the table,) I was content to talk football and watch boats. It was only when something exciting happened on the pitch and the crowd cheered, we even realised the second half had been in progress, for a little while. Slightly regrettably, we parted, arranged to meet at the club dinner and watched the rest of the game.

Marks match report

It wasn't quite end-of-season fare at the Cottage today – there were enough crunching tackles in there to ensure that – but there was a lack of tension that eventually robbed an injury time equaliser of any real meaning with Palace fans frankly barely breaking rhythm in their songs. Shame to see Fulham go down – a decent, inoffensive club that hasn't really bought into the "All The Money You Can Grab" League who, weirdly, were the only team to serve us a thrashing by score line only.

Despite pre-match rumours that Fulham would be playing the kids who'd just lost the F.A. Youth Cup Final while Pulis would be giving the likes of Parr, McCarthy & Gabbidon some Premier League game time, the teams turned out pretty much as expected, with (as far as I could tell) playing one youngster with the rest of the team the experienced lot who'd got them relegated. Pulis brought Gayle (no great surprise after Monday), Ince & Hennessey (wonder what Julian thought of missing out on completing an entire league season) into a 4-4-1-1 formation with Gayle up front & Chamakh in the hole.

Palace started brightly with an early break that saw Ince on the right shoot narrowly wide, whilst Hennessey's first involvement was not leaving his line for a cross followed by an awkward save at his near post. Palace generally played the more attacking football with Bolasie excelling until the final ball, but our rearguard wasn't as clued up as usual and Fulham managed to miss a series of half chances with one badly missed header followed by an air shot in the same attack – to be honest if they had a decent striker instead of Rodallega the game would have been completely different. Meanwhile Bolasie and Dann both drew good saves from Stockdale before Ward hammered in a shot from outside the box – it appeared from my PoV to go straight through the keeper into the net but Gayle peeled away in celebration so guess he got the final touch. Chamakh was having a series of misunderstandings with referee Mr. Friend who kept penalising Marouane when he seemed at least as much sinned against. An exceptionally long & accurate throw from Hennessey nearly saw Bolasie open his seasonal account but Fulham nearly snatched an equaliser just before half-time only for Hennessey made a smart save.

The second half saw Palace again slip into a series of quick breaks, especially from Bolasie & Ward down the left, but from a Fulham corner a good header across the box saw Rodallega's own firm header beat Hennessey but strike the far post. Possibly the key moment in the match came when Jedinak took a knock and was withdrawn, thus ruining his record of being on the pitch for every minute of the league season, with KG coming on. Within a couple of minutes Palace lost the lead, ironically immediately after a fast-flowing move the length of the pitch that just lacked the final pass, when Rodallega made space on the edge of the box and fed Woodrow in on the right; the young striker dummied Ward to make space then finished into the far top corner; on chances made it was about fair.

Palace withdrew Ince & Chamakh for Murray & Puncheon and soon started to gain a slight ascendancy, with Gayle in particular surprisingly winning a lot of balls played long to him against Heitinga & Hangeland. Murray was fouled just outside the box by Scott parker (a shadow of the player of a couple of years ago) and the free kick by Gayle curled outside the wall but inside the near post, a mark of brilliance. It could have been a hat-trick after another quick break from Puncheon saw Murray strike the bar from an angle, with the rebound dropping to Gayle a couple of yards out; unfortunately it came down far too fast and hit Dwight before bouncing wide. That was to cost a final win bonus as in the last seconds of stoppage time substitute David hit what looked like an unstoppable effort from the corner of the box that flew over Hennessey into that same far top corner with what was almost the last kick of the season. In fact with the literal last kick Gayle got on the end of a break straight from the restart only to shoot just over. In the end a draw was a fair result as neither side deserved to lose although Gayle was the outstanding player.

Hennessey - 6

Ward – 7
Mariappa – 6
Delaney – 7
Dann – 7
Jedinak – 7
Ledley – 6
Ince – 6
Bolasie – 7
Chamakh – 6
Gayle – 8
Dikgacoi – 6
Murray – 6
Puncheon – 5

The Temperance Fulham Away

From an editorial prospective, it would obviously have been better, if our visit to Fulham had provided a pivotal moment in the clubs history, a Stockport, Wembley, or Jimmy Glass. Unfortunately, one of the reasons why these memories are so memorable, is that for most fans each of these high tension season finales, is normally surrounded by 5 or 6 'oh well that was a nice day out wasn't it ' moments. At Palace, we have been quite lucky in the proportion of our seasons, which have gone down to the wire, and I am sure that there are some fans, who have finished in mid-table obscurity for 10 years, who would like a bit of our tension. So as I left the Cottage and headed back towards the Temperance, at Putney Bridge, I was not ungrateful to the players getting the job done early. It did after all, allow us to sit back and enjoy a nice day out. However, I cannot but help feel that you might have stopped reading about three games ago.

 Whilst I know that if somebody had put, "baby in the corner" twenty minutes before the end of Dirty Dancing, it would have saved me having to watch the end, over and over again, it wouldn't have been quite the same. (Please don't get all masculine bravado on me, just as we get to the end; I know that you all love it really) However, football isn't a Hollywood script and I can't do anything about the way the book ends, as my boss is often keen to point out, 'it is what it is'.

I suppose I could lie and say that back at the Temperance, where our boat organiser Karen had apparently hired a room, we partied until the early hours, singing Palace songs and I met my future wife. I could say this, but it would be a lie. The Holmesdale Fanatics were I believe there, and it was suggested to me that some of them had been there all afternoon. The suggestion was that they hadn't been to the game on mass, in protest about the price of the tickets. I'm not sure how true this was, but it would explain our relatively quiet and uncoordinated singing. If this was the case, on one hand I admire them, but I also think it is a bit sad that the crass stupidity of football ticket pricing, (I had to get it in, one more time) made them feel they needed to make this stand. Their sterling efforts have after all, created the atmosphere that has added so much to the season.

Their absence at the game, did however allow the rest of us to turn all 'old school,' and introduce a little bit of 'ole, ole' into a period of possession football, which I'm sure they would have found a little passé. I admit that I might also have formed this opinion, had the team in possession been Palace. As it was, it was Fulham passing the ball, and I think that in the away end, we all considered that the Fulham players needed some encouragement from somewhere, as they were receiving very little, if any, from their own fans.

So without the late appearance of Kylie, Taylor or Lily, I just had a quiet pint, thanked Karen for organising the boat and then headed back towards Putney Bridge Station and the Tube home. I didn't really know anybody, I had drunk quite enough for one day, and I was tired. It had been a long season. I wasn't exactly, 'Glad all over,' more kind of; glad it was over, for at least a few months.

On the way back to the station, I met some lost tourists, looking for the station and told them to follow me, I really wanted to just put my headphones on and listen to a good book, but I just couldn't help myself.

Marks Season Summary

In August my hopes were that, regardless of where Palace finished, we would develop as both a club and a team, so that even if we went straight back down we would be equipped for another promotion campaign. Expectations were slightly more pessimistic, anticipating at best a brave if unavailing fight against relegation. Our squad, despite the bargain basement supermarket sweep, looked the weakest on paper compared to other Premier League teams, although the arrivals of Gayle & Campaña were intriguing.

The first four league games of the season were promising, our early first home win removing the usual albatross - perhaps the Premier League wouldn't fulfil its reputation. Yet the League Cup defeat at Bristol City highlighted lack of depth, and Swansea handed out as one-sided a 2-0 thrashing as possible before Southampton easily saw us off. Holloway didn't know what his best team or formation was, and the nadir came with a shocking home defeat by Fulham, the only time all season the Selhurst crowd was silenced. Olly fell onto his sword, and I was sad to see him go; stories of Tony Pulis coming in had me shaking my head.

Keith Millen deserves a lot of praise, with a fighting defeat home to Arsenal followed by a battling 0-0 home to Everton, restoring morale on & off the pitch, but we were bottom when Pulis arrived. His first official game in charge saw perhaps the most vital result of the season, a 10-man win at Hull that prevented us falling away from the relegation pack. Results & performances started to pick up immediately, although the home win against the hapless Hammers was one of the worst games witnessed at Selhurst, while Newcastle did stroll to an easy victory, about the only time the team failed to show up under Pulis.

For naysayers like me there was no immediate sign of the long-ball apocalypse. It was being transferred slightly more directly upfield, while we seldom saw Speroni rolling the ball out to the back four.

Certainly Pulis did not have the ammunition to follow the Stoke template even if he wanted to, but certain players started to become essential to the new Palace tactics. The hard running if light scoring Jerome turned out to be far more valuable than the injured Murray or (temporarily) discarded Gayle, while the previously hapless Puncheon started to put in the odd outstanding performance. A deserved Boxing Day win at Villa, thanks to sub Gayle's tremendous finish, was followed by a fighting performance at the Etihad where opposition keeper Hart was named Man of the Match.

Still, following a defeat at Spurs when Puncheon spurned an early penalty, Palace had slumped back to the bottom of the table. Two important if scrappy home wins followed before the transfer window slammed shut, but we bemoaned the lost opportunity to hit an under strength Everton thanks to the weather. In contrast to the mass immigration of the summer Palace restricted themselves to four new signings. While Hennessey was one for the medium term, and Ince proved to be too lightweight at this stage of his career, Pulis accomplished a masterstroke with the arrival of Dann & Ledley, and we saw the immediate dispatch of West Brom.

Pulis was very much sticking to a 4-2-3-1 formation that could occasionally be deployed in a more attacking 4-3-3 or defensive 4-5-1, but the plan was to play pretty much on the counter attack, given that in almost every game Palace conceded 60% (or more) possession to the opposition. The back four soon took a permanent look with Mariappa at right back in place of the less defensively minded Parr or Moxey, the outstanding Ward switching to the left, while Delaney – another candidate for player of the year – and Dann completed perhaps our best defence since the 1978/79 side. The gates were locked securely behind them by Julian in the form of his life, managing to pull off some brilliant point-saving saves in most games. The midfield was barred by Jedinak alongside either KG or Ledley, whose versatility gave the team greater scope for flexibility. With Jerome alone up front, and the flanks secured by Bolasie, who grew into the season, and the improving Puncheon, the bellwether of our attacking outlook was if Chamakh played in the hole or one of the more prosaic midfielders. There was no room for the more inventive play of Bannan, Williams or Gayle, all short in stature if not skill.

The position though was still uncertain when a point
earned at Swansea by a late penalty from the returning
Murray was followed by a dire home defeat to the
Saints, then two trips to the north East for an
appalling 0-0 at Sunderland followed by late heartbreak
at St James' Park. It looked like our chances were
blown with our run-in looking far more difficult than
most relegation rivals'. Yet Chelsea solved our
goalscoring problems in a cup tie atmosphere inspiring
one of the great home displays as Selhurst rocked.
Better came the following week when hapless Cardiff
were slain in a febrile Welsh capital, a second key
game of the season, before another remarkable Speroni
save saw three points garnered against Villa.

Apparently the best display of the season came when
high flying Everton were defeated 3-2 at Goodison.
Annoyingly I was following this match from a restaurant
basement in Amiens, having been in the stadium when the
original fixture was postponed. Amazingly Palace were
on the brink of safety before April was out, and this
was confirmed when another outstanding counter-
attacking display saw off West Ham to give Palace five
straight league wins. Yet the best was yet to come in
the final home game at a packed Selhurst, when this
amazing crowd roared Palace back from a three goal
deficit to shred the Scousers' title hopes, with
Gayle's two goal salvo highlighting his potential,
which was confirmed with another double at Fulham.

Tony Pulis had built a team that could fight (in the
honest sense) and not Stoke Mk. II, proving those
doubters like me thoroughly wrong, wringing
performances from a squad that still looked weaker than
any other on paper. It was this, allied with the
exceptional atmosphere at Selhurst and the large
following on our trips that deservedly saw us for once
not below the dotted line on a Premier League table.
While some of our less abrasive players had slipped out
of the picture, and we hadn't brought on any of our
younger lads, this was a minor quibble given the
ultimate result. It was equally difficult to chose a
player who stood out from the rest; this was a real
TEAM effort from everyone one on & off the pitch that
made this season one of the most remarkable, unexpected
& joyful I can recall.

Player of the Year Awards

It is customary at the end of any sporting season, to have Player of the Year awards and I have attended many of these over the years. The first that I can really remember, took place in the old supporters club. on what is now the Sainsbury's car park. I was a founder member of the Palace Guard and a whole host of players were in attendance including: as a very faded photo reminds me, Jerry Murphy and Vince Hilaire. These evenings, became more raucous as I represented a variety of football, cricket and rugby clubs, over the next 30 years. The sophisticated and respectable only really returning this year, as I attended the Alleyn's Old Boys F.C 125th Season Dinner at Dulwich and Sydenham Golf Club. However, despite all of these evenings, what I had been most looking forward to when I returned to London, was attending the CPFC player of the year awards, in a marquee on the pitch. My brother, Hazel, Mum and Dad had attended for a number of years and they always came home with lots of great photographs, a hangover, (not Mum and Dad obviously,) and a lot less money in the bank than they started with. (Shirt auctions after a few bottles of Vino, can have this effect.) The first couple of years after I came back to Sarf Landon, were a struggle financially and I could not afford the outlay of the dinner. I had saved up in 2013, and was hoping that I would be able to go. My brother had already organised a second table and I made sure that I was top of the waiting list. Unfortunately, the club decided, that they wanted to widen the appeal of the event, and make it more financially accessible to all supporters. I understand why this was, but given the choice of a black tie Dinner Dance at £65, or a seat in a theatre at £25, I personally would always go for the dinner. I know that some people considered the dinner elitist, and not everybody's cup of tea, but as a coach 1 traveller, I am used to this accusation. Not everybody can sit in the directors box and not everyone would want to, but it doesn't mean you rip it out. One thing that I have missed since moving back to the smoke, is the opportunity to get all poshed up, every now and again. It is rather amusing, that despite some Londoners views that everybody outside the capital, is some local yokel. Country folk are actually quite good at organising these sort of smart, glad rags events. Hunt Balls, Captains Balls, Lions Balls or general Fund-raising Balls, are all part of the social calendar, that I miss. Although these events, are still not everybody's perfect night out in rural communities, they are however not seen as elitist. They are just part of the fabric of the community. You either go or you don't, my Rugby Club Ball used to sell out 500 tickets, without one single jot of advertising. In fact it used to sell out so quickly, that long standing players were sometimes disappointed, to miss out. It certainly wasn't a night for toffs and snobs, just a right good old knees up with good food, good music and good company.

I always considered the CPFC Player of the Year night was similar, but in this, "everything must be accessible to everybody" world, you actually sometimes create a, "some things aren't accessible to anybody" situation. For my 40th, my brother gave me a signed picture of Kenny Sansom, my all-time favourite player. This was signed at the Player of the Year awards. Similarly, Ian and Hazel have a variety of photographs taken over the years, in which the players look very relaxed, and Hazel brushes up alright, as well. I am not sure how you can replicate this in the Fairfield Halls. However, the kids will all be able to go, so that's all great then. I like being surrounded by my nephews and nieces, but not everything needs to be accessible to children. They need to have things to look forward to: being taken to a pub, travelling away on their own, singing the rude version to a song and not having to insert their own words. My youngest niece is actually so adept at this last activity now, that the phrase "I can't hear, any thing" automatically takes on an extra syllable, when I use it myself. That being said, putting my poets head on for a moment. I think I would probably prefer, the more rhythmically correct, "I can't hear a, dropping pin." Whatever the reasons behind the decision in 2013, it was highly unlikely to change, now that we are in the Premier League and have to installed undersoil heating. This is so that, when it snows, the game is called off because of, the safety of the crowds travelling to the game and not any risk to the players on the pitch. (Possibly the only time that fans are.. put before players or the TV companies.) Last year, Hazel was pretty annoyed about missing out on one of her big nights of the year,and buying another new outfit. After the expense of the play-offs, it was pretty unanimous in my family, that no one was going to the POTY. This year I was equally nonplussed about the whole thing. However, I did consider that there was one way it could be made a bit more special, assuming I could sort out suitable tickets, that is.

As soon as they went on sale I went on line and unlike an away trip, was able to highlight exact seats which were bookable. As one of the first on the booking site, I wasn't offered only the back row of the balcony, but could pretty much choose what I wanted. This was all very modern and sophisticated, but as you probably realise, I am an awkward bugger. The seats I really wanted weren't available. A quick call to the Fairfield Halls, was answered promptly and I explained that I would really like to book one of their boxes. The box office staff, after a quick inquiry, informed me that these were being reserved for the club itself.

Unperturbed by this news I dropped a line to the club directly. A quick reply came back, that they weren't sure at the moment, which of the boxes were actually going to be used. Despite this, I was reassured that I would be top of the list, for any that weren't needed.

In the end I was either forgotten about, or all the boxes were taken. My nice idea, to reward my family for all their support over the last few years, couldn't be realised. I will just have to wait for that executive coach trip to Eastern Europe, once we again earn the place, that was so harshly denied us 20 years ago.

The Awards

Hopefully by now you will have realised that there is an order to this book. I write a load of old guff, then Mark comes in with some insightful analysis of the game and the players. It may not be perfect but it works. However, as this book is about a journey into the Premier League, just when you are comfortable with the format, I'm going to change it. You might think that as the paying public, you might get a say in this, but you don't. I'm in charge, so I get to make the decisions and it suits me to have Mark's Awards now and mine last. A bit like Sir Gary, I am the anchor man, so however interesting other people are, I get to have the last word. As it was when we were all younger, it's my ball, so I make up the rules.

Marks Player of the Year

```
This should be easy! Just tot up the (stingy) marks
I've given this season, divide by the number of
appearances, and then we have a mark for each player.
Can't you tell I work in Accounts armed with
spreadsheets & love statistical data! Except that over
40 games (37 league matches i.e. missing Everton away
which I missed and three cup matches) the marks will
tend to average out between 5 & 7, with 6 being an
average performance, which really won't give an
indication of true worth to the team. So, deleting the
Excel file, the marks below should be taken as
indicative of how I saw each player's worth to Crystal
Palace this season rather than an analysis of their
actual performances as viewed by me. In order to
differentiate more widely over nine months of games
I've taken the liberty of using half marks.

I'll start with the managers as it only seems fair...

Holloway - 5.5
Millen - 7.0
Pulis - 8.5

The Players

Dann - 8.0
Delaney - 8.0
Ward - 7.5
Speroni - 7.5
Mariappa - 7.0
Gabbidon - 7.0
Ledley - 7.0
```

```
Bolasie - 7.0
Chamakh - 7.0
Jedinak - 7.0
Dikgacoi - 6.5
Puncheon - 6.5
Gayle - 6.5
Jerome - 6.5
Hennessey - 6.0
Parr - 6 .0
Moxey - 6.0
McCarthy - 6.0
Wynter - 6.0
O'Keefe - 6.0
Bannan - 6.0
Boateng - 6.0
Murray - 6.0
Guedioura - 6.0
Williams (the short one) - 5.5
Ince - 5.5
De Silva - 5.5
Wilbraham - 5.5
Alexander - 5.0
Ramage - 5.0
Campaña - 5.0
Garvan - 5.0
Thomas - 5.0
Phillips - 5.0
Appiah - 5.0
Dobbie - 4.5
Kébé - 4.5
Marange - 4.0
Grandin - 4.0
```

For those of you who are really interested from those who appeared more than once, top of my actual averages was Delaney (6.78) followed closely by Gabbidon (6.65), Dann (6.62), Bolasie (6.61), Speroni (6.57) and Ward (6.56). Interesting that, with the exception of the mercurial Bolasie, defensive players predominate, which reflects the fact that Palace often played without the ball with pressure on the back four and keeper.

Special Achievement Award.

One of the major beefs expressed by supporters about the Player of the Year is the way that the voting is only available to those who attend. this has resulted in Julian Speroni winning the award, for the seven hundred and fifty-sixth time at this year's official awards. I am not sure if this is a reflection on the rest of the team, that our goalkeeper keeps winning this award or on Julian himself.

It could also be as a result of a certain travelling companion, standing at the entrance of the Fairfield Halls, with a stack of pre-filled voting forms, a balaclava, a special sharpened white stick and a home-made sign stating, "vote for Jules, or the little kid gets it". Joniesta, chained to wheels of her chair, would be encouraging this voting, by vigorously handing out the said forms. Whatever the reason, he does deserve a special award, of some kind:

As is often the case at awards nights I will start off the proceedings with this Special Achievement Award. 10 years ago, when he came madly rushing out of his goal to gift Everton a simple tap in, I am not sure that anybody would have expected us to have the same No 1, a decade later. This individual, has without doubt, been one of the most dedicated and talented players of my generation. The tradition of this particular award is also that you get it, when you have won everything else. People want to recognise you, but don't want the whole awards thing to get boring. There is also a tendency, to give it to people who are coming to the swansong of their career. I am not sure that this is relevant to Jules, as I have been impressed with the way he continues to develop as a goalkeeper, particularly concerning moving out of the area of his 6 yard box. I know that my own trauma, in some outpost of the West Sussex League in 1987, made me far less inclined to venture out of my goal and wonder if this is also, some kind of psychological block for Jules. Alternatively, he just knows he is not very good at it. The old adage that you can't teach an old dog new tricks, has not been completely disproved, but our own old faithful is definitely giving it a good go.

Despite these accolades to Jules for his playing performances, one of the major reasons for my decision to give him this award, is actually related to him not playing. My own Special Achievement Award, goes to Mr Julian Speroni, for not punching Tony Pulis in the face, on the morning of the Fulham match. Whatever the tactical and team reasons for dropping Julian, for the last match season, there can in my mind, be no justification. At the start of this book, I praised Ollie for sticking with the team that won us promotion, for our first game against Spurs. It is quite neat to be able to repeat at the end of this book that, in my opinion, there is room for sentiment in football. Julian had played every league game up until Fulham and would I imagine have been hoping to join Mile Jedinak, as having played every minute of every game, in this fantastic season.

Miles injury must have been personally very hard to take, as he also could not eventually complete this feat. Unfortunately, injuries are a part of the game, being left out of the team, in these circumstances, is not. If Jules or Tony Pulis are reading this and would like to set the record straight, then I will gladly insert a retraction. Maybe, Jules gladly offered his place. Somehow, I doubt this was the case. It struck more of someone trying to exert there authority, in an unnecessary way. (and I wrote that before the first game of the 2014/15 season, imagine how I feel now). If Tony, really wanted to play Hennessy that badly, I personally might have been inclined to play Jules up front anyway. Come to think of it, I might also have left Jedi on the pitch and moved him upfront as well. It didn't work out so badly for Danny Butterfield, did it. I once experience something very similar, for a cricket club. I had worked tirelessly for them over 7 years and although I continued to play, it was never quite the same. I hope that Julian, is thicker skinned than I am and we see him back between the sticks, at Selhurst next year.

Young Player Of The Year – Not Awarded During Premiership Seasons

Crystal Palace have a fantastic record in bringing through young players that goes back at least as far as Johnny Byrne. In my generation, there was the team of the 80's and this tradition has continued with the likes of Wilf and Joniesta. In fact, as mentioned previously, it was another young debutant Ibrahim Sekaja, who secured our survival up at Hull just three seasons ago. Such is the number of young players, who have made first team debuts for Palace that many slip from distant memory. When I started my new job back in 2012 I started playing 5-a-side with the company team and found that one of our engineers, was one such player, who I admit I had never even heard of. A quick search through the programme archive and Ian Kings amazing 'The complete record'[xv], gave me the details and I was able to take him the programme of his one and only Palace appearance. Unfortunately, his call up was so late that he didn't even make it onto the team sheet on the back page. However, a picture of Tariq Nabil appeared in the programme for our next home match, so I was able take him that as well. With this fine tradition of producing young and talented players, who break into the clubs first XI, it is great regret that my Young player of the year awards are suspended until further notice. The club, at the official awards night, did still try to concoct an award for a young player, but in my opinion, this was a bit like calling John Burridge into the England under 21's squad, at the age of nearly thirty.

If I was being very pedantic I would probably have given the award to Johnny Williams, on the basis that he is by far the best young player that we have on our books. Anybody who can play for his or her country at 19 (Even Microsoft word's grammar checker has gone all P.C. on Me.) and be awarded Man of the Match, in a team that included Gareth Bale, is obviously a special talent. It is just a shame that the desire for results, means that he has not been able to feature for us. Ipswich Town were instead, the lucky recipients, of his wonderful ability and all around niceness.

To move things on a bit I will just mention two other young players who I will look out for over the coming seasons, although they were not yet candidates for this award. Sully KaiKai looks like an exciting attacking prospect and he can certainly take a free kick. My personal favourite from the development games that

I saw this year was Conner Dymond and although I am not sure that he will be able to break into the first team anytime soon, there will always be a place for his tenacious tackling at some level in professional football. (Until F.I.F.A. outlaw tackling altogether, that is.)

Before I announce my two main awards, it is traditional to have a whole host of minor awards. These normally involve long speeches that interest only a very few people but do offer a good opportunity to go to the bar, the toilet or have a fag. As you have not been drinking, whatever wine on the table that looked like producing the best yield, you may not need any of the reasons for this interlude. I will therefore skip the speeches and announce the awards.

- Favourite ground visited: The Liberty Stadium, Swansea
- Least favourite ground visited: **Carrow Road, Norwich**
- Best concessions: Carrow Road, Norwich
- Favourite goal: OG John Terry v Chelsea
- Best performance : **Everton Away**
- Worst stewarding performance : **The MET v Brighton U 21's**
- Best stewards: **Wigan Athletic**
- Best theatrical performance: **Ashley Young** (Ashley Young now retains the trophy)
- Best Home Fans: **Hull City**
- Favourite Sandwiches: Smoked salmon and cream cheese
- Fan of the year: **MY MUM**

Player of the Year

Amongst the discussions about voting for Player of the Year that have taken place on the BBS has been the type of player that Palace often choose. Looking back over the list of winners it is a fair argument that we have often mostly chosen goal scorers, goalkeepers or combative workhorses. There is however, the occasional exception, Jerry Murphy (1983), could never really be considered in any of these categories. As we have not exactly had a prolific goal scorer, this season and I have already made it clear that Jules has already received, all he is going to, this leaves us back with combative workhorse. The most obvious choice would be Mile Jedinak, but I am sure that he will get many plaudits from other places. Instead, my Player of the Season is Damien Delaney. As somebody who is myself blessed with limited ability, I am always impressed by anybody who uses whatever ability they have, to the absolute maximum. I think that Damien has done this. As a mathematician, I general hate it, when anybody is described as having given more than one hundred percent, but on this occasion I will make an exception.

Clubman Of The Year

It is perhaps more common to have the Player of the Year award, last in the running order. I do however, like to do things a little differently, which is something my family have had to deal with, over the last 40 years and so you can deal with now. Despite this general tendency, there is also a method in my madness. Firstly, this is the award, which I have won most times, over my own playing career. West Sussex IHE F.C., Kington CC and most recently this year, Alleyn's Old Boys Vets F.C., have all decided that although I am a bit rubbish, I turn up and help out quite a lot. Consequently, I tend to consider that this award is the most important and should come last. Secondly, I have been conscious throughout the book not to alienate too many readers; I am aware that my choice for Clubman of the year may at the very least, surprise some. As we approach the final few pages, I feel more confident that if you have made it this far, you will make it to the end.

In any organisation, there are people with exceptional talent and skill. They will be obvious in the contribution that they make and they are normally, rewarded commensurately. They will often rise in their level of influence, in the club or company until they reach a ceiling. Alternatively, their abilities will contribute to the organisation expanding, or increasing its significance and their existing role will become more complex or difficult. Unfortunately, at this point, they are sometimes stuck in a position, that they or those around them, no longer feel that they are suited too. It is often the case, in a business environment, that these individuals then flounder around not being able to do the job but not wanting to admit it either. In a footballing context, the reverse is often true and this is particularly the case with managers. They are often sacked, before they have had the opportunity to come to terms with new challenges. In both the business and footballing worlds, it is very rare that somebody would admit their deficiencies and walk away. They prefer to act in the best interests of themselves, rather than their employers. On the 23rd of October 2013 Ian Holloway took the brave step to resign as manager of Crystal Palace. I have heard nothing in the intervening months, to convince me that this was done, for any other reasons than the best interests of Palace. Ian in his press conference looked physically drained and I am sure that he had done everything within his power to improve our results. In this decision, at a relatively early stage of the season, he gave the club the opportunity to regroup and appoint a manager, with the experience to turn things around. Now that we know, how successfully this was achieved, this decision can be seen a pivotal in our season. For me, a Clubman of the year, is someone who makes these kind of decisions. They might involve a financial or other disadvantage to the individual at a personal level, but they are in the best interest of the club. One of my awards cost me a partner and much of my sanity. I hope that the award of Clubman of the year to Ian Holloway, came with the preservation of his marriage, his family, his sanity (although some have suggested, incorrectly IMO, that he doesn't have any) and in the knowledge, that it was the right thing to do. Even if, I didn't think so at the time. I for one will always thank you for that and wish you good luck for the future.

The Toast

In the best traditions of awards ceremonies, it is time to stand and raise your glasses, with a toast to my club Crystal Palace, its fans, players, employees and owners. I would also like to extend these good wishes, to all similar clubs around the country, who hope for, but do not expect great successes. Over the course of this season, I have travelled six thousand seven hundred and twenty-six miles following the team. In total, it has cost £1576, which in fairness was a bit less than I was expecting, but this doesn't include Costa coffee, beer, thirty pence a time for toilets at Victoria or Mums spend on the sandwiches. My home season ticket is also, very reasonably priced. There have been times over the season when I wondered if it was all worth it, Sunderland and Norwich away, particularly come to mind. However, if we did not go to football on a Saturday, what would I do? I haven't committed myself to every game next season, yet. However, when the away season ticket application, comes pinging into my in-box, at some point in the summer, I am sure all self-control will disappear. So the grumpy old fan, his Mum, his stupid hat and most importantly Crystal Palace Football Club, will be back again next year, doing it all again and "Out staying our welcome"

Tottenham Home

Speroni – 7 – Not as overworked as one would expect, with one athletic tip over and some brave blocks.

Ward – 6 – At times was left outnumbered on the right as Palace could not quite get the hang of the new formation, and Lennon did a fair impression of Zaha late on in turning Joel inside out, but the right back kept going and made a number of good challenges. Also tried hard to offer width down the right in attack.

Moxey – 6 – The penalty decision was one of those things; it is difficult to keep arms at your side when sliding in, but those are the rules. Several times in the first half Dean was left exposed but he tried hard to cover back, mostly successfully. Worked hard up and down the left in both halves and provided much needed width.

Delaney – 7 – Until late on the centre of the defence held up quite well, only being caught out by one good passing move and a run by Defoe that saw the defence part.

Gabbidon – 6 – Solid for much of the match but exposed late on by Defoe's pace.

Dikgacoi – 6 – His passing at time was poor but he put in a good shift, covering the right side with Ward, but often too deep to be an influence in creative terms. Had a late chance but denied by Lloris.

Jedinak – 8 – Outstanding but not quite perfection, as he too succumbed to the occasional terrible pass straight to an opponent. Otherwise broke up numerous Spurs' attacks with anticipation and a bit of steel – surprisingly Clattenburg seemed to allow harder tackles than in the Championship. Jedi's form & fitness will be crucial this season.

Garvan – 6 – Looked good with the ball, and laid off some lovely passes, but again from a deep-lying role which made the through balls easier to defend against. Was outmanoeuvred down the left a little too often for my liking but did put in one lovely strong challenge that made me check it wasn't the Jedi.

Dobbie – 5 – Looked too slow & lightweight, including breaking up a quick counter by twice stumbling over the ball. Knocked off the ball far too easily.

Gayle – 4 – As mentioned above Dwight looked quite lost and was more of a liability than an asset, conceding possession far too cheaply. It appeared that he wasn't sure of his role, and some of the errors betrayed his lack of professional football experience. Yet there is undoubtedly raw talent there, as he showed with his run and shot in the second half, which may be because he found himself playing more in a central striker's role and he could act naturally. As with Dobbie was muscled off the ball far too easily.

Wilbraham – 5 – Difficult to see Aaron as the striker whose goals will give us a decent chance this season, as he is far too slow, and was another who when he won the ball too often knocked the ball into the space where no team mate existed. Some of this can be laid at the feet of his supposed support from deep, but again it meant that the ball kept coming back after we cleared it.

Williams – 7 – Made an immediate impact when he came on as the only Palace player to run past opponents with the ball, and although Spurs learnt quickly and closed him down in numbers.

Phillips – 6 – Shame his pace is also 40 years old as Kevin twice found himself with chances where that extra second cost us. However the attack gained a focus that Wilbraham couldn't supply when KP came on, making runs that gave the midfield options.

Chamakh – 6 – Looked very handy when he came on, although deployed more down the right than through the middle.

Speroni – 7 – Absolutely brilliant first-half save, but let down by his kicking, which was atrocious, and possibly should have come for the ball in the build up to the winner.

Ward – 7 – Continued his impressive run of form from the end of last season, especially when making great runs down the right, but seemed to tire late on and was more exposed in defence.

Moxey – 8 – Was unquestionable my Palace Man of the Match until I saw replays of both goals. Should he have been marking Adam instead of one of the forwards? How much pressure was he under when under hitting his pass to Gabbidon? Neither is clear-cut and, in the second case, Palace still had plenty of opportunities to deal with the threat. Otherwise Dean defended manfully (note who pressured Crouch into heading over) and his attacking play down the wing was a delight, especially the wonderful passing move that he initiated and nearly finished.

Gabbidon – 6 – Generally solid, although was caught by lack of pace at least twice, and could conceivably dealt better with Moxey's pass instead of conceding the fateful throw-in.

Delaney – 7 – One superbly sliding tackle in the first half, and generally had a good game, although Stoke's play early in the second had his struggling.

Dikgacoi – 7 – Quietly efficient and helped Palace win the midfield battle in the first half, and fought manfully in the second. Unusual choice to mark Crouch at set pieces.

Jedinak – 8 – Made some poor passes in the second half but generally played up to the high standards he has set, although as the game concluded he had dropped deeper and often took the ball behind the central defenders.

Campaña – 7 – Someone compared him to Fabregas, and not just in appearance. Jose looks a real gem, with some lovely short passes, good movement and willingness to work hard. Perhaps too hard as we wondered how long he could keep up such efforts, and he palpably tired after the interval. Could be the creative key with KG & Jedi as the locks.

Puncheon – 7 – Another impressive debutant whose movement and work rate were outstanding. The way he made a space for the effort that nearly squeezed under Begovic was classy. Only blemish was being one of those culpable for the second goal.

Gayle – 6 – Played in a more attacking role and showed that he does have the raw material & talent to make a success of his Palace career. What he does need to do, similar to Wilf in his early days, is learn the art of using the ball and losing the blinkers, with a couple of poor choices made in promising positions.

Chamakh – 7 – Until he tired Marouane ran rings around Huth & Shawcross, switching positions with Gayle or Puncheon, and the way he took his goal was a reminder of Glenn Murray's play. Dithered fatally at the back for their second and his weak effort at a block was worrying.

Williams – 7 – Made Stoke fearful for their lead with some clever running, and nearly opened them up until bundled over.

Garvan – 6 – Made a couple of good passes, and a couple of ambitious ones that were cut out. Looked more at home than against Spurs.

Phillips – 6 – Involved in some clever link play but dragged his only chance well wide

Bristol city Away (LC)

Alexander – 5 – A poor debut: his kicks at times were weak, especially from the ground; he flapped at crosses; and he hesitated to come to collect simple balls. A parody of Scottish goalkeeping. I would be seriously worried on this sole display if Julian was indisposed.

Wynter – 7 – Possibly the only plus point of the night, he appeared composed and put in some good tackles. Less successful in providing width in attack.

Jerome Williams – 6 – Decent debut at left back that was up against City's best player on the night in Reid, but he stuck to his task and did not let anyone down.

Ramage – 5 – Strong showing in the first half, but sadly embarrassed for pace and positioning for the two goals. Took his role as skipper well, taking time to make sure the two inexperienced full backs knew what was expected of them in a quiet manner, unlike McCarthy's bellows.

Marange – 6 – Looked a little small for a centre back & possibly a tad overweight, but did not seem to don anything wrong or anything outstanding.

O'Keefe – 5 – Solid but unspectacular first half, then his game fell apart, his errors setting up both Bristol goals. Booked for a couple of wild challenges and perhaps lucky to stay on as, frustrated, he made a third. Ended up out of position at right back as we chased the game. A let down after his strong showing at Wembley: I expected more with this chance to show he should be in the squad for Saturday.

Garvan – 5 – I thought this should be the chance for Owen to show he can control a game with his passing, but sadly he was as mediocre as most of his colleagues, barely registering for much of the game. Poor pass put O'Keefe in trouble for the second goal. At least did have a shot and a good one too, to score our goal.

Dobbie – 4 – Even more put out in that this should have been the game that Stephen could have dominated. Instead he flickered weakly, with his set piece delivery being no more than reasonable, with one early wildly over hit free kick. Worse than against Spurs.

Grandin – 5 – Not entirely sure what his role was as he popped up on both wings and through the middle in the first half without suggesting he would make in difference in any area. Apparently not the answer to our current lack of wingers.

Jonny Williams – 6 – A real disappointment, given a chance to showcase his abilities, yet hardly causing the Bristol defence any concern. Did a lot of work in deep positions that did not hurt City, and often found his efforts wasted by colleagues. Also the victim of some cynical challenges. Did not disappear like some team mates but needs to impose himself on this type of match & opposition.

Wilbraham – 5 – Received hardly any service and did not constitute a threat on goal. Still surprised he was withdrawn given our lack of height.

Phillips – 5 – Another from whom I expected more. Caught offside on several occasions and wasted one chance with a shot dragged wide. Later dropped deeper trying to set up moves but was no more successful there.

Appiah – 5 – Had one opening and wasted it with a snatched effort. Still hardly received great service.

De Silva – 6 – Thrown in to recover a lost situation, made a couple of decent runs and had our first shot on target, even if it hardly stung Parish's hands.

Sunderland Home

Speroni – 6 – No, I'm not being miserly, but Julian had relatively little to do apart from a couple of routine saves. His command of the box and distribution was greatly improved from last week, and at the end it was obvious how much the win meant to him and his colleagues.

Ward – 8 – With the exception of that one slip against Colback, Joel gave a tremendous display, both defensively and in supporting the attack.

Moxey – 8 – At the moment Dean is playing at a level far above anything we've seen from him during his time at Palace. Like Ward he has both defensive & offensive duties, and his raiding down the left in the second half in particular was outstanding. Important clearing header in the period we were under pressure. When did we swap him for Bale?

Gabbidon – 7 – There were a couple of silly free kicks given away in dangerous positions but otherwise Danny read the game well and made several important interceptions. Unwittingly scored the first goal.

Delaney – 7 – Does like the long, raking, diagonal clearances that must be a tactic agreed upon by Olly. Solid at the back, although still question whether he or Gabbidon should have assumed responsibility for marking Fletcher. Also showed a willingness to bring the ball out from the back.

Dikgacoi – 8 – Outstanding at the less flashy aspects of the game, with several tackles and interceptions that wrought midfield control away from Sunderland. I thought he'd scored the first goal, such was the confusion, but there was no doubt who had that thunderbolt from distance, touched over by Westwood. Looks far more comfortable at this level that he did at times a division below.

Jedinak – 8 – Would have been a "9" but for losing Fletcher for their goal. That aside, possibly the most complete performance from a Palace midfielder I have ever seen. A rock in front of the back four, with numerous interceptions and tackles, and showing a great engine to keep going at that level for 90+ minutes. Often dropped behind the two central defenders to maintain possession and build moves. It was a shock when he actually misplaced one pass – and I was one who was critical of this aspect of his game in his first 2 years here – so controlled was his distribution; the cross field pass to Ward early in the first half could have been played by Bobby Charlton or Glenn Hoddle so accurate was it. Also made several breaks and unlucky with two efforts that just drifted wide & over.

Campaña – 7 – Not quite as impressive as at the Britannia, and occasionally lost the ball, but worked hard and showed some impressive touches in tight situations. Looks the perfect complement in midfield to KG & Jedinak. Dead ball delivery good as well, including the corner that caused such confusion for Gabbidon's goal. Has picked up the pace of the English game even if, at the moment, he cannot last the course for 90 minutes.

Puncheon – 8 – I take back all those things I said about Jason after his hat-trick display against us for Millwall. Looks like another exceptional (temporary) acquisition by Holloway, adding pace & skill to the side. Made several breaks and two shots slipped wide. His hard work, and another kindly rebound, set up the opening for O'Keefe.

Gayle – 7 – Continued gradual improvement from Dwight, who showed great anticipation to win the penalty and even bigger balls to take it. Always a threat to the Sunderland defence. Let's hope that, like AJ, that first goal takes some of the weight of expectation off his shoulders and he can play with more natural freedom.

Chamakh – 8 – Hardworking display with no little skill, although oddly despite the number of efforts on goal, none appeared to come from Marouane. That should not matter as he made several openings for colleagues and led the line well, taking & giving knocks. Also showed at the back that he might have taken on board criticism from Holloway for his "defending" last week.

Williams – 7 – That horribly screwed shot aside, Jonny provided a strong rebuff to critics like me of his display at Bristol City. Not so much running with the ball at feet but found space, made great runs off the ball, and several touches of class to set up colleagues. Unlucky with the volley saved by Westwood.

Wilbraham – 6 – Only paled in comparison to his colleagues, Aaron showed some neat touches when he came on.

O'Keefe – 7 – Another I criticised at Ashton Gate, came on and had also made some good contributions before that terrific finish with his left foot.

Manchester United Away

Speroni – 7 – Did all he could and didn't make a mistake, making several good saves with the ball moving in the air.

Mariappa – 5 – Struggled against Ashley Young in the first half, often finding himself minding two opponents. Badly exposed in the second half when the ball was played behind him several times. Hope he's a better centre back than full back.

Moxey – 6 – Struggled at times when Rooney drifted wide, but stuck to his task and made some important blocks. Found it more difficult as the game wore on but kept going until the end.

Delaney – 6 – Good marks for his defensive work, with lots of desperate blocks and decent challenges, but as for some of his decision making and passing ability... Also has this habit of making at least one awful error per game that nearly cost us a goal.

Gabbidon – 7 – Had a moment of madness when trying to play football in the wrong part of the pitch, but defended manfully and was not as exposed for pace as I thought be might be.

Jedinak – 5 – His role in breaking down the opposition's attacks worked well, but wasted this good work with some appalling passing; twice in the first 15 minutes, under no apparent pressure, he passed the ball straight to an opponent. The first goal & KG's red card can be directly attributed to a later similar error in judgement. Was one of the key players in slowing down our play and often sought to play conservatively.

Dikgacoi – 7 – One of our better outfield players in the first half in his role as defensive shield, and not as profligate with the ball as others. Twice denied Young scoring opportunities with the England man resorting to diving. Can't castigate him for the sending off as even if it was a foul (not seen the replay yet) he had to try to tackle Young.

Campaña – 6 – Good in patches but another who wasn't as positive as I'd like on the ball, and did give it away more than once. Busy and tried to help out Moxey down the right. Thought he might be replaced with the more muscular Jerome given the situation, but it looked like another like for like change on the hour, although Jose didn't look as tired as in the previous two matches.

Puncheon – 5 – Made little impact on the game, although the lack of adequate service could explain that; often missing when Mariappa needed help. Another who conceded possession too cheaply & too readily.

Gayle – 6 – Showed good anticipation in making two chances in the first half, although was also guilty of poor use of the ball, and a lack of movement. Twice good passes were played through towards him: on one occasion he made no run; on the other he turned the wrong way. Would a more experienced player have anticipated the passes? Had about our only shot in the second. Still a work-in-progress.

Chamakh – 7 – Worked hard in all areas of the pitch, often dropping deep or wide to pick up the ball, in part because it wasn't played forwards too much. Also made some important clearing headers from corners. Unlucky to be booked considering what Young got away with, and ran himself into the ground for the team, not something he was renowned for at Arsenal.

Guédioura - 6 – A couple of nice touches but also guilty of giving the ball away. Not a fair test given the situation.

Jerome – 5 – Never got into the game, but again not easy to given the state of the match.

Kébé – 5 – Exactly the same as the other two subs, not really found a role to play.

Swansea City Home

Speroni – 6 – If Julian is being harsh on himself he might be critical of his efforts on both goals, but from a rank amateur there didn't seem much he could have done: The first was smashed at him from short range and he nearly blocked it with his legs, only to find the ball bounce down then end up in the roof of the net; the second looked like a good save from the first effort but the rebound didn't go out of play. Did make one excellent save from a 25-yard effort that he saw late, but on the debit side his kicking at times was poor.

Mariappa – 5 – Found Routledge a problem from the start and caught out early for the first goal. On the attacking side never really tried to overlap and provide width apart from one cross in the first half.

Moxey – 6 – Fought hard, especially against Dyer with not much help from Jerome, and unlucky to be booked for a slightly miss-timed tackle when more cynical fouls from both sides went unpunished in the first half, although nearly added a second caution on a couple of occasions, while nearly giving away another Spurs-like penalty. Tried hard to work the left side in attack but received little service from an out-gunned midfield.

Delaney – 4 – Evident confusion between Damien & Jedi over who was responsible for picking up Michu when he drifted out of the attack and these arguments continued for several minutes. Also had a spell where his attention was on venting his displeasure at referee & linesman over an admittedly poor decision, but one that was not costly and when we needed clearer heads. A poor afternoon finished sourly when a miss-timed tackle saw him injure himself on half-time.

Gabbidon – 5 – Tried hard but his lack of pace was exploited at times, and when pressed on the ball couldn't be relied upon to get safely rid of it. Yet without some good interceptions and headers it might have been worse.

Jedinak – 5 – Lost the midfield battle early on, and although he did try to interrupt Swansea's lines of communication, he was neither able to stem the flow or open up our own attacks. Looked a liability at the back in the second half when several times found a Swan sneaking in behind him; not surprising against a technically proficient and quick attack when lacking the ingrained knowledge of angles & lines of defence.

Guédioura – 5 – Made little impact as a holding midfield player and unable to offer much to start attacks, one effort from a free kick aside.

Puncheon – 4 – Increasingly failed to take on his man and seek space on the right flank, in the second half pushing inside & making the oppositions' job far easier. Use of the ball was generally appalling. Surprised he was not replaced by either Thomas or the unused Kébé.

Jerome – 4 – Is powerful, has pace, looks like the perfect forward but somehow has not managed to make an impact yet in his career. Being generous we can put today's display down to a lack of practice with a new team, but too often his positional play lacked intelligence, being either too far away from Chamakh or failing to anticipate & gamble on the Moroccan winning a flick-on.

Bannan – 6 – Looked useful but rarely in areas that hurt Swansea. At least looked to run with the ball and commit defenders, and looked the most likely of the starting XI that would fit into Swansea's team.

Chamakh – 5 – Worked hard but seldom found a team mate in close support until Gayle came on. Worryingly I reckon that's 3 full matches now where Marouane hasn't had a chance on goal, but a lot of that was due to a complete lack of service.

Campaña – 6 - Jose looked useful when coming on, and tried to use the ball creatively, but also lacked the bite of Jedinak or KG to try and wrest midfield control away from Swansea; with Guédioura provided a pretty soft centre. At least took the responsibility of a shot on goal that drifted over.

Gayle – 5 – Added pep to a tired attack and nearly got onto the end of a header & a pass that looked promising, but was unable to control the ball.

Thomas – 5 – Came on but didn't stay out wide, and was unwilling to shoot when finally allowed a glimpse of goal.

Speroni – 5 – An early hesitation nearly gifted Schneiderlin a goal; Julian either had to come straight away or stay at home – instead he was caught in no-man's-land only to be bailed out by Ward. Made what looked an untidy save from one Lambert free kick but in hindsight the ball probably reached him on the volley and was the most expeditious means of protecting his goal; he had no chance on Earth of saving the second one. I think he'll be disappointed not to have done better with Osvaldo's gaols as he seemed to get a large hand to it.

Ward – 7 – Good to have Joel back, although for a few brief seconds it looked like his acrobatic goal line clearance might have crocked him again. Had a busy day defensively and also tried hard to provide some width upfield. One excellent first half tackle to close down a break.

Moxey – 7 – Continued good run of form. Also busy at the back but generally sound. Made a lot of runs to support the attack, especially in the second half, when he often appeared the only player willing to shoot.

Mariappa – 7 – Looked far happier in central defence than at full back and did a good job, generally keeping the Saints' strikers at bay. Some neat play at the back when on the ball.

Gabbidon – 7 – Made the odd mistake but nothing costly, although still looks uncomfortable with the ball at his feet. Worked well in defending in open play and helped repel the corners.

Jedinak – 5 – A poor game by his standards. In the first half he carried out his defensive duties well enough but his passing drooped below the quality level we've come to expect. Started the second half by losing the ball on the edge of our box and seeing Osvaldo score. As Palace chased the game he dropped deeper & deeper to collect the ball, but his passing grew worse, often consisting of stabbing the ball upfield hopefully.

Dikgacoi – 6 – One of our best performers in the first half where his powerful game had been missing against Swansea. Outshone Jedinak although not error-free with his passing either, and made one terrific run to support a break. After the break was one of the players who failed to clear in the build up for their first goal and conceded an unnecessary free kick for the second. Like Jedi not at his best when having to force the pace.

Kébé – 6 – Probably our best player in the first 45 minutes causing Southampton problems down the right without managing to profit from them. Showed some pace & a good touch. Needs to be a little stronger when challenged and didn't look at his best when tracking back. Completely disappeared after the two goal volley at the start of the second half, which may be down to lack of match fitness, and subbed.

Gayle – 5 – Tried hard and showed glimpses of pace, but still a lack of understanding with Chamakh when pushed up alongside the Moroccan. It's a vicious circle – Dwight needs game time on the pitch but isn't ready for the Premier League at this stage.

Bannan – 6 – A quietly efficient game, not many mistakes and made one or two good passes, but never able to turn this into chances.

Chamakh – 5 – Started well but his game started to fray at the edges in terms of temperament, shoving Moxey in the chest when debating how to defend corners. Sulked a little after that, then more so after being booked for diving, and after that seemed to flit in & out of the game as his moods shifted. If he did go down easily then he's double-damned: It was our best chance of scoring, so why didn't he just shoot? And he's cut the moral high-ground out from under both manager & Chairman. When he was in the mood he worked hard and won a fair number of headers, but ended the game a frustrated figure, his dummy eight yards out summing up his (and our) day.

Thomas – 5 – Looked lightweight & short of pace when coming on down the left. Moxey looked far more dangerous.

Jerome – 5 – Saw little of the ball, although hard work & refusal to give up prised an opening that Chamakh declined, but his appalling finish in stoppage time was in line with the team's second half display.

Phillips – 5 – Looked a veteran off the pace.

Liverpool Away

Speroni – 7 – No real chance with any of the goals, and made a couple of good saves in the first half, and collected some dangerous low crosses in the second.

Ward – 6 – Struggled down the right as he was often outnumbered in defence. Tried hard to help Kébé down the right in attack.

Moxey – 6 – One of our better players who had a real tussle with Sterling, but what was he thinking with that ridiculous little tug for the penalty? Worked hard down the left and put in one dangerous cross.

Mariappa – 6 – Unsurprisingly found it difficult up against Suarez but stuck to his task and didn't let anyone down. Often dragged out wide to help Ward leaving gaps in the middle.

Delaney – 7 – Was comprehensively beaten by Sturridge's twists & turns for their second, but redeemed himself with no end of important challenges & interceptions.

Jedinak – 6 – Did well in a defensive role, although I would have preferred him to close down Gerrard more. With the ball his poor passing game continued, too often winning the ball only to give it back.

Puncheon – 5 – Showed the odd flash of form, but generally conceded the ball far too easily either through wrong decisions, poor passing or running up blind alleys.

O'Keefe – 5 – Was often found on the right behind Kébé and looked uncomfortable in this unfamiliar role, if that is where he was meant to be. His general play was OK although he did give the ball away more than once.

Chamakh – 5 – Played wide left most of the match and although he had a couple of powerful runs nothing came of them. I thought he looked lazy in the second half but it could have been a groin strain.

Kébé – 6 – Looked dangerous but somehow didn't seem to have the confidence to follow through, his weak finish when clean through summing up his match.

Jerome – 5 – Suffered from a lack of service and didn't really seem to be operating on the same wavelength as Chamakh.

Campaña – 7 – Initially his impressive passing game made an immediate improvement to Palace's ball retention, although later in the game he too started to give the ball away regularly. Worked hard down the left with Bolasie and delivered a perfect free kick for the goal.

Gayle – 7 – Ran hard and closed down Liverpool's defenders, something that didn't really happen with Jerome & Chamakh. Missed one chance from the edge of the box but his headed finish for the goal was excellent.

Bolasie – 7 – Gave Liverpool no end of problems when he came on, even if all his tricks didn't come off. Finally we had a winger playing out wide and what a difference it made.

Speroni – 5 – Must take the blame for the disastrous five minutes at the start of the second half with an awful clearance; that his brilliance simply denied the blow by seconds is of little account. Might have done better with the fourth although he claimed obstruction / holding prevented him getting across the goal faster (I was watching the flight of the ball – as did the Palace defence – and didn't see anything). Was he also slow to cover back from behind the wall for the second, giving Sidwell an empty net to hit? Made one excellent late save but when one of your old reliable is looking shaky, it's not good.

Ward – 6 – A decent game from Joel, who tried hard in defence and also to support the attack. More of Fulham's attacks came down our right so was under more pressure than Moxey.

Moxey – 6 – One who showed plenty of spirit for all 90 minutes, often being the player furthest forwards as we pushed for a late consolation, at least getting Stekelenburg's knees dirty with a late shot that moved. Wasn't pushed as much defensively on his flank.

Mariappa – 5 – Scored a goal beating the giant Hangeland, but was beaten in turn by Berbatov for their third. Can't blame him for Kasabi's goal of the season as there was barely a yard of space allowed. Like many his head dropped after the fourth.

Delaney – 5 – Not the worst player on the pitch, and not directly to blame for any of the goals, but had an unhappy evening none the less. Did his interactions with Fulham's attackers immediately before both fatal corners help distract the defence? Even when he made attacking runs forward he was stopped by a combination of foul & a linesman's flag. Night summed up when Jedinak misplaced a short square pass that just ran into touch as Delaney slipped over.

Jedinak – 5 – Played far too deep for much of the game, and his passing grew steadily less reliable, as Delaney can testify. As a skipper is showing incipient signs of McCarthyism by volubly balling out his team mates, which can work for some but not others. It would have helped his case had Senderos not been left unmarked as Jedinak let him drift beyond the far post.

O'Keefe – 6 – Another who fought to the end, and caused a couple of moment's discomfort for Fulham, but his game was dragged down with the rest in the second half. Signs of a decent player but not one to rely upon for creativity.

Campaña – 4 – Sadly disappointed his supporters – of whom I am one – who see a lot in this young lad. Started well with some good passes and free kicks, but the accuracy of his passing dropped alarmingly & quickly. He also looked very slow, both in thought & deed – was there an injury as he was laboured over short distances, or – even worse – was he knackered inside half an hour?

Bolasie – 6 – Palace's greatest threat although his trickery didn't bring many immediate results, and can't really claim an assist given the huge deflection on his cross. Perhaps did deserve the rough edge of Jedi's tongue over trying to play Brazilian football on the edge of one's own penalty area, even if the foul was a soft one. Second half he tried hard but saw little of the ball.

Puncheon – 5 – I struggle to recall Jason doing anything exceptionally good or exceptionally bad; a complete mental blank...

Gayle – 5 – As early promise of decent passing moves gradually morphed into long balls to Dwight it's no great surprise that his game wilted, even though he does have a decent jump for a little 'un. Service dried up but again he kept on to the end.

Thomas – 6 – Decent display in a side that was struggling provided decent width on the left, especially with Moxey's help.

Chamakh -5 – Originally came on and went wide left; gradually he came inside & allowed Thomas the wing. Not easy to try to play well in a team that's almost given up.

Phillips – 5 – A couple of decent touches, one shot way wide, but never an influence.

Arsenal Home

Speroni – 6 – Had one sharp save to make from Ramsay, and a couple of dashes off the line to save the ball at an attacker's feet, but surprisingly under employed, especially given the first 10 minutes. Nearly spilled a spiralling Gabbidon header in the wind. No real chance with either Arteta's penalty or Giroud's close range header.

Ward – 7 – Another outstanding display from one of our more impressive & consistent performers this season. Defensively pretty good although was embarrassed by Monreal. Got forward well on the right and only denied his first Palace goal by a combination of Polish fingertips & the woodwork – and that from a left-footed effort!

Moxey – 7- Had far more defensive work to do down the left against Gnabry & the impressive Sagna, when Thomas & Jedinak weren't always switched on defensively. Showed great drive for the 90 minutes, especially in the second half when tried hard to work the left flank, including a strong cross-cum-shot.

Delaney – 7 – Did allow Giroud two headers that the Gunner missed but also put in some solid defensive work, although perhaps a shade lucky with a silly challenge on Gnabry that might have been a penalty. Was carrying an injury from some time out of 90 minutes.

Gabbidon – 7 – The defence did look more solid with Danny back, and he made more than one important challenge, although his misjudged header nearly gave Arsenal an opening. Was caught out by Ramsay's pace & skill at the death.

Dikgacoi – 6 – Good defensively but his passing was often a liability, including one on the edge of the box that nearly saw Cazorla score. Also missed an excellent headed chance in the first half, but did find a nice touch to set up Ward's shot. IMHO played too deep once Arsenal went down to 10 men; either he or Jedi should have been playing at least 10-20 yards further forwards, if not both of them.

Jedinak – 7 – A difficult judgement to make on Jedi's display. Immense in a defensive role with plenty of headers won and tackles made, although was sleeping when Ramsay crept in behind him to force a save from Julian. His passing varied from brilliant – the long ball to Chamakh that saw the red card offence and the cross that Chamakh missed – to the ridiculous – many short passes played too far ahead or behind their intended recipient, and the long ball towards Kébé cut out in the build up to Arsenal's second.

Guédioura – 7 – I was seriously impressed with Adlene's performance – with one notable exception – after taking 10-15 minutes to find his feet. He was tough, both in shielding the ball and not afraid to put in some hard tackles, and showed no considerable skill & pace – who was steaming down the middle when Chamakh had the ball, perhaps prompting Foy's decision to send off Arteta? Unfortunately a Palace Man of the Match performance was thrown away along with a potential point or three with a forward's diving challenge in our own box. Still some potential shown although shooting from 40+ yards was perhaps over-optimistic.

Bannan – 7 – Another who had seen little employment under Holloway to come in and give a determined performance. Down the right he linked well with Ward and looked good coming inside, even finding time to break into the box and have a headed chance. Shame his curling effort fell between the far post & Delaney running in. Leaps well for a little man. If fitness was not an issue, I would have preferred to see Barry stay on and sacrifice KG in the move to 4-4-2.

Thomas – 7 – Thought it by far his best display for Palace, as it was his runs that first indicated Palace were not settling for a damage limitation formation designed to stifle Arsenal. Made Gibbs look second class at times.

Chamakh – 6 – Another curate's egg from Marouane: worked hard most of the time, but at others looked uninterested. Played well in wide areas & breaking down the middle, then showed little interest in closing down Szczesny from an under hit back pass (given the keeper's history got to be worth the effort); found great space inside the box only to completely misjudge his leap. At least had a shot on goal, a real rarity this season, which forced the keeper to dirty his kit.

Bolasie – 6 – Started well, and made Sagna concentrate upon defence instead of attack, and looked the man most likely to unlock Arsenal's defence. Then found himself starved of possession and wasn't a factor for the last 10 minutes.

Kébé – 5 – Had a couple of touches but barely saw the ball.

Gayle – 5 – A couple of decent touches around the box but another who saw little of the ball late on.

West Bromwich Away

Speroni – 6 – Underemployed and with little chance for either goal due to Berahino's accuracy & McAuley's close range header. Made some scrambling saves in the second half.

Ward – 6 – Solid if unspectacular performance, generally good at the back & trying hard down the right to support Bannan. Unluckily caught upfield when Chamakh gave the ball away and consequently out of position for their first goal.

Moxey – 6 – Tried hard as usual at both ends of the pitch but with little reward. Made a couple of mistakes in giving the ball away in dangerous areas but wasn't punished, partly due to his speed of recovery. Looked like he picked up a knock late when making an important block.

Delaney – 6 – Made some very important interceptions but not sure about his positioning & decision making in the move for their first goal, when he effectively removed himself from the equation by marking the 6-yard line & leaving Berahino free lurking on the edge of the box. Not sparing of effort and almost scored a late consolation with an overhead kick. Some of his passing was awful.

Gabbidon – 6 – Thought Danny hesitated when he could have got to the ball before Sessegnon in the move for their first, and as a result was unable to prevent the cross. Apart from that was another solid performer, again making important interceptions.

Jedinak – 6 – Showed plenty of drive and power in the middle, and for a time in the second half established control there, but missed our best chance and was unable to prevent McAuley thundering in their second. His passing was inconsistent at times.

Dikgacoi – 6 – Quiet but effective in breaking up the opposition's play. Looked more effective after half-time when the midfield moved 10-20 yards further up the pitch.

Bannan – 6 – Lively display that didn't earn as much as it should. Is match fitness an issue?

Thomas – 5 – Mediocre display from a winger who never beat his man on the outside and rarely caused problems when almost invariably cutting inside.

Guédioura – 7 – Was looking sharp and dangerous, and miraculously appeared to have struck up an understanding with Chamakh, before he was carried off after a collision with Myhill.

Chamakh – 5 – A really frustrating display. Won some – but by no means enough – headers to create the odd opening, especially for Guédioura, but at other times barely bothered to try. His ball control could be awful – and it was Marouane who lost possession to set up their first goal – but then he worked some openings with neat touches. Lack of confidence showed when presented with a chance on his right foot but preferred to run left towards the defenders. To be honest no matter how good he could be, we need a striker who can hold the ball up and work damned hard.

Puncheon – 4 – Awful: lazy, slow, unaware of space, lacking perception or anticipation, yet still managed to create a couple of openings for himself & others. Even allowing for the latter, we can't afford luxury players on the hope that they might show up once or twice. After good showings against Stoke & Sunderland has regressed badly.

Bolasie – 6 – Saw little of the ball but worked one opening, although a cross instead of a shot might have been a better choice.

Gayle – 5 – Don't think he touched the ball.

Speroni – 6 – One good save and a little luck at the end thanks to the bar &/or Moxey. Not as busy as I expected him to be.

Ward – 7 – Hard a hard time in the first half as Everton often overloaded their left side, and with Bolasie often losing track of Baines. A little more comfortable in the second and even had time to make a couple of attacking forays.

Moxey – 8 – On a couple of occasions nearly undid his hard work & diligent defence with some less than stellar clearances, but got away with it. Never stopped working and was found in attacking situations either side of the interval. Was willing to put his head in when Julian decided to stay at home in the last minute & was clattered for his pains.

Delaney – 8 – Mostly kept the dangerous Lukaku quiet, but was turned an a few occasions and needed help in shutting down the outcome.

Gabbidon – 8 – A rock in the last 10 minutes when Everton kept penetrating our box, with a couple of crucial late interceptions.

Dikgacoi – 7 – Worked hard in the first half, and made a couple of late runs into the box not picked up by the Toffee's defence; missed one glorious chance with a risible header.

Jedinak – 8 – Quiet start but gradually grew to be the matching force to Gareth Barry, especially as the second half wore on. Plenty of headers & tackles won, and not so feckless with his passing.

Bannan – 7 – Hard working and with a belligerence that belies his unimpressive stature. The cross that Chamakh put wide reminded me of all those corners he whipped in at Bloomfield Road a few years back, setting up any one of four colleagues to finish the job. Earned a rousing applause when tackling then winning a header in the second half.

Bolasie – 6 – Overshadowed by Thomas in the first half when his tricks seldom lead to an opening and often gave away the ball in some promising positions. Seemed to lose concentration & Baines at times. Improved in the second with an excellent through ball to Thomas.

Thomas – 7 – Best performance since his arrival, surprisingly proving more effective in the first half than Bolasie with a desire to chase down balls and hassle defenders. Deserved his first goal with an effort that Howard clawed away from the top corner; missed a great chance in the second when sent clear.

Chamakh – 7 – Worked so hard that he might silence Savage (& me) for an hour or two; was unlucky in nearly controlling two long balls to create openings that weren't really there. Linked well with the midfield & Thomas, and didn't give the ball away anywhere near as often as recently. However the headed miss was truly awful. Less involved in the second half and withdrawn for Jerome.

O'Keefe – 7 – Spiky midfield display that was effective if unspectacular.

Jerome – 6 – Made some good runs down the wings but lacked support to force home any advantage. Two notable headed clearances in defence.

Puncheon – 5 – late sub for Thomas who had little chance to be involved.

Hull Away

Speroni – 7 – One slight error at the end when conceding a corner following a misunderstanding with Moxey, but otherwise as solid as a rock. Two relatively easy saves in the first half, one excellent block in the second. Took crosses & actually dominated his box.

Ward – 6 – Efficient but not error-free, as he played at least two "million pound" balls out of defence that were cut out. Struggled at times in the first half but stuck to his task.

Moxey – 7 – Made some mistakes but always recovered in time to get back in position & make the block or interception. Also showed up well on the break. Vital clearance in stoppage time.

Delaney – 8 – Terrific defensive display, mostly in the air, but there was one crucial interception early in the second half.

Gabbidon – 8 – Showed all his experience in manning the rearguard, showing some cal play when in tight situations. Unexpectedly showed up on the right wing in one counter attack!

Dikgacoi – 6 – Solid display and showed a willingness to break at times, but his distribution was patchy.

Jedinak – 8 – Stand out display from the captain. Showed all his usual destructive properties when he seemed to be everywhere in repelling attacks in the second half, but also showed a greater willingness & freedom to break forward, and his interceptions often sparked Palace's counter attacks.

Bannan – 8 –Influential display from Bannan, who linked well with Gayle down the left in the first half, then in the second was more based on the right after O'Keefe replaced KG. His corners were dangerous and well aimed, although why there was not a team mate positioned in the centre of the box to receive them does make you wonder what they practice! Hard working & stayed on for the full 90+

minutes, which was just as well as he found himself in the perfect position to score his first Palace goal.

Gayle – 7 – Very good in the first half, when he formed some excellent interplay with Bannan & Bolasie. Took a nasty knock just before half-time & seemed to fade in the second half before recovering. His finishing was poor when presented with two half chances, his shots being scuffed badly, but only a fine challenge ruined his best chance. Linked well with Jerome and played a wonderful return pass to open up the defence for the goal; also calmly dummied to set up Bolasie's chance / dismissal. Worked hard tracking back defensively even if a little shaky in positioning & the challenge.

Bolasie – 7 – Very much a mixed performance. Always a threat with his pace & trickery, but too often there was no end product as he either blazed away with colleagues unmarked in the middle, or fired in crosses when his mates hadn't made up the ground in the middle. But when he got it right he terrorised their left back. Like Gayle he worked hard in the defensive duties, unlike against Everton. I thought at the time the red card was harsh but can see why it was given; again if his control had been good he would have had an excellent chance (to score / shoot wildly wide) but ended up being dismissed.

Chamakh – 6 – Worked hard even after the very early blow to his head, and can't knock his work rate or bravery, but again too often too deep to be a threat.

Jerome – 7 – Seriously impressed with Cameron's display – at times looking a little ungainly & reminding me of Emile Heskey, his muscularity and effort denied Hull's defenders any rest. Used his strength & pace well, and fashioned one second half chance only to send a strong shot off target. His work for the goal was superb; his move to create a better angle instead of blazing away at goal was unexpected & executed perfectly. Deserves to start the next game and perhaps really impress his new boss (same as the old boss!)

O'Keefe – 6 – Second half sub for KG who put in a good effort.

Puncheon – 6 – Late sub for Gayle who showed ability to hold the ball up.

Speroni – 7 – Rode his luck with the effort crashing against the bar, and then produced a very sharp save to deny Redmond. There were a couple of moments of miscommunication with defenders but Julian was sound taking crosses.

Ward – 6 – Started poorly when sleepy defending gave away a corner, and had trouble facing Hoolahan, never looking totally secure. Some better defending in the second half, especially when Norwich continued their nasty habit of swift counter attacks. Also had one excellent run down the right that ended with a disappointing cross & collision with the advertising hoardings.

Moxey – 5 – Was really exposed by Redmond and – at times by Hoolahan, with most of Norwich's most dangerous attacks coming down our left. Lost possession deep in City's half and so was out of position for the goal, although he nearly caught up, and some of the blame is shared by Bannan. An attacking force in the second half when his dangerous cross nearly led to an own goal.

Gabbidon – 7 – Restricted Norwich to few chances after the first 30 minutes, and made plenty of important interceptions and headers. There was some pinball defending in the first half and I'd like to see the goal again to find out if we could have done better once the first cross went in.

Delaney – 7 – Pretty much the same as Gabbidon, although could have revitalised the team with a headed equaliser if he'd taken a half-chance. Often seemed to end Norwich attacks flat out on the ground!

Dikgacoi – 5 – Overall a disappointing display from KG whose control & passing often let him down. Yet nearly fashioned an early goal, although his "strike" was a weak one easily gathered by Ruddy. Also found himself putting in a great cross from the right that Jerome missed by an inch before being expertly claimed by the keeper.

Jedinak – 7 – Playing slightly more advanced than usual and avoided dropping deep when we were in possession. Didn't see so much of the ball in the first half, when the defence chose to use the two wide midfielders or play more directly, which is one reason why he was overshadowed by Howson. Yet pushed on in the second half, winning plenty of balls and trying hard to get into the box. Picked up a silly yellow card for throwing the ball away after committing a foul.

Puncheon – 5 – Started well, and made a couple of incursions down the right, but too often in the second half promising moves were stymied when he received the ball, and he lost possession too often.

Bannan – 6 – Worked hard all game, unlucky with the effort deflected onto the bar, and usually found a clever ball through to Chamakh or Jerome. But committed too many fouls (according to referee Foy) in dangerous areas while trying to help shore up the left flank and was also culpable in the misunderstanding with Moxey that led to the only goal. Slowly faded in the second half.

Chamakh – 6 – This is going to sound strange, but Marouane worked very hard in his new role, yet often when collecting the ball wide and making the play, he was slow to rejoin the action, and as a result was seldom seen in the opposition penalty area and suffered another game when (IIRC) he didn't have an effort on goal. There were some good moments of interplay with Jerome as well as some confusion, which was to be expected.

Jerome – 6 – Cannot criticise his work rate but suffered from a lack of close support, and when working out wide often had no-one in the box to aim for. Strong on the ball but seldom allowed a sight of goal by Bassong, his one late chance came too quickly to him to fashion a stronger effort on goal.

Williams – 5 –Apart from winning then delivering a couple of free kicks after replacing Bannan down the left, Jonny barely featured.

Kébé' – 6 – One very good turn & shot that exuded more menace than the rest of the team had all match, but also a weak cross from a promising position.

Gayle – 5 – Another late sub who made little impact.

West Ham Home

Speroni – 6 – Solid enough, not required to do anything spectacular, although his save from Downing's free kick was more difficult than it appeared. Perhaps sums up West Ham's lack of a proper striker when his biggest problem of the night was an unattached goal-net.

Ward – 7 – Made some crucial interceptions in both halves; at times found Diamé difficult to handle but stuck to his task, as well as some clearing headers. Made a couple of good runs forward.

Moxey – 6 – Note sure why he kept showing Downing inside onto his good foot, but assume in must have been under instructions. Made a couple of dangerous breaks in both halves, only to be caught out of position & stranded upfield when invariably we lost the ball. Kept running and again showed his tenacity with important clearances as the game closed.

Delaney – 8 – Some brave blocks and had a real battle with Cole (Carlton) but led the rearguard fantastically well.

Gabbidon – 7 – Solid performance with one mazy attacking run in the first half. Also put his body on the line to keep a clean sheet.

Jedinak – 6 – Won enough challenges & headers but then on numerous occasions almost immediately gave the ball away carelessly, perhaps explaining why he had to work so hard. Noticeable that in the first hour played about 10-20 yards further up the pitch than under previous regimes, rarely dropping deep to pick up the ball from the defence. Spent the last 30 minutes in more familiar territory guarding the zone in front of our penalty area.

Dikgacoi – 5 – Defended well but his passing was even more awry than usual, and missed one great chance from a Bannan cross.

Bannan – 7 – First half saw some nice touches but also a couple of woefully-misplaced passes in keeping with the game. Produced two perfect crosses for Chamakh's goal and KG's miss. Kept running all game and summed up by virtually his last contribution when, covering a swift break from our corner, he interposed himself between the ball and their attacker for about 30 yards to block access to Julian. Surprised he was withdrawn. I thought his was a strange substitution when he still looked to have mileage in his short legs, and had proven his use defensively.

Puncheon – 5 – Very similar to Norwich in that he started okay and had Palace's first effort on goal, but then faded badly and was one of those unable to keep possession. Strange to say he nearly scored straight at the start of the second half with an excellent shot deflected just off-target.

Chamakh – 6 – Worked very hard but still doesn't look to be a player who will score many goals, despite last night's effort. Even that looked as though he had mistimed his header, going across goal when the easiest and most open route was to thump it straight down. Worked even harder in the second half.

Jerome – 5 – Didn't enjoy much success in the air against Tomkins, but occasionally embarrassed the defender on the ground with his muscular athleticism, and should really have scored at least once, if not twice, early in the second half. Cannot knock his work rate but occasional inspiration will be needed as well as perspiration.

Kébé – 6 –. Decent replacement for Puncheon, although perhaps lacking the Jason's little piece of defensive fortitude, Jimmy had a decent spell, creating a couple of half chances for others before blowing one he made all for himself.

O'Keefe – 6 – A late substitution to stiffen midfield, which he did well enough.

Williams – 5 – A switch to a five man midfield, Jonny had one short run but that was the limit of his real involvement.

Speroni – 7 – Possibly the crucial moment when saving Campbell's header; remember the deflating effect when Swansea scored at roughly the same time? Only had one more non-routine save in the second half, otherwise controlled his box well. A couple of dodgy kicks and some miscommunication with the defenders were not punished.

Ward – 8 – Didn't see much action at right back apart from one good headed clearance under pressure, but played superbly when switched to the left. Perhaps this helped his two runs down the inside-left channel that nearly created goals.

Moxey – 6 – Steady game with some surging runs down the left, but suffered an early strain or pull and was subbed in the first half.

Delaney – 8 – Another outstanding performance, ready to put his body on the line in a brave first-half block. Was given an easy ride by Cardiff's attempts at a long ball game but still did it professionally. Could have added a goal with a header over from a corner.

Gabbidon – 7 – Only a step behind Delaney in his showing, although there was one worrying moment when he went down in the second half holding his leg. (I've seen O'Keefe play full back & it wasn't pretty, while Jedinak's fill-in at centre back still makes me shudder.) Cardiff's tactics played right into his hands.

Jedinak – 7 – Strong display with plenty of tackles and headers, and his passing accuracy was higher than it has been, perhaps helped by not facing a flat five-man opposition midfield.

Dikgacoi – 8 – Inspired by Nelson's departure? A really strong showing from a player whose recent displays have paled in comparison. Strong in the tackle, KG also laid off some lovely passes, setting Jerome free on more than one occasion. Also threatened the goal with a couple of shots and a header.

Puncheon – 6 – As he has done recently started well, picking up the pieces of Jerome's blown chance to beat his man and fashion a cross of the highest accuracy, then not long after snapping in a shot. But he does seem to drift out of games (isn't that the way with Palace's wingers?) then pop up with a deft touch, as he did in the second half. Worked hard too defensively. I may seem harsh his colleagues did more for longer.

Bannan – 8 – His crossing wasn't as laser-guided accurate as it can be, but he had enough opportunities that a fair number were perfectly placed. His work ethic is also excellent, although his shooting needs a little polish, with one first time volley from an acute angle that even a Suarez or Van Basten might have blanched at.

299

Chamakh – 8 – I've been on his case for his mixed displays where he will work hard one moment, then the next lay the ball off and wander around having done his bit for the move. Well, there was none of that today. Perhaps emboldened by his goal on Tuesday Marouane didn't stop running all game, pressing & closing down Cardiff's defence, never giving them a moment's rest. His goal, a cross-shot from the left, was the finish of a man high on self-belief.

Jerome – 7 – Worked just as hard as Chamakh in the more advanced role, but lacked just that little bit of control or luck to really kill off the game. I thought his confidence would be rock-bottom after blowing the second of two early runs on goal, but in an instant was burying a header and in the following celebrations it looked like a weight had been removed from his shoulders. One bad moment when a long ball found him looking suspiciously offside, yet he decided too late to chase the ball when the linesman ruled he was onside – play the whistle!

Mariappa – 7 – Not a natural full back but Cardiff's wide men were strangely subdued and bypassed for much of the game, so not really tested. Made one brave headed clearance where the boots were flying.

O'Keefe – 6 – Difficult to attune himself to the pace of the game when coming on as late substitute for Bannan & playing in a wide role.

[Sorry – seem to have worn out the key between 7 and 9 – gives the lie that my keyboard is in base 7!]

Chelsea Away

Speroni – 7 – At first I thought Julian could have done better with Willian's effort, the ball seeming to slip through his hands onto the post for Torres's goal – having seen a replay it was actually a fine save not rewarded with good fortune. He made quite a few smart saves, especially late in the first half from Willian, and from an offside Oscar, but saved the best to last, when somehow defying Schürrle & Demba Ba at point-blank range.

Mariappa – 6 – Looked the weak link in the defence and more than once lacked the positioning sense & was caught napping, especially by the hazardous Hazard, although kept going and made some important interceptions. Decent long throw though!

Ward – 8 – Was embarrassed once early on but provided a strong flank defence and an ability to support the attack, highlighted by his run and excellent cross for our goal. Worked very well in tandem with Puncheon.

Delaney – 7 – Was stuck on his arse by the speed and skill of Torres, and never looked truly comfortable, but made up for this with determination & spirit. Shame his trio of headers weren't better as his runs were not picked up by the Chelsea defence.

Gabbidon – 7 – Another who was never at ease with Chelsea's fluid attacking movement but rarely made a mistake, instead making some timely tackles.

Dikgacoi – 6 – Was playing very effectively with some good challenges and a couple of decent passes further up the pitch than normal before forced off early by injury.

Jedinak – 8 – Always involved and always influential, making plenty of important challenges both on the ground & in the air, although will be disappointed he didn't close down Willian's shot. Was often the man charged with covering the defence and also starting many of Palace's counter attacks. It was his recovery of the ball that led to Chamakh's goal.

Puncheon – 7 – Probably his most effective display for Palace, worked hard defensively but also showed some great moments of skill and perseverance when attacking. Involved in the move for Chamakh's goal and created the chance for Bolasie; his dead ball deliveries were dangerous too, while he forced Cech into a good save cutting in from the right.

Bannan – 6 – Worthy if unexceptional display, not as influential as in recent games. The side looked better balanced when he was replaced by Bolasie.

Chamakh – 8 – Hard working in an unfamiliar deeper role than I've seen him play before. Put himself about, especially in an entertaining duel with Essien, and was a most effective link man, especially in the second half when play came through him instead of over him. Excellent finish for his goal. Suffered from cramp at the end that reduced his effectiveness.

Jerome – 6 – No-one worked harder than Cameron but his decision making & execution at most times was poor. Not helped by being exceptionally isolated for much of the first 30 minutes. Good run set up O'Keefe's triple chance.

O'Keefe – 8 – Was inspired by the opposition into a brilliant, if not totally error-free, performance in the middle against far weightier reputations, not frightened to put in hard challenges. Also showed plenty of nous in some excellent running off the ball and good passing. A real plus from this game. Shame he couldn't quite force the ball past Cech and half the Chelsea team.

Bolasie – 7 – Blazed into action with an early run that exposed Azpilicueta for pace, then went to sleep defensively and nearly let Ivanovic in, which sums up his qualities & deficiencies, although redeemed himself with a nice bit of tracking back that put a Blue into the hoardings. Always a threat but really should manage a better effort than the leaden-footed header at the far post. Didn't see so much of the ball late on.

Gayle – 5 – Late sub who didn't see anything of the ball.

Speroni – 6 – On the surface had little chance with either goal from open play, and nearly saved Ben Arfa's penalty, while making a couple of smart saves. Yet the communication, or lack of it, with his defence must be questioned given Gabbidon's disastrous intervention, while his long kicks were too often over hit.

Mariappa – 5 – Apart from one uncharacteristic run down the line and excellent cross, looked like a central defender playing out of position.

Moxey – 4 – In hindsight a mistake to bring Dean back as he was palpably off the pace, being passed by Debuchy as though running in treacle, and he barely brought his attacking runs to the game. Also guilty of a poorly directed defensive header in the build up to the first goal, and was one of the guilty parties in a free kick shambles that caught us out of position.

Delaney – 7 – Might have been the unlucky defender whose touch sent the first goal past Julian's left hand, but generally had a good game, with plenty of interceptions, and the odd driving run upfield. Nothing wrong with his commitment.

Gabbidon – 6 – Struggled a little with Rémy's movement when drawn out to the right, but had a solid game spoiled by the enormous faux-pas of his own goal.

Ward – 5 – A decent game in a limited sense in that he was a combative midfielder, but lacked the tools to turn possession into worthwhile attacks, and was guilty at times of sitting off the opposition's midfielders. A waste of a talent when we had less fit / experienced full backs and a couple of proper, if rather less spiky, midfielders in the squad.

Jedinak – 6 – Tried hard but another guilty of giving the opposition too much time on the ball without being closed down. A little more creative than Ward but not by much.

Bannan – 4 – Ineffectual on the right when he could have filled a berth in the middle, although Pulis does tend to like a solid two in the middle when playing 4-4-1-1 or 4-4-2. Looked a little off the pace and despite some decent dead ball deliveries, including a free kick that a smaller keeper might have had to work harder at keeping out, his game has dropped off a little recently.

Puncheon – 5 – Some decent touches but too often on the periphery as Palace launched long balls down the middle. Nearly made an important intervention with a good shot that was blocked early in the second half.

Chamakh – 6 – Worked really hard and was the one player in midfield who showed some creative touches, but this resulted in him being too far away from Jerome to offer more than fleeting support. Looked to be pushed forward more in the second half and had an early chance that was headed over.

Jerome – 5 – Cannot deny his commitment & work rate that nearly fashioned an equaliser when he somehow worked in a shot that Krul scrambled away. Yet his lack of a cutting edge in front of goal blew Palace's best chance when a routine chance was put over the bar.

Parr – 7 – A little unlucky with the penalty (not the decision itself) that marred a good return from Jonny, who put in a number of good tackles down the left. Also tried to push on to support the attack. Again 20/20 vision suggests he should have started the match.

Bolasie – 5 – Started strongly but soon guilty of running down blind alleys and over elaboration, losing possession and wasting good field position.

Gayle – 5 – Came on for the last 15 minutes and barely saw the ball.

Aston Villa Away

Speroni – 7 – There were another couple of moments where keeper & defender didn't seem to be on the same wavelength, but nothing really worrying. Saves were routine with a little acrobatic twist towards the end. Handling of crosses was immaculate.

Mariappa – 6 – Had a pretty good display on the right side of defence until tested late on and linked well with Bolasie in the second half on the attack. Also made some important headed clearances.

Parr – 6 – Caught out of position early on and resorted to a cynical / professional foul to protect his flank. After that worked hard but was just a little lacking in pace at times. Tried hard to support the attack, especially in the first half.

Gabbidon – 6 – Nearly gifted Villa a goal with a slip when trying to be too clever in dealing with the long clearance of our corner; fortunate that Villa's forwards' footwork was just as poor. Made several safety first clearances into row Z and was solid in the second half.

Delaney – 7 – Made a number of interceptions and headed clearances that halted Villa attacks and generally held the line well.

Ward – 7 – Looked far more comfortable in this showing in central midfield, probably because we had an extra man and the creative responsibilities were assumed by Bannan. Showed strength in winning & protecting the ball, often by turning away from an opponent. Nearly opened his Palace account with a shot that just flew over.

Jedinak – 7 – As with Ward his strength in the tackle and the air was important; has a different method of winning the ball by just stepping in over the ball &

interposing his body between opponent & ball. Also showed up in a couple of swift breaks.

Bannan – 8 – Excellent creative display that should nail down a central spot, his passes to the wingers were often well timed. His corners were not quite as deadly as usual. Nearly scored against his old team with a shot that was pushed agonisingly onto the post. Featured well in all the counter attacks we launched.

Puncheon – 6 – Immensely frustrating as Jason often showed touches of great skill, then let himself down by a completely contrary heavy touch or poor decision. How a player with his light touch in killing a ball and knocking it clear of an opponent cannot did the ball out from under his feet baffles me – he really should have scored twice in the second half. Credit for his defensive duties.

Bolasie – 8 – The real difference between the two teams, was a bit hit and miss in the first half with moments of brilliance when running with the ball followed by a poor cross, but started to find his range from the left. Switched back to the right in the second half and unhinged Villa's entire defence, creating many chances and linking well with Bannan, Ward & Mariappa, setting up a chance for Bannan & two for Puncheon.

Jerome – 5 – Worked bloody hard, often in isolation from any support, but too often betrayed a lack of touch when with the ball, or made the wrong decisions and more than once running the ball out of play. It is also impossible to visualize Cameron smacking home the type of winner we saw today.

Williams – 7 – Came on for Puncheon but played more inside-left than outside-left, strong when on the ball & tenacious when challenging for it.

Gayle – 7 – As with other recent late substitute appearances I could not remember him touching the ball; he worked hard when closing down the keeper & their defenders but as our midfield had dropped deep this was often in vain, and he looked like a young puppy vainly chasing the ball. But when he received it at his feet... well, a Matt Jansen or Ian Wright would have been proud of the finish!

Moxey – 7 – Another late sub out on the left, only touched the ball a couple of times, but made ground and laid off the perfect ball for Gayle's winner.

Speroni – 7 – Solid again and surprisingly not as busy as his opposite number, so diligently was he protected by the massed ranks of defenders. Safe handling of a shot taking a slight deflection off Delaney was important, while his acrobatic tip over was perhaps a little easier than it appeared. Annoyed the home fans with lengthy preparations for his dead ball kicks.

Mariappa – 7 – Faced problems on the right flank and was beaten more than once but was often able to get back in position and put in some vital interceptions. Best display from him in the unfamiliar role of full back.

Parr – 7 – Was occasionally embarrassed by Navas but equally put in some wonderfully timed tackles which had our hearts in our mouths fearing tumbling attackers & penalty awards. Found time to raid down the left & nearly set up a chance for Jerome.

Delaney – 7 – Early on was turned & beaten easily by Dzeko, yet kept his cool and led the defence wonderfully well, with plenty of blocks, headers, interceptions & tackles. Might carry some blame for the goal as his initial headed flicked wide & not away, and along with Gabbidon didn't catch Dzeko's movement.

Gabbidon – 8 – Outstanding display – pretty much the same said for Delaney applies here; wonder if he might have picked up Dzeko for the goal as seemed to be the nearest defender, but that would be a moment's hesitation in an otherwise completely professional display.

Jedinak – 8 – Like much of the Palace midfield did little but defend for the first 30 minutes but carried out that role in his normal efficient manner. Some excellent tackles and led several breaks in the second half, including forcing a save from distance out of Hart.

Ward – 7 – Was occasionally caught in possession in the middle, but often worked hard to win the ball back. Like the entire midfield spent a lot of time stationed in front of the back four, but found time to bring another annoyingly good save from Hart; shame about the awful far post header...

Bannan – 7 – Worked very hard in a defensive role and also set up some promising attacks, nearly bursting into the box one time to be denied by a fine tackle. His corners were excellent.

Puncheon – 8 – Made some mistakes but had some lovely creative touches and thoughtful use of the ball. Lots of effort in the first half when helping out Mariappa. Came close twice to opening his Palace account in the second half.

Bolasie – 6 – Was amazed to find a hard and well-timed tackle made in our box came from Yannick, which sums up both the individual & team effort today. Showed some attacking prowess late in the first half, but didn't continue that in the second, when his corner taking wasn't good enough, especially when compared with Bannan's.

Jerome – 5 – Isolated for almost the entire time he was on the pitch, and marked by two excellent defenders, it was no surprise that Cameron seldom held onto the ball. Brave in his challenge on Hart but looked like a nasty knee injury. Couldn't he just have fallen on Hart, just a little..?

Chamakh – 6 – Was more involved than Jerome, more able to hold up the ball, but also received a little more support from his colleagues. Did miss with a header that should have been on target. Worked hard in closing down City players.

Williams – 6 – One decent run but not really an attacking threat as City were under less pressure when he arrived.

Gayle – 5 – Not sure Dwight touched the ball when arriving as a late sub.

Norwich Home

Speroni – 6 – As with the Newcastle game, not easy conditions for goalkeepers, but Julian looked sound throughout, one moment of lack of communication apart. A couple of easy saves in both halves, and one piece of luck when Hooper's shot cannoned off his knees. Appeared to be unsighted for the first goal; even if not it looked to be perfectly placed out of his reach.

Mariappa – 7 – I doubted Adrian would make a good full back but the last few games indicate he's getting the hang of it. Worked especially well with Puncheon in the first half and nearly as well with Bolasie in the second. Defended well.

Ward – 6 – Played well at left back in the first half, although his crossing after a good start deteriorated. Won plenty of ball in midfield in the second, although also lost a few balls through a lack of awareness or simply miscalculations, but also laid off some good short balls as well as a couple of good runs with the ball.

Gabbidon – 6 – A player of Danny's experience should not be caught out as he was for their goal, even allowing for the conditions – in fact, experienced players should know how to play the conditions. Sadly in this league you are often punished for that one mistake. I thought otherwise he had a decent game against an elusive opponent in Hooper.

Delaney – 7 – Good solid performance in difficult conditions for defenders.

Jedinak – 7 – Always seemed to be there denying Norwich's midfielders any time to breathe, although needs to be careful with those stray elbows. Was seen flying across their penalty box – didn't see if flight was assisted or unaided! Was always a threat from set pieces, setting up Jerome's chance in the second half.

Dikgacoi – 5 – Started OK but ran out of steam by half-time, perhaps being brought back from injury too soon. Again the defensive stuff was fine but lacked any creative spark.

Bolasie – 6 – Immensely frustrating as made plenty of opportunities to deliver the decisive ball, but his crossing was poor and his corners even worse.

Puncheon – 7 – Possibly Palace's most creative player, as even if his crosses ended up with the same final result, they were delivered into dangerous areas that just missed colleagues. Showed some lovely touches, close control, tight turns & lay-offs that often threatened to free a team mate. His first effort on goal was unpromising but showed nerves at the vital time when converting the penalty. Could have grabbed a second with chances in the second half blocked or saved by Ruddy. Worked well with all the full backs today.

Chamakh – 7 – In the first half wasn't always interested in working, berating colleagues for poor deliveries or failing to choose him ahead of passing to others. Perhaps fired up by his confrontation after Norwich's goal when he was very lucky not to receive a red card. Second half was outstanding; his control of the ball and ability to turn his marker, combined with a willingness to run with the ball & commit defenders made opportunities for others.

Jerome – 5 – Cameron's limitations are outweighing his athletic ability & willingness to work hard up front on his own. His first effort on goal was perhaps one Van Basten might score once in 20, but his last was the sort Murray or Phillips would get on target 4 times out of 5 – a lack of skill or confidence resulting in a volley over the bar.

Parr – 6 – Played at left back in the second half and was involved in some promising attacks.

Gayle – 6 – Had some fine early touches when replacing Jerome, using his pace to create a couple of openings.

Williams – 6 – Another who looked like making an impact with his runs but perhaps replaced Bolasie too late to be decisive.

West Bromwich Away (FAC)

Speroni – 7 – Already noted his two errors in a fumbled cross and weak punch, but otherwise his keeping was top class. It couldn't have been an easy pitch to deal with low shots, but he smothered any that he stopped. Excellent save from Vydra in the second half, although difficult to tell in a grey shirt against a grey background from 120 yards away! Who needs Hennessy?

Mariappa – 7 – Was rarely beaten on the right flank and made some important clearances in the second half, as well as linking well with the right wingers in attack.

Parr – 6 – Good first half when he was often seen breaking up attacks and starting counter attacks down the left. Found life a struggle when Scott Sinclair (or Amalfitano – bloody difficult to read their red numbers on striped shorts) came on and was beaten more often than he held the attacks off.

Delaney – 7 – Struggled for a time with long balls aimed for Long but managed to keep the danger at arms' length. Improved in the second half when desperate defending was the order of the day. Made a couple of Beckenbauer (well, Jim Cannon) like breaks that nearly came to grief when colleagues lost the ball with our number one defender upfield.

Gabbidon – 7 – Was up against the skilful Berahino and generally restricted the youngster to shots from outside the box. Made a lot of important clearances and blocks, especially in the second half.

Dikgacoi – 6 – Provided a solid shield for the defence in the first half, perhaps tired in the second when he dropped too deep.

Boateng – 6 – Good first half display, good anticipation to intercept the defender's poor pass and a nice pass to set up Gayle's goal, but made a couple of poor errors late in the first half that could have been costly. Had an early chance in the second half when curled a shot wide, and faded quickly before being replaced by O'Keefe; probably not helped by the yellow card he picked up.

Bannan – 7 – More proof that his best role is in the centre of midfield, but only when partnered by two holding players. Created most of Palace's best moves in the first half, especially in concert with Jonny Williams, and had a good chance to open the scoring when making a well-timed run into the box before finding the angle too tight. Also proved effective when defending.

Bolasie – 6 – Another extremely frustrating game from Yannick as he bamboozled defenders and burst away from them, yet at other times out sprinted by the reserve centre back. Set up chances that were netted by both Gayle (didn't count) & Chamakh (did) but also blew great chances on the break with poor decision making or lazy execution. Another lamentable headed chance missed. Also was at times a liability at the back, in the first half twice inside 30 seconds giving away possession deep in our own half, and conceding a number of cheap free kicks.

Williams – 7 – Worked well with both Bannan and Gayle, and also with whichever full back whose flank he turned up on. Sometimes a little too clever for his own & the team's good. Booked for a professional foul.

Gayle – 7 – Set up Bannan's early chance and then finished, perhaps a little luckily, but put the ball in the one place Foster had no price for reaching. Found life difficult at times when finding himself surrounded by three defenders when receiving the ball, and should look to Chamakh for as example of how to hold up a ball. Thought he too dropped far too deep in the second quarter of the game and failed to provide even a sniff of an outlet for besieged defenders, but that may well have been under instructions. As the game stretched his pace on the break was a vital ingredient and only an offside flag ruled out a second goal.

O'Keefe – 6 – Came on and didn't seem to do much with the ball, instead fulfilling a mostly passive defensive role.

Chamakh – 7 – Looked a class above the other attackers on show with his ability to control a ball, turn and provide excellent lay-offs, and his introduction should have resulted in more goals than his with the final kick, but was one who preferred to find a better placed colleague than shoot, even if no-one filled that category.

Puncheon – 7 – Effective display down the right that set up two good chances.

Tottenham Away

Speroni – 6 – One good save in the first half and some brave collections of the ball at feet in the second. Exposed by both goals inside the box and well beaten by Bentaleb's first half effort but no real chance with any of these.

Mariappa – 6 – Like most of the team had a good first half, but let down by risible quality of crossing when supporting Puncheon. Had more problems in the second half and was caught out of position when Eriksen was played in for the first goal.

Parr – 6 – Excellent going forward and involved in several chances, including having one shot blocked, and worked well with Bolasie. However struggled against Lennon's trickery in his main defensive role, and was beaten by Defoe for their second.

Delaney – 8 – Immense game where he had an effective game against Adebayor, nearly set up a goal for Jedinak with a header from a corner, and it was one of his many runs upfield after intercepting a Spurs' move that created the penalty incident.

Gabbidon – 6 – Only made one real slip but that was the key moment when he allowed Eriksen to get goal side of him for the first goal. Otherwise kept the unimpressive Soldado very quiet.

Jedinak – 7 – Ran the match for the first 30 minutes, then involved in a far more equal struggle for the last hour. Nearly fashioned a messy opener but unluckily his effort struck a motionless Lloris and stayed out. Picked up a really stupid and obvious yellow card late on, probably out of pure frustration.

Ward – 7 – Although my preference would be for a more creative player alongside the Jedi (why is Bannan suddenly out of the team?) I can't knock Joel's efforts. He won plenty of ball and generally used it well. Let down by his corners (another area where Bannan was missed) which often didn't get past the first man, and a late shot that drifted horribly wide.

Puncheon – 6 – Worked hard and often unhinged the left side of Spurs' defence in the first half, but was less in involved in the second half as Palace possession dried up. Let down by his inconsistent crossing – a key ingredient for a winger – and... I'm sure there was something else...

Bolasie – 7 – With Parr Yannick ripped Tottenham apart time & again in the first half, often winning or retaining the ball when he had no right to, and showing some nice touches. Unfortunately when it came to crossing & corners his radar was skewed, which is rather important for a winger. Worked very hard defensively in the first half, one reason why Lennon was not as big a factor as he could have been, but was less diligent in the second in this area.

Chamakh – 7 – The way Marouane turned defenders with his back to goal was simply amazing; one twist and suddenly the defender was two yards away. Sadly much of his best work came to nothing as he played in Puncheon, Bolasie or Jerome when he rarely found himself inside the box. When he did he earned a penalty despite losing the chance to shoot, which he may now regret. Continued to play well in the second but why was it in the last minute of stoppage time that he found himself on the end of crosses? Really needs to get into the box more!

Jerome – 6 – I won't moan about Cameron's work rate and attitude, and he fashioned chances in both halves of varying degrees of difficulty. Yet he is another who doesn't tend to get inside the box anticipating a cross (getting a decent one is another matter!) and the difference between a natural goal scorer in Defoe and a limited if willing participant in Jerome is stark. If those two players swapped sides, Palace would probably have won.

Gayle – 5 – Came on with over 20 minutes to play but I don't think he touched the ball for at least 15 minutes, not necessarily Dwight's fault given the lack of meaningful possession. When he did at the end he showed some nice touches. Can only be the more muscular approach of Jerome & the latter's ability to hold up the ball that keeps Gayle out of the side, as I know which one looked most likely to threaten a goal.

Williams – 6 – Came on at the same time as Gayle & also took time to get up to the pace of the game, but then he did start to make openings down the left, and again found Parr a willing & able partner.

Guédioura – 6 – Late sub whose touch and vision – and ability to deliver a corner – promises more.

Speroni – 7 – His early save was crucial and although the ball bounced nicely for his dive & to turn the ball past the post, we've seen enough keepers beaten from that range to appreciate the skills involved. Showed courage when diving on the ball for low crosses and headers that bounced, while collecting the ball from crosses. One moment of miscommunication was not down to him: we all heard his shout but the Jedi did not.

Mariappa – 6 – Was turned inside out by the impressive Assaidi – we never really got to grips with their wing-back formation. Made some important clearing headers but was twice beaten in the air from corners, although a little illegality might have been used. Helped create Puncheon's goal and generally worked hard to support his winger.

Parr – 6 – Generally excellent going forward, several times making good overlapping runs and finding space in the box, while his crossing was generally better than Bolasie's (not saying much – mine is probably too!). On the back foot defensively when faced by the speedy Cameron but the left side generally hung together better than the right. Also looked like Stoke had figured he was a weak link in the air as several times he was isolated one-on-one with Walters. Exemplified his approach with a late 80-yard run to set up a chance for Wilbraham.

Delaney – 8 – Worked hard at the back against Crouch & Walters and generally was solid & reliable. Strange how he & Ward, defenders both, seemed more comfortable running with the ball through the middle, although twice let down by his colleagues who lost possession with him caught upfield. Silly moment in the second half when presented with the ball 10 yards out but chose to leave it as he thought he was offside: just play the bloody ball as no-one else was there to take advantage!

Gabbidon – 7 – One horrible early sliced clearance that shot over our bar, but apart from that faced up manfully to challenging taller players in the air, and always managed to get in the way if he didn't win the ball. May not be the most cultured central defender we've ever had but is proving himself mightily effective at the highest level.

Ward – 7 – Still on occasion looks like what he is – a defender playing in midfield – when he lacks the positional awareness and natural decision making required. Yet was still effective overall, playing some good short passes and making some short penetrating runs. Denied his first Palace goal by yet another inspired piece of goalkeeping. His corner routines need more work!

Jedinak – 6 – A hard day in the trenches for the skipper as Palace never subdued Stoke's midfield and for long periods were either on the back foot or dropping deep; the latter was especially noticeable when it allowed Adam to run the game from 35-40 yards out. Even in the first half Jedinak was found sitting inside our own half, just ahead of the central defenders, while Palace sought to build an attacking position when in possession. Did the hard work in terms of challenges but his passing wasn't quite true today, although was involved in the final break when Puncheon was denied by Butland.

Bolasie – 6 – Another extremely frustrating display from Yannick who showed a high level of skill accompanied by the odd heavy touch, appalling delivery or moments of sheer stupidity. Worth having on the pitch as he often looks the most dangerous weapon in our arsenal, and at least needs to be treated as such by the opposition.

Puncheon – 8 – Pulis kept faith with Jason after last week's little faux-pas and repaid the manager with the crucial goal. Had a very good first half, even if his corners were occasionally erratic, and worked especially well in conjunction with Mariappa, and helped defend that flank against Assaidi. Second half took his goal well, finding space to shoot just when it looked like he'd run out of it. Only Butland prevented him adding another couple to the score.

Guédioura – 6 – Some nice touches but if he was meant to be supporting Chamakh he was playing far too deep, and these moments were often too far out to pose any immediate threat to Stoke's goal. Good first start since his injury comeback although in the end cramp did for him.

Chamakh – 7 – Yet again gave a fine display of the lone striker's arts in holding the ball up & winning a fair percentage of balls in the air, but seldom posed a direct threat on goal – I thought it was his early header but apparently it was Joel! Was the victim of some heavy challenges, some of which went unpunished, but after one early trek to the sideline kept coming back for more. I was one who doubted his appetite for the fight but he has proven me wrong over the last few months. If only we had someone alongside to take advantage of his hard work...

O'Keefe – 6 – Solid display from Stuart who committed himself into the fray with gusto, and nearly grabbed a late goal.

Wilbraham – 7 – As a late substitute had nearly as many chances as he did at Wembley, although this time the connections made were firmer & the keeping even more praiseworthy. Did an excellent job in holding the ball up but had far more time than he realised with one late chance.

Moxey – 6 – Late substitute for Bolasie who helped seal up the left flank.

Wigan Away (FAC)

Speroni – 6 – Solid & brave display who had no chance with Watson's goal (no keeper would have) but should perhaps have done better with McLean's winner as the shot appeared mis-hit and beat him at his near post.

Parr – 4 – Truly awful day for Jonathan who was roasted by McManaman, nearly gave Watson a goal from an incredibly stupid & inept pass, and even failed to offer his usually outlet on the left. It got worse thanks to McManaman's unlawful challenge.

Mariappa – 4 – Not quite as poor as Parr but was twice caught by McLean for their goals, although had taken a hard knock on the ankle minutes before their winner. Did make a couple of good headed clearances and was able to offer Puncheon some support down the right in the second half.

McCarthy – 6 – You wouldn't think Paddy had been out for 18 months or so, as he didn't appear rusty at all. Played a simple game well and was one of the better defenders, although caught out by Espinoza's pass for the winner. Had a late chance to equalise but could not put any power on the header.

Delaney – 6 – Probably the best of the starting XI with some important clearances, although at time his long range passing was spectacularly off-target. Also had a headed chance at 1-0 down but the cross was just too high for him.

O'Keefe – 5 – Proved too lightweight to help hold the middle on his own (so poor was Adlene) and was regularly outnumbered by two or three opponents. Did have a couple of efforts on goal that were comfortably saved by Al Habsi.

Guédioura – 4 – Never got into the game, giving the ball up on several occasions with poor control or passing, and lacked the steel to win some of his own. It was his error that gave the ball away for McLean's winner.

Bannan - 6 – Looked the most creative player in the first half, although not immune to some poor control, but faded late in the second, although did help make Gayle's chance on the beak with some excellent running off the ball to make a gap. Cannot decide if his low near post corners were a deliberate tactic or two spectacularly lucky flukes!

Puncheon – 6 – Like so many was not in the game for the first half, but became a factor in the second when Palace's best attacks came down the right. Denied a goal by a fine save, and then ruined a late chance by trying to take too much time.

Chamakh – 5 – A peripheral figure after setting up an early chance for Jerome, who never really offered close support to the striker. Appeared uninterested.

Jerome – 4 – Started brightly with a shot that was curling inside the post until Al Habsi intervened, but then suffered from a lack of support, while his own game fell apart. Summed up when actually received a perfect through ball from Chamakh only to find it hitting his heels as he was looking in another direction.

Moxey – 5 – A slight improvement on the stricken Parr and offered a little more going forward, but his defending against McManaman was hurried and never safe.

Wilbraham – 7 – Made a real difference when he came on if just for his appetite for the game. Was on hand to knock home a loose ball in the box, denied a possible second by a crafty nudge in the back, and fell over when presented with our last chance. Also struck up a decent partnership with Gayle.

Gayle – 7 – Showed real zeal when arriving, so much so that it is a valid question as to why he did not start as at West Brom. Involved in Wilbraham's goal with a quick flick and nearly seized a second similar to his goal at Villa with a break and shot. Also should have won a penalty when beating Boyce in the box only to be pulled back, although perhaps the fall might have put off the (admittedly shoddy) referee.

Hull Home

Speroni – 7 – Was iffy under a couple of crosses but continued to come out for them making some good catches and punching well. Was clattered late by Jelavic in the second half for which no yellow card was shown. Made an awkward looking reaction save in the first half from Huddlestone's free kick, but the best was a scrambling save of Boyd's shot that seemed to be creeping in, although the ball did bounce clear for Long to miss from an offside position.

Mariappa – 6 – Linked well with Bolasie down the right in the first half, not so well with Puncheon in the second half. Had a rough time against Elmohamady defensively but did put in some good challenges.

Moxey – 5 – Looked good going forward in the first half but defensively struggled against Hull's wing-back system as the left side creaked all night. His passing was often poor and on more than one occasion allowed Hull opportunities that went unpunished.

Gabbidon – 6 – Found it a struggle against Jelavic who too often managed to get goal side of the defender. Still made some good tackles & clearances.

Delaney -7 – Kept Long quiet for most of the game before switching to Fryatt, and also made the usual number of good challenges. Doubly stupid (but thoroughly understandable) kick on Jelavic for a yellow card & free kick in a dangerous position.

Jedinak – 5 – Came close to scoring three times from two corners & a direct free kick and heavily involved in defensive work, but his passing grew increasingly erratic and was lucky not to be punished for it.

Ward – 6 – Good first half but, as with Jedinak, came under pressure in the second half and his passing deteriorated as well, although not to the same degree. Corners looked dangerous and should have led to at least one more goal.

Bolasie – 7 – Dangerous in the first half, and his skill & tenacity made Puncheon's

314

goal; still needs to work on his shooting though. Less impressive in the second half as starved of possession and was withdrawn in a tactical substitution.

Puncheon – 8 – Another good game from Jason and another important goal, well taken after his initial header was blocked. Showed moments of good close ball control and also worked hard defensively in helping out his full back and closing down Hull's defence.

Chamakh – 6 – Worked exceptionally hard in the first half and had some good touches that nearly set Jerome free. Also suffered from Palace's lack of ball in the second half and was a more peripheral figure.

Jerome – 6 – Another who worked hard in closing down Hull's defenders and at times looked ion the verge of making things happen, but never really had a clear cur scoring opportunity.

McCarthy – 7 – Played as though he had not been out for over 18 months and helped tighten up a defence that was just starting to wobble. Did lose Long once but glad his flying attempt at a clearance did not result in another own goal!

O'Keefe – 6 – One lovely through pass late on to set up a chance, but a little lucky with his late challenge on McGregor as a weaker referee might have sent them both off.

Wilbraham – 6 – Came on late in a left wing position and did some good defensive work in both halves.

Arsenal Away

Speroni – 6 – Very good first half with those three saves, had little chance with the first goal but might have done better with the second, getting a hand to the shot but not able to turn it around the post.

Ward – 6 – Was a very good display let down by finding Oxlade-Chamberlain the wrong side of him for both goals. Midfield also has some responsibility for not picking up the runs (assume Chamakh & Bannan were the guilty parties).

Parr – 7 – Strong showing from a player who kept running for 90 minutes and worked hard in both defence & the rare occasions he ventured forward.

Delaney – 7 – Continued a fine string of performances against a more mobile attack than usual. Did have one headed chance late on that went wide. Picked up a caution in the second half for a tackle that looked well-timed but caught the opponent.

Gabbidon - 8 – Just seemed slightly more involved in the frenetic defending on the edge of our box and always seemed to get in the way of those little reverse passes Arsenal love to play.

Dikgacoi – 6 – Thought KG had a strong first half, another who held the line around the edge of the area, although his passing is a weak link. Let down by giving the ball away for the second goal.

Jedinak – 6 – Defensively good but once again his passing was poor, something we can't afford when only having 30% of the ball.

Bolasie – 5 – A latent threat with his runs but too often the final touch, pass or cross lacks quality.

Puncheon – 6 – Good outlet in the first half and not as profligate with the ball as Bolasie. Not as used in the second but did set up Jerome's chance with our one decent cross.

Chamakh – 6 – Cannot fault his effort but too much of his good work was carried out on or behind the halfway line. One good chance spoiled by a poor touch allowing the keeper to beat him to the ball. Failure to track back allowed Oxlade-Chamberlain a free run for the first goal.

Jerome – 5 – Very isolated but another who worked hard. Could he have done better with that headed chance?

Bannan – 6 – The midfield play did improve when Barry arrived, although he may have been the man who didn't pick up the Ox's run for the second, though if he was he was sold short when KG gave the ball away.

Gayle – 5 – Hardly saw the ball.

West Brom Home

Speroni – 7 – I believe Julian must bear a large share of blame for the goal, as it appeared to go straight through him at his near post. More than made up for that with his save from Morrison – sharp from distance – and then the close range effort when he saved to his right while initially moving to his left. Showed some bravery at the feet of opposing forwards as well.

Ward – 6 – Another who was caught napping for Albion's quick opening to the second half, moving too slowly to close down his man. Worked hard down his flank but still looked short of his pre-Christmas form.

Ledley – 7 – Surprising (to me) choice of left back who was solid first half and capped that with a fine run and strong header for his goal. Didn't offer much going forward and faced harder work in the second half before switching to midfield.

Dann – 7 – Nearly had a poor start to his Palace career when allowing Anichebe to get goal side of him, but then turned in the sort of performance we required. It was difficult to knock the solid Anichebe off the ball but Scott stuck to his task, only being caught out by the rebound leading to Speroni's crucial save. Did like one first half clearing header where he deliberately steered his header to an unmarked Chamakh 15 yards away; not much to think of but compare it to the usual standard of clearing headers we have where we are just grateful to have the ball move away from our goal.

Delaney – 7 – Relatively easy first half but more pressured after the interval, although Albion were seldom allowed a sight of goal. Nearly picked up his first goal of the season from an Ince corner.

Dikgacoi – 6 – Fulfils an unglamorous role well, although his low standard of passing can be a liability. Nothing outstanding but a lot of simple work done well.

Jedinak – 6 – A game of two halves from the Jedi. Excellent in the challenge, but his passing grew increasingly & dangerously slipshod, and this increased the pressure on our defence in the second half. Did take one brilliant late free kick which, if it had bounced a yard or so further from Foster, could well have confounded the keeper in the blustery conditions.

Puncheon – 6 – Some very good touches down the right but another whose game grew increasingly erratic, mixing skill with some appalling passing and close control. Worst moment was standing still waiting for a long pass to reach him when shifting just a couple of feet would have prevented him being robbed of the ball.

Bolasie – 6 – I do seem to keep repeating myself regarding Yannick. There were flashes of brilliance, and I am still trying to work out how he contorted his neck to get an early header on target, and not sure how much he meant of the ball through to Ince for the first goal. But far too often there was no end product, his decision making and sometimes execution too being wildly off target.

Ince – 7 – A different sort of player to Wilfred Zaha, more pace than the ability to twist an opponent's blood, but looked at home in the hole and often switched position with Chamakh. Not distracted by the foul on Bolasie he played to the whistle & it was a cool finish with enough power to lift it over Foster and find the net. His corner taking too was excellent, pin-point accurate for Ledley's goal and then completing the now Palace speciality of a low near post corner. Looked equally adept when moved to the right wing, burning defenders with a neat touch and speed. Can forgive him the one truly awful cross that missed by about 40 yards!

Chamakh – 8 – Took a lot of punishment but did his job well, holding the ball up and bringing the wingers & Ince into play, as with the first goal. Still didn't threaten the goal as often as a forward should but won the important penalty and showed steel in taking the kick himself.

Murray – 7 – Palace did seem to carry a more potent threat when he came on but that was probably just the game stretching in its final phases. Great to see him back and moving without any apparent lack of pace.

Parr – 6 – Came on to close down the left flank & release Ledley into midfield, and did well except for a moment when he was mugged (one of Foy's rare poor decisions) and left on the floor.

Thomas – 6 – Surprised to find Jerome was near to full fitness and made a couple of decent moves.

Manchester United Home

Speroni – 6 – Strangely underemployed given how much ball United had, really only having crosses and through balls to collect. When called into action was safe but nothing too difficult came his way until around the hour mark. Beaten easily by the penalty & had no chance with Rooney's goal or Van Persie's effort when the bar came to his rescue. Kicking was sometimes awry.

Ward – 6 – Good first half with an early run but was kept busy by Januzaj. Was twice a spectator to Evra's runs down his flank which set up both goals. Corners were good & better than Ince's efforts.

Parr – 7 – Worked hard although United found space behind him a couple of times in the first half. Made several runs to support the attack and nearly worked an opening goal turning up unannounced on the far post.

Delaney – 6 – Made one good clearance of Rooney's effort in the first half and never shirked his duties, but United rarely offered a straightforward challenge, preferring to cut our defenders out of the game with passing moves around the edge of the box.

Dann – 6 – As with Delaney often found they were both marking one striker, and an elusive one at that. Both men were drawn away from Rooney by Evra's run for the second goal.

Jedinak – 5 – One of his poorer performances this season. Made some good interceptions but too often conceded possession with poor short passes, setting up more than one United break. Was often seen to be looking over his shoulder trying to trace Rooney's runs. Not enough tackles, like his colleagues seemingly happy to stand off and block. Was drawn out of position for Rooney's goal by United's play on our right.

Ledley – 6 – Pretty anonymous although was one of those who failed to close down Evra for the second goal.

Puncheon – 4 – Very poor, too often choosing the wrong option and giving the ball away. Had the opportunity to run at Ferdinand more than once – and he's nearly as ancient & slow as I am! – but never had the confidence to do so.

Ince – 5 – Started well with some excellent dangerous crosses and off the ball movement, but faded in influence as Palace were increasingly starved of ball. His corners were hit & miss, some being over hit and others not beating the first man.

Chamakh – 5 – Worked hard and showed some good touches up front, linking well with Murray, but made two crucial errors. First his awful header from Ince's cross when you would have put money on Murray forcing De Gea to at least sweat if not pick the ball out of the net. Second his poorly executed & timed tackle that floored Evra a fraction inside the box; I thought this challenge was unnecessary as Evra appeared to be going nowhere, but given what happened for the second perhaps that opinion should be reviewed.

Murray – 7 – The difference between a striker used to the sole role, even if not match-fit, and someone of limited ability was clear today. Murray added a focal point for Palace, being strong enough to win & hold the ball up then brining his colleagues into play, something Jerome singularly fails to do. Made an experienced defender in Vidic panic at time with plenty of manhandling & shirt-pulling.

Jerome – 5 – Good start with an early shot that De Gea made sure went wide, but too often his idea of play was to flick the ball forward and run after it instead of playing with is back to goal and laying the ball off. Thought he should have done better with a far post headed chance late on.

Bolasie – 6 – Actually had a shot on target, even if easy for De Gea. At least provided some pace even if the crossing & decision making were characteristically inconsistent.

Gayle – 5 – Late sub who barely saw the ball.

Swansea Away

Speroni – 7 – There was one moment of panic when lack of communication with his defenders nearly served Bony up a chance on a plate, but that was Julian's only error on what must have been a greasy pitch. Had little chance with the goal – although so brilliant has his form been in 2013 & 2014 you half expected the miracle – but possibly kept us in the game with a fine reaction save from close range, pawing Bony's effort aside.

Ward – 5 – Had a tough time against Routledge in the first half but at least the right side didn't fall apart. Didn't get forward too often as a result.

Parr – 4 – Had one early run that set up Bolasie for a great crossing opportunity, but after that Jonny's game went downhill fast. Dyer and the full back Davies just sliced our left side apart and too many times Parr found Dyer played in behind him.

Delaney - 6 – Very difficult to mark Bony when the forward drops off and the midfield runners pour through the middle. Completely taken out of the game for their goal by the Swansea interplay. Less pressured in the second half and his much-favoured long diagonal ball from left to right was for once an effective weapon, thanks to work from Murray and often finding Bolasie in space.

Dann – 5 – Defensively suffered as much as his partner against Swansea's mobile attack. Nearly caught on the break in the second and took a yellow card for the team by bringing down the attacker wide right.

Jedinak – 5 – Rarely a factor in the match, like the rest of the midfield trio unable to stem the flow of Swansea's attacks in the first half, or spark anything in retaliation. His passing was shocking, even in the second half when Swansea eased off. First half booking for a chest-high challenge that was destined to be nothing other than a caution, another cheap yellow card – how close is Mile to a second suspension?

Dikgacoi – 6 – Anonymous for about an hour then started to influence the game with his strong play, winning balls, hustling mistakes out of the opposition and making good runs to support the attack.

Ledley – 5 – Appeared in three different positions – central midfield, left midfield & left back – proving his versatility but was equally disappointing in all of them. Like the rest of our midfield sans Yannick was outplayed in the first half, overshadowed by Bolasie in the second, and not really asked to do much as left back except return the ball long towards the opposition's goal.

Bolasie – 7 – Was the most latent threat Palace possessed and while his first cross of the match was so wildly over hit one wondered if this was to be another inconsistent display, he kept hammering away, first on the left and then on the right. Second half unhinged the whole left side of Swansea's defence and it is no exaggeration to say it was almost like Zaha reborn. If only his quality of delivery could improve as Wilf's did! At least the crosses were generally driven in low from the goal line and he provided us with the hope something could be snatched from the game. Did set up two late chances for Thomas & himself.

Ince – 4 – After a couple of early touches faded completely from the game, proving far too lightweight on both the right wing & later in the hole. Needs a touch of his old man's grit – he would have been riled up by the abuse from the home crowd. As it was there was a tremendous cheer when his half-time withdrawal was announced. Not sure he would have got into Swansea's team ahead of either Dyer or Routledge on this form.

Chamakh – 5 – Worked hard but saw little of the ball and took a couple of knocks before limping off.

Jerome – 6 – At first as isolated as Marouane had been, worked hard without a hint of quality, but pressed hard on Swansea's defence & there were hints of a partnership developing with Murray.

Murray – 7 – Showed what Palace have missed all season with an exemplary display of hard work, holding the ball up and again allowing the defence no respite. Won the penalty through a combination of these qualities and dispatched it perfectly.

Thomas – 4 – Was not much of a factor until that ridiculous, ill-judged dive. What is wrong with taking a shot from 18 yards?

Southampton Home

Speroni – 6 – Two good saves in the first half from Speroni, although one was offside anyway, and so nearly bailed Puncheon out with a sliding challenge that knocked Rodriguez over but didn't see the ball bounce kindly – mind you it was looking for a second like a possible red card for Julian! Twice rushed kicks from the ground when he had more time to trap the ball but got away with it.

Ward – 6 – Mixed performance from Joel who had some good moments with sharp tackles but whose passing was sometimes misdirected. His corners were equally variable in quality.

Moxey – 6 – Plenty of effort but his passing & positioning was suspect at times as ever. I don't think he could do anything over the goal, expecting Puncheon to deal with the ball, but would be interested to see the replay.

Dann – 7 – Important defensive work often dealing with crosses into the box. I thought his lack of pace might be a weakness today but his positional play helped a great deal.

Delaney – 6 – Only marginally behind his central defensive colleague but defended well against a varied attacking force.

Jedinak – 4 – I thought he looked a yard off the pace today, perhaps a legacy of the week's international, not winning as many balls as usual, while his passing was generally poor, although there was one exception that set Bolasie free. Summed up his & the team's performance with a woeful apogee of a free kick.

Dikgacoi – 4 – Anonymous in the first half but at least pushed on in the second.

Ledley – 6 – Didn't do much in his starting position behind Murray but worked hard in all other areas of the pitch, both defensively and later on out wider.

Puncheon – 3 – Started poorly then made the unforced error that set up the goal. After that it just got worse... It would have been a mercy to take him off – he was walking long before the board came up for him – but for reasons unknown Pulis kept him on long after there was any chance of redemption.

Bolasie – 7 – Again Palace's most potent threat, although that is comparatively speaking. Like most wingers promises more than he delivers, but there has been a gradual improvement in the last few games. He even managed to keep a shot low & on target! Some magic movement set up his run on goal ended by Louvren.

Murray – 6 – Worked hard but often far too isolated until Jerome arrived. Was caught offside a few times early on and never really saw a sight of goal.

Ince – 5 – Came on but had absolutely no influence on the game, barely seeing the ball apart from a couple of decent free kicks.

Jerome – 5 – Tried hard but caught offside far too often.

Thomas – 6 – Managed far more in terms of crosses in his limited time on the pitch than Puncheon managed in over an hour.

Sunderland Away

Speroni – 7 – Comfortable first half, only one shot on target and dealt well with a couple of crosses, although one moment's miscommunication with the defence nearly let Fletcher in at the cost of a corner. Second half two sharp saves from Altidore (even if one would not have counted) but best when dealing with a late break by coming swiftly off his line to head clear.

Mariappa – 6 – Started poorly, being booked early on for two poor challenges, and was often caught by the ball over his head to land in his quarter, but then settled down and very little came down that flank for the rest of the game.

Ward – 7 – Like his fellow full back picked up an early caution which didn't bode well for 90 minutes against Adam Johnson, but managed to keep him quiet for much of the match, although slow to pick up on short corners from that side.

Delaney – 6 – Found Fletcher a handful in the air, but probably drew that particular duel. When faced with Borini in the second half lost him for the effort that came off the bar. Picked up a yellow card in frustration at giving the ball away.

Dann – 5 – Coped well with Borini in the first half but found Altidore a far more difficult opponent in the second, twice being beaten to crosses only to be saved by Julian. Also tried to run the ball out of our half only to be caught in possession.

Jedinak – 4 – The quality of his passing, even the short ball, continues to deteriorate, too often giving the ball to a colleague under pressure or, worse, cutting out the middle man and giving it straight to a red & white shirt. Bailed out by Delaney, Speroni and Sunderland's lack of a cutting edge.

Dikgacoi – 4 – Not quite as profligate with the ball as Mile but not far off it, setting up more than one Sunderland break by conceding possession. Also missed a great chance to steal the three points late on by not hitting the target from 10 yards out – admittedly at an angle but poor nonetheless.

Ledley – 7 – Helped Ward police the left side defensively. Not as attacking as Yannick but popped up in one good move in the first half only to fail to get his shot away, then missing from a decent position in the second half. Would prefer to see him in the middle three with Bannan & one of KG or Jedinak.

Bolasie – 6 – Worked hard, particularly defensively, which are words I don't think I could have recorded a year ago, as he had to cover the space behind Mariappa. Didn't show as much up front as in recent matches, although set up a chance for Murray in the first half and had one shot on target in the second.

Ince – 4 – Continued a run of performances which could not even be described as peripheral. One or two nice touches, setting up Ledley's first half sight of goal, gut once again found wanting in the challenge, either knocked too easily off the ball or lacking aggression in the tackle.

Murray – 5 – Saw little of the ball in the first half, and when he did usually coughed up possession, sometimes under "unfair" challenges not so ruled by the ref. Not much better in the second half but did have a header wide under pressure and set up a chance for Bolasie. Looked tired by the time he was substituted.

Jerome – 6 – Provided a more direct threat when he came on and that little extra pace did force a couple of half chances.

Guédioura – 6 – Started poorly with his first two interventions being to give the ball away then giving away a cheap free kick in a dangerous area. Then settled down and provided a good link to Jerome, helping set up KG's chance. Had a free kick that curled just wide but lacked the pace to embarrass Mannone.

Puncheon – 6 – Not much time to do anything but a couple of good moves down the right and a shot that was easily saved by Mannone.

Newcastle Away

Speroni – 7 – His kicking game was occasionally dicey, and he had one moment of complete miscommunication with Delaney along the lines of: "Why didn't you call?" "I did!" "No you didn't!" as well as almost gifting the ball to Cissé. Yet his overall shot (& header) stopping was excellent, denying the Toon several times in both half, and may have touched Tioté's shot onto the bar. The best were the close range blocks, one in each half, from Gouffran & Cissé. No chance with the goal. Gets my vote as Palace MotM as I can't decide which defenders need to be sent to the naughty corner for the goal.

Ward –¬ 6 – Had some difficult moments at left back with Gouffran often infiltrating behind him and more when Ben Arfa came on. Had some better moments raiding down the left. Was it Joel or Joe who should have closed down Ben Arfa for the goal?

Mariappa – 6 – A quieter time on Adrian's flank and had a good if unexceptional game.

Delaney – 6 – Defended well in general and made one excellent break upfield, but where was he when Cissé popped up in stoppage time? Was badly beaten by one far post corner in the first half that led to a penalty shout.

Dann – 7 – Had an excellent 90 minutes, one seemingly missed header from a corner in the first half aside, and in the second half put in excellent headers and interceptions. As with Damien will need to see MOTD to see what he was doing in the minutes beyond 90.

Jedinak – 7 – I have been one of the harsher critics of Mile over the last few months but he was really back to his best, snapping into tackles, winning headers, and – more importantly – his use of the ball was far, far better. He broke up attacks and also sprinted upfield to support the attack. Not error-free but no-one will win every tackle or header, or never misplace a pass, but the error rate was way down.

Dikgacoi – 7 – Like Mile, KG's performance saw a whole lot of good and not much bad. One early long pass that set Jerome free was possibly the Palace Pass of the Season. Defensively did a lot of work and supported the attack when required, setting up chances for others but sadly his poor touch helped Krul deny him with his own.

Ledley – 7 – Another good display in central midfield as Joe, Jedi & KG almost took turns to push up or sit back; if he had a right foot there may have been an opening at the start of the second half. Moved to left flank, possibly to help close down Ben Arfa, so may be one of the guilty parties for the goal.

Puncheon – 6 – Worked damned hard but often turns away when pushing straight on would be the best option. Set up good chances for Jerome & KG but wasted his own with a wild shot.

Bolasie – 7 – At one stage halfway through the second half, 100+ yards away and 100 feet below us, a Palace player threw himself into a challenge on the edge of our box. KG surely? Ledley possibly? No – it was Yannick! Summed up his approach as he worked tirelessly down both flanks although his final ball sometimes didn't match his approach play. Sadly think he was sacrificed for defensive reasons and we never looked quite the same after he left.

Jerome – 6 – Gave us different qualities to Murray, Chamakh or Gayle but his hard work often created time & space for others to exploit. Had one header wide, then found himself clear but unsupported & his shot was blocked. Second half made even more of a difference but Palace didn't take advantage. Was knackered when subbed.

Bannan – 5 – Didn't too enough when he had the ball and looked off the pace when closing down opponents.

Murray – 5 – Unable to fulfil the same role as Jerome and the team did not play to his strengths.

Guédioura – 4 – Had one shot from a good position that dribbled wide, and blocked one attack by not playing the ball. Unfortunately his lack of movement off the ball but colleagues like Murray & Bannan under pressure and he too seemed lackadaisical when closing down opponents.

Chelsea Home

Speroni – 8 – Immaculate – if we overlook, as we should, those late kicks curling straight into touch. Solid in the first half, brilliant in the second. The first save from Hazard was exceptional as he saw the ball so late and required his full length to turn the ball away; I cannot believe the second as his positioning & reflexes denied what seemed a certain goal. Also bailed out O'Keefe by giving Torres no time to think.

Ward – 8 – Had some problems with Schürrle in the first half, and found it hard going in the second, but there were three moments of brilliance. First his decisive block of Schürrle's close range effort, even if the referee did miss it; the supporting run & cross that led to the goal; and the sublime impersonation of Cristiano Ronaldo as he danced around experienced internationals in about a foot of space.

Mariappa – 8 – Excellent return from an ersatz right back, although in the second half I did wish he wasn't so keen to tear down the wing to support the attack. I thought he had good claims to be the best performer in the first half.

Delaney – 8 – Led the defence well with some crucial interceptions and clearances in both halves, despite taking a hard knock in the first half.

Dann – 7 – Solid and took a yellow card for the team in the second half.

Jedinak – 7 – Didn't win every tackle or header, and not every pass found its target, especially as he tired late on, but did more than enough to repel opponents.

Led more than one fast break that could have been rewarded with a goal. His two shots in the first, especially the free kick from an excellent position, lacked venom.

Dikgacoi – 7 – Worked hard in the less glamorous roles, and although sometimes caught out by Chelsea's swift interpassing in the second half, contributed a lot to defending the lead. In the first half also turned up on the edge of Chelsea's box to make chances.

Ledley – 7 – If he was supposed to be playing in the hole behind Jerome, Joe wasn't much of an influence and hardly featured in the first half in an attacking sense, although did plenty of work defensively. Second half saw him more deployed on the left of the midfield trio, although too often Chelsea's attacks came down that channel. It was a different story attacking, as he not only put Terry under pressure that led to the goal – and made good ground to challenge for the cross – but also had two late chances that he put wide.

Puncheon – 6 – Poor first 30 minutes when he gave the ball away cheaply too often, but slowly grew in confidence with the rest of the team and nearly created an opening for Bolasie. Far better in the second half when catching Chelsea out on the break.

Bolasie – 7 – Didn't see the ball for the first 15 minutes then became our most potent threat, dragging one shot wide from a good position, then being robbed inside the box by a fine tackle, before just filing to control a driven cross. Also did some good work defensively, especially in the second half, and can be considered a little unlucky to be sacrificed in order to shore up the left side of the defence.

Jerome – 8 – Impressive performance of non-stop effort, never giving Terry or Cahill a minute's peace, and would have crowned the display if his finishing had been a little better and not struck the post. Also held the ball up well and laid it off, creating chances for colleagues.

O'Keefe – 5 – Almost a disastrous substitution, obviously not up to the immediate pace of the game, conceding possession cheaply and then there was that kamikaze back pass under no pressure... At least nearly repeated his Sunderland goal, forcing Cech to tip over a shot from the same point.

Murray – 6 – Came on late to hold the ball up and did so when required.

Parr – 6 – Even later sub to hold the right flank – saw the ball once and dealt with the threat confidently.

Cardiff Away

Speroni – 7 – Strangely underemployed given the match situation and Cardiff fielding an over-attacking team, which will indicate how well the outfield defenders (including midfield) performed. One save that looked untidy but was effective on a damp pitch; one mistake when beaten to a cross but the header was cleared; dealt well with anything else that came near him.

Mariappa – 8 – Outstanding display especially when pushing forward, playing a small role in both Puncheon's goals. Defensively only faced Zaha a couple of times but closed Wilf down and also made some important headed clearances.

Ward – 7 – Had to curb much of his attacking instinct when Zaha was deployed on his flank, and early on was outflanked three times by Wilf who beat him on his weaker left side. That Zaha was less of a factor after this indicates that Joel gradually gained the upper hand in that individual duel.

Delaney – 7 – Solid as usual, cannot remember an error that was in any way seized on by Cardiff.

Dann – 8 – As with Delaney but made a couple of very important headed clearances in potentially dangerous situations.

Jedinak – 8 – His passing was still a little ropey but his tackling was excellent, he closed down Cardiff's midfield and won the battle for the centre, while his height was invaluable in helping deal with crosses. Realistically it was the midfield three that won the battle and allowed Puncheon to seize the game.

Dikgacoi – 7 – With Mile shut down most of Cardiff's moves down the middle and also helped out defending crosses. Made a couple of breaks upfield as well, but shame his early effort on goal was nothing like that blistering finish last season at the Valley.

Ledley – 8 – Can't recall a mistake by Joe, so it was good to see the "immutable law of the ex" strike for us for once! Excellent in midfield, creating a goal for Puncheon and being in the right place to unwittingly score the crucial second. Nice touch not to celebrate but did have us fearing it had been disallowed! Picked up a late injury.

Bolasie – 6 – Yannick's turn to be the relatively disappointing winger, as he saw quite a bit of ball but there was little end product. Probably not helped by Ward staying back more often than usual.

Puncheon – 8 – There were times in the second half when he appeared to be easing off and not tracking back – and that was the only mild criticism I can make! Think he had 5 shots on target, with his second goal an unstoppable placed curler, while the first goal was hit early and hard. It was also his free kick that led to the second goal. Was always a danger to Cardiff's defence, especially when linking with Mariappa.

Jerome – 7 – As against Chelsea ran himself into the ground and had some nice touches but not many near the opposition goal. Always provided an option when the defenders or midfield won the ball.

Chamakh – 7 – Some lovely touches on the ball, especially in the last 20 minutes when the whole team was relaxed. His height was important too in clearing headers and the one attacking one that led to Ledley's goal.

Parr – 6 – Came on as left midfield for Ledley and didn't let anyone down.

Murray – 6 – Good swap for the run-out Jerome in a period where the game was all but won and held the ball up well.

Aston Villa Home

Speroni – 7 – Hardly a save to make for an hour, and then those he did make were generally routine, with the exception of another full length effort to deny Weimann from close range. I think we've underrated Julian this season as we are so used to his quality by now, the match- or point-winning save expected.

Mariappa – 5 – Thought Adrian didn't reach the quality of performances he's produced of late with some particularly careless passing and some less than solid challenges, especially in the first half, and didn't really improve until the last 30 minutes.

Ward – 7 – Solid in defence and helped Bolasie a lot on the attack.

Delaney –7 – Another quiet contender for Player of the Year with a couple of vital tackles. Looked to be beaten once by Holt to set up Weimann's chance but otherwise kept a lid on Villa's admittedly toothless attack. Lovely through ball to Jerome in the first half.

Dann – 8 – Quietly impressive, forming a very solid pairing with Delaney, with again a few important tackles and clearances.

Dikgacoi – 6 – Short time on pitch marked by a couple apiece of tough challenges and awful passes.

Jedinak – 6 – I thought it took Mile some time to get into the flow of both halves, marked by some less than shuddering challenges and a greater number of poor passes than usual, and sitting deeper than I'd like. When he did hit his stride Palace dominated the middle and looked a far better team, marked by some lovely passes. At the end added weight to the defence in repelling Villa's late charge.

Ledley – 7 – Another good professional performance from Joe, the only downside a little lack of pace. Held it together when KG departed & Jedinak wasn't on top of his game.

Puncheon – 7 – Good showing bar a strange 10-15 minutes after half-time when his lax approach was a real danger in defence. First half was the main outlet for the first 20 minutes, creating chances. Second half less obvious but still scored a vital goal and hit the post.

Bolasie- 8 – Excellent performance from Yannick who terrorised Villa's right back position either side of half-time, although I'm sure he could have done better with that free kick move when he appeared to mis-kick (look forward to the replay). Created openings for Jerome, which was spurned, and Puncheon, which was accepted gratefully. Didn't understand the substitution unless he really was injured.

Jerome – 6 – Ran his heart out and didn't allow Villa's defence a moment's peace, but missed a really great chance after Guzman's less than impressive save left him virtually a free shot on goal from reasonably close range.

Chamakh – 7 – Improved Palace's attacking play with his ability to hold up the ball and nearly scored with a fine far post header. Also proved useful once again in defending set pieces.

Murray – 6 – Came on just before Palace went 1-0 up and had a couple of nice moments but still looks a little short of pace.

Parr – 6 – Looked like a defensive substitution by Pulis but it worked out fine.

Everton Away

Giving everyone 0 as first game I miss all season the silly b*ggers go and turn in a performance like that!

West Ham Away

Speroni – 7 – On a couple of occasions I thought Julian could have helped out his defenders against Carroll by coming for crosses, but then that's never really been his style, and he did grab all those that threatened his six-yard box. Apart from this minor nit-picking, he again did nothing wrong and made two important saves inside a couple of seconds, the later one keeping out Carroll's header with a fine reflex reaction. Second half saw him collect some easier efforts.

Ward – 7 – Had some difficulty against Downing in the first half, and some of his clearances lacked power &/or direction, causing more problems, but he also made at least three important interceptions in the first half. He also found it easier against Jarvis in the second half. Was an important factor is supporting Bolasie's attacks.

Mariappa – 7 – First half generally handled Jarvis well and made some important clearances, not least with his head. Second half was more stretched as first

Downing then Diamé caused him problems, but he was also prominent in supporting Puncheon in attacks down the right.

Delaney – 7 – At first looked to have the upper hand over Carroll but the big man escaped him three times and nearly made Palace pay. More difficult to tell from the far end who should have been picking Carroll up in the second half when he had his half chances. On all other occasions was a rock with plenty of headers and one sublime back-heeled clearance.

Dann – 7 – Looked to have handled Carroll better overall than Damien although the second half was more difficult to tell when he was taking the big man. Another impressive performance but perhaps should have done better with an early header.

Dikgacoi – 6 – Solid enough game but sometimes his passing was woefully poor, and still trying to figure out how his header didn't go in. Also missed a good chance with a wayward shot in the first half.

Jedinak – 8 – Alright, his passing wasn't perfect but he played enough good ones to make a real difference. Where he really shone was in his tackling and especially his aerial prowess with some important headers at the back. His penalty wasn't too shabby either!

Ledley – 6 – Thought he had a quiet game overall, with his lack of pace handicapping his ability to support Jerome. Did the dirty work well with solid tackles in the centre.

Puncheon – 8 – Looks a completely different player to that from the turn of the year, playing with confidence – perhaps too much confidence given his penchant for over elaboration after we went a goal ahead. Still it was that skill that helped remove the left hinge of the Irons' defence and he tormented Armero.

Bolasie – 8 – Did pull out his usual box of tricks but also decided the best way to attack McCartney was to knock the ball past him and turn on the afterburners. In the second half this pace didn't unhinge the defence as much as knock the whole door in. How he did not end up with a goal or at least an assist beats me, and perhaps his colleagues wasted some of his effort with an unwillingness to shoot when given the chance. Also continued to work hard at tracking back, something Pulis (& Millen) can take credit for.

Jerome – 7 – Lots of hard running as usual and some excellent link play with both wingers, although again didn't get many chances on goal and could have been better served on occasion by colleagues who didn't pass when he'd found space. Did draw an unwise challenge from Armero to win the penalty.

Murray – 6 – Replaced Jerome and committed a couple of fouls but never really had a sight of goal as Palace dropped a little deeper & withdrew the speedy wingers.

Gabbidon – 6 – Late sub to help repel the East End Air Force and marked it with one firm header.

Parr – N/A – Injury time sub to help Mariappa shore up the right.

Speroni – 6 – Given City's seeming dominance actually didn't have a lot to do. No chance with the first goal, he perhaps made it slightly easier for Toure but given the midfielder's run he probably felt he had to come out. There were obvious moments of miscommunication with both Dann & Delaney and some strong words and even stronger body language betrayed an uncertainty over coming for crosses. Perhaps moping over Nelson Muntz's inexplicable failure to offer the customary "ILY" – can we expect a transfer request over this lack of support!?

Ward – 5 – Found James Milner powering past him on the outside more than once in the first 15 minutes and had probably his most discomfiting 90 minutes all season. I'll admit to not being a fan of Milner but he did tie Joel up in knots in one second half attack. Slightly better coming forward but unable to make a telling cross.

Mariappa – 6 – Not so threatened by Nasri on the left so was both able to hold his flank and also support the attack – usually Puncheon – with some good moves. Can't blame him for Dzeko's opener and he was just too late to cover Dann's loss of his man, and also made what might have been important interceptions when Palace were wobbling in the first half.

Delaney – 5 – Never did get to grips with Aguero, but to be fair there are a lot of defenders who will own up to that failing. Made a ricket of a back pass that the whole ground saw would be cut out by Aguero and his composure also ruffled by some disagreements with Julian. Not sure but think Kompany may have beaten him to the corner for what should have been City's second. Was outstripped by Toure for the second goal but managed to slow the midfielder up without preventing the final decisive shot. Still without some brave defending the score could have been worse.

Dann – 5 – Day started poorly when he gave Dzeko a couple of yards space for the first goal. Later was well beaten by Dzeko for another header, then after a moment's panic in the defence gave a calm header back to Julian (obviously hadn't watched the Everton defence yesterday then!) followed by an exercise in finger-pointing. There were instance of good & brave defending but by then the damage was done.

Jedinak – 6 – Fought hard all game, winning the ball or at least holding up City's advance, and both took and gave some hard knocks. Also gave the ball away with some poor passing under pressure but not nearly as often as some of his colleagues.

Ledley – 5 – Struggled to make a mark on the game, especially after twice finding he was responsible for Aguero in the opening minutes only to lose the little blighter just as fast. His lack of pace was really show up, especially by Toure's goal: Joe was in the scramble in their half when Toure came away with the ball; while the City player made a curving detour Joe seemed to ease back on the pedal and found that, despite running in a straight line, he was still beaten to the edge of the box. Too many passes were played laterally and Joe was one of many who seemed to need an engraved invitation to shoot.

Bolasie - 6 – Palace's most potent threat in the first half when he gave Zabaleta real problems down the left, although again too often the crosses lacked precision. Was sometimes missing when Zabaleta & Milner were attacking Ward in the first half. Faded in the second as City sat deeper and Palace lacked the ability to play him in behind the full back.

Puncheon – 5 – Had Palace's two shots on target – one that bobbled through to the Shampoo Advert in the first half, and a second half effort that forced Harmony Hairspray to a full length dive. Apart from a couple of nice touches he was unable to make much of a dent in Kolarov's defending, while his corners were predominantly useless. Was perhaps due a poor game after his run of excellent ones.

Chamakh – 6 – As usual a bit of an enigma from Marouane, who when he ran with the ball seemed to ghost through opponents, but too often the lay-off was poor or he ran into more solid defenders. Held the ball up well on occasions but never struck up an understanding with Jerome, either being too distant from the striker or misdirecting headers too far ahead of him.

Jerome – 5 – Hard game for Cameron who received little decent ball, and on the one occasion he did run at the defence Mr. Webb (the sooner he departs for Brazil the better!) saw nothing wrong when he was chopped down. Lacked close support and was often 10-20 yards away from Chamakh's flick-ons, or when the ball was in close proximity had wandered offside.

Gayle – 6 – Looked impressive with some good touches, particularly with his chest, although too distant from goal to worry Hart.

Murray – 5 – Would be difficult to make an impression in 20 minutes when the service up front all day had been intermittent at best.

Ince – 5 – Even less time to impress and suffered a couple of hefty challenges; I think Tom needs to spend some time at a good Championship side next season to put his game together and become tougher, just as Wilf did, as I can't see him getting game time with a decent Premiership team at this stage.

Speroni – 7 – Strange mark for a keeper who conceded three, but I don't think he had much chance with any of the goals, although he appeared upset with himself for the third goal which he nearly blocked. Some moments of panic & confusion with his defenders, but made one excellent save from Sturridge (although ultimately it had little impact on the actual game), two important tip over's of shots, and one good dive at Suarez's feet.

Ward – 6 – Thought he had another hard game at the back, often faced with Sturridge, and never really closed the striker down for their second goal. Had some good moments supporting the attack.

Mariappa -6 – Struggled against Sterling, especially when Johnson was raiding down that flank with little help from Bolasie, but made some important interceptions & blocks in both halves.

Dann - 7 – No shame in struggling against Suarez, as many supposedly higher-rated defenders have, being beaten for their third, but made some important clearances & blocks in both halves. Had a far post header in the first half that might have been troublesome on better days, but I'm sure it was his long ball that led to the equaliser.

Delaney – 7 – Rumoured to be one of those players struggling with illness before kick off but didn't appear to affect his wholehearted display. Like his colleagues found the pace & movement of Liverpool's attacking trio difficult to deal with but would be fair to say he helped keep their score within reach. Nice way to open his season's account (only leaves Ward and – surprisingly – Bolasie to get off the mark at Fulham) even if not quite as blindingly accurate shot as it first appeared, but the nature of the goal reenergised both team & crowd.

Dikgacoi – 5 – Struggled with the pace of the game, unable to provide the attack with support and too often conceding possession cheaply.

Jedinak – 6 – Difficult to mark the Jedi in this match, as his passing veered from good (nice lay-off for Delaney's goal) to the awful (lots of chips & scoops to no-one in particular) offset by the usual steel in his challenges.

Ledley – 6 – Worked damned hard and carried out sterling defensive duties but lacked the acceleration to get up quickly to support Chamakh and made errors for two of their goals: looked to be the man who lost Allen from the corner for their first; then let the ball rebound off him straight to Suarez for the third. Perhaps summed up his night when he did actually show some pace (perhaps a better engine compared to tired defenders?) but lacked the confidence to have a shot from the edge of the box.

Puncheon – 6 – Worked hard in the first half and forced a good save from Mignolet but faded in the second.

Bolasie – 8 – The battle between Johnson & Yannick was extremely interesting, with the England full back often escaping the winger's attention when pushing forward, as exemplified with that early headed chance, while Bolasie pinned back his ears when he had the ball and for the first 80 minutes looked like Palace's best / only chance of forcing a way back into the match. Switched to the right when Gayle came on but it was on the left that he ran 80 yards on the break to set up Gayle's first goal.

Chamakh – 5 – Some nice touches but with no close support these were often wasted, and he lacked the pace to push beyond the defence. Took quite a few knocks as well.

Murray – 7 – Didn't do much when he came on but set up the equaliser with perfect cushioned ball off his chest. Would like to see him start at Fulham with Gayle to see if they can strike up a partnership with a view to next season.

Gayle – 8 – Loved the finish for the first goal, opening up his body to pass the ball across Mignolet inside the far post. Cool finish for the second, didn't blast it but just knocked it past the keeper. Unlike Marouane looked to run beyond the last defender and take up good & dangerous positions.

Ince – 6 – Late sub who put in a couple of good set piece deliveries and made one excellent challenge on his own goal-line.

Fulham Away

Hennessey – 6 – Unsurprisingly there were a couple of moments when communication between new keeper & defence was poor, with one moment of panic late in the game of note; he probably hasn't had much practice playing behind these four defenders. On the bright side Wayne has a hell of a boot on him and can throw the ball prodigious distances, setting up a couple of counter attacks. There were a couple of crosses he could have come for and his first save looked a little awkward, although he redeemed himself with a smart one just before halt-time and an excellent catch late on. I didn't think he had much chance with either goal from my angle – perhaps Fulham only score these goals against Palace this year.

Ward – 7 – More prominent on the attack than in defence Joel had a fine game, although he will kick himself for working two openings in the second half only to put in weak finishes. When he did get a better shot on target Gayle deflected it past Stockdale so at least he gets some form of assist. Was beaten a little too easily by Woodrow's dummy for their first goal.

Mariappa – 6 – Decent game with some good defending and support for the attack down the right, although at times his distribution could be inaccurate. Many of Fulham's best attacks, especially in the first half, came down our right and behind Mariappa, so had a busy if not wholly successful afternoon.

Delaney – 7 – Another strong game with some good interceptions and challenges, important with a keeper new to the team. From long range in second half couldn't tell who Rodallega won his headers against.

Dann – 7 – As with Delaney, Scott is dependable & seldom lets the team down. Only a fine save by Stockdale prevented him scoring his second Palace goal.

Jedinak – 7 – There was a noticeable difference once the captain left the pitch with a knock to knee or ankle as he did a lot of the unglamorous work. Makes a lot of movement in midfield, either to close down the opposition or to make angles for colleagues with the ball. First half also made some important clearances as Fulham made inroads down our right.

Ledley – 6 – Solid if unspectacular, working hard all game and involved in some of the quick breaks by moving the ball on swiftly.

Ince – 6 – Started well, looking like the player who started against West Brom, and nearly scored an early goal with a fine shot that just crept outside the far post. Also did a lot of defensive work to help out Mariappa and to close down Fulham's keeper & back four when they were in possession. Always available on the break but many of Palace's best attacks came down the other flank. His free kicks & corners looked dangerous; one to the far post finding Jedinak & Dann in space at the far post, but his one short corner with Bolasie was a disaster. Faded a little in the second half before being withdrawn.

Bolasie – 7 – Frustrating for much of the match as he once again tore the left side defence apart with pace & trickery only to be let down by some poor final passes, over elaboration and decision making at time, yet sometimes through sheer persistence & a little luck he'd force a chance for a colleague, and had two decent efforts at his goal of the season only to be foiled by Stockdale.

Chamakh – 6 – Some good touches and worked hard, often dropping back into midfield when Palace didn't have the ball, but conceded a series of free kicks thanks to some inconsistent & often baffling refereeing. Didn't have a sniff at goal.

Gayle – 8 – I was surprised how many times Gayle would receive a long ball at chest or head high, only to kill the ball and lay it back to a colleague, despite the close attentions of Heitinga or Hangeland, and how much work he put into closing down Stockdale or his defenders when they had the ball, forcing quite a few turnovers of possession through wild passes out of play. Looked a different player from the inexperienced lad at the start of the season. Didn't really see his first goal so let's chalk that up to a poacher's instinct, but his second was a brilliant free kick that totally defeated the wall and the keeper. Could have had another two if he'd had a fraction more time to put a rebound away, and a little more care with the last kick of the game when his shot from a tight angle went over. Undoubtedly someone we must persevere with as he knows where the net is and can actually find it.

Dikgacoi – 6 – KG didn't really do anything wrong, with some decent challenges and a couple of good moments on the ball, but he is not as mobile as Jedinak & is generally a worse passer, and the skipper's absence was noticeable.

Murray – 6 – Involved in a couple of good breaks, smashed a shot against the bar late on & nearly set up Gayle for a last-second winner.

Puncheon – 5 – Ruined a couple of good breaks with poor decision making i.e. Deciding running into a thicket of four defenders was better than passing to a number of colleagues breaking forward. Not really reflective of his season as a whole when he was one of the instigators of the recovery.

Annual player summary

This should be easy! Just tot up the (stingy) marks I've given this season, divide by the number of appearances, and then we have a mark for each player. Can't you tell I work in Accounts armed with spreadsheets & love statistical data! Except that over 40 games (37 league matches i.e. missing Everton away which I missed and three cup matches) the marks will tend to average out between 5 & 7, with 6 being an average performance, which really won't give an indication of true worth to the team. So, deleting the Excel file, the marks below should be taken as indicative of how I saw each player's worth to Crystal Palace this season rather than an analysis of their actual performances as viewed by me. In order to differentiate more widely over nine months of games I've taken the liberty of using half marks.

I'll start with the managers as it only seems fair...

Holloway – 5.5 – A sad end to a short stay at Selhurst, Olly perhaps deserves a little more praise. Some of his summer signings were simply disastrous, although that will happen with every manager & we don't know whose input was involved; but four of those ended up as fixtures in the first XI (Mariappa, Puncheon, Chamakh & Jerome) with Gayle showing signs of promise, so it wasn't a complete disaster. What was a disaster was Olly's inability to find his first choice team & formation, culminating in that torrid Monday night against Fulham.

Millen – 7.0 – Steadied the ship and saw an almost immediate improvement in performance and gradually results simply through tightening up at the back.

Pulis – 8.5 – Really made me eat humble pie, not so much in results but in the style of play Palace adopted. We weren't Stoke Mark II – even if Tony wanted to we didn't really have the personnel for those tactics – but a little bit more like a Mourinho side, playing on the counter attack – more importantly, playing with pace. Quickly determined who his main players would be, which sadly saw little use of Williams, Bannan or Gayle, and the formation being a flexible 4-3-3 / 4-2-3-1 / 4-5-1. Made two excellent & important January signings in Dann & Ledley and ended up with a season of achievement that matched Steve Coppell's amazing feats in keeping bankrupt clubs afloat.

Speroni – 7.5 – Most fair-minded folk at the start of the season would admit that Julian was a good shot-stopper with fallibilities in the air & perhaps communicating with his defenders who had struck a particularly good vein of form. The question was whether that form would continue or would the greater exposure he would come under this year, both on the pitch & in the media, find him out? I only noted a couple of dodgy moments early season against Southampton & Fulham, but these are submerged beneath, if anything, an even greater run of form, with vital saves in late season games – Villa, Chelsea & West Ham come to mind.

Alexander – 5.0 – There are several memes about Scottish goalkeepers and on his one appearance Neil sadly lived down to most of them. I wouldn't have been confident if he'd had to replace Julian in a Premier League situation as he didn't seem any improvement on Price.

Hennessey – 6.0 – Decent showing at Fulham but will need more game time to show he is ready to displace Speroni, which is very much a chicken-&-egg scenario.

Ward – 7.5 – Outstanding & versatile performer in both full back berths, another who carried on the form of late last season into the Premier League. Defensively sound but also a great boon to the attack. Given how bare England's cupboard is of right backs he must surely become an international player soon (which will probably wreck his career, but hey...)

Mariappa – 7.0 – A late summer signing who struggled to find a place in central defence under Holloway and was dropped after the Fulham debacle, and looked to be one of Olly's failures. Pulis's desire for full backs that are better at defending than attacking, along with his height, saw him return to the side at right back, where he wasn't as exposed as I'd feared, and he contributed to a defence that looked more solid as the season ran out. Surprisingly also showed good signs when supporting the attack.

Parr – 6 .0 – Unluckily injured before the play-offs and didn't make an appearance until the 17th league match. As usual Jonny didn't let anyone down and had a couple of good performances but had a terrible game at Swansea, after which Pulis chose the more solid Mariappa. I am sorry to see him go as I felt he was a useful squad player covering several positions, but to be honest I couldn't claim he could hold down any one of them.

Moxey – 6.0 – Another of the Play-off heroes to suffer rejection this season, but he like others he started the season as he ended the last in a run of unexpected good form, as most guessed he would be a weak link at the back. Outstanding against Everton but Pulis didn't seem to fancy him and he was soon dropped, first for Parr, and then there was no way back once Mariappa established himself in the team.

Delaney – 8.0 – Unexpected storming success this season, as many doubted he would have the quality to stand up to the standard of attacks he would now face. But, just as he did last season, Damien stepped up and his performances were generally outstanding, and showed the fighting heart that inspired both colleagues & crowd, often throwing himself into blocks & challenges. Had perhaps three poor showings (all at home against Swansea, Fulham & Manchester City) but was a rock in almost every other game.

Gabbidon – 7.0 – Did have the odd 'mare early on (Swansea and an own goal against Newcastle stand out) but after missing Olly's last few games came back into the side under Millen and was an immediate factor in the tightening up of the defence. Unlucky to be dropped when Dann arrived but the decision was proven correct and another hero who added a great deal to the Palace story.

McCarthy – 6.0 – A cup appearance at Wigan and a late substitute who contributed to the home win against Hull. Sadly it looks like his Palace career was wrecked by one injury and the apparent failure of treatment.

Dann – 8.0 – An outstanding signing so kudos to Pulis, Moody & Parrish for taking the plunge on a Championship player with relegation on his CV. It was his defensive partnership with Delaney that helped seal our survival. His positioning and timing were the key as he's not particularly quick, allied to his heading ability, and he provided the perfect foil for Damien.

Ramage – 5.0 – Sad to see such a wholehearted player reduced to an onlooker's role, restricted to one appearance in the shambolic defeat at Bristol City before a loan move to Yorkshire, but it would be difficult to see how he could have strengthened the defence.

Marange – 4.0 – A late (desperate?) signing who didn't even make the 25-man Premier League squad. Poor on his one first team (and that's a debatable term) appearance at Bristol City. Won't be missed as most people haven't even seen him!

Wynter – 6.0 – Looked better than his experienced colleagues in his one showing at Ashton Gate.

Williams (the taller one) – 5.5 – Jerome showed signs of promise in the League Cup tie, his only appearance.

Campaña – 5.0 – A disappointment given the skill that this youngster showed in flashes, especially up at Stoke, but it appears he lacked both the fitness levels and stomach for the fight required in the English game. Substituted at half-time after a terrible display against Fulham and never seen again.

Jedinak – 7.0 – Far more influential than his marks suggest, playing every minute of the league season until forced off late on at Craven Cottage. His quality of his passing could be described as variable at best, but in terms of his being up for the fight he could not be surpassed, leading the way in tackles, interceptions and heading. Had a number of games where he was outstanding, balanced by a few where he was bypassed in midfield more easily (usually when KG was absent), and also produced the coolest penalty to confirm our safety, which perhaps helped when it came to the Dutch this summer...

Dikgacoi – 6.5 – More noted for his absences, when too often our defensive midfield shield appeared lacking, than by outstanding performances when he made the team. Much of his work went unappreciated as it wasn't eye-catching, and his form did start to dip as the season tailed off, but he was key in important victories.

O'Keefe – 6.0 – Surprisingly made early appearances in the Premier League given the squad size and Stuart's lack of experience, and made an impact with a wonderful strike to seal our first home win. Best performance was at Chelsea, and it was perhaps surprising that after that game he was used rarely. Needs game time this season, so will probably need a (temporary?) move.

Garvan – 5.0 – Three early appearances under Holloway before being loaned out; he simply wasn't the style of midfielder we needed in the Premier League.

Dobbie – 4.5 – As with Garvan was given a start against Spurs – whether Olly wanted to give the Play-off heroes one chance or his signings just weren't attuned is a moot point – but disappointed there and was woeful at Ashton Gate.

Guedioura – 6.0 – Could have proven to be an inspired signing of Holloway's until injured at the Hawthorns when just promising to show his abilities playing behind the striker. After that only saw a little bit of action under Pulis.

Williams (the short one) – 5.5 – Not so much for Jonny's performances, which were restricted by injury incurred on international duty (again!), but for the lack of impact such a talented player could have had this season. Not favoured by Pulis – and we can only guess at the reasons why, although stature looks most likely – he ended up being loaned out to Ipswich. In the short-term the decision was correct, but Palace cannot afford to waste such a talent.

Bannan – 6.0 – Sadly underused midfield talent who scored a crucial goal at Hull and was outstanding in the wins over Cardiff & Villa, but hardly saw any action after the New Year. As with Jonny Williams was the problem simply one of size, or were there other factors behind the scenes?

Boateng – 6.0 – Looked good in the FA Cup tie at West Brom.

Ledley – 7.0 – The second of the excellent deadline signings who provided a versatility, covering left back, left wing, behind the striker and holding midfield player, although was far better in the first & last positions. Couldn't start better than scoring on his debut and was outstanding in two crucial late wins against Cardiff & Villa, and also in helping John Terry score past Cech!

Bolasie – 7.0 – Injury prevented his Premier League debut until Anfield, and it is a mark of his performances that he didn't miss a league game when available after that (he was suspended for three games after the red card at Hull). He didn't rate particularly highly in terms of assists, and failed to score, and he could be his usual frustrating self, but he took over from Zaha in the role of (often sole) most potent attacking threat. Twice he tormented Villa and at Upton Park showed up a World Cup defender.

Puncheon – 6.5 – Wildly varying form from Jason, who looked at the start to be another of Olly's failed experiments, with the exception of the match against Sunderland (when everyone looked good!), and was well on his way to being a crowd fall guy. Played well against Chelsea and then had a spurt of decent form and a run of goal scoring. Could still plumb the depths – "miss" doesn't quite describe what happened to the penalty kick at Spurs, while his hapless contribution to Southampton's winner would be hilarious if it hadn't looked to have doomed us – but provided far more moments when his skills were appreciated, and with Bolasie formed a pair of wingers that were barely matched by any other team.

Thomas – 5.0 – Injured in a pre-season friendly and it didn't seem to get any better once he was fit, although unlucky to be injured after his best game against Everton. Took a long time to get back to the squad under Pulis and blotted his copybook when, perhaps lacking confidence, threw away a great chance to win at Swansea in favour of a ridiculous dive that embarrassed both the team & his manager.

Kébé – 4.5 – For a player who often tormented Palace this was an underwhelming signing and definitely one of the mistakes made in the summer.

Ince – 5.5 – An exciting signing who didn't work out. Couldn't have started better than he did with an early debut goal and a couple of assists from set piece deliveries, but soon looked too lightweight at this stage of his career to thrive in the Premier League. Has the talent but perhaps needs a little of his old man's dog in him.

Grandin – 4.0 – Another of our supermarket-sweep panic buys, awful at Ashton Gate and soon dispatched back whence he came.

De Silva – 5.5 – One of the disappointing results of this season was how little exposure our youngsters got, but I guess that's Premier League survival for you. Kyle was one who might have gained from the bench but was restricted to one cup tie.

Gayle – 6.5 – A strange season for our record signing, who must have started under pressure, and there were some good moments among some weak displays. Once Pulis arrived he didn't appear to be favoured, although the sheer quality of his late winner at Villa wasn't surpassed, but by all reports he sorted himself out and gave us the wildly improbably personal double against Liverpool (remember he also scored one at Anfield) , his confidence then soared and he finished with a great free kick against Fulham. Now looks like he might be the player we thought we'd signed, so perhaps Olly deserves some late credit.

Chamakh – 7.0 – Suffered by being deployed as the lone striker, often isolated in the first part of the season, and by his own inconsistencies, but was capable of flashes of quality, which he showed with an excellent goal at Stoke. Looked more used to the role of support in the hole when Pulis could afford to play only two holding midfielders. An important cog in the machine that kept us up.

Jerome – 6.5 – Almost certainly in the Palace Hall of Cult Heroes. Sadly we cannot set aside his poor goal return for someone often played as a lone striker, but in all other parts of his game Cameron provided what was needed. A hard running player who could hold the ball up, despite the odd heavy first touch, he brought to the team qualities that the more potent Gayle & (probably) Murray could not in a 4-5-1 formation. Highlight was his display at home to Chelsea when he tormented their defence and was a post's width away from a career highlight. Also proved pretty good in the air when helping out the defence at set pieces.

Phillips – 5.0 – The Play-Off Final hero deserved one last shot at the Premier League but he was restricted to cameo appearances from the bench, and his last showing was on that unhappy evening against Fulham. In hindsight KP's time had passed, but he left with our best wishes and left some great memories behind.

Murray – 6.0 – Season wrecked by injury, and although he showed sparks of last season's form by winning then scoring the late penalty at Swansea, he was restricted to a handful of appearances off the bench and looked slightly more immobile than is required. Did show signs of striking up a partnership with Gayle, so maybe we will see two up front sometimes this coming season?

Wilbraham – 5.5 – Hardly a look in this season, an occasional sub who looked like he could hold the ball up but not much else. At least doubled his number of Palace career goals with a scrambled effort from two yards at Wigan. Wholehearted but sadly lacking in quality.

Appiah – 5.0 – Looked out of his depth even against lowly Bristol City.

For those of you who are really interested and haven't fallen asleep yet, from for those who appeared more than once, top of my averages was Delaney (6.78) followed closely by Gabbidon (6.65), Dann (6.62), Bolasie (6.61), Speroni (6.57) and Ward (6.56). Interesting that, with the exception of the mercurial Bolasie, defensive players predominate, which reflects the fact that Palace often played without the ball with pressure on the back four and keeper.

Endnotes

[i] http://en.wikipedia.org/wiki/Taylor_Report
[ii] http://hillsborough.independent.gov.uk/repository/HOM000028060001.html
[iii] http://www.youtube.com/user/PalaceFanTV
[iv] http://www.bbc.co.uk/sport/0/football/23821613

[v] http://www.cpfc.co.uk/news/article/pre-season-lazio-at-selhurst-911069.aspx
[vi] http://www.youtube.com/watch?v=oVWTF5mlCus
[vii] http://www.premierleague.com/content/premierleague/en-gb/youth/elite-player-performance-plan.html
[viii] Liverpool 9 (nine) Crystal Palace 0
[ix] http://www.bbc.co.uk/sport/0/24634811

[x] http://www.theguardian.com/football/blog/2013/oct/23/ian-holloway-crystal-palace-resigned

[xi] http://en.wikipedia.org/wiki/John_Bostock
[xii] http://www.theswanseaway.co.uk/2013/09/cold-weather-boots-braces-and-smiley.html
[xiii] http://en.wikipedia.org/wiki/Heysel_Stadium_disaster
http://news.bbc.co.uk/onthisday/hi/dates/stories/june/2/newsid_2494000/2494963.stm
[xiv] http://www.newstatesman.com/politics/2014/02/everyones-equal-eyes-law-unless-you-are-football-fan

[xv] Crystal Palace the complete record by Ian King ISBN 978-1-85983-809-9

17309734R00199

Printed in Great Britain
by Amazon